D0983168

THE SEARCH
FOR
COMMUNITY POWER

THE SEARCH

FOR

COMMUNITY POWER

Edited by

WILLIS D. HAWLEY

Institute of Governmental Studies
University of California, Berkeley

FREDERICK M. WIRT

Department of Political Science
Denison University

PRENTICE-HALL, INC., ENGLEWOOD CLIFFS, NEW JERSEY

Current printing (last digit)
10   9   8   7   6   5   4   3   2   1

PRENTICE-HALL INTERNATIONAL, INC., London
PRENTICE-HALL OF AUSTRALIA, PTY. LTD., Sydney
PRENTICE-HALL OF CANADA, LTD., Toronto
PRENTICE-HALL OF INDIA PRIVATE LTD., New Delhi
PRENTICE-HALL OF JAPAN, INC., Tokyo

To Our Firstborn

KAREN AND LESLIE

PREFACE

That relationship among men which we call "power" has captured the imagination of scholars of western civilization for a period so long that "the memory of man runneth not to the contrary." From earliest times, records reveal inquiry into the nature of power and the ways in which it is obtained, secured, exercised, and lost. Since Plato, philosophers have mused over the questions of who should have power? and to what ends should power be employed? Since Thucydides, historians have chronicled the ways of men in power. In the contemporary period social scientists have peeled off parts of the phenomenona of power for specialized study. Sociologists have examined its social aspects, particularly in terms of class and status; economists have analyzed the amassing and organization of its economic aspects in institutional terms; political scientists have examined the formal and informal aspects of political power in both its institutional and behavioral modes.

Americans, scholars as well as laymen, seem to have a special fascination with the subject, a fascination often tinged with a certain fear. Our Constitution makers, reflecting the attitudes of their contemporaries, were repelled by the evil potential of political power and sought to restrain it in a systematic maze of checks and balances, divisions and separations. In the last part of the nineteenth century the development of highly concentrated economic power produced similar fears of this kind, which led to governmental restraints upon business. In our times the opinion surveys demonstrate that a fear of both political and economic "bigness" is widespread among the populace.

With all this interest in power, it is curious that until very recently few scholars examined the structure of power at the community level. Local "place histories" abound from early times, but these are most often chronicles of good and bad periods, of population rise and economic growth—overlaid by polemics suggesting that the particular history demonstrated the favor of God or manifest destiny in the particular locale. The first American commentaries squarely focusing on the bases of power and the uses of power in the community are to be found in scattered newspaper attacks on corrupt political organizations after the Civil War. Entirely concerned with the machinations of political power, they offer little in the way of comparison, and hence, little theory about the subject.

One of the first consciously comparative analyses of communities was Lincoln Steffens' *Shame of the Cities,* published in 1904. It was a survey concerned less with developing a conceptual or empirical theory than with promulgating a normative attack on the mutually corrupting influences of local political parties and local business. Much of the community analysis which followed in the first quarter of this century was equally concerned with demonstrating that certain reforms in political machinery were all that were necessary in order to overcome corruption.

The first major departures from this tradition appeared in the late 1920s and mid-1930s with the publication of Robert and Helen Lynd's "Middletown" studies. For the first time the total community was in focus, not merely its political institutions. While the Lynds' emphasis upon the dominance of business leaders was not new, their interest in the way in which this control was exercised through many social structures (not least of which were community values) filled in for the first time details of the pervasive influence of a small group across a range of local issues. This analysis (in *Middletown in Transition*) of the dominance of a community by a single family provided a point of departure for the sociological study of community power elites. It is interesting to note that almost a decade earlier two novelists, Sherwood Anderson in *Winesburg, Ohio* and Sinclair Lewis in *Mainstreet,* portrayed systems similar to those found in "Middletown." In the 1940s other sociologists, W. Lloyd Warner in "Yankee City" (228) and "Jonesville" (227) being the most prominent, reached conclusions which paralleled those of the Lynds.

With the appearance of Floyd Hunter's *Community Power Structure* in 1953, however, a new phase in the search for community power commenced. In some respects the most sophisticated study to that time, Hunter's work clearly stated a method for detecting and studying local power structures. His book precipitated a reaction from some dissenting political scientists, setting off a decade-long interdisciplinary debate which has not yet run its course.

Thus in the last few years there has been a growing interest among social scientists in the questions of how and by whom decisions are made in American communities. This interest is manifest in hundreds of articles, monographs, and books. The best of this literature has one or more of these distinguishing characteristics: it provides important insights into the problems of social research; it furnishes the conceptual or empirical basis on which social-system theory (especially political theory) can be developed; it contributes to the normative evaluation of the operation of our democratic society.

There is now a large number of studies which differ significantly in their conceptualization, research methods, and conclusions, so that the study of community power requires increasingly wide reading. In this book we have collected some of the more important commentaries on the search for power in American communities, commentaries which treat major aspects of this special field. Included are definitions, findings, methods, problems, and future research directions. Of course, reasonable scholars will differ with us about both the criteria of importance and the consequent selections in this book—but we do not pretend that what is offered here is necessarily the "last word" or the "best" writing in the field. However, we do believe that the selections herein represent a fairly comprehensive survey of the nature, quality, and problems of community power research. We see these selections as points of departure for a more thorough investigation, and to that end we have provided a lengthy bibliographical appendix.

Section I offers two very significant commentaries on the definition of power. Sections II and III present some major findings on the nature of local power structures, with examples from both the "elite" and "pluralist" schools. Section IV reviews the vigorous debate concerning research methodology and community conceptualization which has sharply divided many sociologists and political scientists. Section V examines some of the special problems in the whole area—the nature of decision-making, the question of "issues" and "non-issues," and the measurement of power. In the concluding Section VI, commentaries are presented, indicating what we consider to be the significant directions in which future research in this area is moving, with particular emphasis upon comparative analysis and general social and political theory.

Each of the six sections is introduced by a brief essay designed to acquaint the reader with the relevance of the subject dealt with in that section to the total field, and to relate the individual selections to this subject. In these introductions we refer frequently to other related readings which are indicated by a number in parentheses corresponding to the numbered item in the bibliographical appendix. Each selection has a short preface which introduces the student to the ideas therein and suggests when appropriate, some important aspects of the material (especially methodological contributions) which are not included in the selections. In some cases footnotes have been omitted; those included in this edition have been renumbered.

It seems to us that the study of community power has much to recommend it to social scientists. Its many methodological problems illustrate the complexity of social research. The problems of theory building suggested in the context of this study have consequence for an empirically based understanding of who gets what, when, and how in presumably democratic societies. The study of community power also helps to evaluate the normative theory of democracy by validating or invalidating the empirical aspects of such theory. In short, the lessons to be learned from the search for power in American communities are important in many ways, and we believe that they have substantial applicability to both larger and smaller social systems.

WDH
FMW

TABLE OF CONTENTS

I

THE NOTION OF POWER

II

COMMUNITY POWER: RULING ELITE MODELS

III

COMMUNITY POWER: THE PLURALIST PERSPECTIVE

IV

LOCATING DECISION MAKERS: ALTERNATIVE STRATEGIES

V

SOME CONTINUING PROBLEMS IN THE SEARCH FOR POWER

VI

TOWARD A THEORY OF COMMUNITY POWER— FUTURE RESEARCH DIRECTIONS

THE SEARCH
FOR
COMMUNITY POWER

I

THE NOTION OF POWER

The concept of power has an elusive quality which has led scholars into intellectual wrangling since first they turned to its study. For the layman, there is an intuitive grasp of its meaning, and indeed, in our daily conversation we use the concept without much thought, assuming that our listeners know what we mean. But like many other general terms by which we seek to encapsulate complex aspects of life, power has many dimensions of meaning. Of citizen Jones we may say, "He is a powerful man," "Jones has a lot of pull," or "Jones runs things in this town." But a thoughtful man may ask what it is that Jones possesses, what is this thing called "power"?

There are other questions about the subject which will be pursued in later sections of this book, but for now let us attempt to clarify the concept of power. At minimum, power analysts agree that power is involved when one person or a group achieves compliance from others in respect to the disposition of a given value. The means used to secure compliance and the consequences for both sides are among the many aspects of the phenomenon of power.

Let us assume that Jones is a banker and Brown is seeking a loan. Ordinary usage would have it that Jones has power over Brown because he can affect Brown's life-opportunities by the decision to grant or not to grant the loan requested. But exactly what is this power and what are its sources? How is it applied? Does the power lie in the bank's funds which Jones may dispense, or in Jones' choice to lend or not to lend the money at his discretion? Does the power, if it lies in the bank's funds, exist independently of Jones and regardless of who is the banker? Is Jones' power po-

1

tential, in the sense of being latent even if it is not used? Or does
his power exist only when it is employed? Further, how does the
banker Jones' power in this case compare to that of the political
ward leader who can swing his district's votes as he wills? Can
power of one sort, for example, control over credit, be converted to
power of a different sort, for example, making public policy? Is
power additive in the sense that every use of it enhances the
possessor's next use of it, or is it depletive in the sense that every
use of it causes a power loss which cannot be replaced without
effort? Many of these questions, as well as others, will be faced in
the selections in this book.

At this point, let us suggest that the various ways of analyzing
the concept of power may be seen to fall on a continuum between
two major approaches to the problem. The first of these approaches
is to focus on institutional bases of influence and to attribute power
to those who have access to these institutions. In other words, certain
institutions—such as political parties, social classes, corporations,
military groups, religious organizations, and the like—are characterized by certain components which may be regarded as power resources. These resources are used to secure from others compliance
with the institution's purpose. Such resources might include wealth,
votes, prestige, physical coercion, etc. Persons who are in a position
to employ an institution's power resources are considered powerful.
*To oversimplify, in this approach power is seen as inhering funda-
mentally in institutions rather than in people.* Thus, when kings
were thought divine, power adhered to kingship whether the incumbent was an idiot in his use of power, like George III, or a
genius, like Peter the Great.

If the approach just discussed tends to focus on institutions
in order to analyze power, *a second approach is to view power as
the result of specific interpersonal relationships.* Here, regardless of
the power resource—money, military might, etc.—or the instruments
by which the institutional base is effected—a loan, armament, etc.
—what is common to all is a relationship between two men, one of
whom induces another to do the former's will. Potential power is
relatively unimportant until it is translated into interpersonal action
to achieve compliance. The qualities of the power holder are the
main focus in this school, which is thought to explain why George
III was not "really" powerful while Peter the Great was. In this
view, it is imperative to discover how men act so as to understand
how, among men possessing ostensibly equal power resources, one

obtains compliance while another fails to or is unwilling to utilize his potential for obtaining compliance.

Of course, what we have said here is a simplification of quite sophisticated analyses. But it is offered as a basic observation to indicate what we believe is a major distinction between the ways in which power is defined. This distinction, though it is seldom as emphatic as we have described it, has influenced much of the analysis of community power which this book presents. If one believes that power is possessed only by a certain stratum of society, such as "the wealthy and well born," or "the bourgeoisie," then he may well view the distribution of power in the community or nation in terms of a pyramid. At the peak of the pyramid are concentrated the few who possess most of a community's resources and determine the life-opportunities for most others. Research based on this outlook involves finding the peak of the power pyramid and detailing the way in which those at the peak shape the lives of others.

But on the other hand, one's outlook may be that power adheres to specific individuals in specific situations involving particular values, bases, and means of power. Then one would view the community as composed of many peaks where different sets of leaders operate in different realms of decision-making. Thus research is focused upon decisions, public and private, in which one can detect some persons compelling others to compliance. Further, this outlook, with its emphasis upon specification of the exact contours of a power matrix, implies the possibility of quantifying some of the relationships involved and hence of measuring the exact nature of the relationships.

The two readings in this section are widely regarded as seminal contributions to the study of social and political power. Each emphasizes one of the two ways of looking at power which we have outlined. However, both authors are certain that one can neglect neither the bases and sources of power nor the ways in which those resources are utilized in one's analysis.

In the first selection Max Weber, one of the intellectual fathers of modern sociology and political science, focuses upon the structural sources and distribution of power, with emphasis on such determinants as the control of markets or economic goods, honor or deference, and communal decisions. While he is one who views power primarily in institutional terms, note the many careful distinctions he draws between bases and instruments of power, and the limitations he offers to an over-simplified Marxist interpretation of society.

In the second article in this section, Herbert Simon emphasizes the individual and interactional nature of power. He describes some of the special problems to be confronted in the study of power which arise from the assymetric nature of power relations and the phenomenon of anticipated reactions. This article previews many of the conceptual and methodological problems that community power analysts have attempted to deal with in the years succeeding its publication in 1953.

Clearly the two articles in this opening section do not cover all the problems involved in defining power. The student will find in our bibliographic appendix material dealing with power which ranges from philosophy to the complex mathematical notation of symbolic logic. Some of the problems of developing an empirical theory of power are discussed below in Section V.

The work of Weber and Simon indicates the complexity of a concept which may seem simple and clear at first consideration. Searching analysis of the concept of power must not be viewed as academic nit-picking—an understanding of the components and dynamics of power is crucial to both sociology and political science, particularly the latter. Harold Lasswell and Abraham Kaplan, in their ground-breaking work, *Power and Society*, [126] put it succinctly: "The concept of power is perhaps the most fundamental in the whole of political science: the political process is the shaping, distribution, and exercise of power. . . ." It is therefore immensely important for that discipline to obtain agreement on the meaning of its most basic concept. As James March will suggest in a later reading (section V), social scientists are far from clear when they use the word "power." Why this is so will be appreciated in the following readings.

Class, Status and Party

Max Weber

*The following selection, like many writings by its author, has had great
impact in shaping an intellectual approach to understanding social life on the
part of later scholars. With great appreciation of the subtlety of distinctions in
life, an historical sweep of supporting evidence which can easily overpower,
and a rigor of logic and argument, Max Weber here explains the elements and
dimensions of social influence. Many of the institutions mentioned above in
the introduction to this section are analyzed to suggest how class, status group
and party affect power's creation, distribution, and employment within a
community.*

1: Economically Determined Power and the Social Order

Law exists when there is a probability that an order will be upheld
by a specific staff of men who will use physical or psychical compul-
sion with the intention of obtaining conformity with the order, or of
inflicting sanctions for infringement of it. The structure of every
legal order directly influences the distribution of power, economic or
otherwise, within its respective community. This is true of all legal
orders and not only that of the state. In general, we understand by
'power' the chance of a man or of a number of men to realize their
own will in a communal action even against the resistance of others
who are participating in the action.

'Economically conditioned' power is not, of course, identical with
'power' as such. On the contrary, the emergence of economic power
may be the consequence of power existing on other grounds. Man does
not strive for power only in order to enrich himself economically.
Power, including economic power, may be valued 'for its own sake.'
Very frequently the striving for power is also conditioned by the social

'honor' it entails. Not all power, however, entails social honor: The typical American Boss, as well as the typical big speculator, deliberately relinquishes social honor. Quite generally, 'mere economic' power, and especially 'naked' money power, is by no means a recognized basis of social honor. Nor is power the only basis of social honor. Indeed, social honor, or prestige, may even be the basis of political or economic power, and very frequently has been. Power, as well as honor, may be guaranteed by the legal order, but, at least normally, it is not their primary source. The legal order is rather an additional factor that enhances the chance to hold power or honor; but it cannot always secure them.

The way in which social honor is distributed in a community between typical groups participating in this distribution we may call the 'social order.' The social order and the economic order are, of course, similarly related to the 'legal order.' However, the social and the economic order are not identical. The economic order is for us merely the way in which economic goods and services are distributed and used. The social order is of course conditioned by the economic order to a high degree, and in its turn reacts upon it.

Now: 'classes,' 'status groups,' and 'parties' are phenomena of the distribution of power within a community.

2: Determination of Class-Situation by Market-Situation

In our terminology, 'classes' are not communities; they merely represent possible, and frequent, bases for communal action. We may speak of a 'class' when (1) a number of people have in common a specific causal component of their life chances, in so far as (2) this component is represented exclusively by economic interests in the possession of goods and opportunities for income, and (3) is represented under the conditions of the commodity or labor markets. [These points refer to 'class situation,' which we may express more briefly as the typical chance for a supply of goods, external living conditions, and personal life experiences, in so far as this chance is determined by the amount and kind of power, or lack of such, to dispose of goods or skills for the sake of income in a given economic order. The term 'class' refers to any group of people that is found in the same class situation.]

It is the most elemental economic fact that the way in which the disposition over material property is distributed among a plurality of people, meeting competitively in the market for the purpose of exchange, in itself creates specific life chances. According to the law of marginal utility this mode of distribution excludes the non-owners from competing for highly valued goods; it favors the owners and, in fact, gives to them a monopoly to acquire such goods. Other things being equal, this mode of distribution monopolizes the opportunities for profitable deals for all those who, provided with goods, do not necessarily have to exchange them. It increases, at least generally, their power in price wars with those who, being propertyless, have nothing to offer but their services in native form or goods in a form constituted through their own labor, and who above all are compelled to get rid of these products in order barely to subsist. This mode of distribution gives to the propertied a monopoly on the possibility of transferring property from the sphere of use as a 'fortune,' to the sphere of 'capital goods'; that is, it gives them the entrepreneurial function and all chances to share directly or indirectly in returns on capital. All this holds true within the area in which pure market conditions prevail. 'Property' and 'lack of property' are, therefore, the basic categories of all class situations. It does not matter whether these two categories become effective in price wars or in competitive struggles.

Within these categories, however, class situations are further differentiated: on the one hand, according to the kind of property that is usable for returns; and, on the other hand, according to the kind of services that can be offered in the market. Ownership of domestic buildings; productive establishments; warehouses; stores; agriculturally usable land, large and small holdings—quantitative differences with possibly qualitative consequences—; ownership of mines; cattle; men (slaves); disposition over mobile instruments of production, or capital goods of all sorts, especially money or objects that can be exchanged for money easily and at any time; disposition over products of one's own labor or of others' labor differing according to their various distances from consumability; disposition over transferable monopolies of any kind—all these distinctions differentiate the class situations of the propertied just as does the 'meaning' which they can and do give to the utilization of property, especially to property which has money equivalence. Accordingly, the propertied, for instance, may belong to the class of rentiers or to the class of entrepreneurs.

Those who have no property but who offer services are differentiated just as much according to their kinds of services as according to the way in which they make use of these services, in a continuous or discontinuous relation to a recipient. But always this is the generic connotation of the concept of class: that the kind of chance in the *market* is the decisive moment which presents a common condition for the individual's fate. 'Class situation' is, in this sense, ultimately 'market situation.' The effect of naked possession *per se*, which among cattle breeders gives the nonowning slave or serf into the power of the cattle owner, is only a forerunner of real 'class' formation. However, in the cattle loan and in the naked severity of the law of debts in such communities, for the first time mere 'possession' as such emerges as decisive for the fate of the individual. This is very much in contrast to the agricultural communities based on labor. The creditor-debtor relation becomes the basis of 'class situations' only in those cities where a 'credit market,' however primitive, with rates of interest increasing according to the extent of dearth and a factual monopolization of credits, is developed by a plutocracy. Therewith 'class struggles' begin.

Those men whose fate is not determined by the chance of using goods or services for themselves on the market, e.g. slaves, are not, however, a 'class' in the technical sense of the term. They are, rather, a 'status group.'

3: Communal Action Flowing from Class Interest

According to our terminology, the factor that creates 'class' is unambiguously economic interest, and indeed, only those interests involved in the existence of the 'market.' Nevertheless, the concept of 'class-interest' is an ambiguous one: even as an empirical concept it is ambiguous as soon as one understands by it something other than the factual direction of interests following with a certain probability from the class situation for a certain 'average' of those people subjected to the class situation. The class situation and other circumstances remaining the same, the direction in which the individual worker, for instance, is likely to pursue his interests may vary widely, according to whether he is constitutionally qualified for the task at hand to a high, to an average, or to a low degree. In the same way, the direction of interests may vary according to whether or not a *communal* action of a larger or smaller portion of those commonly affected by the 'class situation,' or even an association among them, e.g. a 'trade union,' has grown out of the class situation from which the individual may or may not expect promising results. [Communal action refers to that action which is oriented to the feeling of the actors that they belong together. Social action, on the other hand, is oriented to a rationally motivated adjustment of interests.] The rise of societal or even of communal action from a common class situation is by no means a universal phenomenon.

The class situation may be restricted in its effects to the generation of essentially *similar* reactions, that is to say, within our terminology, of 'mass actions.' However, it may not have even this result. Furthermore, often merely an amorphous communal action emerges. For example, the 'murmuring' of the workers known in ancient oriental ethics: the moral disapproval of the work-master's conduct, which in its practical significance was probably equivalent to an increasingly typical phenomenon of precisely the latest industrial development, namely, the 'slow down' (the deliberate limiting of work effort) of laborers by virtue of tacit agreement. The degree in which 'communal action' and possibly 'societal action' emerges from the 'mass actions' of the members of a class is linked to general cultural conditions, especially to those of an intellectual sort. It is also linked to the extent of the contrasts that have already evolved, and is especially linked to the *transparency* of the connections between the causes and the consequences of the 'class situation.' For however different life chances may be, this fact in itself, according to all experience, by no means gives birth to 'class action' (communal action by the members of a class). The fact of being conditioned and the results of the class situation must be distinctly recognizable. For only then the contrast of life chances can be felt not as an absolutely given fact to be accepted, but as a resultant from either (1) the given distribution of property, or (2) the structure of the concrete economic order. It is only then that people may react against the class structure not only through acts of an intermittent and irrational protest, but in the form of rational association. There have been 'class situations' of the first category (1), of a specifically naked and transparent sort, in the urban centers of Antiquity and during the Middle Ages; especially then, when great fortunes were accumulated by factually monopolized trading in industrial products of these localities or in foodstuffs. Futhermore, under certain circumstances, in the rural economy of the most diverse periods, when agriculture was increasingly exploited in a profit-making manner. The most important historical example of the second category (2) is the class situation of the modern 'proletariat.'

4: Types of 'Class Struggle'

Thus every class may be the carrier of any one of the possibly innumerable forms of 'class action,' but this is not necessarily so. In any case, a class does not in itself constitute a community. To treat 'class' conceptually as having the same value as 'community' leads to distortion. That men in the same class situation regularly react in mass actions to such tangible situations as economic ones in the direction of those interests that are most adequate to their average number is an important and after all simple fact for the understanding of historical events. Above all, this fact must not lead to that kind of pseudoscientific operation with the concepts of 'class' and 'class interests' so frequently found these days, and which has found its most classic expression in the statement of a talented author that the individual may be in error concerning his interests but that the 'class' is 'infallible' about its interests. Yet, if classes as such are not communities, nevertheless class situations emerge only on the basis of communialization. The communal action that brings forth class situations, however, is not basically action between members of the identical class; it is an action between members of different classes. Communal actions that directly determine the class situation of the worker and the entrepreneur are: the labor market, the commodities market, and the capitalistic enterprise. But, in its turn, the existence of a capitalistic enterprise presupposes that a very specific communal action exists and that it is specifically structured to protect the possession of goods *per se,* and especially the power of individuals to dispose, in principle freely, over the means of production. The existence of a capitalistic enterprise is preconditioned by a specific kind of 'legal order.' Each kind of class situation, and above all when it rests upon the power of property *per se,* will become most clearly efficacious when all other determinants of reciprocal relations are, as far as possible, eliminated in their significance. It is in this way that the utilization of the power of property in the market obtains its most sovereign importance.

Now 'status groups' hinder the strict carrying through of the sheer market principle. In the present context they are of interest to us only from this one point of view. Before we briefly consider them, note that not much of a general nature can be said about the more specific kinds of antagonism between 'classes' (in our meaning of the term). The great shift, which has been going on continuously in the past, and up to our times, may be summarized, although at the cost of some precision: the struggle in which class situations are effective has progressively shifted from consumption credit toward, first, competitive struggles in the commodity market and, then, toward price wars on the labor market. The 'class struggles' of antiquity—to the extent that they were genuine class struggles and not struggles between status groups—were initially carried on by indebted peasants, and perhaps also by artisans threatened by debt bondage and struggling against urban creditors. For debt bondage is the normal result of the differentiation of wealth in commercial cities, especially in seaport cities. A similar situation has existed among cattle breeders. Debt relationships as such produced class action up to the time of Cataline. Along with this, and with an increase in provision of grain for the city by transporting it from the outside, the struggle over the means of sustenance emerged. It centered in the first place around the provision of bread and the determination of the price of bread. It lasted throughout antiquity and the entire Middle Ages. The propertyless as such flocked together against those who actually and supposedly were interested in the dearth of bread. This fight spread until it involved all those commodities essential to the way of life and to handicraft production. There were only incipient discussions of wage disputes in antiquity and in the Middle Ages. But they have been slowly increasing up into modern times. In the earlier periods they were completely secondary to slave rebellions as well as to fights in the commodity market.

The propertyless of antiquity and of the Middle Ages protested against monopolies, pre-emption, forestalling, and the withholding of goods from the market in order to raise prices. Today the central issue is the determination of the price of labor.

This transition is represented by the fight for access to the market and for the determination of the price of products. Such fights went on between merchants and workers in the putting-out system of domestic handicraft during the transition to modern times. Since it is quite a general phenomenon we must mention here that the class antagonisms that are conditioned through the market situation are usually most bitter between those who actually and directly participate as opponents in price wars. It is not the rentier, the share-holder, and the banker who suffer the ill will of the worker, but almost exclusively the manufacturer and the business executives who are the direct opponents of workers in price wars. This is so in spite of the fact that it is precisely the cash boxes of the rentier, the share-holder, and the banker into which the more or less 'unearned' gains flow, rather than into the pockets of the manufacturers or of the business executives. This simple state of affairs has very frequently been decisive for the role the class situation has played in the formation of political parties. For example, it has made possible the varieties of patriarchal socialism and the frequent attempts—formerly, at least—of threatened status groups to form alliances with the proletariat against the 'bourgeoisie.'

5: Status Honor

In contrast to classes, *status groups* are normally communities. They are, however, often of an amorphous kind. In contrast to the purely economically determined 'class situation' we wish to designate as 'status situation' every typical component of the life fate of men that is determined by a specific, positive or negative, social estimation of *honor*. This honor may be connected with any quality shared by a plurality, and, of course, it can be knit to a class situation: class distinctions are linked in the most varied ways with status distinctions. Property as such is not always recognized as a status qualification, but in the long run it is, and with extraordinary regularity. In the subsistence economy of the organized neighborhood, very often the richest man is simply the chieftain. However, this often means only an honorific preference. For example, in the so-called pure modern 'democracy,' that is, one devoid of any expressly ordered status privileges for individuals, it may be that only the families coming under approximately the same tax class dance with one another. This example is reported of certain smaller Swiss cities. But status honor need not necessarily be linked with a 'class situation.' On the contrary, it normally stands in sharp opposition to the pretensions of sheer property.

Both propertied and propertyless people belong to the same status group, and frequently they do with very tangible consequences. This 'equality' of social esteem may, however, in the long run become quite precarious. The 'equality' of status among the American 'gentlemen,' for instance, is expressed by the fact that outside the subordination determined by the different functions of 'business,' it would be considered strictly repugnant—wherever the old tradition still prevails—if even the richest 'chief,' while playing billiards or cards in his club in the evening, would not treat his 'clerk' as in every sense fully his equal in birthright. It would be repugnant if the American 'chief' would bestow upon his 'clerk' the condescending 'benevolence' marking a distinction of 'position,' which the German chief can never dissever from his attitude. This is one of the most important reasons why in America the German 'clubby-ness' has never been able to attain the attraction that the American clubs have.

6: Guarantees of Status Stratification

In content, status honor is normally expressed by the fact that above all else a specific *style of life* can be expected from all those who wish to belong to the circle. Linked with this expectation are restrictions on 'social' intercourse (that is, intercourse which is not subservient to economic or any other of business's 'functional' purposes). These restrictions may confine normal marriages to within the status circle and may lead to complete endogamous closure. As soon as there is not a mere individual and socially irrelevant imitation of another style of life, but an agreed-upon communal action of this closing character, the 'status' development is under way.

In its characteristic form, stratification by 'status group' on the basis of conventional styles of life evolves at the present time in the United

States out of the traditional democracy. For example, only the resident of a certain street ('the street') is considered as belonging to 'society,' is qualified for social intercourse, and is visited and invited. Above all, this differentiation evolves in such a way as to make for strict submission to the fashion that is dominant at a given time in society. This submission to fashion also exists among men in America to a degree unknown in Germany. Such submission is considered to be an indication of the fact that a given man *pretends* to qualify as a gentleman. This submission decides, at least *prima facie,* that he will be treated as such. And this recognition becomes just as important for his employment chances in 'swank' establishments, and above all, for social intercourse and marriage with 'esteemed' families, as the qualification for dueling among Germans in the Kaiser's day. As for the rest: certain families resident for a long time, and, of course, correspondingly wealthy, e.g. 'F.F.V., i.e. First Families of Virginia,' or the actual or alleged descendants of the 'Indian Princess' Pocahontas, of the Pilgrim fathers, or of the Knickerbockers, the members of almost inaccessible sects and all sorts of circles setting themselves apart by means of any other characteristics and badges . . . all these elements usurp 'status' honor. The development of status is essentially a question of stratification resting upon usurpation. Such usurpation is the normal origin of almost all status honor. But the road from this purely conventional situation to legal privilege, positive or negative, is easily traveled as soon as a certain stratification of the social order has in fact been 'lived in' and has achieved stability by virtue of a stable distribution of economic power.

7: 'Ethnic' Segregation and 'Caste'

Where the consequences have been realized to their full extent, the status group evolves into a closed 'caste.' Status distinctions are then guaranteed not merely by conventions and laws, but also by *rituals.* This occurs in such a way that every physical contact with a member of any caste that is considered to be 'lower' by the members of a 'higher' caste is considered as making for a ritualistic impurity and to be a stigma which must be expiated by a religious act. Individual castes develop quite distinct cults and gods.

In general, however, the status structure reaches such extreme consequences only where there are underlying differences which are held to be 'ethnic.' The 'caste' is, indeed, the normal form in which ethnic communities usually live side by side in a "societalized' manner. These ethnic communities believe in blood relationship and exclude exogamous marriage and social intercourse. Such a caste situation is part of the phenomenon of 'pariah' peoples and is found all over the world. These people form communities, acquire specific occupational traditions of handicrafts or of other arts, and cultivate a belief in their ethnic community. They live in a 'dispora' strictly segregated from all personal intercourse, except that of an unavoidable sort, and their situation is legally precarious. Yet, by virtue of their economic indispensability, they are tolerated, indeed, frequently privileged, and they live in interspersed political communities. The Jews are the most impressive historical example.

A 'status' segregation grown into a 'caste' differs in its structure from a mere 'ethnic' segregation: the caste structure transforms the horizontal and unconnected coexistences of ethnically segregated groups into a vertical social system of super- and subordination. Correctly formulated: a comprehensive societalization integrates the ethnically divided communities into specific political and communal action. In their consequences they differ precisely in this way: ethnic coexistences condition a mutual repulsion and disdain but allow each ethnic community to consider its own honor as the highest one; the cast structure brings about a social subordination and an acknowledgment of 'more honor' in favor of the privileged caste and status groups. This is due to the fact that in the caste structure ethnic distinctions as such have become 'functional' distinctions within the political societalization (warriors, priests, artisans that are politically important for war and for building, and so on). But even pariah people who are most despised are usually apt to continue cultivating in some manner that which is equally peculiar to ethnic and to status communities: the belief in their own specific 'honor.' This is the case with the Jews.

Only with the negatively privileged status groups does the 'sense of dignity' take a specific deviation. A sense of dignity is the precipitation in individuals of social honor and of conventional demands which a positively privileged status group raises for the deportment of its members. The sense of dignity that characterizes positively privileged status groups is naturally related to their 'being' which does not transcend itself, that is, it is to their 'beauty and excellence' [(καλο-κἀγαθια)]. Their kingdom is 'of this world.' They live for the present and by exploiting their great past. The sense of dignity of the negatively privileged strata naturally refers to a future lying beyond the present, whether it is of this life or of another. In other words, it must be nurtured by the belief in a providential 'mission' and by a belief in a specific honor before God. The 'chosen people's' dignity is nurtured by a belief either that in the beyond 'the last will be the first,' or that in this life a Messiah will appear to bring forth into the light of the world which has cast them out the hidden honor of the pariah people. This simple state of affairs, and not the 'resentment' which is so strongly emphasized in Nietzsche's much admired construction in the *Genealogy of Morals*, is the source of the religiosity cultivated by pariah status groups. In passing, we may note that resentment may be accurately applied only to a limited extent; for one of Nietzsche's main examples, Buddhism, it is not at all applicable.

Incidentally, the development of status groups from ethnic segregations is by no means the normal phenomenon. On the contrary, since objective 'racial differences' are by no means basic to every subjective sentiment of an ethnic community, the ultimately racial foundation of status structure is rightly and absolutely a question of the concrete individual case. Very frequently a status group is instrumental in the production of a thoroughbred anthropological type. Certainly a status group is to a high degree effective in producing extreme types, for they select personally qualified individuals (e.g. the Knighthood selects those who are fit for warfare, physically and psychically). But selection is far from being the only, or the predominant, way in which status groups are formed: Political membership or class situation has at all times been at least as frequently decisive. And today the class situation is by far the predominant factor, for of course the possibility of a style of life expected for members of a status group is usually conditioned economically.

8: STATUS PRIVILEGES

For all practical purposes, stratification by status goes hand in hand with a monopolization of ideal and material goods or opportunities, in a manner we have come to know as typical. Besides the specific status honor, which always rests upon distance and exclusiveness, we find all sorts of material monopolies. Such honorific preferences may consist of the privilege of wearing special costumes, of eating special dishes taboo to others, of carrying arms—which is most obvious in its consequences—the right to pursue certain non-professional dilettante artistic practices, e.g. to play certain musical instruments. Of course, material monopolies provide the most effective motives for the exclusiveness of a status group; although, in themselves, they are rarely sufficient, almost always they come into play to some extent. Within a status circle there is the question of intermarriage: the interest of the families in the monopolization of potential bridegrooms is at least of equal importance and is parallel to the interest in the monopolization of daughters. The daughters of the circle must be provided for. With an increased inclosure of the status group, the conventional preferential opportunities for special employment grow into a legal monopoly of special offices for the members. Certain goods become objects for monopolization by status groups. In the typical fashion these include 'entailed estates' and frequently also the possessions of serfs or bondsmen and, finally, special trades. This monopolization occurs positively when the status group is exclusively entitled to own and to manage them; and negatively when, in order to maintain its specific way of life, the status group must *not* own and manage them.

The decisive role of a 'style of life' in status 'honor' means that status groups are the specific bearers of all 'conventions.' In whatever way it may be manifest, all 'stylization' of life either originates in status groups or is at least conserved by them. Even if the principles of status conventions differ greatly, they reveal certain typical traits, especially among those strata which are most privileged. Quite generally, among privileged status groups there is a status disqualification that operates against the performance of common physical labor. This disqualification is now 'setting in' in America against the old tradition of esteem for labor. Very frequently every rational economic pursuit, and especially 'entrepreneurial activity,' is looked upon as a disqualification of status. Artistic and literary activity is also considered as degrading work as soon as it is exploited for income, or at least when it is connected with hard physical exertion. An example is the sculptor working like a mason in his dusty smock as over against the painter in his salon-like 'studio' and those forms of musical practice that are acceptable to the status group.

9: Economic Conditions and Effects of Status Stratification

The frequent disqualification of the gainfully employed as such is a direct result of the principle of status stratification peculiar to the social order, and of course, of this principle's opposition to a distribution of power which is regulated exclusively through the market. These two factors operate along with various individual ones, which will be touched upon below.

We have seen above that the market and its processes 'knows no personal distinctions': 'functional' interests dominate it. It knows nothing of 'honor.' The status order means precisely the reverse, viz.: stratification in terms of 'honor' and of styles of life peculiar to status groups as such. If mere economic acquisition and naked economic power still bearing the stigma of its extra-status origin could bestow upon anyone who has won it the same honor as those who are interested in status by virtue of style of life claim for themselves, the status order would be threatened at its very root. This is the more so as, given equality of status honor, property *per se* represents an addition even if it is not overtly acknowledged to be such. Yet if such economic acquisition and power gave the agent any honor at all, his wealth would result in his attaining more honor than those who successfully claim honor by virtue of style of life. Therefore all groups having interests in the status order react with special sharpness precisely against the pretensions of purely economic acquisition. In most cases they react the more vigorously the more they feel themselves threatened. Calderon's respectful treatment of the peasant, for instance, as opposed to Shakespeare's simultaneous and ostensible disdain of the *canaille* illustrates the different way in which a firmly structured status order reacts as compared with a status order that has become economically precarious. This is an example of a state of affairs that recurs everywhere. Precisely because of the rigorous reactions against the claims of property *per se*, the 'parvenu' is never accepted, personally and without reservation, by the privileged status groups, no matter how completely his style of life has been adjusted to theirs. They will only accept his descendants who have been educated in the conventions of their status group and who have never besmirched its honor by their own economic labor.

As to the general *effect* of the status order, only one consequence can be stated, but it is a very important one: the hindrance of the free development of the market occurs first for those goods which status groups directly withheld from free exchange by monopolization. This monopolization may be effected either legally or conventionally. For example, in many Hellenic cities during the epoch of status groups, and also originally in Rome, the inherited estate (as is shown by the old formula for indiction against spendthrifts) was monopolized just as were the estates of knights, peasants, priests, and especially the clientele of the craft and merchant guilds. The market is restricted, and the power of naked property *per se*, which gives its stamp to 'class formation,' is pushed into the background. The results of this process can be most varied. Of course, they do not necessarily weaken the contrasts in the economic situation. Frequently they strengthen these contrasts, and in any case, where stratification by status permeates a community as strongly as was the case in all political communities of antiquity and of the Middle Ages, one can never speak of a genuinely free market competition as we understand it today. There are wider effects than this direct exclusion of special goods from the market. From the contrariety between the status order and the purely economic order mentioned above, it follows that in most instances the notion of honor peculiar to status absolutely abhors that which is essential to the market: higgling. Honor abhors higgling among peers and occasionally it taboos higgling for the members of a status group in general. Therefore, everywhere some status groups, and usually the most influential, consider almost any kind of overt participation in economic acquisition as absolutely stigmatizing.

With some over-simplification, one might thus say that 'classes' are stratified according to their relations to the production and acquisition of goods; whereas 'status groups' are stratified according to the principles of their *consumption* of goods as represented by special 'styles of life.'

An 'occupational group' is also a status group. For normally, it successfully claims social honor only by virtue of the special style of life which may be determined by it. The difference between classes and status groups frequently overlap. It is precisely those status communities most strictly segregated in terms of honor (viz. the Indian castes) who today show, although within very rigid limits, a relatively high degree of indifference to pecuniary income. However, the Brahmins seek such income in many different ways.

As to the general economic conditions making for the predominance of stratification by 'status,' only very little can be said. When the bases of the acquisition and distribution of goods are relatively stable, stratification by status is favored. Every technological repercussion and economic transformation threatens stratification by status and pushes the class situation into the foreground. Epochs and countries in which the naked class situation is of predominant significance are regularly the periods of technical and economic transformations. And every slowing down of the shifting of economic stratifications leads, in due course, to the growth of status structures and makes for a resuscitation of the important role of social honor.

10: Parties

Whereas the genuine place of 'classes' is within the economic order, the place of 'status groups' is within the social order, that is, within the sphere of the distribution of 'honor.' From within these spheres, classes and status groups influence one another and they influence the legal order and are in turn influenced by it. But 'parties' live in a house of 'power.'

Their action is oriented toward the acquisition of social 'power,' that is to say, toward influencing a communal action no matter what its content may be. In principle, parties may exist in a social 'club' as well as in a 'state.' As over against the actions of classes and status groups, for which this is not necessarily the case, the communal actions of 'parties' always mean a societalization. For party actions are always directed toward a goal which is striven for in planned manner. This goal may be a 'cause' (the party may aim at realizing a program for ideal or material purposes), or the goal may be 'personal' (sinecures, power, and from these, honor for the leader and the followers of the party). Usually the party action aims at all these simultaneously. Parties are, therefore, only possible within communities that are societalized, that is, which have some rational order and a staff of persons available who are ready to enforce it. For parties aim precisely at influencing this staff, and if possible, to recruit it from party followers.

In any individual case, parties may represent interests determined through 'class situation' or 'status situation,' and they may recruit their following respectively from one or the other. But they need be neither purely 'class' nor purely 'status' parties. In most cases they are partly class parties and partly status parties, but sometimes they are neither. They may represent ephemeral or enduring structures. Their means of attaining power may be quite varied, ranging from naked violence of any sort to canvassing for votes with coarse or subtle means: money, social influence, the force of speech, suggestion, clumsy hoax, and so on to the rougher or more artful tactics of obstruction in parliamentary bodies.

The sociological structure of parties differs in a basic way according to the kind of communal action which they struggle to influence. Parties also differ according to whether or not the community is stratified by status or by classes. Above all else, they vary according to the structure of domination within the community. For their leaders normally deal with the conquest of a community. They are, in the general concept which is maintained here, not only products of specially modern forms of domination. We shall also designate as parties the ancient and medieval 'parties,' despite the fact that their structure differs basically from the structure of modern parties. By virtue of these structural differences of domination it is impossible to say anything about the structure of parties without discussing the structural forms of social domination *per se*. Parties, which are always structures struggling for domination, are very frequently organized in a very strict 'authoritarian' fashion . . .

Concerning 'classes,' 'status groups,' and 'parties,' it must be said in general that they necessarily presuppose a comprehensive societalization, and especially a political framework of communal action, within which they operate. This does not mean that parties would be confined by the frontiers of any individual political community. On the contrary, at all times it has been the order of the day that the societalization (even when it aims at the use of military force in common) reaches beyond the frontiers of politics. This has been the case in the solidarity of interests among the Oligarchs and among the democrats in Hellas, among the Guelfs and among Ghibellines in the Middle Ages, and within the Calvinist party during the period of religious struggles. It has been the case up to the solidarity of the landlords (international congress of agrarian landlords), and has continued among princes (holy alliance, Karlsbad decrees), socialist workers, conservatives (the longing of Prussian conservatives for Russian intervention in 1850). But their aim is not necessarily the establishment of new international political, i.e. *territorial*, dominion. In the main they aim to influence the existing dominion.*

* The posthumously published text breaks off here.

Notes on the Observation
and Measurement of Political Power

Herbert A. Simon

In this selection we shift from an emphasis on the bases or sources of power to a discussion of the problems of defining and assessing power. Herbert Simon conceives of power in terms of causation, i.e., power is causing change in behavior. He is fundamentally concerned with understanding the inter-personal 'action involved in a power situation and with proposing ways in which such interaction may be quantified. As the reader proceeds to subsequent selections in this volume, he will note that Simon's statement of the three requirements of observable data in power analysis is later to be translated into three methods of analyzing community power systems, i.e. in order, the decision-making analysis, the stratified distribution of the resources of influence, and the reputational methods. This article was a pioneering effort to quantify the interpersonal elements of power. The basic concepts it develops preview a substantial body of later theorizing, especially by political scientists, as we shall see in later selections.

If political power is taken as one of the central phenomena to be explained by political science, then the propositions of political science will necessarily contain sentences and phrases like "the power of A is greater than the power of B," "an increase (or decrease) in the power of A," "the distribution of political power," and the like. And if the empirical truth or falsity of such propositions is to be tested, there must be agreement as to the operational definition of the term "power" and the operational means that are to be used to determine the degree of its presence or absence in any situation.

All of this is elementary enough—but how far has the task been carried out; to what extent have the operational tools of observation and measurement been provided us? That a great deal remains to be done can be made clear, I think, by an outrageous example. Suppose that, in the presence of a boorishly critical skeptic, we were to assert: "Peron holds

From Herbert Simon, "Notes on the Observation and Measurement of Power," *Journal of Politics*, XV (November, 1953), 500–512, 514–516. Reprinted by permission of the publisher and the author.

a monopoly of power in Argentina." Suppose that our skeptic were to reply: "Prove it." We could, of course, adopt the tactics of Dr. Johnson who, when asked to prove the existence of the table at which he was sitting, suggested that his disputant kick it. While this reply has never been adjudged entirely adequate by metaphysicians, kicking a table would certainly settle the question of its existence to the satisfaction of most empirical scientists. But how, precisely, does one "kick" a dictatorship to find out if it exists? If I kicked Peron, I would go to jail; but I would also if I kicked the King of England, who is not usually regarded as a dictator.

Now I do not doubt that Peron is dictator of Argentina; nor (a slightly more difficult point to establish) that the King is not dictator of England; nor (an even more subtle point) that Stalin was dictator of Russia at a time when he held no official governmental position whatsoever. Nor will I ask the reader to doubt these propositions. I will ask the reader, however, to join me in an inquiry into the meanings of propositions like those just stated, and into the means for establishing the truth of such propositions—which truth, in spite of the appearance of self-evidence, can certainly be confirmed only by empirical data. In general, our inquiry may be regarded as a series of footnotes on the analysis of influence and power by Lasswell and Kaplan in *Power and Society*, which we will take as the starting point.

Sketch of a Definition of the Term "Power"

Like Humpty Dumpty, we will insist that a word means what we want it to mean. But if our aim is to construct a body of science, and if we already have in view the general range of phenomena to be explained, our definitions may be willful, but they must not be arbitrary. If we were to say that we would measure a man's power by his height, this would be an internally consistent definition, but one hardly useful in exploring the phenomena referred to in common speech as the phenomena of power. If we were to say that we would measure a man's power by his wealth *or* his ability to influence the behavior of others, the definition would not even be internally consistent, for these two criteria might in fact be only imperfectly correlated.[1]

---

[1] As we shall see, Harold D. Lasswell and Abraham Kaplan, in their otherwise very incisive analysis of power in *Power and Society* (New Haven: Yale University Press, 1950) came dangerously close to this latter error, being saved from it only by distinguishing between "influence" and "exercise of influence." Since their terminological convention is certainly inconvenient and confusing, I shall not follow it. Instead, I shall retain "value position" and "value potential" in place of their "influence," and use "influence" for their "exercise of influence."

Power and Value Position. I think that definitions which equate influence or power [2] with the values an individual possesses are unsuitable for political science. The difficulty is revealed when we try to state what we mean by a "value." If we list specific values—wealth, wisdom, or what not—then the statement that "A possesses certain of these values" is not what we mean when we say "A has power." For if these two statements are regarded as identical by definition, then a proposition like "the wealthy are the powerful"—dear to Marxists and anti-Marxists alike—ceases to be an empirical proposition in political science, and becomes true simply by definition.

A second defect of such definitions is that they confront us with the necessity of inventing new values to account for persons whom we wish to regard as powerful, but whose values lie outside the usual lists—Gandhi is a good example.

The situation becomes even worse if we admit power into the list of social values that define power. That power is a value, i.e., something desired and valued, is generally admitted; but if so, to define power as value position renders meaningless propositions like: "We can measure a person's power by his ability to acquire power." [3]

To summarize, I propose to define power and influence in such a way as to distinguish these concepts from value position. In doing so, I believe I am conforming to common usage, because (a) propositions, intended to be empirical, are often asserted with respect to the relation between power and value position, and (b) power is often asserted to be a value (but not the only value) that is desired.

If, having made a distinction between power and value position, we are able to establish an empirical relationship between the two, we can then use value position as an *index* of power—which is something quite different from using it as the defining operation. I think that we can conjecture what the relationship is likely to be. When a society is in a state of stable equilibrium, there is likely to be a close correspondence between the distribution of power and the distribution of value. If this is so, then, *in equilibrium situations,* we can use the value distribution as an index of the power distribution when the latter is difficult to ascertain directly.

Power and Value Potential. Objections similar to those just mentioned can be raised against defining power or influence as synonymous with value potential. Value potential (see Lasswell and Kaplan, p. 58) is simply value position referred to some future date. As before, such a definition would transform from empirical propositions to definitional

[2] It is not necessary, for present purposes, to distinguish between influence and power, and I shall continue to use the two words as synonyms.

[3] On the other hand, if power is independently defined, this proposition becomes an empirical statement about the dynamics of power.

identities such statements as: "Those who have power will employ it to improve their value position"—which is roughly equivalent to: "Those who have power have high value potential."

In fact, the two definitional proposals examined thus far—relating power to value position and value potential, respectively—reveal that even at the empirical level we are not certain as to the relationship between the possession of values and of power. Does possession of power imply high value position or high potentiality of improving value position? In the previous section I suggested that, in equilibrium situations, we assume an empirical relationship to exist between value *position* and power in order to predict the latter from the former. In non-equilibrium situations, we often employ an assumed relationship between power and value *potential* to predict the latter from the former. These empirical dynamic relations may be represented diagrammatically thus:

Value Position —> Power —> Value Potential (Future Value Position).

An Alternative Definition. As an alternative to the definitions just discarded, we propose the definition of "influence process" employed by Lasswell and Kaplan: "The *exercise of influence* (influence process) consists in affecting policies of others than the self."

This definition involves an asymmetrical relation between influencer and influencee. Now we are wary, in the social sciences, of asymmetrical relations. They remind us of pre-Humeian and pre-Newtonian notions of causality. By whip and sword we have been converted to the doctrine that there is no causation, only functional interrelation, and that functional relations are perfectly symmetrical. We may even have taken over, as a very persuasive analogy, the proposition that "for every action, there is an equal and opposite reaction." If, in spite of this, we persist in thinking that there is something asymmetrical about the influence (or power) relation, it may be reassuring that quite similar relations can be introduced into the most respectable of physical systems.

It should be noticed also that the Lasswell-Kaplan definition refers to processes of change rather than to a state of equilibrium. Presumably, we observe the influence of A over B by noting the differences between the way B actually behaves and the way he *would* behave if A were not present (or if A's desires changed). Influence belongs to the theory of dynamics, or of comparative statics, rather than to the theory of equilibrium.

ASYMMETRY OF THE POWER RELATION

The notion that the power or influence relation of A to B is asymmetrical carries with it some implication as to how the phenomenon of power can be observed and measured. Let us first consider the case where the asymmetry is supposed to be complete; i.e., A influences B, but B does not influence A at all. Then, if we are dealing with a determinate system, the behavior of A can be predicted without any reference to his relation to B, while the behavior of B follows once we know the behavior of A. Stated otherwise, the social system as a whole must contain a subsystem, that determines the behavior of A, but in which B does not appear (or at least B's reactions to A's behavior do not appear).

Now to determine the influence of A upon B, we simply observe a number of situations in which the behavior of A varies, and note what is the concomitant variation in B's behavior. As a concrete example, let us suppose that a dictator is "unilaterally coupled" to his subjects—his decisions determine their behavior, but there is no "feedback" from their behavior to his. Then, if by manipulating the variables that determine his own expectations or desires we can change his decisions, we can also observe what changes this brings about in the behavior of the subjects.

Power in the Presence of Feedback. It will immediately be objected that we are never faced with a situation involving unilateral coupling in this extreme sense—that there is always some feedback from the influencee to the influencer. This difficulty can be handled in either of two ways: (1) we can give up the idea that the relation is asymmetrical; or (2) we can add an asymmetrical relation operating in the opposite direction from the first. *If the processes of influence take time,* and particularly if the time lags associated with the two asymmetrical relations are different, there is at least the possibility that we can make separate empirical observations of the two relations.

If, in our previous example, our dictator makes a decision, and if he is sensitive to public approval and disapproval, then we will observe in sequence: (1) the decision, (2) subsequent changes in behavior of the subjects, (3) expressions of approval or disapproval by the subjects, and (4) modifications in the decision if it proves to be unpopular. In favorable cases, the feedback may involve large time lags. If, instead of a dictator, we have an elected president, the feedback might take the form of a change in the holder of the office at the next election.

Now, if there is any feedback at all, measurement of influence requires the observation of disequilibrium as well as equilibrium. In a state of equilibrium in the case of the elected president, the last previous election would have already put in office a president whose decisions would be acceptable to the citizens—it would be impossible to determine whether the chicken was mother or daughter of the egg.

The Rule of Anticipated Reactions. But an even graver difficulty must be admitted. Because of the phenomenon that Friedrich has christened "the rule of anticipated reactions" and that the servomechanism engineer calls "anticipatory control," the time lags upon which we depend for measurement may be destroyed. If the President is elected, his decisions may be affected not only by what the citizens did in the last election, but also by his expectations of what they will do in the next.

I think it can be seen that the possibility of measuring the separate links in the chain of influence depend, in this instance, on the presence of some ignorance in the system. So long as the President is able to form exact expectations of the citizens' reactions, and they of what a candidate will do if elected, his influence on them cannot be distinguished from their influence on him, but let his or their forecasts be in error and the possibilities of disentangling the relations are re-established.

Fortunately for political scientists—who would otherwise be largely debarred from observation of the central phenomenon of their science— the members of the body politic are often far from accurate in their predictions. If President Roosevelt had foreseen the outcome of the 1938 "purges" he might not have undertaken them, and we should have been deprived of valuable information about influences on voting behavior. If the assassination of Lincoln had been anticipated, we would have lost instructive insights into the relative powers of President and Congress provided by the administration of Andrew Johnson. The unpredicted and the unexpected provide a break in the usual chain of intended connections and, serving as something of a substitute for controlled experimentation, permit us to observe the construction of the separate links.

Implications of the Definition. Apart from the question of measurement, the habit of viewing a social structure as a network of (generally) asymmetrical relationships can help to clarify some of the ambiguities that are commonly found in statements of power relationships. This formulation teaches us that, when we wish to speak of the influence of a particular element in a social system upon that system, we must specify whether we mean the influence of the element considered as independent, with all the reverse feedback relations ignored, or whether we mean the net influence of the element, taking into account all the reciprocal influences of other elements upon it. Concretely, how powerful we consider the President to be depends on whether we ignore, or take into consideration, the fact that he is an elected official, and the fact that he is advised by a corps of permanent civil servants.

If we regard the President as an "independent variable," then we arrive at one assessment of his influence. If we add to our system the environmental influences created by the administrative bureaucracy, which greatly restrict the variability that differences in personal qualities and beliefs would otherwise produce in the behavior of different presidents, we arrive at a smaller estimate of the influence of those personal qualities and beliefs.

As an exercise for developing his skill in handling both this distinction and the rule of anticipated reactions, the reader may like to test his wits on the proposition: "The power of the President can be measured by the number of bills he vetoes where the veto is not overridden."

The interpretation of influence as unilateral coupling corresponds reasonably well with our everyday intuitive notions. We would ordinarily argue that it makes a greater difference to events in the United States if a Justice of the Supreme Court or a United States Senator is replaced than if John Jones, an Idaho potato farmer, retires and turns over his farm to his son. What we are saying here is that the personal characteristics of the individual occupying a particular position (a judgeship or a senatorial seat) constitutes a variable upon which other variables in the system depend. The influence of any position, according to this notion, is proportional to the amount of change induced throughout the system by a change in the characteristics of the individual occupying the position in question.

The Exercise of Influence and the Influence Base

Direct measurements of influence are obtained when we can observe the ratio of change in behavior of influence to change in behavior of influencer. If, starting with such measurements, we are able to determine empirically the conditions that make for influence—the characteristics of individuals and situations that permit us to predict that the influence of a particular individual will be large—then we can derive from these empirical relationships additional indirect measurements of influence. In particular, if we can measure the magnitude of the influence *base,* we can infer from this the magnitude of the influence. (E.g., if wealth is the principal influence base in a particular situation—the principal means for exercising influence—then in that situation we may measure influence by wealth.)

Dynamic Relationships. Now there are generally intricate relationships among the bases of influence and the values that are sought. In the first place, influence is the means, in rational social behavior, of securing the values that are desired. Hence, influence itself, and consequently the bases of influence also become something valued as means to other values. Moreover, many of the bases of influence may be valued *both* as means for the exercise of influence and for other reasons as well.

Wealth will serve as an example. Wealth, in most societies, is a base of influence, hence, a means for securing values. But wealth is also valued for the consumption it permits and the deference it commands. Now consider the extreme case of a society in which wealth is the only influence base, and where consumption and deference are the only values. In such a society, *investment* is the use of influence to augment the influence base, *consumption* is the use of influence to augment other values without increase in the influence base.

Similar dynamic relationships apply to influence bases other than wealth. Political power, too, can be "invested"—control of a legislature may be employed to gerrymander legislative districts in order to ensure continued control. It can also be consumed, to obtain desired legislation, sometimes at the expense of future power.

I have spelled out these dynamic relationships to emphasize the point made earlier that it is essential to distinguish between the operations that measure influence directly, and the indirect estimates of influence that can be inferred from measurements of the influence base. It is often true that influence is used to obtain value. (This accounts for the relationship between influence and value potential.) It is often true that value position provides the influence base. (This accounts for the relationship between influence and value position.) It is often true that influence is employed to augment future influence. In the scheme proposed here, these are all empirical relationships that should not be confused with definitional identities.

Comments on the Nature of the Influence Base. The term "influence base" has been used here to refer to the conditions for the exercise of influence. The influence base is by no means synonymous with the value position, although there are two significant connections between them. First, when values are exchangeable, they can be given to others in return for desired behavior. It is in this sense that values provide a base for influence. Second, any condition that gives its possessor influence is likely to become a disideratum—a value. It is not because being a Supreme Court Justice is valued that such a Justice has influence; but, conversely, it is because he has influence that the position is valued.[4]

Because the connection between influence base and value is not always the same, a classification of influence bases in terms of the values related to them is rather superficial. A more fundamental basis for classification is with respect to the motivation of the influences that leads him to accept influence. On this basis, Lasswell and Kaplan define three successively narrower terms: (a) influence (encompassing all motivations

---

[4] To be sure, the connection can be even more complicated in a society where persons having a high value position are regarded as possessing the legitimate right to exercise influence. An example would be a prestigious scientist whose pronouncements on theology and politics are given respectful attention. But, properly speaking, the influence base in this case is not prestige but the rules of legitimacy in the society. I think the point will be clear after we have discussed, in the next paragraphs, the concept of legitimacy.

for acceptance); (b) power (acceptance motivated by sanctions); and (c) authority (acceptance motivated by attitudes toward legitimacy).

There has been some tendency in the literature of political science to regard ordinary sanctions, like money and physical force, as the bases of "effective" power; and legitimacy as the base of "formal" power. The implication of this kind of language is that "effective" power is what determines actual behavior, while "formal" power is some kind of epiphenomenal rationalization of the power structure—window-dressing, so to speak.[5] Some political scientists, however, Charles Merriam being a notable example, insist on legitimacy as an important independent motivation for the acceptance of power.

Which of these viewpoints is correct—and to what extent—is an empirical question. The definitions we have thus far constructed indicate, at least schematically, what kinds of data would be needed to answer the question. What is required is a situation in which we can observe: (a) the distribution of power as indicated by behavior changes of influencees as a function of behavior changes of influencers; (b) the distribution of monetary, physical, and similar sanctions among the influencers; and (c) the attitudes of influencees toward legitimacy, and their beliefs as to where legitimate power lies. Situations where there is the greatest possible discrepancy between the possession of sanctions and the possession of legitimacy would be the most rewarding. Many clearcut examples of the discrepancy between power bases can be found, of course, in revolutions. An example of a more subtle situation that could profitably be examined from this viewpoint is the behavior of the United States Senate in the 1937 fight over the Supreme Court bill. I will not try to prejudge the evidence except to state my personal conviction that legitimacy will turn out to be a far from epiphenomenal aspect of the power structure.

Expectations and the Power Base. An empirical study of this problem will not proceed very far without disclosing another crucial behavioral variable: the *expectation* of each of the participants about the behavior of the others. I refer not merely to the obscuring effects of the rule of anticipated reactions, discussed earlier, but to the fact that the consequences an individual thinks will follow on his actions depend on what action he thinks other individuals will take.

A political régime prescribes appropriate behavior rôles to its participants; these rôles include appropriate actions to constrain any particular

---

[5] Lasswell and Kaplan take a middle ground on this question. According to them, legitimacy has real force (pp. 121–3, 134), but the holders of effective power, because they can interpret the essentially ambiguous rules of legitimacy, can rationalize almost any power structure they prefer (pp. 126–130). But the authors, while tending to discount the limits on the process of rationalization, do recognize that limits exist (p. 130).

participant (or small group of participants) who departs from his rôle. But the constraints will be applied only if the remaining participants (or most of them) continue to play their rôles. Hence, most of the sanctions a political régime has at its disposal—whether they consist of money, force, attitudes toward legitimacy, or what not—disappear at once when a large number of the participants act in concert to depart from their rôles.

To each individual in a political régime, consequently, the régime looks exceedingly stable so long as he expects the other individuals to support it; it looks exceedingly unstable when he pictures himself as acting in concert with a large number of others to overthrow it. Hence, estimates of the stability of a political structure depend not only on observation of the distribution of actual power, or of the distribution of the power base; but equally upon estimates of the capacity of subgroups for co-ordinated action.

It follows from this that power and influence, measured in terms of the definitions we have proposed, are not additive quantities. Every observation of a power relationship makes an assumption, whether explicit or implicit, as to the pattern of expectation and of group co-ordination. Such an observation will have predictive value, in general, only so long as this assumption holds.

To take a specific example, if we were to make some observations as to the power of a political party to discipline an individual member, we would probably reach conclusions that would be completely inapplicable to the question of the party's power to discipline an organized dissenting clique.

Expectations as a Means of Measuring Power. At this point we might revert to a point raised at the beginning of this paper: how do we know that Peron is dictator of Argentina? If we accept the proposition we have just been urging, that expectations of consequences are a major determinant of behavior, then we can use such expectations, so long as the situation means stable, to estimate where power lies.

We are faced here with an example of a self-confirming prophecy. Suppose we are able to ascertain that the people of Argentina really believe that Peron is dictator. It follows that they will expect sanctions to be applied to themselves if they do not accept the decisions of the Peron régime. Hence, so long as these expectations remain they will behave as if Peron were dictator, and indeed, he will be.

It seems to me that this is the valid core of the naive method we commonly employ as political scientists when, seeking to determine the power structure in a particular situation, we ask the participants what the power structure is. This procedure is valid to the extent that the expectations of the participants constitute the power base. It gives us, in fact, an indirect measure of influence in the same way that data on wealth, or on attitudes of legitimacy, give us indirect measures of influence.

Now if this technique of observation is to be used sophisticatedly, certain cautions must be observed. First, such observations fail to reveal wheels within wheels in the power mechanism. Peron decides for Argentina, but who decides for Peron? Second, when expectations diverge from the other elements in the power base, they may conceal the fragility of the power structure. We have seen that revolution involves, above all, a change in the expectations, and this will be revealed only at the moment of revolution.

Both of these points can be illuminated by looking at the phenomenon of the "figurehead." The holder of power begins to move toward the status of figurehead when his behavior is no longer an "independent variable" but is itself determined by his submission to power. This can take place in at least two ways. First, he may be aware of sanctions to which he is subject that are not apparent to others (if he makes the wrong decision, the secret police will assassinate him, or his mistress will refuse to sleep with him). In this case, he becomes a figurehead when the existence of these sanctions becomes known, for this knowledge will alter the expectations to conform to the "real" power structure. (Of course, other power bases enter to modify the course of events—he may continue to wield power because feelings of legitimacy attach to him.)

Second, the power holder may sense that the system of expectations is fragile—that revolution is imminent unless he anticipates the reactions to his exercise of power and restrains it within limits. Again, when awareness develops of his self-restraint, expectations will begin to change and he will begin to lose his power. It can hardly be doubted that this was a central process in the movement of England from a monarchical to a democratic government.

With this we may close our comments on the influence base—the conditions for the exercise of influence. We have seen that influence and the bases of influence are distinct and separately observable concepts; and that independent observation of them is required to assess the relative effectiveness of various influence bases in the influence process. Finally, we have seen that observations of the exercise of influence must, to be meaningful, be accompanied by observations of the expectations and capacities for co-operative action of the various subgroups acting in the power arena.

THE UNITS OF OBSERVATION

Our definition of influence leaves quite ambiguous the kinds of units in which degrees of influence might be expressed. The quantities with which we are most familiar are those measured in *cardinal numbers:* A weighs 200 pounds; he weighs twice as much as B. Sometimes we deal with a "weaker" kind of number, the *ordinal number,* which permits us to say that: "A is cleverer than B," but not: "A is twice as clever as B." We may also be aware of quantities that are not single numbers but pairs, triples, or n-tuples of numbers (usually called *vectors*). If A has five oranges and three apples, we may denote his possessions by the vector (5,3). We can say that A has more than B, who has (4,2); but we cannot compare A with C, who has (4,5). We cannot say that D has twice as many as A unless he has exactly twice as many apples *and* twice as many oranges.

All of these kinds of quantities, and others as well, occur in the physical sciences. Mass is a cardinal number, hardness an ordinal number, and force a vector. We should expect to find at least as rich a variety of quantities in the social sciences. Hence, we must ask ourselves what "kind" of a quantity best represents influence and power.[6]

I do not propose to tackle the problem in all its generality, but will, instead, examine one broad class of situations that I think is of significance. The particular class of power relations with which I shall be concerned is usually denoted by the term "authority," and I shall retain that term although it is used in a very different sense by Lasswell and Kaplan.[7]

We will say that an individual accepts *authority* when his choice among alternative behaviors is determined by the communicated decision of another. The acceptance of authority may stem from any combination whatsoever of the bases of power—monetary inducements, force, legitimacy, or any others. Authority is never unlimited—the range of alternative behaviors from which the superior may select the particular choice he desires of the subordinate is a finite range. The limits within which authority will be accepted we will call the *zone of acceptance.*

It is clear from the definition that authority is a form of influence: when A exercises authority over B, he exercises influence over B. Hence, a measurement of authority will be a measurement of at least one form of influence.

Let us regard each possible behavior that B can perform as an element in a set, and let us designate the set of all such possible behaviors

---

[6] I believe that most of the arguments against "quantitizing" or "measuring" the "qualitative" variables encountered in the social sciences stem from ignorance of how flexible the concept "quantity" is, and how indefinite the lines between quantity and quality. Such arguments are particularly suspect when it is asserted in one sentence that a particular variable is "essentially qualitative" and in the next that the adjectives "more" or "less" can be predicated of it.

[7] As has been stated previously, in *Power and Society,* authority denotes power based on legitimacy.

by V. The set of behaviors that B will perform at A's command (the subset of V corresponding to B's zone of acceptance) we will designate by S. Then we can use the size of the set S as a measure of A's authority over B.

But what kind of a quantity is the size of S? Suppose that at one time B will accept any order in the set S, but at some later time he will only accept orders in S', which is a part of S. Then we are surely justified in saying that A's authority has decreased. Under such circumstances, comparisons of "greater" and "less" are possible. But it may happen that the zone of acceptance changes from S' to S' ' where these are intersecting (overlapping) sets neither of which entirely includes the other. In this case we cannot say that A's authority has increased or that it has decreased—our sets are not completely ordered. The kind of quantity that appears most suitable for measuring the degree of authority of A over B is what the mathematician would call a "partial ordering."

Now this may seem a disappointing result—we started off with brave talk about "measuring" and have ended with some statements about more or less inclusive sets. The point is that whatever quantities we construct must reflect the characteristics of the phenomena we propose to measure with them. Ordinary cardinal (or even ordinal) numbers possess the property that they are completely ordered. If power relations are only partially ordered, then we shall certainly end up by talking nonsense about them if we insist that they should be represented by cardinal numbers, or that we should always be able to predicate "greater" or "less" of them. If we feel disappointment, it should be directed at the phenomena with which we are confronted rather than at the kind of quantity that appears to represent them.

I must hasten to point out that the above discussion does not in any sense prove that it is impossible to associate cardinal numbers with authority relations. It often happens that, starting with sets of elements, we can associate a cardinal number with each set in such a way that the resulting complete ordering is consistent with the partial ordering defined by the sets themselves. (The cardinal number associated with each set measures, in some sense, its "size.") This is precisely what the tax assessor does when he associates with Jones' set of tangible possessions a number that represents the (presumed) amount of money for which these possessions could be exchanged in the market.

Putting aside the question of using cardinal numbers to measure the "sizes" of different zones of acceptance, we may ask how the sets themselves may be observed and measured. The procedure is relatively straightforward; we observe what kinds of decisions are accepted and what kinds are not. If His Majesty's first minister decides that several hundred additional lords shall be created to establish the supremacy of the House of Commons, will His Majesty accede to the request? The observation falls within our general definition of influence: how does the behavior of the influencee vary with the behavior (in this case the decision) of the influencer?

The difficulties that are generally involved in the observation of influence are present here also. Because of the rule of anticipated reactions, the influencee may behave in accordance with the anticipated decision, never expressed, of the influencer; and the influencer will seldom issue commands that he knows in advance lie outside the zone of acceptance of the influencee—the limits will seldom be observed except when predictions are faulty. Because of the effect of expectations, the zone of acceptance may be suddenly narrowed when the influencee judges that he will be joined in resistance to authority by others.

To pursue these matters further would carry us rapidly into some rather difficult mathematical questions. If we attempted to construct mathematical models for formulating and analyzing authority relations we would be led, I think, to models resembling very closely those employed by von Neumann and Morgenstern in their *Theory of Games and Economic Behavior. . . .*

CONCLUSION

Let us now draw together the threads of our discussion. The problem posed at the outset was how we can make observations and measurements of the distribution of influence and power. The definition of the key terms—"influence" and "power"—is the first step toward an answer. The position taken here is that the phenomenon we wish to measure is an asymmetrical relation between the behavior of two persons. We wish to observe how a change in the behavior of one (the influencer) alters the behavior of the other (the influencee).

We have seen that in most situations, all sorts of reciprocal power relations are present, and that their observation is complicated by the anticipation of reactions. The more accurate the predictions of participants in the system of the reactions of others, the more difficult it becomes to observe influence. Our main hope must be that human beings will remain fallible in their predictions.

To the extent that we can establish empirically the conditions for the exercise of power, these conditions, or influence bases, provide an indirect means for measurement. Observations of the distribution of values and of attitudes regarding legitimacy constitute two significant kinds of indirect evidence about the distribution of power. A third, of critical significance, are the expectations of the participants in the power situation.

In a final section we examined the types of units in terms of which measurement might be expressed. Our principal conclusion here is that we must be prepared to admit into our measurement schemes many other kinds of units besides cardinal numbers. In particular, certain notions from set theory, such as the concept of partial ordering among sets, may be suggestive of fruitful schemes of measurement.

II

COMMUNITY POWER:
RULING ELITE MODELS

From earliest to recent times, scholars have observed that economic, social, and political power invariably rests in the hands of the very few. The concern of scholars with patterns of elite rule is not only a result of their interest in describing reality, but sometimes reflects a number of different normative views about the question whether an elite *should* rule.

Almost all recent studies of community power find that the actual distribution of power falls far short of the ideal type of democracy popularly associated with Athenian Greece, the nineteenth-century New England township, or the Swiss cantons. And yet the conclusions of these studies differ in important ways, which correspond with what we have broadly distinguished as "elite" and "pluralistic" systems. By elite rule we mean that the key decisions in the community are dominated by a fairly autonomous few whose interests are relatively cohesive. In addition, the concept of elite rule usually has a class component; that is, those who rule are economically or socially privileged. On the other hand, political pluralism implies that the distribution of power is somewhat dispersed and that class lines are not the determinants of that distribution. Moreover, in a pluralist political system the balance of power is not invariable over time. It tends to adjust to new levels of equilibrium in response to demands from those who seek a greater share of the rewards that power brings.

Most contemporary students of social influence do not merely report things as they are; they accompany their findings with criticism or justification in normative terms. When criticism or justification is a component of community study, it seems that those authors who find elite systems are more likely to see their role as that of the critic or reformer; those who report pluralist findings, though not always satisfied with things as they are, are more likely to view themselves as defenders of democratic theory. This possible distinction between community power analysts is interesting, and the literature on the normative aspects of this empirical work is extensive.

Another difference between elite and pluralist studies lies in the methodology generally utilized by the authors of each type. By and large, elite studies have sought to determine which individuals in the community have a reputation for being influential "for getting things done." Sometimes such studies seek to identify those who hold positions which are thought to provide their incumbents with power resources. Cadres so identified are then shown to share similar values which they protect or promote. Occasional incidents, frequently anecdotal in character, are utilized to illustrate the degree and manner in which this elite exercises its influence. The approach of the pluralist studies, however, which we will examine in greater detail in the next section, is to regard position and reputation as incidental, secondary, or even irrelevant, and to focus on concrete manifestations of influence in the process of political decision-making.

Finally, elite studies seem to differ from pluralist studies in that the frame of reference of the former is often broader. Those who find elite rule are concerned with the exercise of power in social, educational, religious, political, and economic institutions, with greatest emphasis often placed on the last of these. Pluralist studies, on the other hand, tend to focus on the way in which social, economic, religious and educational influences, etc., are manifested in more or less structured political decisions. As a result of these emphases, elite studies often center on economic dominants while pluralist studies often center on political dominants.

These distinctions, however, can easily be overstated. *As will become increasingly clear in this book, and especially in section IV, the distinctions between elite and pluralist systems are matters of degree rather than of mutually exclusive contrasts.*

The four articles which comprise this section are arranged chronologically and reflect the increasing awareness of the complexity of political power that characterizes the literature in general. Although each selection concludes that the community studied was dominated by a "general purpose" political elite, the three most recent studies note in various ways that political power is not exercised without some limits. These limits include competition, real or potential, as well as the sheer enormity of the task involved in exercising power. However, unlike the pluralist conclusion that leaders have constituencies to which they must be at least moderately responsive, those who find elite rule are more likely to see the relationship between leaders and the community as a whole as the relationship between "players" and "audiences." As in the theater, there is an interaction, but the audience rarely, if ever, pulls the player off the stage.

The first selection below is from the "Middletown" studies of Robert and Helen Lynd. The first of the community studies which utilized the approach of social anthropology, *Middletown* and *Middletown in Transition* are now the classics in this genre. "Middletown" remains the prototype of the city in which one group —in this case the "X Family"—has a virtual monopoly on all aspects of 'community power.

Floyd Hunter's *Community Power Structure* represents another landmark in that he popularized the use of sociometry to demonstrate interpersonal behavior patterns related to community influence. In his study of Atlanta, Hunter describes a city seemingly controlled in all major decisions by financial and social elites, with a sub-layer of personnel who effectuate those decisions. While Hunter was not the first to employ panels of persons knowledgeable in community life who nominate decision-makers, his particular technique was an important step in the systematic study of the community, and led to replication and refinement. This selection reveals the structure of power as Hunter found it, although his full discussion of the extensive sociometric work on which his conclusions were based has been abridged.

The small town has been the subject of much glorification and abuse in the American myth system. For some, it embodies the best of our culture—warm, personal relationships, awareness and interest about issues affecting local life, freedom from the crushing pressures of an impersonal big city, etc. For others, however, the small town is characterized by a homogeneity and conformity which cramp the spirit, by public apathy which allows a few old families or the wealthy to dominate public life, by the absence of cultural and social diversity, etc. Drama and literature have generally emphasized the latter themes, although conventional wisdom has usually preferred the former. We present a selection from *Small Town in Mass Society* by Arthur Vidich and Joseph Bensman which reveals a community of shared values in which an elite can dominate by reflecting and reinforcing those values. (In section III, we will examine a study of another small town where the structure is perceived in a very different way.)

Finally, in the article by Donald A. Clelland and William H. Form, we see an example of the more highly refined methodology of recent years applied comparatively. This is a sophisticated statement of some of the variables which may determine the degree to which those with substantial economic influence dominate the public life of various types of communities.

Many Americans apparently believe (is it that we prefer to believe?) that "the country club set," "the big brass," "the best families," "city hall" (the one you can't fight), and the ubiquitous "they" are the people who *really* run things. It would appear that studies such as those presented here have either shaped or reinforced—probably both—popular notions of the distribution of privilege and prerogative in our society.

As the reader examines the selections in this section he will want to examine critically the research methods utilized by the authors, and the interpretations made of the evidence they find. How does each approach affect the evidence gathered? To what extent are normative biases evident, and do these biases shape the conclusions? How do these studies coincide with the reader's own experience? Most importantly, do these studies (and others like them) require us to be more "realistic" about the value of democratic participation, or to come to grips in some fundamental way with the apparent incongruity between democratic theory and the actual nature of our political and economic institutions?

Middletown's "X" Family:
A Pattern of Business-Class Control

Robert S. and Helen M. Lynd

Robert and Helen Lynd's studies of Muncie, Indiana (population 35,000 at the time of research), were among the first efforts to understand in depth the culture of an American community and to describe how that culture is affected by, and shapes the lives of, its people. The studies continue to be widely read and are almost unrivaled in the scope of their concern. The Lynds were not explicit about their research design except to say that they sought to examine all aspects of life in the community. The data upon which their conclusions were based were obtained primarily from observations by the authors and three associates, from personal interviews, and from the study of records, maps, and newspaper accounts of life in Muncie. While the Lynds denied that there was any such thing as a "typical" American community, Muncie was selected because it was, in their judgment, "as representative as possible of contemporary American life."

The first report on Muncie appeared in 1929 under the title Middletown *and was based on research undertaken in 1925. The Lynds returned to Muncie in the mid-1930s to assess the impact of the depression on the life of that community. They found, among other things, that it was controlled much as it had been a decade earlier, by a small business elite which in turn was dominated by one family. In the selection below, taken from their second report,* Middletown in Transition, *the Lynds show the extent of the "X Family's" influence in Middletown and the ways in which that influence is exercised and maintained.*

"If I'm out of work I go to the X plant; if I need money I go to the X bank, and if they don't like me I don't get it; my children go to the X college; when I get sick I go to the X hospital; I buy a building lot or house in an X subdivision; my wife goes downtown to buy clothes at the X department store; if my dog stays away he is put in the X pound; I buy X milk; I drink X beer, vote for X political parties, and get help from X charities; my boy goes to the X Y.M.C.A. and my girl to their Y.W.C.A.; I listen to the word of God in X-subsidized churches; if I'm a

Mason I go to the X Masonic Temple; I read the news from the X morning newspaper; and, if I am rich enough, I travel via the X airport." (*Comment by a Middletown man, 1935.*)

Since *Middletown* was published, some local people have criticized it for underplaying the role of the X family in the city's life. This group of wealthy families, along with four or five others, was not characterized as an "upper class" in 1925, because "these families are not a group apart but are merged in the life of the mass of the businessfolk." Whether or not the earlier study was entirely right in so largely grouping them with the rest of the business class, certainly no local prompting was necessary in 1935 to call attention to their overshadowing position. For, after ten years' absence from the city, one thing struck the returning observer again and again: the increasingly large public benefactions and the increasing pervasiveness of the power of this wealthy family of manufacturers, whose local position since 1925 is becoming hereditary with the emergence of a second generation of sons. . . .

In and out of the picture of Middletown in 1925 wove the influence of this family of brothers who had come to the city with the gas boom, begun with modest capital and become millionaires, and had ever since held an unostentatious but increasingly influential place in the city's life. . . .

Half a dozen other family names in Middletown are associated with the city's industrial development, but none of them so completely symbolizes the city's achievements. Of the original five brothers, four remained in 1924; and when shortly thereafter another died, the entire business of the city stopped during his funeral. Two of the brothers remain today, both men in their seventies, alert, capable, democratic, Christian gentlemen, trained in the school of rugged individualism, patrons of art, education, religion, and of a long list of philanthropies; men who have never spared themselves in business or civic affairs; high exemplars of the successful, responsible manipulators of the American formulas of business enterprise. In their conscientious and utterly unhypocritical combination of high profits, great philanthropy, and a low wage scale, they embody the hard-headed *ethos* of Protestant capitalism with its identification of Christianity with the doctrine of the goodness to all concerned of unrestricted business enterprise. In their modesty and personal rectitude, combined with their rise from comparative poverty to great wealth, they fit perfectly the American success dream.

Every American city has its successful businessmen, but the American success story has been kaleidoscopic in recent years. Local giants, the boys who have grown up with the town and made good, have shrunk in stature as rapid technological changes, the heavy capital demands of nation-wide distribution, and shifts in the strategic centers for low-cost production in a national market have undercut their earlier advantages of location, priority in the field, or energy; and as Eastern capital has forced them out or bought them out and reduced them to the status of salaried men, or retired them outright in favor of imported managements. One can classify American small manufacturing cities into two groups: those in which the industrial pioneers or their sons still dominate the local business scene, and those in which "new blood" has taken over the leadership; and it is likely that a census would show today a numerical predominance of the second group among cities containing major industries.

Middletown is, therefore, probably a minority city in this respect. The two remaining X brothers, reenforced by the active entry into the family business of four of the sons and two of the sons-in-law of the family, not only still own and control completely their wide business interests, but have become, amidst the local havoc of the depression, far more locally influential than ever before. It so happens that their industry, the making of glass fruit jars, is one that thrived on the depression; the great plant was not only kept busy, often employing night shifts throughout the lean years, but it returned profits reported to have been among the largest in their forty-five years of business. As the general level of the surrounding ground fell away in the depression, their preeminence increased. Their financial liquidity has been such that, with their public spirit, they have been able to cushion the local impact of the depression at a number of points; and a by-product of their strength in the midst of general weakness has been a marked increase in their banking and personal penetration into a number of areas of the city's business life. Both because of their generous help and this resulting increase in control, and because of a very human awe in the presence of a prestidigitator who can make money out of a business depression, the power and prestige of the X family among the business class in Middletown has grown decidedly with the depression. The fact that a local citizen could, late in 1934, characterize as "the one big point about this town" the fact "that the X's dominate the whole town, *are* the town, in fact" suggests the reason for the separate treatment of the family in this chapter.

Middletown has, therefore, at present what amounts to a reigning royal family. The power of this family has become so great as to differentiate the city today somewhat from cities with a more diffuse type of control. If, however, one views the Middletown pattern as simply concentrating and personalizing the type of control which control of capital gives to the business group in our culture, the Middletown situation may be viewed as epitomizing the American business-class control system. It may even foreshadow a pattern which may become increasingly prevalent in the future as the American propertied class strives to preserve its controls.

The business class in Middletown runs the city. The nucleus of business-class control is the X family. What the web of X wires looked like in 1935 may be seen from the following necessarily incomplete pattern of activities lying more or less on the surface of the city's life:

1. Getting a Living

(a) *Banking.* . . . On the board of directors of the one remaining bank are three members of the X family, with one of them as chairman; while on the board of the trust company are the X member who is chairman of the bank's board, one of the sons, and a son-in-law. In addition to the members of the X family, seven of the remaining eleven members of the board of the trust company are also members of the board of the bank. Middletown's credit facilities are therefore very centrally controlled. In addition, one son is a director in one of the city's building-and-loan associations and two other sons are directors in a small "Morris Plan" loan company.

The ramifications of this banking control of the community's credit resources are wide and subtle. Only the insiders know its details, but one picks up constantly the remark in conversation that "The banks now control the Jones plant"—and the Smith plant and the Brown plant. There is probably some measure of truth in the statement by a businessman, who in the earlier study had always proved a reliable source of information, that "If you don't join up with the inner ring, you can't work with them and you can't work against them, and you won't get the credit to run your business if they are not for you." Another member of the business class commented: "It's a one-bank town now. People don't dare complain about the way the Community Fund and other local affairs are run because all of these stem straight back to the people who control our local credit resources."

Remarks like these must not be taken too literally and sweepingly, and it would be grossly unfair to read into the situation personal malevolence, least of all on the part of the X's at the center of the local control group. This inner financial group is simply the hub of a wheel engaged in running a city.

(b) *Legal Talent.* Middletown's best law firms are retained in one or another of the interests of the X family. This renders understandable the comment of a local paper during the depression that "Lawyers and banks get along here. They maintain a happy relationship here as compared with their conflict in other cities." The personal attorney of a leading member of the X family is city attorney.

(*c*) *Industry.* The X family has not followed a policy of deliberately seeking financial control of other industries in the city. While they have an interest, direct or indirect, in some of the city's industrial plants other than their glass plant, paper-board plant, and the city's interconnecting trunk railways (which they own entirely), their power in Middletown industry is otherwise largely banking power and the commanding power of prestige and example. No secretary of the Chamber of Commerce could hold his position against X opposition. . . .

(*d*) *Retailing.* During the depression Middletown's largest department store failed. Since it occupied a building owned by the X family, the most conspicuous retail building in the city, the family has reopened it as the "X Store." And, like all X activities, it is a far better store than it was ten years ago under the former management, and a decided asset to the city. The family is reported to have an active interest in at least one other retail business, the leading furniture store in which one of the X brothers is a director, while its indirect banking controls in the retail field are particularly pervasive. Two dairies, run as playthings by younger members of the X family, squeezed the local milk market by pressing X milk into use in local institutions supported in part by X charity, and in 1934 a large independent dealer capitulated and sold out his business to the X's and became the manager for them. This kind of move, again, represents a specific gain to Middletown, as some of the city's milk is bad while the X milk is very superior. The output of a brewery in a neighboring city, in which the X family has a large interest as an outlet for its glass bottles, is said to be heavily pushed against all rivals in the local market.

2. Making a Home

Since 1925 the X family has literally moved the residential heart of the city. An outstanding change in these ten years is the development of the northwest section of the city, the section where the X's live and the section most remote from local industrial plants, into the outstanding residential section. This shift has been carefully engineered by members of the X family. . . .

The X residential development in the West End is related to two other major developments engineered by the X's in that section, adjoining the new subdivisions: the purchase and transformation by the X's of the haggard old normal school into a cluster of beautiful buildings now bearing the name "X State Teachers College," with an associated handsome new laboratory grade and high school that is the envy of the rest of the school system; and the location, adjoining the college, of the new million-and-a-half-dollar hospital, an outright gift to the city by the X family. These combined developments give a distinction to Middletown's West End which no section of the city, grimy with soft coal smoke, had in 1925.

And yet, as one watches this flowering forth of the city under the guiding hand of the X family, one must bear in mind the comment of a local man that "The X's are about the only people I know of who have managed to augment their fortune by the art of philanthropy." . . .

3. TRAINING THE YOUNG

A member of the family is president of Middletown's school board, and a prominent X attorney is school attorney. Middletown feels comfortable with a member of this family at the head of its schools. An editorial comment in June, 1936, says: "There is still a feeling among women's organizations that there should be one woman on the [school] board, but that it is not likely to come about until a year hence, if then, or ever. Mr. X's term will expire a year hence *and there is no likelihood of replacing him if he still wants the job. . . .*" (Italics ours.)

The local college, though a State institution, is said to be X controlled both in its larger policies and in occasional small details. From both faculty and students, very guardedly in the former case and more openly in the latter, one heard of the pressure from the X's against radicalism in the college. . . .

It is not intended here to suggest that X State Teachers College is under deliberate repressive control. Its student body contains the most politically liberal force in the city. What is here suggested is that the college, though a State institution, is so closely watched by the X family and is so dependent upon their power and influence that it tends to follow officially their intellectual and political emphases. This does not, however, mean that all liberal teaching is stifled.

The family's authority in local educational matters is enhanced by the fact that it has also given $1,000,000 to the State University. One brother is president of the University's board of trustees.

4. SPENDING LEISURE

Both the Y.M.C.A. and the Y.W.C.A. buildings are X philanthropies. . . .

Personnel and policies in the case of both "Y's" are closely controlled by members of the X family. . . . The family's other contributions to the leisure-time activities of the city are . . . extensive. . . .

5. Religion

A number of local churches, including working-class churches, have been helped in their building programs by X generosity. The X family, particularly the older generation, believes in the goodness of religion and in steady churchgoing. The influence of the older generation is, on the whole, theologically conservative. It would be unfair to say that their aid to local churches—from contributions to building programs to playground equipment—is given in order to influence these churches' teachings. Their gifts are undoubtedly prompted by a desire to make Middletown a better place in which to live, and to them as people of long religious tradition the church is an important community civilizing agency. But, though not so intended, their philanthropy here as elsewhere operates as part of the local business-class control system. All of business-class Middletown, including its ministers, hesitates to come out in the open against X causes or X points of view. One stubborn "liberal" minister is reported to have been "broken" by the family ten years ago. . . .

6. Government

. . . Middletown is a Republican stronghold. The business leaders tend to be solidly Republican, and in this the X family sets them a conspicuous model. A member of the family is Republican National Committeeman for the state; the family contributes heavily to Republican campaign funds and to the Liberty League; and they pull a consistently heavy oar financially and personally for the G.O.P. ticket, national, state, and local.

In the face of this established situation, a small sensation was created among Middletown Democrats when, after the turning of the state and nation to the Democratic party in 1932, one of the abler members of the second generation of X's suddenly bobbed up as an influential local Democratic leader and head of the (Democratic) Governor's Commission on Unemployment. The Democratic weekly paper commented in the summer of 1935:

> Young X has done pretty well for a new Democrat who voted the traditional X Republican ticket as late as the last general primary. He has laid himself up a job on the school board, as a Democrat, controls the Democratic mayor and county chairman, is the final word in hiring hands in relief work in ten counties, and the acknowledged boss of the Democratic party hereabouts.

This paper, the erratic personal organ of an old-time swashbuckling editor who was mayor from 1930 through 1934, and the one paper in town that deals baldly with messy local affairs, headlined this situation with characteristic colorfulness:

> Democratic Party Here Now a Possession of the Mighty X Kin: Ruthless in Business and Piratical Forays in Realms of Finance, They Play Both Political Parties on Theory That Heads We Win, Tails You Lose; [and again, in a later issue:] Smooth-running Politics Makes New-fledged Democrat President of School Board; Strides Past D—— and Keeps G——, Republican, as School Attorney over Weak Protest of the Mayor; Young X Tells the Democrats Where to Get Off, but His Millions and Influential Family Surround Him With Groveling Servitors.

The present mayor, a Democrat who was reelected in the fall of 1935, after having served as mayor fifteen years earlier, is now sometimes spoken of as "X-controlled." . . .

On their part, the X family does not seek to exploit Middletown politically in the sense familiar to students of American municipal administration, nor need one read skulduggery, as one local commentator suggested, into the refund of a $52,000 income-tax overpayment by the Hoover administration in December, 1932, to the one of the X's who is a Republican National Committeeman and a heavy contributor to Republican campaign funds. It seems more probable that we are simply confronted here by a situation of conflict between two ostensibly separate but actually interdependent sets of cultural institutions: on the one hand, a set of lagging political institutions fallen into disrepute because of the meager calibre of the men who find it financially worthwhile in this culture to run for municipal office and because of the patent waste and graft incident to their operation; and, on the other hand, a set of economic institutions more ably manned by the best abilities in the male population, somewhat more efficient, and more central to the concern of an industrial community. The operators of the economic institutions do not want to bother with the political institutions; but, on the other hand, they do not want too much interference with their central economic concerns from the political institutions. They, therefore, bother to inject just enough control over the confusion of local politics to insure a tolerable tax rate, support for "sound" municipal cooperation in maintaining an open-shop town, control over the numerically dominant working class, and similar broad policies calculated to enable their central business of money-making to go forward without too much interference. And all of this is done by men like the X's with a strong sense of their actions being "in the public interest."

7. Caring for the Unable

The strong arm of X philanthropies supports all Middletown charities.

8. Getting Information (the Press)

The X family has held for some years a powerful stock interest, loosely described locally as "controlling," in Middletown's morning paper. This paper is sometimes spoken of locally as "the X paper." The family also has an interest in a leading daily in the state capital.

In connection with the dissemination of information, one other point deserves note. A local labor man pointed out in 1935 that the X's now control, through their connection with the school board, Masonic Temple, and college, all the large meeting halls in Middletown. Such "control" is at present incidental and inconsequential. This type of situation can, however, assume real significance if, for instance, a labor or radical movement should become marked in Middletown. . . .

The picture of family-wise control by the X's presented in the preceding pages may have given the impression of close, coordinated planning among the members, old and young, of the family. The situation is actually much more informal than this. Even within the family a considerable degree of rugged individualism exists. There is a common sense of direction, but no family "general staff" mapping the strategy of investment and control. . . .

We obviously confront here a highly complicated situation regarding which no positive summary judgments are possible. It is the impression of the investigator:

That the lines of leadership and the related controls are highly concentrated today in Middletown.

That this control net has tightened decidedly since 1925 and notably with the depression.

That the control is at very many points unconscious and, where conscious, well-meaning and "public spirited," as businessmen interpret that concept.

That the control system operates at many points to identify public welfare with business-class welfare.

That there is little deliberate effort from above to organize local bankers, businessmen, and leaders of opinion into a self-conscious "we" pressure group; but that this sharply centripetal tendency of Middletown's businessmen is normal behavior in a capitalist, credit-controlled culture where there is a potential control-center in the form of vast personal resources of demonstrated willingness to lend a friendly hand.

That, so long as the owners of such vast personal resources exhibit a public-spirited willingness to help with local problems, leadership and control tend to be forced upon them by circumstances, and their patterns tend to become the official guiding patterns.

That, viewed at any given time as a going concern, this centrallyhubbed control agency both may and does operate in many subtle and even ordinarily unintended ways to "welcome little fishes in with gently smiling jaws," with an accompanying loss to the latter of independent leadership. Those who try to be independent tend to be regarded, as the local phrase puts it, as "gumming the works." As the local Democratic editor, who loves mischievously to pin his victims to the wall not with pins but with broadswords, remarked editorially: "The ownership of banks, factories, colleges, breweries, dog pounds, hospitals, mayors, and county chairmen, centered in this millionaire group, has produced an appalling economic pressure on citizens who find themselves in the house of bondage. However, it is a benevolent protectorate extended over all who come into camp gracefully. But the stuffed club is always at hand, to penalize dissenters. 'Treat 'em right and they'll be good to us' has been preached here long enough."

What the future of this X control system will be is hard to guess. Within another decade the two remaining giants of the first generation will probably be out of active life. At present the policy of the family seems to be that it may as well give away a generous part of its income because it would be taken in taxes anyway. But the family's wealth will pass along fairly intact to the four sons and two sons-in-law now in their early thirties and forties. There is more diversity among these second-generation men, and one gathers that the intentness upon business that characterized the pioneering first generation is finding competition among the second generation from political ambition, activities involved in living as country gentlemen, and other distractions. The second-generation men are in no sense mere "rich men's sons" or "wasters," but are alert, able, and responsible. The fact that they have not removed to larger cities but remain in Middletown, taking their places as wheel horses in the family team, suggests the carrying forward of the *ancien régime*. A local minister expressed the belief that the younger generation of the X's is "even better than the old," though two businessmen concurred in stating that "The younger generation of X's don't stack up in ability with the fading generation." The supporting power of their wealth will remain, but one suspects that the intensity of devotion to local causes will inevitably be somewhat less among these younger families that have not fought shoulder to shoulder with the city's business pioneers to build a city from the boom town of the 1880's. Meanwhile, hereditary, as over against first-generation, wealth offers Middletown the possibility of increasing class stratification and the softening of local fiber that tends to accompany the passage of first-generation wealth into second-generation power. . . .

Community Power Structure

Floyd Hunter

Whereas the Lynds found that "Middletown" was dominated by a single family, Floyd Hunter found, almost twenty years later, that "Regional City" (Atlanta, Georgia) was controlled by a small, relatively cohesive, economic elite. Hunter's study of this city of over 300,000 persons (in 1950-51 when the research was carried out) was a seminal contribution to the study of community power. Indeed, the study's title, Community Power Structure, *has become a common term, used by scholar and layman alike, and has had an important effect on the impression many have of the way cities and towns are "run."*

But the importance of Hunter's research lies not so much in his picture of the distribution of power in Atlanta, as in the methods he employed to identify and describe the pattern of influence which he reports. He sought to develop an operational and economical research technique which would lend itself to quantification. His basic approach, described in the opening paragraphs of this selection, is to ask presumably knowledgeable persons to identify those individuals who are most "influential" and to ascertain the relationship between these individuals. This technique, which has come to be called the "reputational" method, and which has undergone substantial refinement in recent years, has been the focus of considerable controversy which we will examine in section IV of this book.

. . . No pretense is made that the group to be discussed represents the totality of power leaders of the community, but it is felt that a representative case sample is presented, and that the men described come well within the range of the center of power in the community.

The leaders selected for study were secured from lists of leading civic, professional, and fraternal organizations, governmental personnel, business leaders, and "society" and "wealth" personnel suggested by various sources. These lists of more than 175 persons were rated by "judges"

From Floyd Hunter, *Community Power Structures* (Chapel Hill, N.C.: University of North Carolina Press, 1953), excerpts from Chapter 4. Reprinted with permission of the publisher.

who selected by mutual choice the top forty persons in the total listings.*
These forty were the object of study and investigation in Regional City.
Some data were collected about the total number. Twenty-seven members of the group were interviewed on the basis of a prepared schedule
plus additional questions as the investigation proceeded. Any figures used
in the study will need to be tied fairly rigidly to the twenty-seven members on whom there are comparable data. Thirty-four Negro citizens are
included in the study. The fourteen under-structure professionals in civic
and social work who were interviewed have also provided data which
may be considered comparable. . . .

The system of power groups which is being examined may not be
called a closed system. The groups are links in a total pattern, which
may offer suggestive clues to total power patterns in the operating system
of Regional City. There are gaps in the power arc which investigation
may not be able to close. Actually the discussion here is primarily concerned with the structuring of power on a policy-making level. Only a
rudimentary "power pyramid" of Regional City will be presented. One
may be content to do this because I doubt seriously that power forms a
single pyramid with any nicety in a community the size of Regional City.
There are *pyramids* of power in this community which seem more important to the present discussion than *a* pyramid. Let me illustrate this
point.

In the interviews, Regional City leaders were asked to choose ten top
leaders from the basic list of forty. The choices of the twenty-seven persons answering this question showed considerable unanimity of opinion.
One leader received twenty-one votes out of a possible twenty-seven.
Other leaders received nearly as many votes. Some received no votes
at all. One could pyramid the forty leaders on the basis of the votes cast
for them . . . but the pyramid is not a true expression of the existing
relationships between the top leaders of the community. George Delbert,
for example, was chosen eight times more than Charles Homer, and
Homer is consequently six places down the scale from Delbert. Delbert
is considered a "big man" in Regional City affairs, but he is not as big
as Homer, according to most of the informants in answer to the simple
question, "Who is the 'biggest' man in town?"

The question on which Delbert came to the top of the voting poll was
phrased, "If a project were before the community that required *decision*
by a group of leaders—leaders that nearly everyone would accept—which
ten on the list of forty would you choose?" Delbert came out on top in
this question, but not on the one related to who is the biggest man in

* Ed. note: There were fourteen judges, selected by the author, who represented
three religions, were male and female, young and mature people, business executives
and professional people, and Negro and white.

town. Thus the pyramid scheme suggested by the voting poll of leaders, related to making projects move, must be modified in relation to the factors which weigh in Homer's favor in other areas related to power. Quite possibly some of these factors are Homer's wealth, his social position, and his business position. . . .

The validity of the question concerning who might be chosen to "decide" on a community project cannot be measured purely in terms of a pyramid-structuring. Its validity for this study lies in the fact that the question determined, in some degree, "how near the center" this group was that could "move things" in the affairs of the .community. Each man interviewed was asked to add names of persons he considered as powerful as or more powerful than the men listed. Sixty-four names were added to the list. Thirty-seven of the additional names were mentioned but once by informants. Sixteen were mentioned twice; five, three times; five, four times; and one, five times. Eleven informants added names, but there was general agreement that the list was a fairly comprehensive one as it stood, with the exceptions mentioned.

The high consensus regarding the top leaders on the list of forty, plus the lack of any concerted opinion on additional individuals, would indicate that the men being interviewed represented at least a nucleus of a power grouping.

The question was also put to interviewees, "How many men would need to be involved in a major community project in Regional City 'to put it over'?" The answers to this question varied from, "You've got the men right here on this list—maybe ten of them," to "fifty or a hundred." . . .

. . . [T]he "men of independent decision" are a relatively small group. The "executors of policy" may run into the hundreds. This pattern of a relatively small decision-making group working through a larger under-structure is a reality, and if data were available, the total personnel involved in a major community project might possibly form a pyramid of power, but the constituency of the pyramid would change according to the project being acted upon.

In other words, the personnel of the pyramid would change depending upon what needs to be done at a particular time. . . . The men in the under-structure may have a multiplicity of individual roles within the totality of the community structure which can be set in motion by the men of decision.

As I became familiar with the list of forty names through the interviewing process, it became evident that certain men, even within the relatively narrow range of decision leaders with whom I was dealing, represented a top layer of personnel. Certain men were chosen more frequently than others, not only in relation to who should be chosen to decide on a

project, as has already been indicated, but the same men interacted together on committees and were on the whole better known to each other
than to those outside this group. Through analyzing the mutual choices
made by those interviewed, it will be shown that there is an *esprit de
corps* among certain top leaders, and some of them may be said to operate
on a very high level of decision in the community; but this will not necessarily mean that one of the top leaders can be considered subordinate to
any other in the community as a whole. On specific projects one leader
may allow another to carry the ball, as a leader is said to do when
he is "out front" on a project which interests him. On the next community-
wide project another may carry the ball. Each may subordinate himself
to another on a temporary basis, but such a structure of subordination
is quite fluid, and it is voluntary. . . . It would seem from this evidence
that the under group defers to the upper group, and that there is some
solidarity in the upper echelons of policy-makers.

As shown earlier, power has been defined in terms of policy leadership, and the data given in the present chapter make a beginning at
defining structural power relations. A group of men have been isolated
who are among the most powerful in Regional City. It has been shown
that they interact among themselves on community projects and select
one another as leaders. Their relations with one another are not en-
compassed in a true pyramid of power, but some degree of ranking, even
in the top-level policy leadership group, has been indicated. Let us
now look at policy personnel patterns in another way.

In sizing up any individual one often asks, "What do you do for a
living?" The reply to this question allows one rather quickly to rank
another in a rough scale of social values. The men under discussion hold
commercial, industrial, financial, and professional positions in Regional
City that tend to classify them in the minds of any observer. . . .

. . . [M]ost of the leaders hold positions as presidents of companies,
chairmen of boards, or professional positions of some prestige. Generally
speaking, the companies represented in the listing are of major enterprise proportions. More than half the men may be said to be businessmen,
if the term is used broadly. The major economic interests of the community are overwhelmingly represented in the listing. The pattern of
business dominance of civic affairs in Regional City is a fact. No other
institution is as dominant in community life as the economic institution. . . .

[One informant] was asked to tell how [decision-making groups] would
operate in relation to one another on a community-wide project, and he
outlined the procedure very clearly. . . . [R]epresentatives from each
[group] are drawn into any discussion relative to a major community decision. Each man mentioned as belonging to a [group] also belongs to a major

business enterprise within the community—at least the clique leader does. His position within the bureaucratic structure of his business almost automatically makes him a community leader, if he wishes to become one. The test for admission to this circle of decision-makers is almost wholly a man's position in the business community in Regional City. The larger business enterprises represent pyramids of power in their own right, as work units within the community, and the leaders within these concerns gather around them some of the top personnel within their own organization. They then augment this nucleus of leadership by a coterie of selected friends from other establishments to form knots of interest called "crowds" by [the informant]. The outer edges of any crowd may pick up such men as Percy Latham, the dentist, who in turn picks up others in relation to any specific activity in which the crowd may be interested. The top men in any crowd tend to act together, and they depend upon men below them to serve as intermediaries in relation to the general community. . . .

Several of the top leaders within the crowds would "clear with each other" informally on many matters. The older men, as mentioned earlier, tended to get their heads together on most matters, as did the younger group, but such relationships were not completely stable. Each man at the top of a "crowd pyramid" depended upon those close to him in business to carry out decisions when made. An older man, for example, could not command another older man to do something, but within his own crowd there would be a hierarchy he could put to work. In most instances decision-making tended to be channeled through the older men at some point in the process of formulation, but many things may be done on the initiative of any combination of several powerful leaders in the crowds named. None of the leaders indicated that he could work alone on any big project, nor did any feel that there was any man in the community with such power. The individual power leader is dependent on others in Regional City in contrast to mill or mining company towns where one man or one family may dominate the community actions which take place.

Society prestige and deference to wealth are not among the primary criteria for admission to the upper ranks of the decision-makers according to the study of Regional City. The persons who were included in the listing of forty top leaders purely on the basis of their wealth or society connections did not, with three or four exceptions, make the top listing of persons who might be called upon to "put across a community project." As has been mentioned before, a distinction is made between persons of wealth and social prestige who engage in work and those who do not. The persons of wealth are perhaps important in the social structure of the community as symbolic persons. They may be followed in matters of fashion and in their general manner of living. Their money may be important in financing a given project, but they are not of themselves doers. They may only be called decisive in the sense that they can withhold or give money through others to change the course of action of any given project. . . . If there is power in the charitable foundation structures, it resides in the lawyers who operate them, rather than in the donors who are largely inactive in the affairs of the foundations.

Political eminence cannot be said to be a sole criterion for entry into the policy echelons of Regional City's life, generally speaking. The two exceptions to this statement are embodied in Mayor Barner and County Treasurer Truman Worth. Both Barner and Worth were successful businessmen before becoming involved in local politics to the point of seeking public office. Their interests may be said to be primarily business in the strict sense of the word. Both have a popular following that has kept them in office, but their close associates are businessmen. Mayor Barner had only one picture in his office—that of Charles Homer, the biggest businessman in the community. Both Barner and Worth look to businessmen constantly for advice before they make a move on any project concerning the whole community. Furthermore, they do not ordinarily "move out front" on any project themselves, but rather follow the lead of men like Delbert, Graves, or any one of the other leaders of particular crowds.

The point made at this turn of the discussion is not a new one. Businessmen are the community leaders in Regional City as they are in other cities. Wealth, social prestige, and political machinery are functional to the wielding of power by the business leaders in the community. . . .

In the general social structure of community life social scientists are prone to look upon the institutions and formal associations as powerful forces, and it is easy to be in basic agreement with this view. Most institutions and associations are subordinate, however, to the interests of the policymakers who operate in the economic sphere of community life in Regional City. The institutions of the family, church, state, education, and the like draw sustenance from economic institutional sources and are thereby subordinate to this particular institution more than any other. The associations stand in the same relationship to the economic interests as do the institutions. We see both the institutions and the formal associations playing a vital role in the execution of determined policy, but the formulation of policy often takes place outside these formalized groupings. Within the policy-forming groups the economic interests are dominant.

The economic institution in Regional City, in drawing around itself many of the other institutions in the community, provides from within itself much of the personnel which may be considered of primary influence in power relationships. A lengthy discussion on institutions per se is not proposed. Their existence as channels through which policy may be funneled up and down to broader groups of people than those represented by the top men of power is easily recognized. . . .

The idea was expressed several times by interviewees that some minister *ought* to be on the listing, but under the terms of power definitions used in the study they did not make "top billing." It is understood, however, that in order to get a project well under way it would be important to bring the churches in, but they are not, as institutions, considered crucial in the decision-making process. Their influence is crucial in restating settled policies from time to time and in interpreting new policies which have been formed or are in the process of formulation. Church leaders, however, whether they be prominent laymen or professional ministers, have relatively little influence with the larger economic interests.

One cannot, in Regional City at least, look to the organized institutions as policy-determining groupings, nor can one look to the formal associations which are part of these institutions. . . .

None of the men interviewed considered any of the associational groupings [private clubs] crucial in policy determination. Their role, like that of the organized institutional groupings, is one of following rather than leading. They may provide a forum for discussing and studying community issues, needs, and policies; but, when decision is called for, another structure must come into play before action becomes the order of the day. The organizations may serve as training grounds for many of the men who later become power leaders. Most of the leaders had "graduated" from a stint in the upper positions of the more important organizations. Most associational presidents, however, remain in the under-structure of the power hierarchy. The organizations are not a sure route to sustained community prominence. Membership in the top brackets of one of the stable economic bureaucracies is the surest road to power, and this road is entered by only a few. Organizational leaders are prone to get the publicity; the upper echelon economic leaders, the power. . . .

One more organizational component must be analyzed before tying together the units of the community structure. This component is what may be termed a fluid committee structure.

The committee is a phenomenon which is inescapable in organized community life in American hamlets, villages, small cities, and great metropolitan centers. Almost every activity of any importance in our culture must be preceded by committee work, carried on by committee work, and finally posthumously evaluated by a committee. Regional City is no exception to the general rule. . . .

Meetings are often a substitute for group action. As one Regional City professional phrased it, "There are those who believe in salvation by luncheon!" There is great faith manifest in certain quarters of our society that if people can just be got together in a meeting all problems will be solved. And there is some justification for this faith, since so many matters of community business, as well as private transactions, are brought to successful conclusions in meetings.

Meetings have the functions of clarifying objectives of a group and of fixing and delegating responsibilities for action on any matter. They may in like manner hold action in abeyance. Decisions reached in meetings may be solemnly binding, or they may not be. Decisions arrived at in one meeting may be changed in the next meeting. Responsibilities may be shifted and membership changed according to the will of the group as a series of meetings proceeds. Rarely are committee meetings bound by "constitutional" prohibitions or heavy legalistic trappings which characterize so many associational and institutional gatherings. The outstanding characteristic of the ordinary committee meeting is its fluidity and its adaptability in adjusting to changing conditions, which are so essentially a part of our modern urban culture. The importance of the committee in power relations cannot be overstressed.

While it is important to stress the fluidity of committee structure, it must also be pointed out that there is a stable base of personnel who are seen time and again in a variety of committee meetings. There are men in any community who devote large portions of their waking hours to attendance at one meeting or another. Public-relations men in industry and associational secretaries are paid to devote considerable of their time to meeting attendance. It becomes commonplace among this latter personnel group to see one another at committee meetings, and such personnel become familiar with community leaders who operate on a similar level with them. There is a tendency to judge the importance of these meetings by who is in attendance.

Most of the top personnel of the power group are rarely seen at meetings attended by the associational understructure personnel in Regional City. The exception to this general statement may be found in those instances in which a project is broad enough so that the "whole community needs to be brought in on the matter." Such meetings as bring in the under-structure personnel are usually relatively large affairs, rather than the smaller, more personal meetings which characterize policy-determination sessions. The interaction patterns of the two groups discussed here have shown a much higher rate of interaction among the top group than between the top and lower groups.

In matters of power decision the committee structure assumes keystone importance. The committee as a structure is a vital part of community power relationships in Regional City. Let us illustrate graphically in Figure 1 the place of two hypothetical policy committees in relation to institutional, associational, and corporate groups. . . .

We have also indicated in the figure that some institutions and associations are more frequently drawn upon for power personnel than others. The dotted lines represent those groups that are potential contributors to the policy-making structure. The cultural association group has been so designated, for example, since policy is formulated around some cultural activities which may have bearing on power relations. As an illustration, the status factor operating when a leader becomes a patron of the arts may have some relation to his general power position.

A few generalized remarks may be made concerning Figure 1, using a hypothetical example. . . .

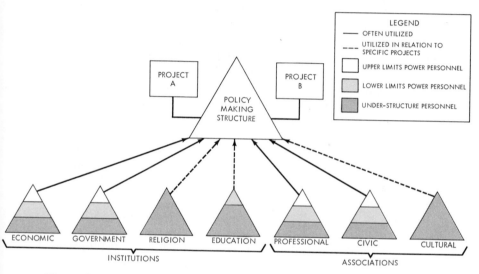

Figure 1. Generalized pattern of policy committee formation utilizing institutional and associational structures.

If a project of major proportions were before the community for consideration—let us say a project aimed at building a new municipal auditorium—a policy committee would be formed. This may be called Project Committee A. Such a policy committee would more than likely grow out of a series of informal meetings, and it might be related to a project that has been on the discussion agenda of many associations for months or even years. But the time has arrived for action. Money must be raised through private subscription or taxation, a site selected, and contracts let. The time for a policy committee is propitious. The selection of the policy committee will fall largely to the men of power in the community. They will likely be businessmen in one or more of the larger business establishments. Mutual choices will be agreed upon for committee membership. In the early stages of policy formulation there will be a few men who make the basic decisions. As the project is trimmed, pared, and shaped into manageable proportions there will be a recognition that the committee should be enlarged. Top-ranking organizational and institutional personnel will then be selected by the orginal members to augment their numbers, i.e., the committee will be expanded. The civic associations and the formalized institutions will next be drawn into certain phases of planning and initiation of the project on a community-wide basis. The newspapers will finally carry stories of the proposals, the ministers will preach sermons, and the associational members will hear speeches regarding plans. This rather simply is the process, familiar to many, that goes on in getting any community project under way.

Project B might be related to changing the tax structure of the community. Much the same organizational procedure will be repeated, but different associations may be drawn into the planning and execution stages. The policy-making personnel will tend to be much the same as in Project A and this is an important point in the present discussion. There will be a hard core of policy leadership on Policy Committee B that was also present on Project Committee A. This relative stability of the top policy-making group is a pattern quite apparent in Regional City civic affairs. A similar pattern of stable committee membership exists in the under-structure of the associational and corporate bureaucracies in the community which interact in a chain of command with the top power leaders on given projects.

It must be stressed that the same policy leaders do not interact repeatedly with the same under-structure personnel in getting projects put over. The interaction is based entirely upon a given project that is under consideration at a given time. The under-structure personnel may be likened to a keyboard over which the top structure personnel play, and the particular keys struck may vary from project to project. The players remain the same or nearly so, however.

A variation in the pattern of structuring a top-decision committee may be found in those policy committees in which the decision is made by individuals who are not to be out front on the project. In other words, the men of policy may wish to remain anonymous in relation to the action phases of the program in question. In such cases, the policy group remains informally intact, and "second-rate" or "third-rate" men are advertised as the sponsors of the particular project. This pattern may occur when a project is somewhat questionable as to its success. The policy-forming group is just as real, however, as if it were named publicly.

The men upon whom falls the burden of carrying the project into its action stages are well aware of the persons who chose them. . . .

Of course the affairs of the community do not stop at its borders. There are relationships between personnel in the city and persons in state and national power groups. Robert K. Merton has observed that community leaders fall into "cosmopolitan" and "local" groupings.[1] This generalized concept seems to hold true in Regional City. Some men tend to confine their activities almost entirely within the community, while others are active on state and regional matters. . . .

The community politicians almost entirely operate locally on boards and committees, but the Mayor has many individual contacts with the two levels of government above him on a less formalized basis than boards and committees of policy would imply. . . . He is not the most influential man in Regional City in local-national policy matters, and when the dynamics of the power structure is elaborated upon, this will become apparent. The Mayor denies much influence in state matters. . . . State and local politics are differentiated, but not entirely distinct. As in the other states where a large metropolitan center is located there is much friction and conflict of interest between the two political groupings. The two are joined often at that point at which major economic interests are involved, and the leaders of economic bureaucracies have much personal influence in bridging the formal structural gaps between the levels of government on specific matters.

In one of our postulates it is stated that, "Power is structured socially, in the United States, into a dual relationship between governmental and economic authorities on national, state, and local levels." In the light of the present analysis, there is less of a "dual" relationship than had been assumed. This is particularly true in Regional City, where the dominant factor in political life is the personnel of the economic interests. It is true that there is no formal tie between the economic interests and government, but the structure of policy-determining committees and their tie-in with the other powerful institutions and organizations of the community make government subservient to the interests of these combined groups. The governmental departments and their personnel are acutely aware of the power of key individuals and combinations of citizens' groups in the policy-making realm, and they are loathe to act before consulting and "clearing" with these interests. . . .

There is evidence, too, that the local economic interests tie into larger groupings of like interests on the state and national levels which tend to overshadow the policy-making machinery of government at all levels.

[1] Paul Lazarsfeld and Frank N. Stanton, (eds.), *Communications Research* (New York: Harper and Brothers, 1949), p. 192.

The structure is that of a dominant policy-making group using the machinery of government as a bureaucracy for the attainment of certain goals coordinate with the interests of the policy-forming group. . . .

The structural relationships between the economic policy-determining groups and the operating units of government have often been looked upon as inherently immoral. The ethical implications of the domination by one set of men in manipulating government for specific and limited purposes may be avoided, but some concern must be expressed in relation to a functional difficulty which such domination presents in our society. . . . There are gaps in the power arc which are closed on many issues by the narrower-interest groups. In other words, it has been pointed out that the power personnel do not represent a true pyramid of political power. The power personnel may decisively influence most policies that concern legislative groups, and they are acutely aware of their own interests in such policy matters. However, on many issues they are not interested, and there is consequently no continuing structure which may transmit to the legislative bodies the general interests of the underlying groups within the body politic. This is no new problem, but it is a structurally significant one. If the formalized structures of government are under the domination of a group of policy leaders who are isolated from direct responsibility to the mass of people in a democratic society, then, values aside, the scheme is at best dysfunctional. No patent remedy is suggested in this writing but there is a structural weakness in the policy-making machinery and power-wielding mechanism as it has been observed in a particular locality. Correction of the difficulty may come from an open recognition of actual operating elements in power relations unobscured by abstract value descriptions which do not fit reality. Simply put, power structure is looked at here, not from the point of view of what one may think we have, or what one may think we ought to have, but rather in terms of what we've got. . . .

[A]n obvious question is, "What holds the system together?" This question was asked of our informants. The question was put in this way: "It is evident that we are dealing with a small group of policy leaders in this study, but the whole community of Regional City is comprised of some half million persons. What holds the whole group together in relation to the influence exerted by so few leaders?" . . .

Within the primary groups, or separate crowds clustered around specific interests, it is evident [from the answers to the previous question] that similar interests and resulting common sentiments have a great deal to do with holding the groups together. Men who work together over a long period of time become comfortable in their working relationships with one another. Mutual sentiments of liking will grow up between them, and these sentiments in turn will lead to further interactions.[2] The ability of a top leader to retain a position of prestige depends to some extent on how well he conforms to the norms of the group he leads. The men of Regional City tend to be exponents of the "common man" in appearance and manner of speech, at least during the workday. Some of the men of top wealth and position are spoken of as "common as an old shoe." Their private lives hidden from the general mass of people may be uncommon, but their everyday behavior tends toward a confirmation of what one Regional City professional in the under-structure has called the "patched pants theory." "The biggest ones act like they have patches on their pants," he said. . . .

Common interests, cutting across the lines of all separate crowds, tend to hold the community structure intact. . . . [M]oney represents power in a stable economy when it is backed by tangible resources. With this limitation noted, it must be admitted that money still has meaning in power terms in Regional City. It is an important element.

Force is also an element of power but it is not an independent element. . . . One must look deeper than the elements of money or force to analyze adequately the power structure of Regional City. Both of these elements have their place, but both are interconnected with a complex set of habitual relationships of men which are described in terms of group relations. . . .

The leaders of Regional City tend to protect themselves from too many demands by channeling policy execution through an under-structure on matters of policy. This under-structure is not a rigid bureaucracy, as has been pointed out, but is a flexible system. It has elements of stability and tends to operate by levels. The men at each level are spoken of as first, second, third and fourth rate by the power leaders, who operate primarily in conjunction with individuals of the first two ratings. The types of personnel which may be found in each rating by a sample classification are as follows:

Examples of Personnel from First to Fourth Rate in Regional City

First Rate: Industrial, commercial, financial owners and top executives of large enterprises.

Second Rate: Operations officials, bank vice-presidents, public-relations men, small businessmen (owners), top-ranking public officials, corporation attorneys, contractors.

Third Rate: Civic organization personnel, civic agency board personnel, newspaper columnists, radio commentators, petty public officials, selected organization executives.

[2] George C. Homans, *The Human Group* (New York: Harcourt, Brace and Co., 1950), p. 112.

Fourth Rate: Professionals such as ministers, teachers, social workers, personnel directors, and such persons as small business managers, higher paid accountants, and the like.

These ratings might be expanded. They are given simply to indicate a suggested ranking of selected personnel who operate below the policy-making leaders in Regional City. The first two ratings are personnel who are said to "set the line of policy," while the latter two groups "hold the line." . . . The top leaders are conserving their time and energies for the primary role they play—policy-determination. They are also interested in holding a balance of power in the community. . . .

The "little fellows" are continually moved to perform their proper tasks by those above them. The roles defined for the under-structure of power personnel are carefully defined in keeping with the larger interests. Their movements are carefully stimulated and watched at all times to see that their various functions are properly performed.

Stability of relationships is highly desirable in maintaining social control, and keeping men "in their places" is a vital part of the structuring of community power. . . . If one of [the] under-structure men should be presumptuous enough to question policy decisions, he would be immediately considered insubordinate and "punished," first by a threat to his job security, followed possibly by expulsion from his job if his insubordination continued. . . .

There may be isolated dissatisfactions with policy decisions in Regional City, but mainly there is unanimity. The controversial is avoided, partly by the policy-making group's not allowing a proposal to get too far along if it meets stiff criticism at any point in decision-making. A careful watch is kept for what "will go" and for what "will not go. . . ." When criticism is open it is generally directed toward some of the under-structure men who are fronting for the larger interests. If criticism is directed toward the top leaders, the critic is liable to job dismissal in extreme cases or more subtle pressures in less flagrant cases. The omnipresent threat of power sanctions used against recalcitrant underlings is recognized by the lower echelons of power, and they generally go along with most decisions, grumbling in private with close associates, if at all. Most of these third- or fourth-rate leaders rationalize their behavior—particularly when upper decisions are in conflict with their professional or private value systems. . . .

Small Town in Mass Society

Arthur J. Vidich

Joseph Bensman

Arthur Vidich and Joseph Bensman studied the daily life of "Springdale," a small town of 2500 people in upstate New York, during a period of three years. Their research design was closer to that employed by the Lynds than by Floyd Hunter. Like both "Middletown" and "Regional City," "Springdale" was apparently dominated by a small elite whose values were quite congruent.

While Vidich and Bensman's findings and approach are similar in many ways to those of the earlier studies, their analysis of the elements of power and the manner of its exercise adds important elements to the literature. Their use of leadership "roles" provides a foundation for comparative study, and their attention to the "costs" of leadership suggest some ways of conceptualizing the limits on personal power. The authors illustrate that those with power maintain their influence not only through their own energy and the skillful exercise of their resources, but also by meeting the general needs of the community—at least to the extent that effective opposition to their hegemony cannot be mobilized. In many respects their picture of small-town life fits the popular notion of the homogeneous community in which the maintenance of harmony is a fundamental objective of community leaders.

. . . The interlocking, duplication and overlapping of leadership roles tend to channel community policy into relatively few hands, and it results, at the level of the personalities of the leaders, in some degree of community coordination. That is, a wide range of community activities are coordinated simply because a small number of individuals are engaged in a wide range of leadership positions.

The extent to which this coordination is effective, however, is an interesting question which is open to exploration on the basis of our data. Moreover, the roles of leaders and would-be leaders that are not coordinated is also an important part of the leadership process since the

From Arthur J. Vidich and Joseph Bensman, *Small Town in Mass Society* (Princeton, N.J.: Princeton University Press, 1958), pp. 258–267, 272–284. Reprinted by permission of the publisher.

65

activity represented by these roles may help to account for innovation, diversity and change.

Four of Springdale's leaders have appeared and reappeared in almost all contexts in our previous discussion. These leaders are Jones, Lee, Flint and Young. Jones is the farm feed and mill operator, Lee the editor of the paper and town clerk, Flint the lawyer and legal counsel to organizations, and Young the county committeeman and high-order Mason.

When one reviews the organized public life of the community from the perspective of leadership, it is quickly apparent that this small number of individuals occupies a great many of the available positions. In fact, one encounters the same faces over and over again in almost every community context. This is as true for the political, educational and religious spheres already described as it is true for other community activities. . . .

The extent to which such overlapping of leadership constitutes domination, the extent to which some areas of community life are free from the influence of this central leadership group and the extent to which different leadership groups appear to dominate in different institutional spheres—all these are separate problems subject to special analysis. However, looking only at the summation of such leadership roles, we can gain another view of the structure of the public life of the community.

Primary and Secondary Leadership Roles

Not all of the positions which the dominant leaders hold are equally important. Some can almost be called honorary positions which an individual gains by being dominant in other positions. When Lee is elected to the presidency of the Community Club and when Flint is made president of the business bureau, they are being given a form of social recognition for their community work in general. A nominating committee decides that "it is about time Lee is made president because of everything he's done." In this sense such positions are honorary and are thrust upon "generalized leaders," even though their occupancy involves work and even though it may be flattering to receive such recognition.

While a given leader may occupy a great many positions, not all positions are of equal importance to him. The occupancy of some serve simply as legitimations for the occupancy of still other positions. Being a church member and a lay church leader establishes prestige and an identification with an institution whose purposes are held to be materially disinterested. All of the generalized leaders maintain church affiliations. Moreover, they carry this identification further by giving financial and verbal support to almost any religious activity. Similarly, they occupy positions in charitable money-raising drives and community projects designed to "benefit the whole community." As individuals they feel they must occupy these positions not because of the positions themselves but because of other dominant positions: Flint's church and charitable activities support his party and village board positions, Lee's community work and fire-fighting activities support his town board position.

It can be said that of the numerous positions an individual may occupy some are master positions in the sense that they account for the dominance of a public personality. The other positions—the honorary and the legitimizing and the unwanted positions—are mere reflections of the master positions. The secondary positions are meaningful because they support and sustain the positions of generalized leadership. In order to understand the leadership dynamics of the community, it is always important to locate and distinguish one type of leadership position from the other.[1]

The Dynamics of Secondary Leadership Roles

The qualifications for leadership in a given sphere are to a certain extent based on an individual's being situated in a special set of circumstances so that it is strategically possible for him to be available, prepared and, perhaps, indispensable for a number of different positions. Moreover, once an individual has acquired the halo of being a public leader, he is drawn into additional positions just because he is known as a leader.

Men like Lee, Flint, Jones and Young, simply on the basis of past experience, are walking libraries of community history, of similar organizational problems encountered in the past and of other people's capabilities and personal problems. They are experts on legal procedures and policy matters and have an experiential basis of judgment in such matters; and they are recognized by others as having such attributes. They are in a position to put specific issues, policies and conflicts in the broad framework of the total community and its past and, because of this, lesser individuals will not or are not able to act without them. As a result of these processes, leadership accumulates leadership even when the individual does not desire the position of leadership. Flint, particularly because of his knowledge of legal forms, is constantly called upon to serve in advisory capacities in a great variety of organizations. He is called in as a consultant, for example, by almost all the committees of the Community Club, by the fire companies and by the library association, and he accepts all such calls either by attending the meeting or by

[1] Floyd Hunter, *Community Power Structure: A Study of Decision Makers* (University of North Carolina Press, Chapel Hill, N.C., 1953), and H. H. Gerth and C. Wright Mills, *Character and Social Structure* (Harcourt, Brace and Co., N.Y., 1953).

conferring with committee and organizational heads. Although he complains about these demands on his time, he is forced to accept such secondary duties, even when they are not desired, in order to sustain and follow through on what he regards as his primary positions. He tries to resist such demands on his time and frequently publicly complains about being overburdened and overworked, but invariably he accedes "because I know nobody else will do the job—there aren't enough leaders in this town."

Thus it happens that the general leader is called into consultations and discussions in which he is not *primarily* interested. Were he to refuse such demands over a period of time, he would not possess the knowledge of community affairs necessary to the leadership positions which he regards as important, especially the various governing boards and the Republican committee.

Community leaders, regardless of their reluctance to extend their leadership into secondary positions, are forced to submit to pressures to become involved in unwanted and alien activities because, if they do not accept such secondary positions, they are likely to be thought of as selfish power grabbers who want only to take and not to give. Hence, there is always the risk of losing power in the primary spheres if they refuse to extend themselves into secondary spheres. Seen from their own perspective, however, this is not a coldly and rationally derived calculus. It is important to note that these community leaders believe in social participation and public service as a basic form of self-legitimation; though they may complain of overwork and burdensome responsibility, these are also statements of self-justification which reveal the psychological importance of the activity for the self-image.

However, this overwhelming occupancy of so many important positions by so few men places stresses on other potential leadership groups. People who aspire to generalized leadership or people who are interested in leadership in only one area find access to preferred positions blocked by generalized leaders who are frequently not primarily interested in holding the positions to which the potential leadership aspires. . . .

Supporting Leadership Positions

The multiplication of leadership roles by a relatively small number of unspecialized leaders has a further consequence. Simply because these top leaders are involved in such a wide and continuous range of activities—literally day and night—the amount of time they can give to any one activity is necessarily limited. That is, they are not in a position to do leg work, administration and other forms of detailed work. Their leadership tends to involve the intangibles of consultation, policy discussions, advising and the informal bringing together of information and data based on all their "positions" as all of their background bears on a particular situation. This is simply to say, for example, that Flint in his role as village counsel or Lee in his role as town clerk is able to coordinate in his own person all facts and factors in the total life of the community which bear on the particular problem being considered. At any one time Flint is the only man who is in a position to coordinate the decisions of the Community Club and the village board. Indeed in the combination of Flint, Lee, Jones and Young one could gain almost a complete picture of the major activities, plans, personnel and decisions that make up the life of the community at any given moment.

In order for such a leadership complex to operate, a secondary type of role complex exists which supports and sustains and makes possible the efficient leadership of top leaders. These are the roles of the workers, the doers and the executors. When decisions are made, when top leaders have decided upon a course of action, they call upon others to do the actual work: they themselves are concerned only with checking work as it is done, and are continuously involved in a succession of other policy matters in other spheres of community life. For them leadership is a continuous shifting between receiving reports on actions relevant to past decisions and making new decisions which result again in receiving new reports. Below the top layer of leadership there exists a varied assortment of people upon whom generalized leaders can rely to carry out programs. These consist of professionals, particularly teachers, young wives of industrial workers who are willing to spend part of their day in organizational activities, a few industrial workers and a host of people with specialized interests in sports, education, culture, community betterment and so forth. In other instances they may be people (particularly women) who are simply known to have time and an interest in getting out and doing something. Each community leader knows who these people are and to a certain extent each has his own private constituency of workers whom he can call upon when necessary. . . .

This second group of technical leaders enlarges and magnifies the number of individuals that constitute the leadership corps of the town. They are selected and recruited on a number of bases. Each of the aspirants to such indispensable but secondary positions is assessed and scrutinized in his various capacities as he performs a successive number of technical tasks. On the basis of past performance, an image of him as an organizational personality arises in the "leadership mind" and in the "public mind." Once this image forms and crystallizes, he wears it as a public definition and as a yoke for the rest of his life in the community. . . .

FORMAL LEADERSHIP AND ORGANIZATIONAL POWER

There is no clear relationship between technical or secondary positions in formal "offices" or chairs and the actual control of policy within the community. The highest political leaders in the community, for example, may have no formal political positions, though they may have a position in a church. Jones and Young hold no political office and Flint is only the appointed clerk of the village board. Similarly, many of those who are simply technical implementers and who make no major policy decisions may occupy what appear to be the top official positions. The mayor, for example, and frequently the president of the Community Club are persons who have no voice in the determination of community affairs. There is, hence, no way to decipher the relationship between position and power except by detailed ideographic examination of the lines of decision making and policy formulation.

SPECIALIZED LEADERSHIP ROLES

The appearance that power is monolithic, even within the limitations noted above, would be false if we did not consider the community's specialized leadership roles. There are a great many leaders who are interested in and oriented to only one institutional sphere. In a sense, for such leaders, the interest in leadership flows from an interest in that sphere rather than from an interest in leadership itself. For instance, the interest may be purely occupational; a given occupational position qualifies an individual for a position as a leader for roles surrounding and appropriate to that occupation. Leadership stops at the limits or at the boundary of the impact of the occupation. Teachers and ministers both fall within this category. . . .

SPECIALIZED LEADERSHIP AND SOCIAL CHANGE

Although the organizational powers of specialized leaders are limited, power takes many forms in addition to the organizational. As noted previously, the power and influence of specialized leaders is very great in effecting diffused styles of life, patterns of taste and consumption, agriculture, religion and education—all of the higher levels of values—but it does not effectively penetrate the channels of organizational control and policy making. *It is for this reason that the more diffused collective life of the town has a different dynamic than does its organized life. For this reason the town can change in its external appearances, in its demo-*

graphic composition, in its cultural content and in the whole nature of its public life and character without experiencing any change in the individuals and groups who exercise organizational and political control.

But, in addition, there are definite processes which account for changes in the importance of generalized leaders in the community. Unlike more diffuse changes which result from the activities of specialized leaders, those changes which affect the character of social classes always affect the character of life and the image of it which general leaders mirror. Thus the recent rise to dominance of farmers colors the community's self-image, though this is only in degree. At the political level this is expressed in the predominance of farm-oriented leaders in all important aspects of the organized life of the community. The relative decline in the social and political influence of businessmen in the last forty years goes hand in hand with the increasing influence of farmers and the social, but not organizational, influence of the consumption-minded middle class: all this leads to a reshaping of the community's character. Although the pyschological characteristics of the businessmen are still present, they do not dominate community life except in the purely political segments of village politics. . . . The psychological characteristics of the farmers have percolated through almost all aspects of the public life. The farmer's importance is seen in purest form in the general symbolization of the community as an agricultural community, the equation of the town with the farmers and their interests and the belief that the prosperity of the town rests on the prosperity of the prosperous farmers. At the inter-personal level this is reflected in the willingness of all groups to talk to the farmer in his language and on his terms even when this is alien to one's own language and life circumstances.

CLASS AND LEADERSHIP

The Businessmen

A number of small businessmen occupy formal leadership positions, but it is precisely they who are not the real leaders. Yet it is remarkable that in politics, at least at the village level, the political perspective of the small businessman is the dominant one. The gap between their lack of actual leadership while holding formal political positions and the dominance of their perspective in village politics is bridged by the political brokers. Flint and Jones are the primary brokers for the business-men, though it is Flint who is most exclusively oriented to the business community.

From the standpoint of the leadership process it is important to consider the special characteristics of the political broker. What precisely is his function? To what extent is he an errand boy and to what extent does he impose his leadership? How does he respond to various types of tensions and pressures?

Economically Flint is dependent on the businessmen since they constitute an important part of his legal clientele and since he receives fees from public funds which they administrate, but this does not mean that he is an errand boy. For any specific issue the businessmen do not actually know what they want or how to get it. They do know, in a general way, what kind of end result would be satisfactory. It is Flint who has to tell them what is desirable from their point of view in specific situations. Moreover, he definitely and indispensably is the only person who can tell them what are the most efficient techniques for reaching their goals. When the railroad announced a plan to eliminate its Springdale service it was Flint who coordinated their views, convinced them that the issue pertained to them and provided them with the technical know-how for organizing and conducting their defense before the Public Service Commission.

What is more, Flint talks more to the individual businessmen than they talk to each other, so that at any given time he has more information about them than they have of each other. He knows more what they think as a group than any one of them. He sees issues and events from a perspective which includes all the individual perspectives of the businessmen, while each businessman has a perspective which arises from the peculiarities of his own position. This means that Flint more than any single businessman is in a position to create a favorable atmosphere for one or another side of an issue. He can give a businessman ideas which the businessman otherwise would not have had and, by knowing beforehand what each individual businessman thinks, he can compromise the conflicting views of different businessmen before they individually know that they have differences of opinion. In this way he creates an *atmosphere* by creating a business viewpoint on an issue where without him such a viewpoint might not come into being.

This, of course, does not mean that the broker possesses unlimited power. The major limit on his power as a broker is that he cannot be obviously and demonstrably wrong in a way that the error can be definitely attributed to him. That is, the ultimate check on his power and leadership is the possibility of not being able to cover up his mistakes. It must be remembered that his power and leadership is largely informal and hence rests simply in the confidence of the conferring group.

However, the business group is only one of the reference groups that Flint faces. The other referent group that he faces is, as it were, a referent group of one, namely, Jones, who is the gatekeeper to almost all upper levels of politics. Jones, himself a businessman but an economic giant among midgets, is much more than a businessman. Because of his peculiar position, as we have noted, he faces all groups in the community. But, as we have also noted, Jones does not deal directly with the businessmen, but rather deals with them through Flint. This is necessary for him because he cannot afford to be identified with any one faction in the town. It is for this reason that Flint is placed in the position wherein he has "to clear it with Jones."

The test case in political dominance arises when Flint is placed in such a position that his interests as a representative of the business group are at odds with the interests of Jones as a representative of other groups. Such conflicts ordinarily revolve around the town tax rate or some indirect expression of the tax rate such as an appropriation for roads or road equipment. The question is: How does Flint resolve the conflict? First, he attempts to mediate the two sets of interests and to placate both—to assure the businessmen that a proposed new road will improve business and to encourage attempts to build the road without a noticeable tax increase. But when conflicts cannot be resolved at this level, Flint must defer to Jones and, what is more, he must justify his action to the businessmen. This is not always difficult since the businessmen recognize the dominance of the other interests represented by Jones.

The Prosperous Farmers

Lee operates at almost the same level with reference to the farmers, but in this case both Lee and Jones face the farmers directly. Both meet them personally, but they do not necessarily compete with each other. Lee deals with the farmers as a political figure who makes political contacts. The farmers identify him as a political figure and his concerns are the immediate and direct issues in the politics of the town board.

Jones, the dominant political figure in the community, does not have to discuss politics with the farmers. His relations with the farmers and their relations with him take place in what appear to be non-political contexts. He circulates among farmers both in his place of business and in visits to farmers' homes on occasions which are quite natural to the conduct of his business and to his personal likes and dislikes. Since he occupies no political office, no one has any direct excuse to approach him on purely political terms except Flint, Lee and Young. This means that he does not have to discuss politics publicly at the level of immediate issues and procedural conflicts. Yet, through his "non-political" contacts and discussion and from reports from others, he continuously "knows" and understands the big political picture for the entire area. There is thus no occasion for him to be publicly political except to those others who are openly identified with the public process of politics. This has numerous consequences.

Everyone in the community knows that Jones is the most powerful man in town and that he is the political boss, but only a few can deal with him directly as a political boss. His personality reinforces his un-approachability. He is a shy, quiet, unassuming man who never appears to stand out in public situations. This role of political unapproachability and "open public anonymity" has the following political consequences:

1. There are almost no occasions on which he is forced to play a public political role (to "stick out his public neck") in conflicts between the various interests he represents. His subordinates are forced to fight publicly among themselves, and when the issue is resolved in favor of one group, he has never been openly involved even though the resolution of the conflict could not occur without his private intervention. Only on the rare occasion when his machine is directly threatened by outsiders like West will he show his hand publicly. An open public gesture on his part is a formidable act and is understood by all as a *caveat*. Jones acts publicly only when his own political existence is threatened.

2. In instances where unanimity is achieved by all parties to a conflict or where there is no conflict, Jones identifies himself with the unanimity and publicly takes his stand. He avoids a public stand on any divisive issues.

3. Due to these factors, Jones appears to have very little shape or form to most segments of the population. Groups who wish to influence policy or share power recognize that Jones is the major blockage, but, because of the very shapelessness of his political profile and his apparent abstinence from politics, he is not even accessible for public attack. Since he cannot be explicitly linked with politics, it is impossible to organize opposition against him—there is nothing explicit that can be opposed— and it is futile to attack his subordinates because they do not have the power.

4. As a further consequence of the formlessness of his political sway, it is not easy to place limits on the extent of his power. It is not even possible for an opposition group to estimate and assess the extent and limits of his power and knowledge within his private sphere of operations. For this reason it is just as easy for groups who would be inclined to oppose Jones to overestimate his authority as to underestimate it. All groups and individuals overestimate his authority, but by this very fact they increase his power, since they act on the basis of their estimation.

Different groups and individuals respond differently to the structure of Springdale's politics. Most groups who are interested in politics simply accept the fact of Jones's authority without attempting to measure it. They rather attempt to work within it by attempting to influence Flint and Lee. Neighborhood groups in rural areas approach Lee when they are interested in road improvements. In all matters pertaining to the village it is almost automatic for people to see Flint.

THE POLITICAL INNOVATOR

The only group which attempts to measure Jones's authority is the "community improvement" group, composed largely of the professional segment of the middle class. This is not a permanent political group, but rather a loose temporary grouping whose personnel changes with changes in issues. Different individuals from within this class organize temporarily around issues in which they have a highly specific interest—the youth recreation program, the swimming hole. The leadership for such temporary interest groupings is not formalized, but, again, varies to a certain extent according to issues. . . .

With the exception of the old aristocratic families who largely serve only in ceremonial functions, this exhausts the groups who provide leadership for the community at any significant level. However, individual members of all the classes, except the shack people, can become workers in the organized social activities of the community:

1. *Traditional farmers* may hold ceremonial positions in the Grange and may serve on various work committees in the churches or the Grange.

2. *Prosperous farmers* may hold higher ceremonial positions in the Grange and the Masons, may occupy some of the higher lay positions in the churches and occasionally serve on committees in the Community Club, or, as in one case, can be its president. When prosperous farmers do not occupy higher positions it is not because they cannot but rather because they are reluctant and feel they do not have time.

3. *The businessmen* carry on the routine program of the business bureau—plan the dinner meetings, secure the speakers and chair the committees concerned with business ethics and outside competition. Some assist in church canvasses and others help on Community Club projects and programs; they may be on a program committee or they may act in plays. Some of their wives are in the ladies' aids and book clubs.

4. *Professionals* and *skilled workers* carry the major burden of the work load in the churches, the Community Club, the P.T.A., the Masons, the library and the dramatic and choral activities.

5. The *marginal middle class*, particularly the aspiring investors and hard-working consumers, carry out the projects and programs of the American Legion and also occupy its higher positions. They also almost exclusively staff and man the positions and activities of volunteer fire companies.

The description of such positions and the classes that fill them tell something about the nature of the organizations, but it tells very little about the dynamics of the community. Primarily, this is because at the very point where important decisions affecting the structure of the community are made, the real decision-makers occupy no important formal positions which are relevant to the decision. The decision-makers may occupy positions which are only a *reflection* of the informal positions they hold, and which are not the positions which announce the decisions.

<h3 style="text-align:center">LEADERSHIP AND SOCIAL CHANGE</h3>

Decision-making in the community is not a specialized function. The decisive leaders of the community do not occupy any specialized positions and are not limited in their decision-making to decisions which affect only one sphere of the life of the community. Rather the same individuals, some of whom occupy no formal positions, are involved in making decisions which affect all aspects of the community. They shift their focus of attention from sphere to sphere as decisions in one particular sphere affect different aspects of the community in different ways.

As a permanent "policy" (although policy is too calculating an expression since they are simply following the logic of their attempt to maintain control) they attempt to limit the areas in which specialized leaders can exercise authority and influence the community. They attempt to restrict the activities of all specialized expert groups except the political expert, that is, themselves. It must be remembered, however, that this attempt to control is with respect to local affairs only. They attempt to retain control within the local community at the same time that the local community is changing and is influenced by the outside world. In spite of the complexities of the problems of local control, these amount to almost nothing in comparison to the changes the community is undergoing with reference to and as a product of the outside world. In a sense, then, the opposition to the local leadership does not consist of dissident groups within the community but rather the whole trend of mass society which impinges on the local arena. In his attempts to deal with such larger trends in modern society, the hardboiled realistic politician takes on as his adversary the major currents of change in modern society that affect the small town. Seen in this light, the political realists become genuine romanticists, and so it appears that it is precisely such romanticism which seems to keep the local society functioning regardless of the stresses and strains under which it operates.

However, one must not overlook the fact that their control in the local community is exercised from the standpoint of a number of real political bases. They draw their support from all the dominant groups in the town. From one point of view, then, it is not their own narrow class interest that they express, though this is not always as clear in the case of Jones, but even he goes much beyond his own immediate class interests in his political concerns. To a certain extent, then, politics and the direction of community affairs have an autonomy of their own. Perhaps this is simply because those who are concerned with politics become submerged in the aesthetics and the sheer rhythm of politics.

But even when they are not directly concerned with their own class interests, the political managers must take into account the class interests of the significant economic groups that impinge upon politics and they must weigh and balance the interests of these groups. They must develop programs which are combinations and compromises that reflect the weight, the interests, the activity and the intensity of feeling of these groups. In a sense the political managers, then, are actors who play to a passive audience and who, after all their histrionics, depend on their ability to please and entertain groups which frequently appear to be only observers. The players aim all their acting at the audience and the audience acts only to approve or reject. Only in extreme situations is the audience seen as the instigator in the interchange between player and audience, but if one follows the plays performed and the manner in which they are played, one can see the relationship between the player and the audience. However, to account for changes in the play and in the acting, it is always necessary to account for changes in the composition of that part of the audience which has the interest and the price of a ticket. At some points the audience changes to the point where certain actors lack the ability and the skills to please it, and these are the crucial points in the history of the town. The dynamics of the town which change the composition and character of the political audience thus, while hidden, are decisive in determining the scene, the cast and the play.

Economic Dominants and Community Power: A Comparative Analysis

Donald A. Clelland

William H. Form

Many early studies of community power, like the preceding selections, found that economic and political power went hand in hand. Robert Schulze was among the first to demonstrate a tendency for economic elites to disassociate themselves from local politics when the companies they managed were absentee-owned or integrated into national markets (196). Schulze's study of this phenomenon—which he called "the bifurcation of power"—in "Cibola" (Ypsilanti, Michigan) appeared in 1958. Shortly thereafter, Donald A. Clelland and William H. Form replicated Schulze's research in "Wheelsburg" (Lansing, Michigan).

Clelland and Form, in comparing their findings with Schulze's, indicate that the "bifurcation hypothesis" is generally valid, but that the different conditions in "Wheelsburg" are associated with a slower rate of withdrawal from community affairs than in "Cibola." In addition to the findings and the apparent thoroughness of the research reported, the article presented below is valuable because it illustrates the worth of comparative investigations of community power modeled on previous studies. It may be that the study of community power would have progressed much further had more of the research been of the type of replication described in this article. (Scholarship in community studies is not alone in its failure to replicate work in order to test the validity of findings and the reliability of methods. Perhaps social science in general would benefit from a Journal of Replication.)

. . . Irrespective of approach, [to the study of American community power] an ideological question has been persistent—whether the community is governed informally by an economic elite or whether the dominant pattern is political pluralism, a situation where decision-makers represent groups with differing interests.

Reprinted from "Economic Dominants and Community Power: A Comparative Analysis," by Donald A. Clelland and William H. Form, *American Journal of Sociology*, LXIX (March, 1964), 511–521, by permission of The University of Chicago Press. Copyright 1964 by the University of Chicago.

One instructive way of posing this controversy is to ask what types of relationships characterize the stratification orders in American communities in the past and in the present.[1] More specifically, the sociological question is: To what extent has private economic power been translated directly into community or public power? Although R. O. Schulze did not formally place his research within the Weberian framework, operationally he did study the question we have posed by tracing historically the place of economically powerful figures in the public life of Cibola.[2] The study reported here attempts to replicate his investigation in a different type of community, which we shall call "Wheelsburg."

Schulze's findings upheld his hypothesis that as a city grows from an isolated, self-contained entity to an urbanized community "increasingly involved and interrelated in the large social complex," its sociopolitical power structure changes from a monolithic one dominated by persons possessing great economic power to a bifurcated structure comprising "two crucial and relatively discrete power sets, the economic dominants and the public leaders."[3] Economic dominants were defined as "those persons who occupy the top formal statuses in the major economic units within the community area,"[4] and public leaders (or top influentials) as those who, in the opinion of community "knowledgeables," exercise major influence and leadership in community affairs.[5]

[1] In the framework of Max Weber as explicated in "Class, Status and Power," in *From Max Weber: Essays in Sociology*, ed. and trans. Hans H. Gerth and C. Wright Mills (New York: Oxford University Press, 1946).

[2] Robert O. Schulze, "Economic Dominance and Public Leadership: A Study of the Structure and Process of Power in an Urban Community" (microfilmed Ph.D. dissertation, University of Michigan, 1956); "The Role of Economic Dominants in Community Power Structure," *American Sociological Review*, XXIII (February, 1958), 3–9; "The Bifurcation of Power in a Satellite City," in *Community Political Systems*, ed. Morris Janowitz (Glencoe, Ill.: Free Press, 1961), pp. 19–80.

[3] "The Bifurcation of Power . . . ," *op. cit.*, pp. 21–2.

[4] *Ibid.*, p. 21. For Schulze's operational criteria for determining economic dominants and public leaders see *ibid.*, Appendixes A and B, pp. 73–75. Essentially the same criteria were utilized to identify the dominant economic units (and consequently economic dominants themselves) in the two cities. Number of employees, capital worth, and assessed valuation were used as measures. However, since Wheelsburg is a much larger city than Cibola, the minimum figures for cutoff points were necessarily larger. In Cibola the only dominant economic units were manufacturing plants, banks, and savings and loan companies. In Wheelsburg a wider variety of economic units was included in the dominant group, e.g., department stores, utilities, and insurance companies. In addition to the heads of the major economic units, all who were on the board of directors of two or more of the major economic units were also identified as economic dominants.

[5] As suggested by Hunter, [*Community Power Structure* (Chapel Hill, N.C., 1953)]. The "knowledgeables" who were interviewed in the two studies differed somewhat. Schulze's knowledgeables were the heads of local voluntary associations. This research relied on the nominations of fourteen high-ranking officials from seven institutional sectors of the community (mass communication, business, union, welfare, education, government, religion). David A. Booth and Charles A. Adrian compared

Schulze tentatively explained the dissociation of economic dominants from local political-civic affairs by the following three trends: (a) the establishment by a growing number of locally-owned industrial units of direct supplier relationships with a small number of large, non-local manufacturing plants; (b) the subsequent introduction into the local economic system of an increasing number of branch plants of large, absentee-owned corporations; and (c) the concomitant dissolution of the extensive networks of interlocking directorates and officerships which had formerly served to link significant numbers of local economic dominants within the community.[6]

These trends have also occurred in Wheelsburg, but to a more limited degree. The greatest variation between Cibola and Wheelsburg is in the first factor, because in Wheelsburg many local supply plants were established to serve the local automobile firms.

COMPARISON OF THE COMMUNITIES

The two communities differ significantly in a number of ways. For most of its history Cibola was a small independent town. It is now a satellite city of approximately 20,000 inhabitants located just beyond the Standard Metropolitan Area of a large midwest industrial center containing more than 3,000,000 people. The five largest of its eight major industrial plants were absentee controlled. Cibola is an extreme example of a city that "has felt the full impact of the metropolitan drift of American life."[7] A period of rapid expansion began during World War II with the establishment just outside the city's boundaries of a gigantic war-production plant which employed over 40,000 workers at its peak. After the war the economic instability of absentee-owned companies occupying this plant caused wide and rapid fluctuations in the local labor force. Consequently, during the 1940's the community experienced rapid fluctuation and high turnover in population. At the time of Schulze's study employment at the main plant had leveled off at 9,500 as it became tied securely to the motor vehicle industry.

Wheelsburg is located about 60 miles west of Cibola. It is an independent city of over 100,000 dominating a metropolitan area with a population of approximately 180,000. Like Cibola, its economy is based primarily on motor vehicle production. In fact, the same motor vehicle company is the largest single employer in both communities. In Wheels-

---

the results of the method used by Schulze with the simpler method we employed, and found almost identical results (see their "Simplifying the Discovery of Elites," *American Behavioral Scientist*, V [October, 1961], 14–16).

[6] Schulze, "The Role of Economic Dominants . . . ," *op. cit.*, p. 6.

[7] Schulze, "The Bifurcation of Power . . . ," *op. cit.*, p. 24.

burg the company employs nearly 15,000 workers. However, significant sections of Wheelsburg's labor force are employed in state government and in a nearby state university. Wheelsburg's period of most rapid industrial and population growth occurred earlier than Cibola's, between 1900 and 1920. This growth largely reflected the success of locally owned automobile and supplier plants. Since 1920 Wheelsburg's growth has been moderate and steady even with the large invasion of absentee-owned companies. Such companies came earlier to Wheelsburg, but entered and grew more gradually than in Cibola.

Currently, thirteen of the twenty non-financial dominant economic units are absentee-controlled.[8] Unlike Cibola, (*a*) Wheelsburg's major firms have been fairly stable operations, (*b*) the vast majority of its labor force has always been employed within the city limits, (*c*) very few of its economic dominants have lived beyond the city's contiguous suburbs, and (*d*) the city is removed from the influence of a large competing metropolis. Wheelsburg, then, is a much more stable and "normal" type of community setting in which to test Schulze's hypothesis.

Following Schulze's method closely, we tested his main hypothesis by (1) reconstructing the formal participation patterns of economic dominants over the past century in the political and civil activities of the community; (2) ascertaining the representation of current economic dominants among public leaders, that is, in the "reputational" power structure; and (3) analyzing the role of current economic dominants in specific community issues and programs.

ECONOMIC DOMINANTS AS POLITICAL AND CIVIC LEADERS

In Wheelsburg, as in Cibola, the proportion of economic dominants who occupied high local governmental offices declined dramatically over the century. . . . [I]n both communities prior to 1900 the economic dominants were highly represented in local government. . . . Although the twentieth century ushered in a sharp decline in the proportion of economic dominants holding public office in both communities, this decline was sharper in Wheelsburg than in Cibola. Moreover, in both cities, but especially in Wheelsburg, the offices held by economic dominants have been increasingly appointive rather than elective. Indeed, no economic dominant has served as mayor since 1899, or as councilman since 1932.

[8] An absentee-controlled company is defined as one having a majority of its board of directors living outside of the local community. In both Cibola and Wheelsburg, slightly less than 50 per cent of the dominant economic units were absentee-controlled —five of eleven units in Cibola and thirteen of twenty-seven units in Wheelsburg. In both cities, all of the financial units (three and seven, respectively) were locally owned.

The trend of these developments in Wheelsburg may be seen more clearly by examining the data in terms of twenty-year periods. A precipitous decline in public officeholding by economic dominants occurred in the 1900–1920 period, with relatively little change thereafter. However, there has been a continuing change in the type of office held. In each succeeding twenty-year period, fewer of the economic dominants who held office were elected. Increasingly, they have come to hold advisory and honorary positions in local government. Since it is probably fair to assume that the power potential of appointive offices is less than that of elective offices, the shift of economic dominants from the latter may be taken as evidence of continuing loss of formal political power.

Schulze suggests that after 1900 the arena of local involvement of the economic dominants shifted from politics to voluntary associations. The Wheelsburg data confirm his observation. . . . [C]urrent public leaders or top influentials regard the Chamber of Commerce as the single most influential organization in the city. Yet . . . direct control of this organization by economic dominants has probably declined over the years.

In both Wheelsburg and Cibola economic dominants reduced their incumbency in public offices at the turn of the century. A similar withdrawal from civic leadership positions began about 1940.[9] A comparative analysis of the economic development of the two communities corroborates some of Schulze's explanations and contradicts others. The evidence fails to support Schulze's position that the growth of absentee ownership and the dissolution of local business ties (interlocking directorates) among the economic dominants account for their withdrawal from public office. In both communities these phenomena occurred *after* the withdrawal. . . . A third factor which Schulze associated with withdrawal, namely, the growth of direct supplier relationships to non-local industries by locally owned plants, must also be discarded, for in Wheelsburg no such growth took place and yet the pattern of withdrawal was similar to that of Cibola. Moreover, in Wheelsburg this withdrawal does not seem to have been forced by the growing political power of ethnic groups as was the case in many American cities.[10] There has never been a large

---

[9] "Withdrawal" is probably an apt phrase, because no evidence is available to suggest that there was community pressure on the economic dominants to reduce their community involvement. However, individual economic dominants were constantly changing. Their withdrawal consisted not so much in dropping civic leadership positions as in the failure of new economic dominants to seek such positions.

[10] E.g., in New Haven, from the late nineteenth century until recently, local politics were controlled primarily by "ex-plebes," individuals on the rise from the ethnic proletariat, who gained office through "the skills of ethnic politics." From 1842 to 1898, New Haven politics were dominated by the leading entrepreneurs. It may be significant that the period of dominance by economic dominants is almost identical in New Haven, Wheelsburg, and Cibola (see Dahl, *Who Governs?* chap. iii and iv).

ethnic proletariat in Wheelsburg, nor have local politics ever been heavily based on ethnic lines or class conflict.

What factors, then, are associated with the sharp decline in political participation by economic dominants (i.e., the bifurcation of political and economic power structure) since the turn of the century? At the broadest level of explanation, the increased involvement of the community and its economic units in state and nationwide social economic systems was, no doubt, an important factor. More specifically, in Wheelsburg, the end of the period in which political and economic power tended to coincide was marked by the rise of a new breed of economic elite, namely, managers and owners of the new automobile and supply plants. Younger, wealthier, operating larger businesses, more directly involved in the day-to-day operation of their businesses, introducing a wide variety of new products, these men did not participate in local politics probably largely because they lacked the time and because they probably found that business was much more exciting. A growing separation of wealth and social honor may have been a second factor, but the new economic elite was partly based on old local wealth and the majority were entrepreneurs rather than simply managers of companies financed by non-local capital. However, in the absence of ethnic and class cleavage in the community, it is doubtful that the new economic dominants, many of whom were classed Horatio Alger success models, lacked the popularity needed for election. They probably did not choose to run.

On the other hand, later withdrawal from civic leadership positions seems to be associated with the introduction of absentee-owned plants and the related decrease in common local business ties (interlocking directorates) among the economic dominants. The importance of the latter factor is underscored in Wheelsburg where economic dominants not only have more local economic linkages but also comprise a larger proportion of the local civic leaders. . . .[11]

COMMUNITY INFLUENCE OF ECONOMIC DOMINANTS

In order to assess the community influence of current economic dominants in Wheelsburg, two procedures were used. First, their reputational influence was investigated by assessing their representation in the list of public leaders (community influentials as determined by the method outlined in notes). Second, their "actual" influence was probed by examining their role in a number of community issues or projects.

[11]Sixty-five per cent of the economic dominants in the 1940–59 period were associated as officers, partners, or directors in at least one other business with other economic dominants.

In 1958–59, thirty-nine individuals were found to be economic dominants, and coincidentally, thirty-nine people were designated as public leaders. The names of twelve persons (31 per cent) appeared on both lists. This overlap is considerably higher than that found in Cibola where only two of seventeen economic dominants were among the community's eighteen public leaders. Moreover, eight of the top fifteen public leaders in Wheelsburg, including the top four, as rated by the public leaders themselves, were economic dominants. Although major absentee-owned corporations were "underrepresented" among the economic dominants who were also public leaders, "U.S. Motors" (the absentee-owned industrial giant in the community) was represented by three executives (two of whom were not defined as economic dominants). From these observations we cannot conclude that two discrete power sets are found in Wheelsburg.

In order to substantiate the basic dissimilarities between the economic dominants and public leaders in Cibola, Schulze examined their patterns of political and civic participation. He found that the economic dominants had held only about half as many governmental offices as the public leaders. The same was true in Wheelsburg, although both groups were less active. Somewhat surprisingly, economic dominants were as well represented as the public leaders in the five most influential associations. [There was a] similar situation of high participation by both economic dominants and public leaders in Wheelsburg's most influential associations. However, the Cibola situation of wide differences between public leaders and economic dominants in the number of officerships held in these associations was not in evidence. . . . [A] higher proportion of economic dominants in Wheelsburg (from both locally and absentee-owned companies) have in the past held office in the five most influential organizations. Differences are small between the two communities in the proportions currently holding such offices. In short, both Tables 4 and 5 document no deep bifurcation in associational participation between Wheelsburg's economic dominants and public leaders. The relatively high rate of participation by absentee-owned corporation executives is especially notable.[12]

One of the reasons for the failure of economic dominants to participate in the civic life of Cibola was that they regarded the city mainly as the locus of their work life and not their community life.[13] Moreover, their

---

[12] Although managers of the largest absentee-owned corporation did not dominate the local scene as extensively as in the case of Bigtown, they did have representatives on most of the local bodies to co-ordinate knowledge of what was going on in the city. For data on Bigtown, see Roland J. Pellegrin and Charles H. Coates, "Absentee-owned Corporations and Community Power Structure," *American Journal of Sociology*, LXI (March, 1956), 413–19.

[13] A large proportion lived in other communities in the metropolitan area and may have participated in the associational life of these other communities.

private economic interests were primarily non-local. This may not be surprising since the city's largest economic units were absentee-owned and oriented toward a national market. However . . . a much more extensive network of economic ties exists in Wheelsburg than in Cibola.[14] Despite a high degree of absentee ownership in Wheelsburg, a fairly extensive network of economic ties unites the interests of the economic dominants and the public leaders. These ties may explain the higher rate of civic participation by its economic dominants and their closer social integration to public leaders.

As a final demonstration of the bifurcation of Cibola economic dominants and public leaders, Schulze analyzed the decision-making process on two important community issues. The economic dominants refused to become involved in resolving either of them, leaving the public leaders autonomous but perhaps without a solid power basis for community action.

In Wheelsburg, an analysis of eleven community issues [15] revealed that eight of the [23] economic dominants who were also public leaders were among those mentioned as influential in initiating and resolving these issues. Economic dominants, including some representing absentee-owned corporations, either initiated or co-initiated programs of action for six of the eight issues in which they were involved. Although this evidence suggests that economic dominants have not withdrawn from community decision-making and that they are not just ceremonial leaders, apparently they do not form a monolithic power elite. Different individuals became involved in different issues, doing so in the process of playing their own "games." [16]

Not all of the broad community issues in which economic dominants were involved were controversial. Some of them may more properly be

[14] "Economic ties" are instances in which a pair of individuals serves as officers or directors of the same firm. Each pair is counted as one economic tie. For example, if four public leaders serve on the board of directors of a bank, there are six economic ties (pairs).

[15] These issues were selected and recapitulated by the public leaders in interviews. They included hospital expansion drive, downtown development, establishment of a metropolitan planning agency, improvement of airport terminal facilities, establishment of a tricounty planning agency, annexation of a school district to the city, widening of a city street, ban on Sunday shopping, proposed shift of location of city hall, proposed sale of bonds by the city to finance construction of parking facilities, and proposed annexation of a suburban shopping center. Our inspection of newspapers and other documents reveals that these indeed represent nearly the full range of community issues during the last five or six years. One or two others might be added by other local interests such as organized labor (see William H. Form and Warren L. Sauer, "Community and Labor Influentials: A Comparative Study of Participation and Imagery," *Industrial and Labor Relation Review*, XVII [October, 1963], 3–19).

[16] Norton E. Long, "The Urban Community as an Ecology of Games," *American Journal of Sociology*, LXIV (November, 1958), 251–61.

called "projects." The major issues in Cibola seemed to involve a higher degree of conflict in the political arena. Perhaps this conflict reflected the inertia of partisan party politics which existed in the community as late as 1947. In addition, both of the major issues in Cibola—adoption of a new city charter and annexation—were the direct results of rapid urbanization and industrialization, processes which had occurred at a more gradual rate in Wheelsburg. There, political life seemed less marked by conflict, for local government not only was non-partisan but it traditionally and customarily responded to the needs of business. [17] It is highly probable that the lack of political conflict and the tendency for community decision-making to be channeled to the private rather than public sphere are interdependent. In Wheelsburg there was little evidence of basic differences in values among the economic dominants, the public leaders, and the elected officials. If representation of conflicting interests or values is chosen as the indicator of pluralism in the power structure, Wheelsburg (and most American communities) will be judged less pluralistic than if a weaker test of pluralism, such as the participation of separate individuals in different issues, is used.[18]

Thus, the social climate of the decision-making roles of the economic dominants in the two cities is not identical. Whether Wheelsburg dominants would become involved in highly conflictful issues should they arise is not known. Certainly they hesitated to publicize their involvement in controversial issues.[19] One large firm, for example, refused to become overtly involved in an annexation issue despite the fact that its economic interests were involved. However, it made its position known. What covert influence this might have had cannot be accurately appraised. Yet, since executives of the absentee-owned corporations were less likely to become involved in community decision-making than economic dominants from locally owned enterprises, possibly Wheelsburg's pattern of influence is evolving toward the type found in Cibola. On the other hand, both economic dominants and public leaders work hard to solve issues without conflict, and controversial issues probably arise less often in gradually expanding cities such as Wheelsburg than in cities which have grown very rapidly and have experienced extreme economic fluctuations,

[17] Form and Sauer, op. cit.

[18] For a fuller discussion of this problem see Marshall N. Goldstein, "Absentee Ownership and Monolithic Power Structures: Two Questions for Community Studies," in Current Trends in Comparative Community Studies, ed. Bert E. Swanson (Kansas City, Mo.: Community Studies, Inc., 1962), pp. 49–59.

[19] The same attitudes were revealed in interviews conducted by Rossi in Mediana. This does not mean that economic dominants had withdrawn from local influence systems because, as Rossi points out, "this is the age of community projects" (Peter H. Rossi, "The Organizational Structure of an American Community," in Complex Organizations, ed. Amitai Etzioni [New York: Holt, Rinehart & Winston, 1961], p. 301).

such as Cibola. Further research is required to determine the power roles of economic dominants in cities differing in size, social composition, economic composition, and economic history.

CONCLUSIONS

Comparative analysis of the roles of economic dominants in power structures of a satellite and an independent city reveals that in both communities the formal political and economic power structures which were once melded have tended to become bifurcated over time. This process seems to have paralleled the integration of local economic units into national markets and the process of governmental centralization. The economic dominants, once highly active leaders in civic associations, have tended to reduce their participation in this area, especially in the satellite community. [i.e., Cibola] This withdrawal coincided roughly with the rapid extension of absentee ownership in both cities. Currently, the nearly complete bifurcation of economic dominants and public leaders (top influentials) found in the satellite city was not as evident in the independent city, where an extensive network of economic ties bound the two groups together. Moreover, unlike the economic dominants in the satellite city, those in the independent city have not abandoned their decision-making role in community issues.

While the evidence cited in this research is not conclusive, it points to variable patterns of relations between economic dominants and public leaders in different types of communities. Apparently the absence of local party politics, a history of local industries becoming absentee-owned rather than the introduction of branch plants from outside the community, the institutionalization of local political controls, and the absence of ethnic, class, or other cleavages which contribute to partisan politics reduce the withdrawal rate of economic dominants from participation in community associations and local power arrangements. The time is ripe for many rapid comparative studies of a wide range of communities to determine more precisely the factors responsible for the bifurcation of persistence of ties between economic dominants, civil leaders, and community influentials.

III

COMMUNITY POWER:
THE PLURALIST PERSPECTIVE

As the readings in the preceding section suggest, many of the studies of community power which appeared in the 1950s and before can be characterized by certain similarities. In most cases the methodologies employed varied only slightly from the approaches used by the Lynds or by Hunter, and most concluded that public policy-making in America's cities and towns was either directly or indirectly dominated by an elite with varying degrees of political autonomy and value consensus. After the publication of Hunter's seminal study of "Regional City" (Atlanta, Ga.), both the methodology and the findings of this earlier research came under attack, especially by political scientists, for example, by Herbert Kaufman and Victor Jones (113), Robert Dahl (48), Nelson Polsby (170–173), and Raymond Wolfinger (236).

While most early critics of the "elite studies" focused their attacks on the methodological aspects of this research, there was invariably an implicit—and often an explicit—alternative theoretical perspective in their writings. This alternative perspective questions the existence of a single center of power, or a cohesive coalition of groups which wield power, in American communities. Instead, the critics propose that there are usually (though not always) *multiple* centers of power, none of which is completely sovereign. In addition, these centers of power do not overlap or coalesce from issue-area to issue-area in any consistent way. In other words, American cities are pluralistic. The power of leaders is significantly limited by other leaders and by those whom they lead, although direct mass participation in decision-making is not required or expected. According to pluralists Wallace Sayre and Nelson Polsby:

. . . in a wide range of community situations, participation in
decision-making is limited to a relatively few member of the community, but only within the constraints of a bargaining process
among elites and of an underlying consensus supplied by a much
larger percentage of the local population whose approval is costly
to secure. (174)

There is also a normative dimension to the pluralist analysis.
The theoretical assumptions of the pluralists seem to carry the implicit judgment that pluralist political systems are "better" (i.e.,
more democratic) than elite political systems. Of course, those who
have found varieties of elite rule have often expressed their distaste
for such structures, as the writings of the Lynds, Hunter, and others
clearly demonstrate. While most of us would agree that a relatively
broad dispersal of political power is preferable to the domination
of community policies by the few, a pluralist structure of leadership is not in itself adequate evidence that the political system is
serving the interests of the many. Indeed, a number of political
scientists have recently become critical of those who have too
readily equated pluralistic leadership structures with democracy.
These scholars have warned that before one can begin to say that
pluralism leads to democracy, it is minimally necessary to demonstrate, and not merely assert, that (1) a balance of power exists
among competing interests and, (2) perhaps more important, that
the leaders of competing groups are in some way responsible to the
wishes of those they lead.[1]

In addition, because of the widespread and understandable tendency of democrats to view rule by the few as "bad" and pluralism
as "good," or at least better, it may be useful to ask whether in
some communities, especially small and homogeneous communities,
dominance of decision-making by an "elite" might not meet most of
the demands of democratic theory. For example high social class
citizens of homogeneous towns may place very few demands on
local public facilities, except for the possible exception of demands
for high-quality education, and the level of consensus on the quality
and quantity of public services may be so high that the citizens
knowingly (and even gratefully) relinquish political decision-
making to the few.

It should be noted that there has been, at least until recently, a
tendency to dichotomize elitist and pluralist models of community

---

[1] For example, see Grant McConnell, *Private Power and American Democracy*
(New York: Alfred A. Knopf, 1966); Peter Bachrach, *The Theory of Democratic
Elitism: A Critique* (Boston: Little, Brown and Co., 1967); and E. E. Schattschneider,
The Semisovereign People (New York: Holt, Rinehart and Winston, 1960).

power. In a sense, the way in which this book is organized may strengthen that tendency, although subsequent sections will illustrate the inadequacy of this dichotomy. As we have already seen in the previous section, the ruling elite model has a number of variations, some of which seem not distinctly different from what other researchers might call pluralism. In short, there are no well-defined boundaries between elitist and pluralistic political systems. Indeed, it may be more useful to view different types of power structures in terms of their relative position on a common continuum than to compel them into one of two presumably polar categories.

Both pluralist and elite structures take many forms which are related to such factors as local history, socio-economic conditions, value patterns and the like. There is a need to begin to refine systematically the criteria by which the various types of pluralism and elitism might be identified. This will facilitate a greater understanding of the relationship between the political system and its policy outputs.

Despite a stream of criticism leveled at the Lynds, Hunter, and those who followed and built upon their pioneering work, not until the 1960s did any sizable number of studies begin to appear which operationalized the methodological alternatives to these previous studies and provided empirical evidence to support the pluralist model of community power.

In this section four studies are examined in which the authors find that the potential influence upon community policies is relatively broadly shared. The section begins with excerpts from *Who Governs?*, Robert Dahl's famous study of New Haven, Connecticut, and is followed by a selection from Aaron Wildavsky's methodological replication and refinement of the New Haven research in Oberlin, Ohio (population 8000). Wildavsky argues that pluralism can characterize small towns as well as large cities. In *Governing New York City*, Wallace Syre and Herbert Kaufman examine the role of groups in the fragmented political system of the nation's largest city. Finally, we will consider Paul Smith's study of a small midwestern city in which he uses guidelines derived from game theory to examine the political process.

In studying these selections the student might compare readings from this and the previous section to note the differences and similarities in research methods, assumptions, and explicit findings, as well as in the authors' interpretations of their findings. It may be especially important to compare the different conceptions of the term "power" that are implicit in some of the selections. The student may also wish to ask how the findings in these articles correspond with his own criteria for a democratic system. Similarly, what other evidence might the researchers have developed that would permit a more precise judgment upon the system investigated? Is it as open and as democratic as they claim it is? Finally, one might compare the studies in this section and contrast them with the four preceding studies, keeping in mind two fundamental questions. What are the basic criteria for distinguishing the various types of pluralist systems? And what are the implications for public policy outputs of the different types?

Who Governs?

Robert A. Dahl

Robert Dahl's study of New Haven, Connecticut (population 150,000) has been a very influential book, especially upon students of political science. In Who Governs? Dahl attempted to develop an alternative to those research methodologies which had so often before yielded evidence that American communities were "run," directly or indirectly, by an elite whose power rested on economic resources or social standing. Even more important, Who Governs? was a comprehensive effort to develop an empirically based theory of democratic pluralism.

In reviewing the following excerpts drawn from throughout the original work, the reader may wish to ask: What is Dahl's concept of power and how is it exercised in New Haven? Are the issues selected for study suited in substance and number to the author's objectives? Is it possible to build a general theory of politics from the New Haven experience or from any case study?

In general, the reader might ask how the findings in other selections in this volume fit Dahl's model of democratic pluralism.

The Definition and Measurement of Influence

During three and a half centuries from Thomas Hobbes to Max Weber little was done to make widely used notions of power or influence more precise. In the last quarter century, and particularly in the last decade, the problem of providing operational meaning and measurements for the concepts of power and influence has received a good deal of attention. Nonetheless, no entirely satisfactory solutions to the numerous problems involved have yet been set forth, and this book necessarily reflects the fact that concepts and methods in the analysis of influence are undergoing rapid changes. . . .

Operational Measures of Influence

One of the most serious problems in the study of influence arises from the fact that, no matter how precisely one defines influence and no matter

From Robert A. Dahl, *Who Governs?* (New Haven, Conn.: Yale University Press, 1961). Reprinted by permission of the publisher.

how elegant the measures and methods one proposes, the data within reach even of the most assiduous researcher require the use of operational measures that are at best somewhat unsatisfactory.

One way to compensate for the unsatisfactory character of all existing operational measures of influence is to be eclectic. In this study, an eclectic approach was adopted deliberately, not only to avoid putting all our eggs in one methodological basket but also in order to take advantage of the existence of a very wide assortment of data. Six methods of assessing relative influence or changes in influence were used in this study. These were:

1. To study changes in the socioeconomic characteristics of incumbents in city offices in order to determine whether any rather large historical changes may have occurred in the sources of leadership. . . .

2. To isolate a particular socioeconomic category and then determine the nature and extent of participation in local affairs by persons in this category. . . .

3. To examine a set of "decisions" in different "issue-areas" in order to determine what kinds of persons were the most influential according to one operational measure of relative influence, and to determine patterns of influence. . . .

4. To survey random samples of participants in different issue-areas in order to determine their characteristics. This method was used to locate the socioeconomic sources of the subleaders in different issue-areas.

5. To survey random samples of registered voters in order to determine the characteristics of those who participate in varying degrees and in varying ways in local affairs. . . .

6. To study changes in patterns of voting among different strata in the community. . . .

Democracy, Leadership, and Minority Control

It is easy to see why observers have often pessimistically concluded that the internal dynamics of political associations create forces alien to popular control and hence to democratic institutions. Yet the characteristics I have described [relatively firm control of an association's direction by a small leadership stratum] are not necessarily dysfunctional to a pluralistic democracy in which there exists a considerable measure of popular control over the policies of leaders, for minority control by leaders within associations is not necessarily inconsistent with popular control over leaders through electoral processes.

For example, suppose that (1) a leader of a political association feels a strong incentive for winning an election; (2) his constituents comprise most of the adult population of the community; (3) nearly all of his constituents are expected to vote; (4) voters cast their ballot without receiving covert rewards or punishments as a direct consequence of the way they vote; (5) voters give heavy weight to the overt policies of a candidate in making their decision as to how they will vote; (6) there are rival candidates offering alternative policies; and (7) voters have a good deal of information about the policies of the candidates. In these circumstances, it is almost certain that leaders of political associations would tend to choose overt policies they believed most likely to win the support of a majority of adults in the community. Even if the policies of political associations were usually controlled by a tiny minority of leaders in each association, the policies of the leaders who won elections to the chief elective offices in local government would tend to reflect the preferences of the populace. I do not mean to suggest that any political system actually fulfills all these conditions, but to the extent that it does the leaders who directly control the decisions of political associations are themselves influenced in their own choices of policies by their assumptions as to what the voting populace wants.

Although this is an elementary point, it is critical to an understanding of the chapters that follow. We shall discover that in each of a number of key sectors of public policy, a few persons have great *direct* influence on the choices that are made; most citizens, by contrast, seem to have rather little direct influence. Yet it would be unwise to underestimate the extent to which voters may exert *indirect* influence on the decisions of leaders by means of elections.

In a political system where key offices are won by elections, where legality and constitutionality are highly valued in the political culture, and where nearly everyone in the political stratum publicly adheres to a doctrine of democracy, it is likely that the political culture, the prevailing attitudes of the political stratum, and the operation of the political system itself will be shaped by the role of elections. Leaders who in one context are enormously influential and even rather free from demands by their constituents may reveal themselves in another context to be involved in tireless efforts to adapt their policies to what they think their constituents want.

To be sure, in a pluralistic system with dispersed inequalities, the direct influence of leaders on policies extends well beyond the norms implied in the classical models of democracy developed by political philosophers. But if the leaders lead, they are also led. Thus the relations between leaders, subleaders, and constituents produce in the distribution of influence a stubborn and pervasive ambiguity that permeates the entire political system.

Some Hypotheses

Given these assumptions, one might reasonably expect to find in the political system of New Haven that the distribution of influence over important decisions requiring the formal assent of local governmental officials is consistent with the following hypotheses:

First, only a small proportion of the citizens will have much *direct* influence on decisions in the sense of directly initiating proposals for policies subsequently adopted or successfully vetoing the proposals of others.

Second, the leaders—i.e., citizens with relatively great direct influence —will have a corps of auxiliaries or subleaders to help them with their tasks.

Third, because a democratic creed is widely subscribed to throughout the political stratum, and indeed throughout the population, the public or overt relationships of influence between leaders and subleaders will often be clothed in the rituals and ceremonies of "democratic" control, according to which the leaders are only the spokesmen or agents of the subleaders, who are "representatives" of a broader constituency.

Fourth, because of the need to win elections in order to hold key elective offices, leaders will attempt to develop followings of loyal supporters among their constituents.

Fifth, because the loyalty and support of subleaders, followings, and other constituents are maintained by memories of past rewards or the expectation of future rewards, leaders will shape their policies in an attempt to insure a flow of rewards to all those elements whose support is needed. Consequently, in some circumstances, subleaders, followings, and other constituents will have significant *indirect* influence on the decisions of leaders. The existence of this indirect influence is an important source of ambiguity in understanding and interpreting the actions of leaders in a pluralistic system.

Finally, conflicts will probably occur from time to time between leaders' overt policies, which are designed to win support from constituents, and their covert policies, which are shaped to win the support of subleaders or other leaders. The keener the political competition, the more likely it is that leaders will resolve these conflicts in favor of their overt commitments.

To determine whether these propositions actually fit the political system of New Haven, I now propose to turn to three "issue-areas" where it is possible to examine decisions to see what processes of influence are at work. Decisions in two of these areas, public education and urban redevelopment, require the formal assent of local government officials at many points. The third, the process of making nominations in the two major parties for local elective offices, is only quasi-governmental, but I have chosen it on the assumption that whoever controls nominations might be presumed to occupy a critical role in any effort to gain the assent of local officials. . . .

Direct Versus Indirect Influence

The six hypotheses . . . seem to be consistent with the processes for making decisions in New Haven, at least in the three issue-areas examined in the preceding three chapters. If one analyzes the way in which influence in these three issue-areas is distributed among citizens of New Haven, one finds that only a small number of persons have much *direct* influence, in the sense that they successfully initiate or veto proposals for policies. These persons, the leaders, have subleaders and followers. Because of widespread belief in the democratic creed, however, overt relationships of influence are frequently accompanied by democratic ceremonials, which, though ceremonial, are not devoid of consequences for the distribution of influence. The choices made by constituents in critical elections, such as those in New Haven in 1945 and 1955, do have great *indirect* influence on the decisions of leaders, for results of elections are frequently interpreted by leaders as indicating a preference for or acquiescence in certain lines of policy.

Assuming one could measure the amount of influence each adult in New Haven exerts over decisions in a given issue-area, . . . many constituents have no direct influence at all; most people have very little. Subleaders of course have much more; the influence of the most powerful subleaders merges imperceptibly into that of leaders. Only a tiny group, the leaders, exerts great influence.

If one were to illustrate *indirect* influence, . . . a few citizens who are nonvoters, and who for some reason have no influential contact with voters, have no indirect influence. Most citizens, however, possess a moderate degree of indirect influence, for elected leaders keep the real or imagined preferences of constituents constantly in mind in deciding what policies to adopt or reject. Subleaders have greater indirect influence than most other citizens, since leaders ordinarily are concerned more about the response of an individual subleader than an individual citizen. Finally, leaders exert a great amount of indirect influence on one another, for each is guided to some extent by what he believes is acceptable to some or all of the other leaders.

Unfortunately, one cannot measure influence so precisely. . . . [There are] ambiguities in the relations of leaders and constituents which are extremely difficult and probably impossible to resolve satisfactorily at present by appeal to direct evidence. These ambiguities are created by the fact that leaders do not merely *respond* to the preferences of constituents; leaders also *shape* preferences.

Suppose the leaders in every issue-area are substantially identical and agree on the policies they want. One may even suppose that although not identical they are all drawn from a single homogeneous stratum of the community and therefore possess identical or complementary objectives—which is rather as it must have been in the days of the patrician oligarchy. The capacity of leaders to shape the preferences of citizens would surely be relatively high in either case. Ordinary citizens would depend on a single, unified body of leaders for information and cues about policies; they would have relatively little opportunity to pick up information about other alternatives. Moreover, if leaders in all issue-areas were substantially alike and agreed on objectives, they could combine their political resources to induce citizens to support their policies through many different techniques of coercion and persuasion. Leaders could, and presumably would, *aggregate their resources* to achieve common objectives.

Suppose, on the other hand, that leaders differ from area to area and disagree among themselves, and that because of their disagreements they actively seek for support from constituents. Then the capacity of leaders to shape the preferences of citizens would—other things remaining the same—be lower. Citizens would have alternative sources of information, and the techniques of coercion and persuasion employed by one group of leaders could be countered to some extent by other leaders.

Clearly, then, in order to answer the question, "Who rules in New Haven?" we need to know more than the *distribution* of influence. We need also to know something about *patterns* of influence. . . .

SPECIALIZATION OF INFLUENCE: SUBLEADERS

Probably the most striking characteristic of influence in New Haven is the extent to which it is *specialized;* that is, individuals who are influential in one sector of public activity tend not to be influential in another sector; and, what is probably more significant, the social strata from which individuals in one sector tend to come are different from the social strata from which individuals in other sectors are drawn.

This specialization shows up most clearly among the subleaders, whose characteristics will be examined in this chapter. In the next, evidence will be presented bearing on the specialization of the top leaders.

Similarities Among Subleaders

Considered as a group, the subleaders in the three issue-areas studied earlier—party nominations, urban redevelopment, and public education—possess certain similarities that tend to distinguish them from the average registered voter.

First, subleaders stand somewhat above their fellow citizens in financial position, educational attainments, and social status. In a society where public life is still widely thought to be a man's world and where men rather than women are generally expected to occupy the positions of responsibility, it is not surprising that two-thirds of the subleaders are men. But they are distinguished by more than merely the conventional privileges of American manhood. Subleadership in New Haven is skewed toward the middling strata. Subleaders tend to live in better than average residential areas. The majority hold white-collar jobs. Even within the white-collar category itself, there are three times as many professionals, proprietors, and managers among the subleaders as among registered voters. The subleaders have received considerably more education. They earn more money. They are more likely to own their own homes.

Considering the electorate of New Haven, the working classes are numerically under-represented and the middle strata numerically over-represented among the subleaders. . . . [Nevertheless] subleaders are much more similar to voters than to the Social and Economic Notability of New Haven.

Specialization of Influence: Leaders

The specialization that characterizes the subleaders is also marked among the leaders. With few exceptions any particular individual exerts a significant amount of direct influence in no more than one of the three issue-areas studied.

Of the various decisions examined in redevelopment, twenty-six actors (persons or groups) succeeded in initiating a policy or vetoing a proposed policy. In party nominations, thirteen actors were successful—four in the Democratic party and nine in the Republican party. In public education, sixteen actors exerted direct influence. Eliminating duplications, fifty different individual actors initiated or vetoed policies in all three.

However, only three leaders initiated or vetoed policies in more than one issue-area. . . .

Of the remaining forty-seven leaders, twenty-seven, or more than half, exerted direct influence in only one instance. Seventeen exerted direct influence in two or three instances in only one issue-area. And three exerted direct influence in four or more instances in only one area. . . .

Altogether, six leaders successfully initiated or vetoed proposals four times or more in at least one issue-area. . . . Of these, only two—the two mayors—exerted direct influence in all three. . . .

Doubtless greater overlap could be found in other sectors of policy— for example, in party nominations, patronage, and city contracts. . . . Despite these qualifications, however, the extent of specialization of influence is striking. In New Haven, it would appear, only the mayor is in a position to exercise much direct influence on more than a few sectors of public policy.

Direct influence is not only specialized. To a great extent it reposes— or at any rate it has in recent years—in the hands of public officials. Of twenty-five persons with high or intermediate influence, sixteen were public officials. . . .

Table I

Sources of leadership

Level of influence	Public officials	Notables or corporations	Others	Total
Low	11 *	8 *	8	27
Intermediate	12 *	4 *	3	19
High	4	1	1	6
Total	27	13	12	52 **

* An individual who was both an official and a Notable was counted in both columns.

** Includes two individuals who were counted both as officials and Notables.

To what extent are the leaders drawn from a single homogeneous stratum of the community? Of the fifty different actors, fifteen were agencies, groups, or corporations; they acted in situations where it was impossible to ascribe the initiation or veto of policy to a particular person. Of these fifteen collective actors, four were business firms, three were citizen groups, and eight were federal, state, or local government agencies. Of the thirty-five individual persons, seven were Social or Economic Notables and the remaining twenty-eight were not. Sixteen of the individual persons were of Yankee, English, or Scotch-Irish stock; six were of Irish stock; four were of Italian stock; and nine were of various European origins, other than Ireland, Italy, or the British Isles. Seventeen were Protestants, thirteen were Catholics, and five were Jews.

As with the subleaders, the issue-area in which a leader's influence is specialized seems to be a function of durable interests or concerns. These interests can usually be traced initially to professional or occupational goals and strivings. Leaders in redevelopment are with a few exceptions officially, professionally, or financially involved in its fate. Most of the leaders in the public schools have a professional connection of some kind with education. The occupational ties of party leaders are more complex. Usually, however, there is reciprocal benefit: party connections advance the leader in his occupational goals, and occupation success in turn enables him to enhance his influence in the party.

Thus the answers to two of the questions set out [earlier] are furnished by the phenomenon of specialization:

First, a leader in one issue-area is not likely to be influential in another. If he is, he is probably a public official and most likely the mayor.

Second, leaders in different issue-areas do not seem to be drawn from a single homogeneous stratum of the community.

Other questions remain. To what extent do leaders in different issue-areas agree on a common strategy? And how do they settle their conflicts? In short, how are the actions of different leaders with specialized influence over decisions in different issue-areas integrated?

Five Patterns of Leadership

The number of theoretically possible patterns of integration is almost infinite. However, because of their familiarity and generality, five possibilities were considered in our study of New Haven. These were:

1. Covert integration by Economic Notables.
2. An executive-centered "grand coalition of coalitions."
3. A coalition of chieftains.
4. Independent sovereignties with spheres of influence.
5. Rival sovereignties fighting it out.

The first of these, covert integration by the Economic Notables, is a common answer suggested by studies of a number of other cities. In this pattern the top leaders consist of a unified group of private citizens who arrive at agreements about policies by covert negotiations and discussions carried on in the privacy of their clubs, homes, business firms, and other private meeting places. Leaders gain their influence from their wealth, high social standing, and economic dominance. . . .

I believe the evidence advanced in previous chapters is sufficient to warrant the rejection of the hypothesis that this pattern applies to New Haven. In every city where Economic Notables are alleged to rule covertly, it is important to note, evidently they do so by means sufficiently open to permit scholars and newspapermen to penetrate the veil; indeed, an inspection of the information contained in descriptions of these cities indicates that the job of probing into the clandestine structure of power has presented few barriers to the assiduous researcher. It is all the more improbable, then, that a secret cabal of Notables dominates the public life of New Haven through means so clandestine that not one of the fifty prominent citizens interviewed in the course of this study—citizens who had participated extensively in various decisions—hinted at the existence of such a cabal; so clandestine, indeed, that no clues turned up in several years of investigation led to the door of such a group.

To abandon the hypothesis of covert integration by Economic Notables does not mean that the Economic Notables in New Haven are without influence on certain important decisions. . . .

A second pattern is envisioned in an alternative hypothesis: that today the top leaders are more likely to comprise a coalition of public officials and private individuals who reflect the interests and concerns of different segments of the community: In this view, a coalition is generally formed and the policies of the coalition are coordinated largely by elected leaders who draw on special skills and resources of influence that leaders without public office are not likely to have. This pattern of integration is usually associated with vigorous, even charismatic elected chief executives; presumably it was characteristic of the presidencies of FDR and Truman. . . .[1]

The third pattern is seen as integration of policies in different sectors by a coalition of chieftains. Something like it fits the various party and nonparty coalitions that control policy-making in Congress and particularly in the Senate.[2] The difference between the second pattern and this one is of course only one of degree; in marginal cases it would be impossible to say whether a particular pattern of integration should be called executive-centered or a coalition of chieftains. . . .

With some reservations as to historical accuracy, the fourth and fifth patterns might be regarded as analogous to a system of independent city-states or petty sovereignties. . . . In this system of petty sovereignties each issue-area is controlled by a different set of top leaders whose goals and strategies are adapted to the particular segments of the community

[1] See Arthur M. Schlesinger, Jr., *The Coming of the New Deal* (Boston: Houghton Mifflin, 1959), Part VIII; James M. Burns, Roosevelt: *The Lion and the Fox* (New York: Harcourt Brace, 1956); Richard Neustadt, *Presidential Power* (New York: John Wiley, 1960).

[2] Recent observers describe Congress in terms that would fit the pattern here, although each offers highly important differences of emphasis and interpretation. Cf. David B. Truman, *The Congressional Party* (New York: John Wiley, 1959), Ch. 4; William S. White, *Citadel, The Story of the U.S. Senate* (New York: Harper, 1956), Chs. 8 and 14; Roland Young, *The American Congress* (New York: Harper, 1958), Ch. 3.

that happen to be interested in that specific area. As long as the policies of the various petty sovereignties do not conflict with one another, the sovereigns go about their business without much communication or negotiation. When policies do conflict, the issue has to be settled by fighting it out; but since the sovereigns live within a common system of legal norms, constitutional practices, and political habits, "Fighting it out" means an appeal to whatever processes are prescribed, whether voting in a legislative or administrative body, decision by judges, executive approval, or elections. The practice of fighting it out increases the likelihood of appeals to the populace for support, and hence the extent to which leaders shape their polices to what they think are the predominant preferences of the populace. However, since fighting it out is mutually costly and the results are highly uncertain, strong spheres of influence may develop with a relatively clear understanding as to the limits of each sphere; in this case, fighting it out is avoided, appeals to the populace are less likely, and policies are shaped more to meet the goals of leaders, subleaders, and special followings.

Thus the way in which petty sovereignties integrate their policies tends to assume one of two patterns, depending on the extent to which the policies of the one sovereign are consistent with those of the other. If the petty sovereigns perceive their policies to be strictly inconsistent, in the sense that a gain for one means an equivalent loss to the other, then conflict is unavoidable and fighting it out is likely to be the method of settlement. This is the case, for example, if the sovereignties are two highly competitive parties, both intent on winning office for their candidates.

However, if the petty sovereigns perceive their policies to be consistent or even complementary, in the sense that a gain for one entails no loss for the other and may even produce a benefit, then fighting it out is likely to be avoided. Possibility of conflict is minimized by mutually accepted spheres of influence, combined with a strong presumption that the *status quo* must be adhered to; it is also understood that if disagreements arise they are to be resolved by implicit, or occasionally explicit, bargaining among the petty sovereigns without an appeal to the populace or other external authorities.

These five patterns of coordination seemed to us most likely to cover the range of possibilities in New Haven, though the likelihood of finding still other patterns could not be excluded *a priori*. During our investigation of New Haven two possible variations on the five patterns became obvious. First, the prevailing pattern might vary with different combinations of issue-areas. For example, the pattern of integration applying to nominations and elections might not be the same as the pattern applying to education and redevelopment. Second, patterns of integration might vary over time. The variations might be long-run changes, such as the decline of the patrician oligarchy; they might be short-run changes; conceivably one might even encounter more or less regular fluctuations in integrative patterns associated with, say periodic elections.

Except for the first pattern (covert integration by Economic Notables), which it now seems safe to reject, all of these possibilities appear to be entirely consistent with the evidence so far. In the chapters that follow I shall demonstrate, from an examination of particular decisions that all of the remaining four patterns have actually existed in New Haven in recent years. Before 1953 there existed a pattern of independent sovereignties with spheres of influence, which I shall call Pattern A. This gave way briefly to a coalition of chieftains and then, under Mayor Lee, to an executive-centered "grand coalition of coalitions," which I shall call Pattern B. Standing quite apart, the pattern of integration with respect to the political parties has been that of rival sovereignties fighting it out, which I shall call Pattern C. . . .

THE EXECUTIVE-CENTERED COALITION

During Mayor Lee's first term the political order was swiftly transformed. The pattern of petty sovereignties he had inherited soon gave way to another of the five patterns mentioned earlier, a coalition of chieftains. However, this pattern proved to be transitional, and we need not concern ourselves with it here. The executive-centered coalition that followed proved to be more durable. In this pattern, only the Mayor was a member of all the major coalitions, and in each of them he was one of the two or three men of highest influence. . . .

The mayor was not at the peak of a pyramid but rather at the center of intersecting circles. He rarely commanded. He negotiated, cajoled, exhorted, beguiled, charmed, pressed, appealed, reasoned, promised, insisted, demanded, even threatened, but he most needed support and acquiescence from other leaders who simply could not be commanded. Because the mayor could not command, he had to bargain.

The centrifugal forces in the system were, in short, persistent and powerful; the fullest and most skillful use of all the resources available to the mayor added barely enough centripetal thrust to keep the various parts from flying off in all directions. Or, to change the image again, the system was like a tire with a slow leak, and the mayor had the only air pump. Whether the executive-centered order was maintained or the system reverted to independent sovereignties depended almost entirely, then, on the relative amount of influence the mayor could succeed in extracting from his political resources. . . .

Thus, although the executive-centered order of Mayor Lee had drastically curtailed the independence of the old petty sovereignties and had whittled down the relative influence of the various chieftains, that order was no monolith. The preferences of any group that could swing its weight at election time—teachers, citizens of the Hill, Negroes on Dixwell Avenue, or Notables—would weigh heavily in the calculations of the Mayor, for the executive-centered coalition was not the *only* important pattern of influence in New Haven. The unending competition between the two political parties constituted another pattern of influence; thanks to the system of periodic elections, the Mayor and his political opponents were constantly engaged in a battle for votes at the next election, which was always just around the corner.

RIVAL SOVEREIGNTIES

. . . The leadership of the two political parties presents a pattern strikingly different from those that have prevailed in other parts of the political system in New Haven.

Within both the Republican and Democratic parties, it will be recalled, nominations for local office have for years been tightly controlled by very tiny sets of leaders. In describing control over nominations, I have also said something of the relations among the leaders *within* each of the two parties. But what of the relations between the leaders of each of the two parties?

In brief, the pattern that prevails in New Haven is one of petty sovereignties in periodic conflict in campaigns and elections. The men who control the nominations and manage campaigns in the Republican party are ordinarily a somewhat different set from those who control nominations and manage campaigns in the Democratic party. The two parties are to a great extent independent and competitive. Probably the competition between them has always been rather vigorous. Although rotation in office is not decisive proof of competition, in the past three-quarters of a century only once, during Mayor Murphy's fourteen-year span from 1931–45, has a single party held the office of mayor for more than a decade. In that same period there have been only four occasions when one party has held the mayor's office for as long as eight years; there have been two six-year periods of control by one party and two four-year stretches. In all the other elections, or almost exactly half, the incumbent party was defeated after only a single two-year term in the mayor's office. . . .

What can we conclude about the specific effects of political competition in New Haven?

First, the elected officials of New Haven have had a significant influence on many policies—on schools and redevelopment, for example. And whatever may be the relation between elections and the preferences of citizens as to local policies, elections do determine—sometimes by an exceedingly small margin of votes—*who* is elected to office. Thus even if recent elections in New Haven were interpreted only as a choice of individuals to hold elective office, the effects on some policies were considerable.

Second, political competition and elections, at a minimum, lead to the rejection of a great range of possible policies, some of which may be discussed in campaigns but many of which are never discussed at all. Thus the assumption, referred to in Chapter 8, among members of the political stratum that the essential characteristics of the socioeconomic system should remain substantially unchanged means in effect that every election is an implicit rejection of all policies that would entail sweeping changes in the social or economic structure of New Haven.

Third, the attempt of political leaders to win the votes of the various ethnic groups in New Haven has had a sizable effect on many policies that are not openly discussed in campaigns—on the ethnic and social characteristics of the men and women nominated for public office and on decisions concerning appointments, contracts, and other public expenditures. Two important side effects of these efforts to appeal to ethnic groups have probably been (1) to speed assimilation, transmit political skills, and gain acceptability among them for the American creed of democracy and equality, and (2) to inhibit the growth of distinctive working-class political identifications, ideologies, and political parties.

Finally, from time to time elections clearly have had a decisive effect on specific policies. Rightly or wrongly—but probably rightly—the election of Celentano in 1945 was interpreted throughout the political stratum as a vote in favor of spending more money on the schools. Rightly or wrongly—but probably rightly—the re-election of Lee in 1955 was taken as a sign that the voters had given overwhelming approval to urban redevelopment.

In short, New Haven is a republic of unequal citizens—but for all that a republic. . . .

The Distribution of Political Resources

. . . The resources available to political man for influencing others are limited, though not permanently fixed. For our purposes in this book, a resource is anything that can be used to sway the specific choices or the strategies of another individual. Or, to use different language, whatever may be used as an inducement is a resource.

How one classifies resources is to some extent arbitrary. It would be possible to list resources in great detail, distinguishing one from the other with the utmost subtlety or to deal in very broad categories. One could search for a comprehensive and logically exhaustive classification or simply list resources according to the dictates of common sense. One could employ elaborate psychological categories derived from theories of modern psychology, or one could use more commonplace terms to classify resources. To the extent that we can explain the patterns of influence in New Haven, it will do, I think, to use categories dictated by common sense; to do more at this stage of our knowledge would be pseudoscientific window dressing.

Some resources can be used more or less directly as inducements. Or, put another way, the kinds of effective and cognitive experiences mentioned a moment ago as peculiarly fundamental and universal depend rather directly on some kinds of resources and more indirectly on others.

A list of resources in the American political system might include an individual's own time; access to money, credit, and wealth; control over jobs; control over information; esteem or social standing; the possession of charisma, popularity, legitimacy, legality; and the rights pertaining to public office. The list might also include solidarity: the capacity of a member of one segment of society to evoke support from others who identify him as like themselves because of similarities in occupation, social standing, religion, ethnic origin, or racial stock. The list would include the right to vote, intelligence, education, and perhaps even one's energy level.

One could easily think of refinements and additions to this list; it is not intended as an exhaustive list so much as an illustration of the richness and variety of political resources. All too often, attempts to explain the distribution and patterns of influence in political systems begin with an *a priori* assumption that everything can be explained by reference to only one kind of resource. On the contrary, the various manifestations of influence in New Haven described in earlier chapters can be explained, as we shall see, only by taking into account a number of different political resources.

Although the kinds and amounts of resources available to political man are always limited and at any given moment fixed, they are not, as was pointed out a moment ago, permanently fixed as to either kind or amount. Political man can use his resources to gain influence, and he can then use his influence to gain more resources. Political resources can be pyramided in much the same way that a man who starts out in business sometimes pyramids a small investment into a large corporate empire. To the political entrepreneur who has skill and drive, the political system offers unusual opportunities for pyramiding a small amount of initial resources into a sizable political holding. This possibility will prove to be highly important, as we shall see, in accounting for changes in influence in New Haven.

Hypotheses

We saw how the monopoly over public life enjoyed by the Congregational patrician families of New Haven was destroyed, how the entrepreneurs without inherited social position and education acquired the prerogatives of office, and how these men were in their turn displaced by ex-plebes who lacked the most salient resources of influence possessed by their predecessors: hereditary social status, wealth, business prominence, professional attainments, and frequently even formal education beyond high school. The change in the New Haven political system from the election of Elizur Goodrich in 1803 to John W. Murphy in 1931—the first a descendant of a sixteenth-century Anglican Bishop, a Yale graduate, a Congregationalist, a lawyer, a judge, congressman, Federalist; the second a descendant of Irish immigrants, a Catholic, a Democrat, and a union official in Samuel Gompers' old Cigar Makers International Union—represented nothing less than an extended and peaceful revolution that transformed the social, economic, and political institutions of New Haven.

This change in New Haven is fully consistent with three of the key hypotheses in this study. First, a number of old American cities, of which New Haven is one, have passed through a roughly similar transformation from a system in which resources of influence were highly concentrated to a system in which they are highly dispersed. Second, the present dispersion is a consequence of certain fundamental aspects of the social, economic, and political structures of New Haven. Third, the present dispersion does not represent equality of resources but fragmentation. The revolution in New Haven might be said to constitute a change from a system of *cumulative inequalities* in political resources to a system of noncumulative or *dispersed inequalities* in political resources.

This system of dispersed inequalities is, I believe, marked by the following six characteristics.

1. Many different kinds of resources for influencing officials are available to different citizens.

2. With few exceptions, these resources are unequally distributed.

3. Individuals best off in their access to one kind of resource are often badly off with respect to many other resources.

4. No one influence resource dominates all the others in all or even in most key decisions.

5. With some exceptions, an influence resource is effective in some issue-areas or in some specific decisions but not in all.

6. Virtually no one, and certainly no group of more than a few individuals, is entirely lacking in some influence resources. . . .

STABILITY, CHANGE, AND THE PROFESSIONALS

New Haven, like most pluralistic democracies, has three characteristics of great importance to the operation of its political system: there are normally "slack" resources; a small core of professional politicians exert great influence over decisions; and the system has a built-in, self-operating limitation on the influence of all participants, including the professionals.

Slack in the System

Most of the time, as we have already seen, most citizens use their resources for purposes other than gaining influence over government decisions. There is a great gap between their actual influence and their potential influence. Their political resources are, so to speak, slack in the system. In some circumstances these resources might be converted from nonpolitical to political purposes; if so, the gap between the actual influence of the average citizen and his potential influence would narrow.

The existence of a great deal of political slack seems to be a characteristic of pluralistic political systems and the liberal societies in which these systems operate. In liberal societies, politics is a sideshow in the great circus of life. Even when citizens use their resources to gain influence, ordinarily they do not seek to influence officials or politicians but family members, friends, associates, employees, customers, business firms, and other persons engaged in nongovernmental activities. A complete study of the ways in which people use their resources to influence others would require a total examination of social life. Government, in the sense used here, is only a fragment of social life.

The Professionals

The political system of New Haven is characterized by the presence of two sharply contrasting groups of citizens. The great body of citizens use their political resources at a low level; a tiny body of professionals within the political stratum use their political resources at a high level. Most citizens acquire little skill in politics; professionals acquire a great deal. Most citizens exert little direct and immediate influence on the decisions of public officials; professionals exert much more. Most citizens have political resources they do not employ in order to gain influence over the decisions of public officials; consequently there is a great gap between their actual and potential influence. The professionals alone narrow the gap; they do so by using their political resources to the full, and by using them with a high degree of efficiency.

The existence of a small band of professionals within the political stratum is a characteristic of virtually all pluralistic systems and liberal societies. The professionals may enjoy much prestige or little; they may be rigidly honest or corrupt; they may come from aristocracies, the middle strata, or working classes. But in every liberal society they are easily distinguished by the rate and skill with which they use their resources and the resulting degree of direct influence they exert on government decisions.

Probably the most important resource of the professional is his available *labor time.* Other citizens usually have occupations that demand a large part of their labor time; they also feel a need for recreation. Measured by the alternatives he has to forego, the average citizen finds it too costly to sacrifice at most more than a few hours a week to political activities.

The professional, by contrast, organizes his life around his political activities. He usually has an occupation that leaves him freer than most citizens to engage in politics; if he does not, he is likely to change jobs until he finds one that fits easily into political routines. Celentano was an undertaker, Lee a public relations man for Yale, DiCenzo a lawyer, Golden an insurance broker—all occupations that permit innumerable opportunities for political work. As a public official, of course, the politician can work virtually full-time at the tasks of politics.

Most citizens treat politics as an avocation. To the professional, politics is a vocation, a calling. Just as the artist remains an artist even as he walks down a city street, and the scientist often consciously or unconsciously remains in his laboratory when he rides home in the evening, or the businessman on the golf course may be working out solutions to his business problems, so the successful politician is a full-time politician. The dedicated artist does not regard it as a sacrifice of precious time and leisure to paint, the dedicated scientist to work in his laboratory, nor the dedicated businessman to work at his business. On the contrary, each is likely to look for ways of avoiding all other heavy claims on his time. So, too, the dedicated politician does not consider it a sacrifice to work at politics. He is at it, awake and asleep, talking, negotiating, planning, considering strategies, building alliances, making friends, creating contacts—and increasing his influence.

It is hardly to be wondered at that the professional has much more influence on decisions than the average citizen. The professional not only has more resources at the outset than the average citizen, but he also tends to use his resources more efficiently. That is to say, he is more *skillful.*

Skill

Skill in politics is the ability to gain more influence than others, using the same resources. Why some people are more skillful than others in politics is a matter of great speculation and little knowledge. Because skill in politics is hard to measure, I shall simply assume here that professionals are in fact more skillful. However, two hypotheses help to account for the superior skill of the politician.

First, the stronger one's motivation to learn, the more one is likely to learn. Just why the professional is motivated to succeed in politics is as obscure as the motives of the artist, the scientist, or the businessman. But the whole pattern of his calling hardly leaves it open to doubt that the professional *is* more strongly motivated to acquire political skills than is the average citizen.

Second, the more time one spends in learning, the more one is likely to learn. Here the professional has an obvious advantage, as we have just seen: he organizes his life, in effect, to give him time to learn the art of politics.

I have just said the *art* of politics. Although politicians make use of information about the world around them, and hence depend on "scientific" or empirical elements, the actual practice of politics by a skilled professional is scarcely equivalent to the activities of an experimental physicist or biologist in a laboratory.

Even the professional cannot escape a high degree of uncertainty in his calculations. If the professional had perfect knowledge of his own goals, the objective situation, and the consequences of alternative strategies, then his choice of strategy would be a relatively simple and indeed a "scientific" matter. But in fact his knowledge is highly imperfect. He cannot be sure at what point rival professionals will begin to mobilize new resources against his policies. When new opposition flares up, he cannot be sure how much further the battle may spread or what forces lie in reserve. He cannot even be certain what will happen to his own resources if he pursues his policies. He may lose some of his popularity; campaign contributions may fall off in the future; the opposition may come up with a legal block, an ethnic angle, a scandal.

Because of the uncertainty surrounding his decisions, the politician, like the military leader, rarely confronts a situation in which his choice of strategies follows clearly and logically from all the information at his disposal, even when he happens to be well-informed as to his own goals.) Surrounded by uncertainty, the politician himself necessarily *imputes* a structure and meaning to the situation that goes beyond empirical evidence and scientific modes of analysis(What the politician imputes to the situation depends, in sum, not only on the information at his disposal but also on his own inner predispositions. His strategy therefore reflects his predispositions for caution or boldness, impulsiveness or calculation, negotiation or toughness, stubbornness or resilience, optimism or pessimism, cynicism or faith in others. The strategies of professionals may vary depending on the forces that generate needs for approval, popularity, domination, manipulation, deception, candor, and so on. The effect of inner dispositions on a professional's strategies is by no means clear or direct. But as one works back from a given situation with all its uncertainties to the professional's interpretation of the situation and his choice of strategies, usually some element in the interpretation or the choice is difficult to account for except as a product of his own special dispositions imposing themselves on his selection of strategies.

Differences in predispositions that result in differences in strategies often reveal themselves in dramatic differences in the style of a chief executive: the differences between a Roosevelt and Eisenhower, for example, or a Wilson and a Coolidge, or the early Truman doubtful of his inherent fitness for the presidency and the later, cocky, self-confident President. Differences also show up at the local level—for example, the contrast between the cautious demeanor of Mayor Celentano and the aggressive, programmatic behavior of Mayor Lee.

Just as individuals vary, so professionals vary in the extent to which they use all the resources at their disposal.) Some professionals seem driven not only to use all the resources they have but to create new resources and thus to pyramid their influence. They are a kind of political entrepreneur. In an authoritarian milieu perhaps the political entrepreneur might even be driven to dictatorship. But in a pluralistic political system, powerful self-limiting tendencies help to maintain the stability of the system.

The Art of Pyramiding

We have seen that in the pluralistic political system of New Haven, the political order that existed before 1953—the pattern of petty sovereignties—was gradually transformed into an executive-centered order. How could this change take place? There were few formal changes in the structure of government and politics. The city charter not only remained unaltered, but as we have seen a proposed charter that in effect would have conferred full legality and legitimacy on the executive-centered order was turned down decisively in the same election in which the chief of the new order was re-elected by one of the greatest popular majorities on record.

The transformation of petty sovereignties into an executive-centered order was possible only because there were slack resources available to the mayor which, used skillfully and to the full, were sufficient to shift the initiative on most questions to the chief executive. Initially, the new mayor had access to no greater resources than his predecessor, but with superb skill he exploited them to the limit. In this way, he managed to accumulate new resources; he rose to new heights of popularity, for example, and found it increasingly easy to tap the business community for campaign contributions. His new resources in turn made it easier for him to secure the compliance of officials in city agencies, enlarge his staff, appoint to office the kinds of people he wanted, obtain the cooperation of the Boards of Finance and Aldermen, and gain widespread support for his policies. Thus the resources available to the mayor grew by comparison with those available to other officials. He could now increase his influence over the various officials of local government by using these new resources fully and skillfully. An executive-centered order gradually emerged. . . .

What then stops the political entrepreneur short of dictatorship? Why doesn't the political entrepreneur in a pluralistic system go on pyramiding his resources until he overturns the system itself? The answer lies in the very same conditions that are necessary to his success. If slack resources provide the political entrepreneur with his dazzling opportunity, they are also the source of his greatest danger. For nearly every citizen in the community has access to unused political resources; it is precisely because of this that even a minor blunder can be fatal to the political entrepreneur if it provokes a sizable minority in the community into using its political resources at a markedly higher rate in opposition to his policies, for then, as with the White Queen, it takes all the running he can do just to stay in the same place. Yet almost every policy involves losses for some citizens and gains for others. Whenever the prospect of loss becomes high enough, threatened citizens begin to take up some of the slack in order to remove the threat. The more a favorable decision increases in importance to the opposition, the more resources they can withdraw from other uses and pour into the political struggle; the more resources the opposition employs, the greater the cost to the political entrepreneur if he insists on his policy. At some point, the cost becomes so high that the policy is no longer worth it. This point is almost certain to be reached whenever the opposition includes a majority of the electorate, even if no election takes place. Normally, however, far before this extreme situation is approached the expected costs will already have become so excessive that an experienced politician will capitulate or, more likely, search for a compromise that gives him some of what he wants at lower cost.

Three aspects of Mayor Lee's situation made it possible for him to avoid costly opposition. These were: the wide degree of latent support for redevelopment that already existed in New Haven and needed only to be awakened; the evident need for a high degree of coordination among city agencies if redevelopment were to be carried out; and the Mayor's unusual skill at negotiating agreement and damping down potential disagreements before they flared into opposition. These aspects of Lee's situation are not prevalent in New Haven all the time, nor, certainly, do they necessarily exist in other cities. In the absence of any one of them, opposition might have developed, and the attempt to transform the independent sovereignties into an executive-centered order might have become altogether too costly.

Thus the distribution of resources and the ways in which they are or are not used in a pluralistic political system like New Haven's constitute an important source of both political change and political stability. If the distribution and use of resources gives aspiring leaders great opportunities for gaining influence, these very features also provide a built-in throttle that makes it difficult for any leader, no matter how skillful, to run away with the system.

These features are not, however, the only source of stability. Widespread consensus on the American creed of democracy and equality referred to many times in the previous pages, is also a stabilizing factor. The analysis in the preceding pages surely points, however, to the conclusion that the effectiveness of the creed as a constraint on political leaders depends not only on the nature of the political consensus as it exists among ordinary citizens but also as it exists among members of the political stratum, particularly the professionals themselves. . . .

Leadership in a Small Town

Aaron B. Wildavsky

There is a popular notion that the small town in America is a cheese press of homogeneity and conformity, in which little competition exists among community leaders. Aaron Wildavsky, drawing upon his close study of the small college town of Oberlin, Ohio, argues to the contrary in this selection taken from a chapter entitled "Who Rules Oberlin and Why." In addition to using and refining Dahl's techniques of decision-making analysis and opinion surveys, Wildavsky considers all the issues of conflict in the community instead of the limited number examined by Dahl. He demonstrates the existence of considerable controversy, engendered by leadership elements who do not fit the pattern of overlapping control found in Vidich and Bensman's study of "Springdale." The author shows that the pluralist perspective can apply to a small town as well as to a larger one, and that conflict appears even in seemingly homogeneous communities. The reader will find Wildavsky's analysis of the nature of power resources and how they are employed especially interesting.

The essential purpose of the case histories and role studies presented in the previous chapters was to present evidence which would enable us to decide what kind of political system exists in Oberlin. We have described every major decision . . . during the period from January, 1957, to June, 1961. . . . If we find that the same participants exercise leadership in nearly all significant areas of decision, that they agree, and that they are not responsible to the electorate, we conclude that a power elite rules in Oberlin. If we discover that a majority of citizens are influential in all or most cases, the proper conclusion is that Oberlin is ruled by the people as a mass democracy. And if we find that the leaders vary from one issue area to the other, with such overlap as there is between issue areas concentrated largely in the hands of public officials, we must conclude that there is a pluralist system of rule in Oberlin. Once having arrived at the correct conclusion, it will become possible for us to attempt

From Aaron Wildavsky, *Leadership in a Small Town* (Totowa, N.J.: Bedminster Press, 1964), pp. 253, 254, 267–271, 272–273, 273–275, 276–281. Copyright © 1964, Bedminster Press Incorporated. Reprinted by permission.

to explain why this particular power structure exists, to account for such changes as have taken place since the 1930's, and to go into the dynamic aspects of how decisions are made in the Oberlin Community.

Following Dahl's procedure, we set up a Leadership Pool consisting of all those who participated in a particular decision and could conceivably be candidates for leadership. Then we separate out those who lost, who got nothing of what they wanted. This leaves us with a Leadership Elite —those who in some way helped secure an outcome they deemed to be favorable. Within this broad category, we seek to distinguish among those who initiated, vetoed, or gained consent for a policy proposal.

Rarely is it possible to trace the first origins of an idea. To initiate a policy in our terms means to seize upon an idea, develop a policy proposal, and pursue it to a successful conclusion. To veto a proposal means either to secure its defeat entirely or to modify or reject a part. To gain consent one must secure the assent of others for a favorable policy outcome. These categories are further divided in order to give some idea of the degree of leadership. This is inevitably somewhat arbitrary and we have sought to do as little violence to reality as is possible by restricting ourselves to three broad degrees—high (implying a major role in initiating, vetoing, or gaining consent), low (a discernible but minor role), and moderate (a residual category).

For analytical purposes the case histories are divided into seven issue areas—housing, utilities, welfare, industrial development, zoning, education, and nominations and elections. After describing leadership in these decisions, we shall compare them to discover the extent of overlap between issue areas and the kind of individuals who exercise influence in more than one area. . . .

We find a clear outline of a pluralist system in accordance with the theory stated in the first chapter. There is no person or group which exerts leadership in all issue areas. To the extent that overlap between issue areas exists, it is held predominantly by public officials—the City Manager, Mayor Long, City Council—who owe their positions directly or (in the case of the Manager) indirectly to expressions of the democratic process through a free ballot with universal suffrage. The one exception is Don Pease, co-editor of the *News-Tribune*, who owes his prominence in the light plant issue to membership on the Public Utilities Commission, who has the kind of dispensable occupation which permits time for leadership, and whose job encourages, if it does not demand, rather wide participation in community affairs. . . .

Although men like Long, Dunn and Comings, who combine public office with unusual activity, are clearly outstanding leaders, none of them has all the influence there is to have in any case. They all require the consent of others. . . .

The number of citizens and outside participants who exercise leadership in most cases is an infinitesimal part of the community. This is necessarily the case since the total number of all those who participate at all in any way is quite small. Meteors who participate in only one or two cases (and that sporadically), and specialists, who confine their participation to one or two issue areas, make up the bulk of influentials. The ability of citizens who devote much time and effort to a single case or issue area to become leaders is clearly indicated as is the initiative and support provided by generalist public officials. . . .

Although leadership is diffused in Oberlin, the outcomes of community decisions are not merely random occurrences but fall instead into a rather well-defined pattern. From inspection of the leaders in the cases we have described it appears that a rather broad coalition of interests, though its members occasionally disagree and suffer defeats, has been victorious on most issues of importance. This combination of the Co-op, some college people, out-of-town businessmen, and Negro leaders has, for the sake of convenience, been called "the planners."

The major analytic tasks confronting us are, first, to account for the success of the planning coalition and, second, to explain why the more oligarchic power structure of the thirties gave way to the pluarlist system we have found today. The explanatory factors we shall employ include differential rates of participation, the structural conditions created by the non-partisan ballot, the existence of several independent centers of influence, and, most important, the more active and skillful exploitation of key bases of influence by the planners.

The planning coalition was in part consciously created—Long, Dunn, Hellmuth, Comings, Blanchard and Ellis set out to recruit commuting businessmen, Negroes, and college people—and partly the result of engaging in conflict and discovering who was on what side. As the various planning policies were debated it became obvious that the cost involved and the constant use of government had led to a split among the activists. Many of the local businessmen were directly affected by the increased water rates, threatened by the possible influx of competing enterprises, and generally fearful of change which might upset the accustomed patterns of affairs in the community. From conversations it appears that some felt that their middle class status was threatened by increased costs which might compel them to become wage earners and reduce their hard-won standard of living. Others objected to changes in the community introduced without their consent, changes which foreshadowed a deprivation of their customary influence and the deference they felt to be their due. At the same time, the commuting businessmen and college people welcomed policies which had the magic label of "planning" and which showed promise of improving community services. The taxes they paid on their houses did not seem onerous to them and they were more than willing to sacrifice a little cash for rewards in terms of better schools, and more attractive housing areas and streets. Negro activists like Wade Ellis made common cause with the planners not only because of a general sympathy with them but also because they saw new industry and a housing code as means of improving the conditions of their race in Oberlin. Their eminence within the Negro sector enabled them to overcome some opposition from Negro homeowners who had low incomes and objected to higher costs. Skill in coalition building was exercised by Dunn and Long as they proposed policies meeting widespread preferences, recruited personnel to promote them, provided a rationale for those who chose to agree, and modified opposition where necessary without giving up essential elements of their program.

If its members had to run together as Republicans or Democrats however, the planning coalition probably would have been impossible. Take the case of Charles Mosher, publisher of the *News-Tribune*. He was a Republican State Senator, a career legislator, a person who worked hard at his job and looked forward to advancement within the party. He would have found it exceedingly difficult, if not impossible, to justify supporting Democrats as Democrats in Oberlin city elections. His allegiance to the party and the expectations of party officials would have been violated by such an action. Under a non-partisan system, however, Mosher could and did support Bill Long and other Democrats on the ground that their party affiliation was not relevant to local affairs. Men like Eric Nord and Homer Blanchard and other commuting businessmen, most of them Republicans, would also have felt uncomfortable at being formally allied with Democrats. Moreover, as is common among middle and upper class individuals, they tend to shy away from active participation as partisans, preferring to avoid the tones of political hostility associated with party strife. They were much more easily recruited under the banner of non-partisan good citizenship than they would have been under party labels.

Central leadership for the planners was provided by tandem, cooperative arrangements between Councilman Bill Long and City Manager Richard Dunn. They helped set the general direction, provided huge amounts of energy, initiated proposals of their own, vetoed some they did not like, and helped gain support for the policies of others with which they agreed. Allied with them on the basis of shared perspectives and mutual agreement were active out-of-town businessmen, the editors of the local paper, some college faculty, a few Negro leaders, members of the Co-op, and a sprinkling of others. The point is not that all people falling within these categories gave their support, but that they provided a corps of activists, mostly specialists, who shared the task of developing policies and gaining public approval. It is doubtful, for example, that the category of out-of-town businessmen numbers more than one hundred individuals. But they provided two-sevenths of the 1959 Council (Nord and Blanchard), four of the eleven candidates for City Council in 1961 (Nord, Blanchard, Griswold, Johnson), and a vastly disproportionate share of commission and committee memberships appointed by the Council.

College people like Ken Roose, George Simpson, and David Anderson performed similar functions. It is probably true that the traditionalists had a substantial minority of support in the faculty, but except for a brief flurry in the 1959 election, these people were not especially active.

Why was the planning coalition successful in getting most of what it wanted? One answer could be that it possessed resources which were superior to those of its opponents. Another answer could be that resources were employed more actively and with greater skill. A third possibility is that it met with no appreciable resistance because others agreed or did not feel strongly enough to bother to challenge the coalition. Let us, then, survey the major resources (bases of influence) which were employed to control decisions in Oberlin and appraise their degree of dominance over others and the rate and skill with which they were employed. We will see that the planning coalition was superior in its possession and use of time, energy, official position, knowledge, persuasion and political skill. And that resources commonly thought to be dominant, such as money, control of credit, jobs, social standing, and the like were not crucial or were mainly in the hands of the losers. . . .

Most of the wealth that exists in Oberlin is not used for any political purpose at all. Hence, those who have little but use what they have are not necessarily disadvantaged. And since all participants (except those at the barest margin of financial existence) have a little cash to spare, wealth is not terribly important. No doubt the existence of financial obligations may help in getting a few signatures on a petition or in obligating an individual to do some work. But these are effects easily obtained by other means. In the secrecy of the ballot box, no one need fear reprisal. There may be some who fear to participate actively lest they incur the displeasure of the wealthy. Yet we know of no such cases and, if they exist, they have not prevented blatant opposition to policies favored by presidents of both banks and wealthy merchants. The victorious planners are in no position to exert financial sanctions over anyone (College faculty and commuting businessmen hire few townspeople, lend no money) unless it be a few employees of the Co-ops who are not noticeably active in town politics.

Social standing appears to be an insignificant base of influence in Oberlin. No doubt there are deference relationships in Oberlin but these do not appear to translate themselves into the political realm. There are some families who frequent a Country Club in Elyria and who hold dances in auspicious surroundings. But most of them are not active at all in the community and the few who do take part are rather equally divided between the opposing factions. Eric Nord and Robert Fauver may gain something from high social standing, but Bill Long, Richard Dunn, Ira Porter or John Cochrane do not. If these activists receive deference, it is due to something other than their social position. To be sure, high social standing may predispose individuals toward activity but no one political group has anything like a monopoly of that resource.

Friendship is a valuable resource which is widespread in the community. . . . While it is difficult to say that anyone made much better use of friendship than others, it does appear that the planners had more success in getting their acquaintances to become active in civic affairs than did the traditionalists, with the exception of the 1959 election.

One reason for the greater activity of people identified with the planners is a consequence of another resource at their disposal—officiality, the holding of elected or appointed public office. This enabled the planners to recruit kindred spirits for positions on the many city commissions and special committees formed to promote policies like the housing ordinance. As these people began to participate, conversations with many of them reveal that they became more interested and engaged in additional activity. They came to know what was going on, developed new friendships, a taste for political "gossip," and even saw some positive results now and then which further solidified their interest.

The most obvious advantage which officiality brings to a Councilman is his vote and to the City Manager, his formal authority. There being few or no effective means of coercion in Oberlin (such as patronage), Councilmen are relatively free agents and can dispose of their votes to secure their preferences. This is evident in the many votes establishing and enforcing housing and zoning ordinances, a new water system, continuing and expanding the light plant, and also in internal bargaining whereby individual members receive concessions, such as modifications of the housing code, in return for their votes. The many examples of the City Manager's use of his office include blocking the Gibson apartments, exercising discretion in enforcing the housing code, and presenting information unfavorable to the Elyria offer to supply water. Officiality is limited, of course, by the official's perception of community sentiment and by desire for re-election and reappointment. Indeed, it would be extremely difficult for any faction to secure its preferences in most areas of community policy unless they were able to occupy public office and they are sensitive to the need for popularity which this entails. Nevertheless, in regard to the general run of decisions which do not occasion much interest, officiality is a crucial resource. This is all the more true when it is recognized that officiality provides access to other resources—knowledge and information, popularity, friendship, development of skills, the expectation of activity and the legitimization of attempting to exercise influence.

In a democratic political system, officiality is largely dependent on popularity with the voters as the 1959 election demonstrates. The planners proved to be more popular. But why was this so? Although this question cannot be answered conclusively, it does appear that the traditionalists were considerably less skillful, and less continuously active. Their decision to run as a group concentrated their popularity and enabled Long to tar them all with the same brush as hidebound and against progress. Time after time they were caught with less than full knowledge of a particular issue and made to appear uninformed. They did not foresee their weakness among college people and Negroes and did little to appeal to these sections of the population. The major difficulty here, it seems, was that they started too late. Their burst of activity at election time could not make up for the continuous activity among the planners to pursue policies which would appeal to college people and Negroes, and, possibly more important, to recruit leaders from among these groups. The opinion leaders in the two communities were overwhelmingly for the planners long before the election, a circumstance which may have made it extremely difficult for the traditionalists to make an impact at election time, as their precinct workers discovered. By contrast, the program of the planners appeared to be considerably more positive and received favorable notice from activists in college and Negro quarters. The slate which the planners put forward was deliberately chosen to make a broader appeal through inclusion of Blanchard and Nord who were known to be conservative businessmen. As the election returns show, the planners appealed to a much wider section of the community than did their opponents.

As the planners were more popular, so were they more persuasive in a context where ability to persuade others is perhaps the chief resource available to anyone who wishes to influence a community decision. . . .

In part, the greater knowledge of the planners was a function of their officiality—the City Manager, Councilmen and Commission members had a right to demand information, were in an advantageous position to receive it, and were required by their positions to be knowledgeable. The advantages this knowledge confers are evident in virtually all the cases under discussion from the water and light plant decisions, where members of the PUC had little difficulty in showing that opposing proposals were illinformed, to the City Manager's ability to help block the Gibson apartment and to further recreation goals by knowing what was happening. To a considerable extent, however, the superior knowledge which the planners possessed was a product of their greater effort to inform themselves. . . .

It would be wrong, however, to think of skill as something esoteric or a composition of various tricks. For the most part, in Oberlin, it consists of rather simple kinds of actions. First, the collection of information so that one is better informed than others. Second, the development of a rationale for approaching those who make the decision. Third, the use of citizens committees and Council Commissions to test community sentiment, to gather support, and to ward-off opposition. Fourth, open meetings to give opponents a chance to vent grievances, to convince the doubtful, and to comply with feeling of procedural due process so that no one can accurately say that he was not given a chance to present his views. Fifth, ceaseless persuasion through personal contact, the newspaper, and official bodies. Finally, and this is perhaps most subtle, an appreciation of group dynamics and a general sense of strategy which includes pinpointing the crucial individuals and persuading opinion leaders of important groups. . . .

The point is not that this general approach reveals the presence of some mastermind but rather that the opponents of the planners had nothing to match it. The traditionalists never quite found a way to combat the use of committees and commissions as strategic instruments. To do so would have required a recognition of the danger they posed and the recruitment of a corps of specialists to compete with them. Only by matching the interest and activity of the planners could they have competed with them on the level of knowledge and persuasion. They did not do so, it appears, partly because they did not think the effort was worthwhile and partly because they could not adjust their thinking to a new type of situation in which participation in public affairs, however limited it might appear, had been significantly enlarged. The planners had pyramided their resources by using officiality, knowledge, skill, time and energy to gain popularity, using this popularity to promote policies expanding their base of support, using this increased support to win an election, using the additional personnel to promote new policies, using time in office to develop more knowledge and skill, and so on. . . .

What emerges most clearly from this discussion of resources is the accessibility of the most effective ones. Most people have time and energy if they care to use it, most can obtain knowledge if they work at it, all have a vote to help determine who holds public office, and virtually anyone who feels he can get support is in a position to run for office. Only a small number take advantage of these opportunities but they are there. Presumably, if sufficient numbers of people felt sufficiently unhappy about the existing state of affairs they would find these resources available to them and could quickly increase the rate at which they were being employed. True, there are some whose socio-economic position or low education have not provided life experiences which would predispose them toward effective participation. There is reason to believe, for example, that members of the Negro community could benefit themselves if they expanded their participation, even though their responses to the questionnaire do not show that there are issues they would like to promote which are not being debated in town. It is true also that interests they have are being promoted by a few of their leaders and by white people who identify with them so that the benefits they receive are greater than their participation *per se* would justify. Should a number of new leaders—men who would help formulate and interpret their demands and explain the connections between what they want and what happens in community affairs—arise from within the Negro community, the disabilities they may suffer today might be lessened.

The basic answer to the question of why the planning coalition was successful is that it utilized commonly available resources at a much greater rate and with considerably more skill than its opponents. Time, energy, knowledge, persuasion and skill were all available to others in quantity. The only resource the planners came near to monopolizing was officiality and that for only a limited two-year period, subject to approval by the electorate.

What about "other factors" in the situation which may have been significant but which we have not mentioned? It is hardly possible to exhaust the total range of conceivable explanations. But it is desirable to consider at least three others: rule by businessmen, social changes, and the presence of a "great man" who molded local history in his own image.

Regardless of our previous analysis, it may be said, the fact remains the most of the influential planners were businessmen and this alone may account for their victory in a capitalist society. Yet as we observe the opposing forces over a wide range of decisions in Oberlin, several issues splitting the community from top to bottom, it becomes strikingly evident that the term businessman is woefully inadequate as a predictor of common interests, complementary strategies, or mutual support. The fact is that men who can all properly be called businessmen have taken opposing sides on most of the controversies in Oberlin. Otherwise, it would be exceedingly difficult to account for the conflicts over the past several years, since most of the activists (with the exception of the City Manager and a few college people) are businessmen of one kind or another. . . .

In an attempt to show whether the change in power structure between the 1930's and the later 1950's could be related to changes in the social composition of Oberlin, an investigation was made on census returns since the turn of the century. What they reveal is that Oberlin appears to be a remarkably stable community. . . . The safest conclusion would appear to be that although social changes may in some degree be responsible for the success of the planners, the available evidence does not suggest that we can lean too heavily on this kind of explanation.

The role of the individual in history has long been the subject of inconclusive debate. Is he a true maker of history or is he merely a manifestation of deeper social currents? The case of Lenin's relationship to the Bolshevik Revolution is instructive on this point. Lenin did not and could not have accomplished the first October Revolution which was a result of such factors as mass upheaval due to a bloody war, breakdown of the Czarist system, and the work of many revolutionaries not including the Bolsheviks. Yet it can be said that without Lenin there would have been no Bolshevik (November) Revolution. For he was the only prominent Bolshevik who was in favor of making the attempt and it was he who convinced his fellow conspirators to go ahead. It can be said, then, that while Lenin could not have created the conditions for Revolution, he was able to seize the strategic moment in a vast cataclysm and turn it to his own advantage. Probably the best that can be done in this famous "chicken-and-egg" controversy is to look upon the conditions of the time as setting broad limits within which the remarkable individual can move, that is, to look upon the remarkable individual as thwarted or assisted in varying degrees by these circumstances.

Had Bill Long come to Oberlin in the 1930's he probably would not have been as successful in community affairs as he was at a later date when his opportunities for gaining allies and pursuing change through planning were greater. . . . To say this, however, may be no more than to suggest that Long might not have tried to do in the thirties what he found feasible in the fifties.

Yet it does appear that if Long had not moved to Oberlin, a number of developments . . . might not have taken place. At least, and this seems to be a safer statement, the changes that he helped bring about might well have been delayed. It is true that [some issues] had been discussed before he came to Oberlin and became active. Yet if he had not participated in hiring a person like City Manager Dunn, nor used great quantities of energy, knowledge and skill in bringing these items up for decision, nor persisted where other men might have stopped, much less would have been done. Of course, Long could not and did not do it alone. But he seized upon and created opportunities which might otherwise have come to naught. Without his presence, Oberlin's political system probably would have been much more fragmented; the existing central direction might have given way to relatively autonomous specialists.

Governing New York City

Wallace S. Sayre

Herbert Kaufman

The notion that the giant cities of today are run by some monolithic political "machine" or "interests," economic or otherwise, should be cast into serious doubt by a thorough reading of the volume from which this selection is taken. Sayre and Kaufman provide us with a clear, systematic statement of the competitive, multi-centered nature of decision-making in New York City. Policy seems not so much to be made as to be extruded from the crevices between semi-autonomous centers of influence. That New York City is not unique in this pluralist pattern may be judged from other volumes dealing with Chicago (23) and Syracuse (142). The counterpoised fears of these decision-makers in New York prevent the development of a cohesive, internally consistent elite who "run the town." The decision centers are numerous and they are kept from flying apart by a series of "balance wheels" in the system.

Sayre and Kaufman examine the election process, the distribution of city positions, and the outcome of specific issues. In addition, they study, over a period of time, the activities of groups and institutions which they identify as key participants in the political process. Basing their selections on historical data and other evidence, the participants they designate are: administrators of line agencies and other key bureaucrats; special authorities and certain agencies; parties and non-governmental groups; the courts; officials of other governments; the city council; the Board of Estimate; and the Mayor's office.

A full view and a fair judgment of New York City's many-faceted political and governmental system has been a matter of national as well as local debate for at least a century and a half. Historians and journalists, statesmen and politicians, social scientists and other analysts, writers in verse and prose have all been fascinated by the power, the variety, the size, and the significance of the city, its politics, and its government. But they have not achieved consensus. The city in the nation, the city in the state, the city in its metropolitan region, the city as a city, the quality of

From Wallace S. Sayre and Herbert Kaufman, *Governing New York City* (New York: Russell Sage Foundation, 1960), pp. 709–716.

its political and governmental life—all these remain, and will continue, as matters of debate and discussion, of interest and concern—for the nation as well as for the city.

The most striking characteristic of the city's politics and government is one of scale. No other American city approaches the magnitude, scope, variety, and complexity of the city's governmental tasks and accomplishments. Nor does any other city represent so important a political prize, in its electorate and its government, in the national party contest. Nor can any other city match the drama, the color, and the special style of the city's own politics. In all these respects the city is imperial, if not unique, among American cities.

The city's politics and government have been more widely known for their defects than for their claims to excellence. This notoriety rather than fame for the city has been the product of many causes. There has been the city's high visibility as the nation's largest urban center. There have been the effective processes of exposure built into the city's political system. There have been the highly articulate voices of dissent and criticism always present in the city. There have been, too, the scale and theatrical qualities of the defects in the city's political system. And the citizens of the city have themselves been more given to eloquence in their indignation at "failures" than in their pride over "successes." Notoriety is, in this sense, perhaps itself a valid claim to fame for the city: the city's political and governmental system has never produced contentment, acquiescence, or a sense of lasting defeat among its critics. The voice of the critic has often had the most attentive audience.

The city's political system is, in fact, vigorously and incessantly competitive. The stakes of the city's politics are large, the contestants are numerous and determined, the rules of the competition are known to and enforced against each other by the competitors themselves, and the city's electorate is so uncommitted to any particular contestant as to heighten the competition for the electorate's support or consent. No single ruling élite dominates the political and governmental system of New York City.

A Multiplicity of Decision Centers

The decisions that distribute the prizes of politics in New York City issue from a large number of sources.

Each source consists of two parts: a "core group" at the center, invested by the rules with the formal authority to legitimize decisions (that is, to promulgate them in the prescribed forms and according to the specified procedures that make them binding under the rules) and a constellation of "satellite groups," seeking to influence the authoritative issuances of the core group. The five large categories of participants in the city's political contest whose roles have been described in this volume—the party leaders, the elected and appointed public officials, the organized bureaucracies, the numerous nongovernmental associations (including the mass media of communication), the officials and agencies of other governments—play their parts upon the many stages the city provides. The most visible of these stages are those provided by the formal decision centers in each of which a core group and its satellite groups occupy the middle of the stage. Every center (every core group and its satellite groups), whatever its stage, must also continuously acknowledge the supervising presence of the city's electorate, possessing the propensity and the capacity to intervene decisively in the contest on the side of one contestant or the other.

Party leaders are core groups for nominations. They function as satellites, however, in many decisions about appointments, and in connection with 'substantive program and policy decisions in their role as brokers for other claimants. The city's electorate is the core group for electoral decisions, where it has a virtual monopoly. Other participants in the contest for the stakes of politics may exert considerable influence on the electorate, but only in the same fashion as satellite groups in other special areas influence each appropriate core group.

In all other decision centers the core groups are composed of officials. Most prominent among these core groups are the officials presiding over the decision centers of the general organs of government—the Mayor, the Board of Estimate, the Council, and the legislators and executives at the higher levels of government. Their decisions spread across the entire spectrum of the city's governmental functions and activities; consequently, all the other participants in the political process are, at one time or another and in varying combinations, satellite groups to these central core groups, trying to influence their actions. Each of their decisions, it is true, evokes active responses only from those participants particularly interested in the affected sphere of governmental activity, but most of their decisions prove to be of interest to some participants in all the five major categories (though rarely to all participants in all categories). In the course of time, most groups taking part in the city's politics apply leverage to the core groups in the general governmental institutions in efforts to secure favorable decisions. The courts are also general organs, and therefore the judges as the core group in that arena are of interest to most contestants at one time or another, but the modes of influence exerted on them are somewhat more restricted and institutionalized than those exerted on the core groups of other general organs.

Functionally specialized officials constitute the core groups for decisions in particular functional areas of governmental action, whether these are in line agencies (such as the Board of Education, the Department of Welfare, the Police Department, the Fire Department, the Department of Health), in special authorities (Transit, Housing, Triborough Bridge and Tunnel, or the Port of New York Authority), or in overhead agencies (the Budget Bureau, the Personnel Department, the Law Department, the City Planning Department, for example). Each of these decision centers is surrounded by satellite groups especially concerned with its decisions—the leaders of the interests served, the interests regulated, professional societies and associations, organized bureaucracies, labor unions, suppliers of revenues and materials, and others. Usually, the groups concerned chiefly with particular functions are uninterested in decisions in other, unrelated functional areas, so that most of the decisions (about appointments as well as programs and policies) in each decision center are worked out by an interplay among the specialized core and its satellite groups.

Most officials have a dual role. They appear not merely in core groups but also as satellites of other officials. From the point of view of the general organs, for instance, the agency heads are claimants endeavoring to influence decisions in the city's central governmental institutions. From the point of view of a department head, the general organs are satellites making demands. Although the general organs' influence on agency leaders is especially strong, it is not by any measure complete domination; the agency leaders commonly preserve a region of autonomy free from invasion by the central organs as well as from other groups and institutions. Department heads also often see their own official colleagues (particularly the heads of overhead agencies), as well as the leaders of the organized bureaucracies, acting as satellite groups, as wielders of influence, and as competitors. Their counterparts in other governments tend to appear in the same light. Other officials (themselves core groups in their own respective areas) are thus likely to appear among the satellites of any particular official core group.

The leaders of the city's organized bureaucracies are, strictly speaking, never members of a core group but always a satellite group seeking to exert influence over one or more core groups. Their role is not without ambiguity in this respect, however, for many bureaucrats also occupy significant decision-making posts in the city government. As members or leaders in their organized bureaucratic groups, these bureaucrats thus occasionally play a dual part; as leaders or members of satellite groups they engage in efforts to influence the actions of a core group in which they are also members. But these are not yet typical situations. In most instances, the leaders of the organized bureaucracies are satellite groups.

The leaders of the city's nongovernmental groups never formally constitute core groups, but appear instead as satellites. Functionally specialized groups, being close to the agency officials whose decisions affect them, are not far from the center of the particular arena in which they operate. But, except when they are coopted into what amounts to a part of officialdom, they cannot do what the core groups do: issue authoritative, official, binding decisions. As satellites, some of the civic groups, and the communication media, are active and frequently highly influential in a broad range of functional spheres. In any specific functional area of governmental activity, however, it is the specialized, well-organized, persistent, professionally staffed nongovernmental organizations that continuously affect the pattern of decisions. Core groups of officials tend to estimate the reactions of other nongovernmental groups that might be galvanized to action by specific decisions, and the officials respond to the representations of such groups when these groups are sufficiently provoked to exert pressure. But the impact of these organizations is more intermittent and uncertain than that of those with sustained and specialized programs of influence. Yet even the specialized are compelled by the nature of the rules to accept roles as satellites.

DECISIONS AS ACCOMMODATIONS

No single group of participants in the city's political contest is self-sufficient in its power to make decisions or require decisions of others. Every decision of importance is consequently the product of mutual accommodation. Building temporary or lasting alliances, working out immediate or enduring settlements between allies or competitors, and bargaining for an improved position in the decision centers are the continuing preoccupations of all leaders—whether party leaders, public officials, leaders of organized bureaucracies, or leaders of nongovernmental groups.

Each core group is constantly bargaining and reaching understandings of varying comprehensiveness and stability with some of its satellite groups, seeking a coalition of forces which will enable it to issue decisions that will stand against the opposition of those outside the coalition. The satellite groups, in turn, are just as constantly bargaining with each other for alliances on specific decisions or more permanent agreements. These accommodations between core and satellite group and among satellite groups represent an infinite variety of bargains, some leaving the core group with considerable freedom of movement, others tying it into close partnership with other members of an alliance, and still others imprisoning it within a powerful coalition of satellite groups.

Since almost all core groups confront a competing and often numerous field of satellite groups, bargaining is perpetual.

Bargaining and accommodation are equally characteristic of the relations between one core group plus its satellites and other core groups with their satellites. These accommodations are necessary since some core groups have supervisory authority over others, some have competing jurisdictional claims, and almost all are competitors for the scarce dollars available through the budget.

Indeed, core groups themselves do not exhibit solid internal unity; each is in many respects a microcosm of the entire system. The central organs of government, for example, are in reality mosaics: The Board of Estimate with its powerful borough representatives, the office of Mayor with its many commissioners and assistants chosen by expediency rather than preference, the Council composed of councilmen representing small districts and operating through many committees—all three are assemblages of many parts. The state legislature, the Governor, and the other elected and appointed state executives are similarly divided when they become involved in the city's government and politics. Even more so are the central institutions of the federal government dealing with the city.

In much the same way, the city's administrative agencies are not monoliths but aggregates of components enjoying varying degrees of autonomy. Each department head must learn to deal with his deputies and assistants, his bureau chiefs, sometimes his organized bureaucracies. The organized bureaucracies are likewise splintered along functional, religious, professional, trade union, rank, and other lines. Party leaders may be described as a class but, in fact, they constitute a large number of rather independent participants in city government, rivaling each other, bargaining with each other, working out more or less unstable agreements with each other. The electorate itself, the sometimes remote and nebulous presence that shapes and colors the entire contest for the stakes of politics, is composed of a multitude of subdivisions—the various geographical constituencies, the regular voters and those who appear only for spectacular electoral battles, the party-line voters and the selective nonvoters, the ticket-splitters, the ethnic and religious voters, the ideological voters of all persuasions, as well as the social and economic class voters.

The process of bargaining, in short, reaches into the core of each decision center and is not confined to relations between core groups, or between core groups and their satellites, or between satellites. If there is any single feature of the system of government and politics in New York City that may be called ubiquitous and invariant, it would seem to be the prevalence of mutual accommodation. Every program and policy represents a compromise among the interested participants.

PARTIAL SELF-CONTAINMENT OF DECISION CENTERS

The decisions that flow from each constellation of groups active in each of the city's decision centers are ordinarily formulated and carried out without much calculated consideration of the decisions emanating from the other centers. They are usually made in terms of the special perspectives and values of the groups with particular interests in the governmental functions or activities affecting them. Only occasionally are they formulated in a broader frame of reference.

This fragmentation of governmental decision-making in the city is partially offset by features of the system tending to introduce more or less common premises of decision into the centers. A major "balance wheel" has been noted by David B. Truman: the overlapping memberships of many groups in society. The same individuals turn up in many contexts and in many guises, carrying to each the viewpoints and information acquired in the others. A second balance wheel is the frequency with which the core groups of one center operate as satellite groups in other centers; no center is completely isolated from the others. Overhead agencies serve as a third unifying element, for they cut across the whole range of governmental functions and activities, introducing, within the limits of their own specialties, a common set of assumptions and goals into many of the decisions of other centers. A fourth unifying factor is represented by the civic groups and the press, which exert their influence on a wide variety of decision centers without regard to the subject-matter specialties of the centers. They are not equally effective everywhere, and they are seldom so effective in any given center as the more specialized participants in it, but they help to relate what happens in every center to what goes on in others. Finally, the central institutions of government (including the courts) operate under relatively few functional restrictions and therefore make decisions with respect to all phases of the city's government and politics. Collectively, their perspectives are broad, their interests are inclusive, their desire to rationalize and balance the actions in all decision centers are strong, and their formal authority to impose a common basis for decisions is superior to that of other groups. These five factors help to keep the system from flying apart.

Yet the autonomous nature of the core group and its satellite groups in each decision center is striking. Although the leaders may belong to many groups, they behave, when particular decisions are at issue, with a remarkable lack of ambivalence. The interests immediately at stake provide the criteria of action, and they often seem unambiguous; at any given moment, group leaders and members act as though they had only one interest, one membership, at that moment. Most participants are galvanized to action by only a relatively narrow range of issues and ignore most others no matter where they occur; as a result, most of the actors in any center share very special interests in the problems at hand, and the casual outsider or the intermittent satellite group has much less effect on the decisions made there than do the strongly motivated "regulars." As modes of integrating the decisions of the city's whole governmental system, the balance wheels have therefore not been spectacularly successful.

What is perhaps most surprising is the failure of the central organs of government to provide a high level of integration for the city's system. The Council has been weak, the Board of Estimate inert, the Mayor handicapped. The government at Albany cannot do the job of pulling the decision centers of the city together, even if it were so inclined. This would mean running the city, a task the state is unable and unwilling to assume, a task that would not win it the thanks of the city's residents or of other residents of the state. Moreover, the state government has not been inclined to strengthen the central institutions of the city, but has enacted legislation and created agencies that intensify the independence of many local officials. State administrative supervision of city agencies has encouraged many city officers and employees to develop close links with their functional counterparts in the state capital, and to rely on these to buttress their resistance to leadership from the city's central institutions. The nature of the judicial process renders the courts incapable of performing an integrative function. Thus, despite the opportunities for integration presented by the formal powers of the city's central institutions, they have generally either officially ratified the agreements reached by the active participants in each decision center, which are offered to them as the consensus of experts and interested groups, or, on an *ad hoc* basis, have chosen one or another alternative suggested when the experts and interested groups have been divided on an issue. It is in the latter role that the city's central institutions have had their greatest significance. Seldom have they imposed, on their own initiative, a common set of objectives on all the centers of decision. The central institutions are important participants in all the decision-making in the contest for the stakes of politics in the city, but they are rarely the prime movers or the overriding forces.

As a result, most individual decisions are shaped by a small percentage of the city's population—indeed, by a small percentage of those who engage actively in its politics—because only the participants directly concerned have the time, energy, skill, and motivation to do much about them. The city government is most accurately visualized as a series of semi-autonomous little worlds, each of which brings forth official programs and policies through the interaction of its own inhabitants. There are commentators who assert that Tammany, or Wall Street, or the

Cathedral, or the labor czars, or the bureaucracy, or even the underworld rules New York. Some of these, it is true, are especially influential in shaping some decisions in some specialized areas. Taking the system over-all, however, none, nor all combined, can be said to be in command; large segments of the city's government do not attract their attention at all. New York's huge and diverse system of government and politics is a loose-knit and multicentered network in which decisions are reached by ceaseless bargaining and fluctuating alliances among the major categories of participants in each center, and in which the centers are partially but strikingly isolated from one another. . . .

The Games of Community Politics

Paul A. Smith

Paul A. Smith, focusing in this article upon a town in transition between sets of leaders, suggests that community decision-making can be conceived of as a "game" involving conflicting interests, differential rewards, and rules of behavior. The author seeks to operationalize game theory in straightforward and relatively simple terms. In later portions of the article, not presented in this volume, he moves toward more formal and quantitative models of game theory.

The reader will note the equation of "political power" and "community power" implicit in Smith's analysis. Smith is well aware that other "games," even more important to most people than those which center on government, determine the distribution of other values in the community. There appears to be no intrinsic reason why the approach used in this article could not be cast in terms that would fit other concepts of community power. Whether game theory constructs are a really useful way of discovering and understanding the distribution of influence in a given area is a question which awaits, and seems to warrant, further research.

. . . Let us suppose that every community is a system of games.[1] Taking a modest-size midwest city as an example,[2] there are business games,

Reprinted from "The Games of Community Politics," *Midwest Journal of Political Science*, 9 (February, 1965) by Paul Smith, by permission of the Wayne State University Press. Copyright 1965, by Wayne State University Press.

[1] Many of the ideas found in this part of the analysis have been lifted directly from Norton E. Long's highly suggestive article, "The Local Community as an Ecology of Games," *The American Journal of Sociology*, 64 (November, 1958), 251–61. I avoid Long's "natural ecology" references in order not to confuse my already highly metaphorical usage of games. [This selection appears in section V of this book. Ed.]

[2] All of the primary data used in this paper are drawn from an Iowa city having just under 20,000 inhabitants and noted by pollsters for its "typical" characteristics. It is the site of several large manufacturing concerns, one employing about one-fifth of the wage-earners in the surrounding county. Vigorous labor, business, fraternal, and civic organizations are present, and the income, occupational, and educational profiles of the community closely approximate those of the state and the United States. Though city elections are formally non-partisan, well organized "citizens

labor games, education games, newspaper and radio games, and so on. Abstracting from our common understanding of the word, each game has rules, players, scores, and often audiences. Usually there also are particular skills and strategies associated with playing the game well, and even more specialized techniques for parts or positions of the game. Thus we can translate virtually any enduring pattern of social interaction involving conflicting interests into game terminology. Furthermore, the fact that an expanded universe of human activities is being so defined makes it clear that there is nothing necessarily trivial or merely entertaining about games. This becomes evident when we give more generalized meanings to the major components of this construct.

The rules provide limits to how a game may be played. They define those patterns of action that *are* the game.[3] Hence, they encompass physical limitations of the players, resource limitations of the environment, and normative restrictions enforced by both social mechanisms and internalized values and beliefs. They may apply to players differentially. Some may be relatively disadvantaged by the rules; and within a general game the rules may distinguish positions having unique limitations of their own.[4] This enables the analyst to achieve either greater specificity or generality, depending on his purposes.

Scores are the "payoffs" of the game. They determine to what extent a player is operating successfully and hence mark the value or utility of the game's outcome. Although games are competitive by definition,[5] it is apparent that this requires that certain outcomes be more desirable than others, and that some players will usually receive greater payoffs

---

groups" support opposing tickets of candidates. Both major political parties are also in a healthy state of repair, with the Democrats gradually gaining in strength, until they are today an immediate threat to Republican superiority. (The county itself, up to the 1960 election, was one of the half-dozen or so in the nation that always voted for the winning Presidential candidate.) In short, this community embodies a wide range of historical, social, and political characteristics. We have chosen the pseudonym, Mayburg, for this city.

[3] Actually, it may be argued that all a game is are rules, other terms being added mainly to clarify our analytical operations and enhance our translations from "real life." While there are substantial similarities, the game components defined here will not be identical to those of formal game theory.

[4] Take the local politics game, for example. The players obviously are limited in their actions by a host of factors, ranging from their physical make-up to their constituencies. Some citizens have a better chance to get what they want than others. Some positions will be more difficult of access than others, and positions will vary in their behavioral requirements (or duties). Some of these points will be developed later.

[5] I am not ruling out cooperation among players. However, all games are marked by competition, if only with nature. Scarcity does not imply that a game must be "zero-sum" (that one side loses what the other side gains), but it does demand competition for the limited positive payoffs (utilities) which are the object of the game.

from the game than will others. Moreover, some games will embody more value and afford greater payoffs than other games.[6] It will also be noted that any *system* of games, with its necessary intersections, requires a certain "community," or common perception of relevant rules and pay-offs.

Strategies are comprehensive plans for playing the game. They involve patterns of "moves" selected on the basis of what other players will do, and thus require interpersonal assessments of intent. This usually introduces considerable uncertainty into the game. Some strategies yield greater payoffs or higher scores than others, and some players are almost always more skillful than others in strategy selection.

Players are those persons (or coalitions) who have certain conflicting interests, actively follow the rules, and reap the payoffs. Though I have distinguished the audience from the players, the former also are rather deeply engaged in the game. In most games, however, it seems wise to maintain the distinction between the two activities of playing the game and of observing—even contributing to—it as part of the audience.

A game thus provides its players with goals, measures of success or failure, and guides to preferable conduct. It also differentiates between more or less successful players, between players and nonplayers, and between non-playing persons with varying degrees of knowledge about what is going on. Once identified, games provide comprehensive explanations for behavior, predictions of social value distributions, and a framework for the construction of "rational" theory.[7]

It is clear that individuals may and usually do play a number of games, though one (ordinarily their occupation) is much more engrossing than the others. Thus in terms of elementary set theory, we can say that certain games intersect. The amount of intersection, that is the number and scope of subsets, depends upon the overlap of players, rules, and payoffs.

[6] It is evident, I think, that this analytic framework comes very close to functional theory in sociology. There we find functional differentiation of human actions and social positions. This will be manifested in performances of distinct roles and ordinarily will generate unequal rewards arising from hierarchical functional evaluations. For several brief discussions of functional analysis see the articles by Harold Fallding, Wilbert E. Moore, and Melvin Tumin, *American Sociological Review*, 28 (February, 1963), 5–28. Moore's remarks, pp. 13–18, make the similarity especially evident.

[7] It should be added that games are intellectual constructs not to be reified. Community players obviously need not be expected to perceive their games as the researcher does. On the other hand, it has been claimed that men are "game-playing animals," and we were continually impressed by the apparent meaningfulness of game terminology to our respondents in the community being studied. This was particularly true for "the political game."

Some games form more subsets than others and there is more intersection among certain games than among others—just how much can be determined empirically by comparing the intersection of players, rules, and payoffs. The more two games intersect, the more they are functionally related.

We, of course, are interested in political games and their intersections with other games in the community. If we take as political games those having in common rules, players, payoffs, strategies, etc., devoted to authoritative allocations of values in the community,[8] the overlap of these games with others will tell us a lot about such things as the structure of power and authority. In order to bring empirical data to bear upon these constructs and to expedite analysis, I shall define the major political game in the city of Mayburg as involving the attainment and manipulation of formal offices of city government. The players of this game attend to the conscious allocation of values for the entire territorial community. They are not, of course, limited to office-holders alone. Those who recruit or influence officials may also be players, depending on their level of activity.

Let us make three major hypotheses: (1) The local (city) government game is residual. That is, it is played as a minor game after the demands of more important games are met. (2) There is no single subset of successful players; in other words, no overlapping group of players that may be called a power elite. (3) Participation and influence in local politics can be deduced from the rules and payoffs of the political game.

If the local political game is entered as a "secondary" activity, its payoffs should reflect this relative value position. What is the status of the political game relative to others? To supplement national survey data concerning the prestige of politics and governmental offices,[9] a representative public sample, government office-holders, and business leaders of Mayburg were asked to make preference rankings of political and other symbols.[10] Several of the relevant sets are presented in Table I.

[8] This definition is taken from David Easton, *The Political System* (1953). More accurately, *the* political game involves the authoritative allocation of values. Various subgames may be specified that perform this function in particular ways or with respect to particular values. For example, the Federal Trade Commission and the local city council are both subgames of the greater political game. However, I shall not maintain this distinction here and will treat subgames as games, thus usually speaking in the plural.

[9] For a summary of national rankings of political and other occupations and a good discussion of the problems of analysis, see William C. Mitchell, "The Ambivalent Social Status of the American Politician," *Western Political Quarterly*, 12 (September, 1959), 683–98.

[10] The public sample used here and elsewhere was a carefully designed area probability sample, in which each household in the city had an equal chance of being selected. Public officials were those members of the city government holding offices of a substantial decision-making sort, i.e., mayor, councilmen, city clerk, city attor-

TABLE I

Preference Rankings of Selected Political Symbols

| Symbols | Mean Rankings By: | | |
	Public Officials [*] (n = 18)	Business Leaders [*] (n = 37)	Public [*] (n = 227)
Business Leader	1	1	2
Church Leader	2	2	1
Political Leader	3	3	3
City Council	1.5	2.5	1
Chamber of Commerce	1.5	1	3
School Board	3	2.5	2
Politics	3	3	3
Business	1	1	1
Farming	2	2	2

[*] For each set of symbols, differences between ranks are significant at the .01 level. Calculations of significance are based on Kendall's S. See Maurice G. Kendall, *Rank Correlation Methods* (1955), pp. 49–53; and Florence R. Kluckhohn and Fred L. Strodtbeck, *Variations in Value Orientations* (1961), especially pp. 124–27, for a specific example of how these data were manipulated. I wish to thank Marie H. Martin for helping with the calculations.

Three things are plain from this table. First, the data confirm the generally modest status of political games in the eyes of both leaders and non-leaders in the community. Second, the prestige of the game varies rather consistently with the way it is labeled—the institutional "City Council," for example, fares better than either "Political Leader" or "Politics." While not surprising, this has an important implication, for what is often postulated as one of the more compelling payoffs of the political game—the value of the play itself—may run a serious risk of being disparaged. Third, different segments of the community place different valuations on certain games. We can see that public officials and businessmen have more favorable views of "Chamber of Commerce" and "Business Leader" than does the public as a whole.

Obviously, it would be difficult to establish a comprehensive prestige order of community games with this sort of ranking device (barring complete transitivity), or to connect verbal reactions (to symbols) with significant behavior patterns. More directly relevant, therefore, is our accumulated evidence that leading players of certain "high value" games,

ney, police-chief, and so on. Business Leaders were those persons who had served on the Board of Directors of the Chamber of Commerce during the preceding decade *and* who remained active business owners or executives.

All respondents were presented with a list of three-symbol sets and for each set asked to "rank these names from one to three according to how *desirable* or *preferred* each name is to you."

such as banking, industrial or business management, medicine, law, and so on, are not only reluctant to move into political games, but also treat them as lesser pastimes when they do play them. City Council membership since World War II shows this rather clearly, with top business executives, civic group leaders, and professional men, being notable for their absence.[11] Moreover, when respondents—both the public and the leaders themselves—were asked why these "top leaders" did not hold official governmental or party positions, their most frequent response was that, after all, such individuals *had more important things to do*.[12] Further evidence was found in a common pattern, wherein a good number of these "top layers" of other games had at one time held positions in local government, but had dropped this activity as the status and demands of their major game positions increased.

Of course, the possibility remains that the "real" political game is played outside the arena of formal government; that these top players of business, professional, etc., games do in fact play the game of authoritatively allocating community values, but do not make their moves in public. Nonetheless, insofar as such value allocations ordinarily require at least the legitimation of formal decisions at some point, this "real" activity must sooner or later affect these decisions. Here, our data, though less systematic, strongly suggest that the top players of other games play politics little more than they do the formal governmental games in the community. Total political participation scores of these top players vary enormously.[13] But their average, while not low, is not extremely high either, being distinctly below that of less successful players (of these other occupations) who, however, participate formally in the political game.

By no means should this be taken to mean that leading players of other games universally eschew politics.[14] But the *degree* to which these players

[11] Of the 29 different members of the City Council since the war, four were top business executives, ten were middle or low-level executives in large business firms, eleven were modest or small-sized private owners, and one had been a successful labor leader. The four top men all served at a time of "economic crisis" in the community, and even then two of them were below the top positions they hold now.

[12] Perhaps the most amusing and palpable instance of this view occurred in a recent election. One of the candidates for a high city office, upon learning that his cement company would no longer be able to do business with the city if he were elected, made a vigorous effort to avoid election, and succeeded.

[13] These were calculated from the respondent's party activity, his interaction with other persons holding public office or known to be politically active, and the amount and intensity of his political discussion. They depend primarily upon the degree to which he engaged in influencing decisions about public issues.

[14] It might be pointed out that Norton Long comes to about the same conclusion for New York City as I do for Mayburg. In both places, public roles are generally unable to elicit the commitments of time and effort characteristic of top business positions, etc. Even in small communities, such as "Springdale," where there appears

also enter the political game will depend upon the relative payoffs of the respective games and their positions in them. Even though top business-men, for example, might find payoffs of political games relatively un-enticing, we have seen that just the opposite might be true for their fel-low players lower down the payoff hierarchy. While the preceding supports our first hypothesis, in that the local political game appears to carry but modest payoffs and to attract players of "modest degree" from

TABLE II

Differences in Rank of Persons Attributed Influence
in Various Policy Areas †

Person	General Influence Rank (n = 84)	Economic Influence Rank (n = 77)	Education Influence Rank (n = 110)	Political Influence Rank (n = 40)(Total Sample n = 234)
A	1	1	12	2
B	2	3.5	22.5°	14
C	3	5.5	22.5°	14
D	4	24 °	1	26.5°
E	5	2	22.5°	19.5
F	6	5.5	22.5°	26.5°
G	7.5	24 °	22.5°	1
H	7.5	24 °	22.5°	4.5
I	9	9	22.5°	19.5
J	10	7.5	22.5°	24.5

† In each policy area there is a rank order of attributions. The rank correlation coefficient of the General and Economic rank orders is .52; for the General and Political, −.12; and for the General and Education, −.34. The rankings were carried out to more than twenty.
° These persons were not even ranked in this policy area. They are assigned tied-rankings below the bottom rank for purposes of illustration.

other games, the possibility remains that the political game has been too narrowly defined in terms of activity; that the players and even payoffs are different if community influence and reputation are taken into ac-count. To examine this, we need to consider the community's identifica-tion of influentials and then the rules of the political game.

to be generalized, integrated leadership, there seems to occur what Schulze has called the "withdrawal of economic dominants from active direction of the political and civic life . . ." Robert O. Schulze, "The Role of Economic Dominants in Community Power Structure," *American Sociological Review*, 23 (February, 1958), 8; and see Arthur J. Vidich and Joseph Bensman, *Small Town in Mass Society* (1958), especially Ch. 10. But this does not obviate the intersection of business and political games. See *Ibid.*, pp. 278 ff.

In Mayburg, the representative sample referred to earlier was asked to name those persons most influential *Generally* in the community, those most influential in the area of *Economic Development*, those in the area of *Education*, and those in the area of *Political Recruitment.* Named persons were then ranked according to the frequencies of their attributions in each policy area. Table II presents the results for the upper part of our list of attributed leaders. If we assume that these data accurately reflect the views of the community as to who has influence and where, it is clear that the sets of persons to whom are attributed General and Economic influence intersect to a greater degree than any of the others. Hence, in terms of community *reputation*, we may infer that successful players of business games are more likely to have reputations for overall community influence than persons who play education or political games. This is borne out by the intersection of the Economic Dominant and Attributed Influential sets.[15] Seven of the top ten and ten of the top twenty reputed to be General Influentials are also Economic Dominants. From the actual names involved in Table II, one thing is clear. In this community, the middle-level executive, the modest store owner, and the rising lawyer and real estate man, who actually play both games, are not attributed as much general public influence as their more advanced teammates.

All this brings us to the inevitable question, if the political game is neither played by or attributed to the top players of other games, why are its players drawn so predominantly from middle-level economic positions and not from other games as well? The answer must lie in the rules. While the determination of intersecting rules among different games is empirically manageable, I shall concentrate here upon the nature of political rules alone. To begin with, the rules of any game may not coincide with its formal prescriptions, something well known to students of bureaucracy and administration. In fact, most rules are defined and en-forced by other players and to a lesser extent by the audience. For rules to be operational, the probable cost of breaking them must exceed the probable gain. This shows that in an important sense the payoffs or rewards of a game are a function of its rules and vice versa. It also implies that some rules are more important (i.e., more costly to break) than others.

Compared to other games, politics has a multiplicity and ambiguity of players and audiences, varying from a clearly identified professional elite and indifferent general observers on the other. All play a part in

---

[15] Economic dominance involves the ownership or control of great economic resources. The criteria of economic dominance, and especially the empirical data available to establish it, leave much to be desired. See Robert O. Schulze, *op. cit.*, pp. 3–9; and Dahl, *Who Governs* (1961), pp. 67–68 and p. 332.

defining and enforcing the rules, thus giving rise to significant uncertainty about what rules actually apply in a given situation. Complex relationships link players with the audience and with players of other games.[16]

The variability of participation in political games is well documented. In Mayburg, a survey of adult citizens [17] one week before the municipal election (to be discussed later), which produced a record turnout and the replacement of a long-established regime with a dissident set of players, yielded the results shown in Table III.

TABLE III

Quality of Public Political Knowledge

Identification of Political Leaders *			Knowledge of Election Issues ‡		Perception of Community Problems †	
Low	0–1	33%	Don't know any	56%	Don't know	20%
	2–3	39%	Personalities	18%	Vague, Unspecific	18%
	4–5	25%	Vague, unspecific	6%	1–2, specific	61%
High	6–7	3%	"Need change"	12%	More, specific	1%
		100%	1–2, specific	7%		100%
			More, specific	1%		
	n = 178			100%		

* Respondents were asked to identify by office and party a list of seven public and party officials in the community. Only office identification is used here.
‡ ". . . What would you say are the main issues in this election?"
† "What do you think is the main problem that this community faces today?

On the whole, the community exhibited little awareness of political players or issues, and only a modest perception of community problems, which presumably form the grist for future political games. And without benefit of a "score card" identifying the players, citizens did even worse. This may be seen in Table IV, which presents the results of interviews with three different sets of respondents, all of whom were asked to name community influentials.[18] At their best (in the area of Education),

[16] The case of a city councilman is illustrative. In this particular sub-game, other players include other councilmen, government officers, party leaders, etc. But these players follow strategies involving the general public in order to maximize their winnings. In doing this, they must use players of other games, such as the newspaper game, and are in turn themselves used by players of such other games. Norton Long makes an important point of this functional interdependence of players in certain different games.

[17] This is not the same population sample referred to earlier and described in Note 10. It was drawn about nine months earlier, using the same area probability methods—that is, it was a random sample of city households—but with a smaller sample n of 200. The interviews were also shorter and 178 were completed.

[18] This Random Sample is the same one referred to in Note 10. The Public Officials, however, here represent all city officials, including members of the School Board, the Planning and Zoning Commission, and so on. Hence the set is larger

TABLE IV

Proportion of Respondents Naming Influentials

Percentage of	In The Area Of:			
	General Influence	Economic Development	Political Recruitment	Education
Random Sample (n = 234)	36%	34%	26%	47%
Public Officials (n = 37)	78	70	57	62
Influentials (n = 36)	82	94	77	94

fewer than half of the public sample named any influential at all. The situation was dismal in the Political area, where almost 75% named no one. In every group, respondents were apparently less knowledgeable about the identity of successful political players than about those of other games. It would seem that while its formal rules (constitutional and statutory) "open up" the political game to a wide variety of players, other limitations have a contrary effect. This suggests that operational community expectations about the playing of politics do little to encourage actual participation. We have already noted that the modest payoffs associated with the game serve to discourage intensive participation by successful players from "prestige" games. More than this, however, the prevailing uncertainty and lack of information about the game make it extremely costly to play for individuals on the other end of the social scale (i.e., the unskilled, low-educated, and poor.) The situation of these persons is such that the costs of the game might become prohibitive—leading them to abstain altogether.[19] The obvious implication that the actual rules do not distribute advantages equally throughout the community cannot be pursued here. . . .

[Our] data point unmistakeably to rules of public conduct that political players break at their peril:

(1) Public decisions should be made carefully, avoiding haste and partiality. (The Prudence Rule)

(2) These decisions should be made in the open, in full view of the community. (The Visibility Rule)

(3) Before final decisions are made, public support should be sought and

than that used in Table I. The influentials are those persons attributed influence by at least five respondents in the public sample and comprise roughly the top 40% of all those attributed influence in all areas.

[19] See especially, Anthony Downs, *An Economic Theory of Democracy* (1957). A major reason for what in some ways might seem a surprising lack of enthusiasm for politics on the part of these low-status persons (in view of the comparatively high payoffs the political game could yield them) is their slender chance of success. This low probability, as we have seen, results from the rules, which favor players with higher (status) occupations, educations, incomes, and so forth.

the opinions of the people given faithful attention. (The Responsiveness Rule)

(4) Politics should not be used as a vehicle for personal gain. (The Disinterest Rule)

From other evidence, four more may be added:

(5) Harsh debate and aggressive argumentation are unseemly in public life. Most issues should be settled in an orderly and essentially quiet fashion. (The Moderation Rule)

(6) Laws, especially as enunciated by courts and attorneys, are the touchstone of correct public behavior and are to be scrupulously observed. (The Legality Rule)

(7) No group (or coalition) should be permanently in power. (The Change Rule)

(8) Leaders should have an "interest" in the community, best indicated by economic commitment, length of residence, and experience. (The Community-Stake Rule)

The first reaction of the political scientist to this set of rules for community politicos is that they have been cribbed from some high school civics book. Since the political game isn't "really" played this way, we have been duped! But in Mayburg accumulated evidence shows that most of the players most of the time do play the game according to these rules. Moreover, this should not be surprising in light of recent findings about political socialization in the United States.[20] It is neatly consistent with the profound constitutionalism associated with the American political culture.

Although fragmentary, the foregoing evidence of the payoffs, players, and rules of the local political game exhibits internal consistency. We have seen that the political game is accorded modest value,[21] that its players are not drawn from the highest positions in other games, and that its rules would not make the life of a "power elite" an easy one (Nor do they encourage populist democracy!). A vital factor in the political game is the inordinate amount of uncertainty, arising from variations in who is playing, how intensely, and by what rules. This, plus the rules

[20] David Easton and Robert D. Hess, "The Child's Political World," *Midwest Journal of Political Science,* 6 (August, 1962), 229–46; and Fred I. Greenstein, "The Benevolent Leader: Children's Images of Political Authority," *American Political Science Review,* 54 (December, 1960), 934–43.

[21] There is one very important payoff I have mentioned only in passing. This is the value of the play itself, and—if successful play is assumed—of power itself. This is difficult to distinguish from other values of the game, but our empirical data provide scant indication that this was seen as a major payoff by the players of Mayburg. The rules, of course, proscribe many of the activities commonly associated with "playing politics," and this is a critical factor in lowering the payoffs of the game.

and payoffs that are understood, makes politics a risky game, especially for the top and bottom economic positions. Even though here displayed crudely and imperfectly, the game construct thus appears to offer both explicit guides to empirical evidence and coherent explanations for the observed events of local political life. . . .

IV

LOCATING DECISION MAKERS: ALTERNATIVE STRATEGIES

The selections in the previous two sections describe two more or less discrete types of community power structures. Of course, variations upon these two general types, as well as alternatives, have been found. Nevertheless, "ruling elite" and "pluralist" models of community influence dominate the literature. In this section we focus upon the apparent gap in findings by researchers, and on the different methods they used, as well as the relationship between the two. The authors of the studies in section II found elite patterns by assessing power in terms of the positions or reputations of those described as influential, while the writers in section III focused on participation in political decision-making to demonstrate a pluralist structure of influence. There has been scholarly debate, sometimes bitter, between the advocates of these two approaches. While this debate in the mid-sixties seems to be leading to an increasing recognition that both approaches (as well as others) yield something of value when combined in field research, the issues that divide the two groups have not yet been resolved completely.

As we have seen, Floyd Hunter, in his study of "Regional City," employed what has come to be called the "reputational" approach to reveal community power. This technique has been used most often by sociologists who have found an "elite" which dominates community policy-making. The basic question guiding this research has been, "Who has the power in the community?" or, in effect, "Who is running this town?" Such questions assume that there exists a set of power holders whose control of a broad spectrum of resources enables them to determine public policies. Operationally, the methodology involves asking "knowledgeables"—those who are in a position to have information about community affairs—for the names of those who are generally most important in getting things done, or whom the "knowledgeables" would enlist if they wanted to get something done. Whether using one or two stages, this technique results in a list of the names of the "influentials" most nominated by the "knowledgeable" panel. In some studies, the members of this list of "influentials" are then interviewed to determine how they exercise power and with whom they interact in public or private affairs (38). A variation upon this technique, often used in conjunction with other approaches as a first step, is the "positional approach," which involves the simple ascription of power to those persons in high formal positions of local public and private groups or agencies. The findings of both the "reputational" and "positional" approaches have generally been similar: American communities are run by a small group of persons, primarily business and social leaders, with the citizenry essentially uninvolved or unimportant in the development of community policies (225).

Herbert Kaufman and Victor Jones, both political scientists, were among the first to attack the validity of "positional" and "reputational" methods of detecting leaders when they reviewed Hunter's book (113). They laid down the basic criticism of both Hunter's approach and findings, criticism which has been further elaborated in later studies by other political scientists. They argued that the answers to Hunter's queries about the holders of power would provide only a picture of the reputation for power, which is not the same thing as establishing that "real" power exists. It was these critics' claim that one could find power holders only by examining instances in which power was actually employed, by individuals or groups, to influence the outcome of a decision in the direction desired. This "decisional approach" was to become the hallmark of the writings of the "pluralist" school, which began to appear in print in noticeable volume after 1960. As we have seen, this school tended to conclude that power was not concentrated in the hands of one group, but was dispersed among a number of groups, each of which tended to be limited to its special sphere, with only the top elected political leader providing some coordination of power resources—if then. These scholars tended to conclude that the mass of citizens have varying degrees of influence upon the outcome of events, even though this influence may be indirect, in the sense that officials tend to anticipate and be guided by citizens' concerns.

Thus there has been little consensus among social scientists on the prevailing structure of power in American cities and towns and on the way that structure should be studied. This disagreement raises an important question in the sociology of knowledge: why do different sets of analysts employ such disparate methodologies and reach such different conclusions? Recent research by John Walton suggests that the answer may lie in part in the different outlook on American society which sociologists and political scientists have adopted as a result of their professional training (223).

Sociologists have been fascinated with the structure of class and status in terms of the division of labor, attitudes, life-styles, etc. This disposition may lead to a hierarchial view of society in which a few people have many resources and much status while many people have very little of either. To the sociologist, furthermore, "power" is likely to mean broad influence exercised through economic and social institutions as well as through the formal structures of government. On the other hand, political science, at least since World War II, has been shifting its focus from the traditional study of formal, legal and governmental institutions to the political behavior of the men operating within such institutions. This new orientation has been concerned with the exercise of power at many levels of government, the making of decisions, and the authoritative allocation of values. When analyzing a community in this context, political scientists tend to focus upon political actors who can be observed actually participating in the decision-making process. For them, the political system is the dominant institution in community decision-making.

Although the professional orientation of political scientists and sociologists may introduce a subtle form of bias into the way they approach their research and analysis, it does not, of course, necessarily invalidate their conclusions. A good scholar is aware of the problem of bias, which is checked by two important controls— his personal and professional standards of scholarship, and the scrutiny of his peers. These two controls sit on his shoulders when he writes, insuring that he does not work completely alone. In community power analysis, moreover, two disciplines are scrutinizing one another.

As the debate over methodology wore on, it became increasingly clear that each method might well be striking at a different dimension of power within the same setting. A number of researchers began to examine empirically the usefulness of the reputational and decisional approaches. Such inquiry has produced by the mid-sixties an awareness of the strengths and limitations of these as well as other research methods. This analysis of methodology has demonstrated that no one method is the sovereign key to wisdom, that each contributes important insights into the phenomenon in which we are interested, and that the best methodology requires a judicious combination of all feasible research techniques.

The articles which follow guide the reader through this interdisciplinary debate. In their selections Robert Dahl and Raymond Wolfinger examine what they regard to be the inadequacies of the reputational and positional approaches. On the other hand, Howard Ehrlich, while acknowledging the inherent biases of the reputational approach, suggests that this research method does provide some important insights, not only about the distribution of power, but about power holders themselves. Thomas Anton attacks the decisional approach in terms of its faulty conceptualization as well as its methodological errors. Then, in the selection from Linton Freeman and his associates, and that from Robert Presthus, we turn to the evolving resolution of the dispute by which scholars compare the major methods within an empirical framework. Freeman does so by examining different measurement techniques and many issues in the same community, while Presthus treats similar techniques within two communities. We believe that Presthus' comments on the utilities of each approach represent the general position toward which both sociologists and political scientists are moving—if they are not already there.

Finally, the reader should understand that this section represents, in what we hope are dramatic terms, a demonstration of the significance of methods of research. Alternative methods may spring from different assumptions about the nature of social "reality" and may lead to different findings about that "reality." We suggest that having read the articles below one may want to examine once again the contrasting findings of sections II and III and to ask how much difference there actually is in the results of the elitists and pluralists. Indeed, is it possible that both sociologists and political scientists see the same phenomenon, but the former calls it elitist and the latter calls it pluralist? Or, are there quite important differences between types of communities? In a very substantial sense these were the questions which Aristotle was pursuing when he analyzed the constitutions of the Greek city-states. The literature still awaits review of that earliest of works in terms of contemporary community power analysis (128).

A Critique of the Ruling Elite Model

Robert A. Dahl

This article, a prelude to the author's now classic study, Who Governs?, *opens the debate over methodology which comprises this section with a direct and incisive criticism of the elitist theory. Dahl argues that the "ruling elite model" assumes the existence of important characteristics of the community without empirical backing. Further, he offers a test of the theory implicit in the model in terms of research requirements, and he asserts that these have never really been fulfilled: "The evidence for a ruling elite, either in the United States or in any specific community, has not yet been properly examined so far as I know. . . . because the examination has not employed satisfactory criteria to determine what constitutes a fair test of the basic hypothesis." Blunt words these, and they outline the battlefield upon which the heated and continuing dialogue takes place.*

A great many people seem to believe that "they" run things: the old families, the bankers, the City Hall machine, or the party boss behind the scene. This kind of view evidently has a powerful and many-sided appeal. It is simple, compelling, dramatic, "realistic." It gives one standing as an inside-dopester. For individuals with a strong strain of frustrated idealism, it has just the right touch of hard-boiled cynicism. Finally, the hypothesis has one very great advantage over many alternative explanations: It can be cast in a form that makes it virtually impossible to disprove.

Consider the last point for a moment. There is a type of quasi-metaphysical theory made up of what might be called an infinite regress of explanations. The ruling elite model *can* be interpreted in this way. If the overt leaders of a community do not appear to constitute a ruling elite, then the theory can be saved by arguing that behind the overt leaders there is a set of covert leaders who do. If subsequent evidence shows that this covert group does not make a ruling elite, then the theory can

From Robert A. Dahl, "A Critique of the Ruling Elite Model," *The American Political Science Review,* LII (June, 1958), 463–469.

be saved by arguing that behind the first covert group there is another, and so on.

Now whatever else it may be, a theory that cannot even in principle be controverted by empirical evidence is not a scientific theory. The least that we can demand of any ruling elite theory that purports to be more than a metaphysical or polemical doctrine is, first, that the burden of proof be on the proponents of the theory and not on its critics; and, second, that there be clear criteria according to which the theory could be disproved.

With these points in mind, I shall proceed in two stages. First, I shall try to clarify the meaning of the concept "ruling elite" by describing a very simple form of what I conceive to be a ruling elite system. Second, I shall indicate what would be required in principle as a simple but satisfactory test of any hypothesis asserting that a particular political system is, in fact, a ruling elite system. Finally, I shall deal with some objections.

A SIMPLE RULING ELITE SYSTEM

If a ruling elite hypothesis says anything, surely it asserts that within some specific political system there exists a group of people who to some degree exercise power or influence over other actors in the system. I shall make the following assumptions about power:

1. In order to compare the relative influence of two actors (these may be individuals, groups, classes, parties, or what not), it is necessary to state the scope of the responses upon which the actors have an effect. The statement, "A has more power than B," is so ambiguous as to verge on the meaningless, since it does not specify the scope.

2. One cannot compare the relative influence of two actors who always perform identical actions with respect to the group influenced. What this means as a practical matter is that ordinarily one can test for differences in influence only where there are cases of differences in initial preferences. At one extreme, the difference may mean that one group prefers alternative A and another group prefers B, A and B being mutually exclusive. At the other extreme, it may mean that one group prefers alternative A to other alternatives, and another group is indifferent. If a political system displayed complete consensus at all times, we should find it impossible to construct a satisfactory direct test of the hypothesis that it was a ruling elite system, although indirect and rather unsatisfactory tests might be devised.

Consequently, to know whether or not we have a ruling elite, we must have a political system in which there is a difference in preferences, from time to time, among the individual human beings in the system.

Suppose, now, that among these individuals there is a set whose preferences regularly prevail in all cases of disagreement, or at least in all cases of disagreement over key political issues (a term I propose to leave undefined here). Let me call such a set of individuals a "controlling group." In a full-fledged democracy operating strictly according to majority rule, the majority would constitute a controlling group, even though the individual members of the majority might change from one issue to the next. But since our model is to represent a ruling elite system, we require that the set be *less than a majority in size.*

However, in any representative system with single member voting districts where more than two candidates receive votes, a candidate *could* win with less than a majority of votes; and it is possible, therefore, to imagine a truly sovereign legislature elected under the strictest "democratic" rules that was nonetheless governed by a legislative majority representing the first preferences of a minority of voters. Yet I do not think we would want to call such a political system a ruling elite system. Because of this kind of difficulty, I propose that we exclude from our definition of a ruling elite any controlling group that is a product of rules that are actually followed (that is, "real" rules) under which a majority of individuals could dominate if they took certain actions permissible under the "real" rules. In short, to constitute a ruling elite a controlling group must not be *a pure artifact of democratic rules.*

A ruling elite, then, is a controlling group less than a majority in size that is not a pure artifact of democratic rules. It is a minority of individuals whose preferences regularly prevail in cases of differences in preference on key political issues. If we are to avoid an infinite regress of explanations, the composition of the ruling elite must be more or less definitely specified.

SOME BAD TESTS

The hypothesis we are dealing with would run along these lines: "Such and such a political system (the U.S., the U.S.S.R., New Haven, or the like) is a ruling elite system in which the ruling elite has the following membership." Membership would then be specified by name, position, socio-economic class, socio-economic roles, or what not.

Let me now turn to the problem of testing a hypothesis of this sort, and begin by indicating a few tests that are sometimes mistakenly taken as adequate.

The first improper test confuses a ruling elite with a group that has a high *potential for control.* Let me explain. Suppose a set of individuals in a political system has the following property: there is a very high probability that if they agree on a key political alternative, and if they all act in some specified way, then that alternative will be chosen. We may say of such a group that it has a *high potential for control.* In a large and complex society like ours, there may be many such groups. For example, the bureaucratic triumvirate of Professor Mills would appear to have a high potential for control. In the City of New Haven, with which I have some acquaintance, I do not doubt that the leading business figures together with the leaders of both political parties have a high potential for control. But a potential for control is not, except in a peculiarly Hobbesian world, equivalent to actual control. If the military leaders of this country and their subordinates agreed that it was desirable, they could most assuredly establish a military dictatorship of the most overt sort; nor would they need the aid of leaders of business corporations or the executive branch of our government. But they have not set up such a dictatorship. For what is lacking are the premises I mentioned earlier, namely agreement on a key political alternative and some set of specific implementing actions. That is to say, a group may have a high potential for control and a *low potential for unity.* The actual *political effectiveness* of a group is a function of its potential for control *and* its potential for unity. Thus a group with a relatively low potential for control but a high potential for unity may be more politically effective than a group with a high potential for control but a low potential for unity.

The second improper test confuses a ruling elite with a group of individuals who have more influence than any others in the system. I take it for granted that in every human organization some individuals have more influence over key decisions than do others. Political equality may well be among the most Utopian of all human goals. But it is fallacious to assume that the absence of political equality proves the existence of a ruling elite.

The third improper test, which is closely related to the preceding one, is to generalize from a single scope of influence. Neither logically nor empirically does it follow that a group with a high degree of influence over one scope will necessarily have a high degree of influence over another scope within the same system. This is a matter to be determined empirically. Any investigation that does not take into account the possibility that different elite groups have different scopes is suspect. By means of sloppy questions one could easily seem to discover that there exists a unified ruling elite in New Haven; for there is no doubt that small groups of people make many key decisions. It appears to be the case, however, that the small group that runs urban redevelopment is not the same as the small group that runs public education, and neither is quite the same as the two small groups that run the two parties. Moreover the small group that runs urban redevelopment with a high degree of unity would almost certainly disintegrate if its activities were extended to either education or the two political parties.

A Proposed Test

If tests like these are not valid, what can we properly require?

Let us take the simplest possible situation. Assume that there have been some number—I will not say how many—of cases where there has been disagreement within the political system on key political choices. Assume further that the hypothetical ruling elite prefers one alternative and other actors in the system prefer other alternatives. Then unless it is true that in all or very nearly all of these cases the alternative preferred by the ruling elite is actually adopted the hypothesis (that the system is dominated by the specified ruling elite) is clearly false.

I do not want to pretend either that the research necessary to such a test is at all easy to carry out or that community life lends itself conveniently to strict interpretation according to the requirements of the test. *But I do not see how anyone can suppose that he has established the dominance of a specific group in a community or a nation without basing his analysis on the careful examination of a series of concrete decisions.* And these decisions must either constitute the universe or a fair sample from the universe of key political decisions taken in the political system.

Now it is a remarkable and indeed astounding fact that neither Professor Mills nor Professor Hunter has seriously attempted to examine an array of specific cases to test his major hypothesis. Yet I suppose these two works more than any others in the social sciences of the last few years have sought to interpret complex political systems essentially as instances of a ruling elite.

To sum up: The hypothesis of the existence of a ruling elite can be strictly tested only if:

1. The hypothetical ruling elite is a well-defined group.
2. There is a fair sample of cases involving key political decisions in which the preferences of the hypothetical ruling elite run counter to those of any other likely group that might be suggested.
3. In such cases, the preferences of the elite regularly prevail.

Difficulties and Objections

Several objections might be raised against the test I propose.

First, one might argue that the test is *too weak.* The argument would run as follows: If a ruling elite *doesn't* exist in a community, then the test is satisfactory; that is, if every hypothetical ruling elite is compared with alternative control groups, and in fact no ruling elite exists, then the test will indeed show that there is no minority whose preferences regularly prevail on key political alternatives. But—it might be said— suppose a ruling elite *does* exist. The test will not *necessarily* demonstrate its existence, since we may not have selected the right group as our hypothetical ruling elite. Now this objection is valid; but it suggests the point I made at the outset about the possibility of an infinite regress of explanations. Unless we use the test on every possible combination of individuals in the community, we cannot be certain that there is not some combination that constitutes a ruling elite. But since there is no more *a priori* reason to assume that a ruling elite does exist than to assume that one does not exist, the burden of proof does not rest upon the critic of the hypothesis, but upon its proponent. And a proponent must specify what group he has in mind as his ruling elite. Once the group is specified, then the test I have suggested is, at least in principle, valid.

Second, one could object that the test is *too strong*. For suppose that the members of the "ruled" group are indifferent as to the outcome of various political alternatives. Surely (one could argue) if there is another group that regularly gets its way in the face of this indifference, it is in fact the ruling group in the society. Now my reasons for wishing to discriminate this case from the other involve more than a mere question of the propriety of using the term "ruling elite," which is only a term of convenience. There is, I think, a difference of some theoretical significance between a system in which a small group dominates over another that is opposed to it, and one in which a group dominates over an indifferent mass. In the second case, the alternatives at stake can hardly be regarded as "key political issues" if we assume the point of view of the indifferent mass; whereas in the first case it is reasonable to say that the alternatives involve a key political issue from the standpoint of both groups. Earlier I refrained from defining the concept "key political issues." If we were to do so at this point, it would seem reasonable to require as a necessary although possibly not a sufficient condition that the issue should involve actual disagreement in preferences among two or more groups. In short, the case of "indifference vs. preference" would be ruled out.

However, I do not mean to dispose of the problem simply by definition. The point is to make sure that the two systems are distinguished. The test for the second, weaker system of elite rule would then be merely a modification of the test proposed for the first and more stringent case. It would again require an examination of a series of cases showing uniformly that when "the word" was authoritatively passed down from the designated elite, the hitherto indifferent majority fell into ready compliance with an alternative that had nothing else to recommend it intrinsically.)

(Third, one might argue that the test will not discriminate between a true ruling elite and a ruling elite together with its satellites.) This objection is in one sense true and in one sense false. It is true that on a series of key political questions, an apparently unified group might prevail who would, according to our test, thereby constitute a ruling elite.) (Yet an inner core might actually make the decisions for the whole group.)

However, one of two possibilities must be true. Either the inner core and the front men always agree at all times in the decision process, or they do not. But if they always agree, then it follows from one of our two assumptions about influence that the distinction between an "inner core" and "front men" has no operational meaning; that is, there is no conceivable way to distinguish between them. And if they do not always agree, then the test simply requires a comparison at those points in time when they disagree. Here again, the advantages of concrete cases are palpable, for these enable one to discover who initiates or vetoes and who merely complies.

(Fourth, it might be said that the test is either too demanding or else it is too arbitrary. If it requires that the hypothetical elite prevails in *every single case*, then it demands too much. But if it does not require this much, then at what point can a ruling elite be said to exist? When it prevails in 7 cases out of 10? 8 out of 10? 9 out of 10? Or what? There are two answers to this objection. On the one hand, it would be quite reasonable to argue, I think, that since we are considering only key political choices and not trivial decisions, if the elite does not prevail in *every* case in which it disagrees with a contrary group, it cannot properly be called a ruling elite.) But since I have not supplied an independent definition of the term "key political choices," I must admit that this answer is not wholly satisfactory.) On the other hand, I would be inclined to suggest that in this instance as in many others we ought not to assume that political reality will be as discrete and discontinuous as the concepts we find convenient to employ. We can say that a system approximates a true ruling elite system, to a greater or lesser degree, without insisting that it exemplify the extreme and limiting case.)

(Fifth, it might be objected that the test I have proposed would not work in the most obvious of all cases of ruling elites, namely in the totalitarian dictatorships.) For the control of the elite over the expression of opinion is so great that overtly there is no disagreement; hence no cases on which to base a judgment arise. This objection is a fair one. But we are not concerned here with totalitarian systems.) We are concerned with the application of the techniques of modern investigation to American communities, where, except in very rare cases, terror is not so pervasive that the investigator is barred from discovering the preferences of citizens. Even in Little Rock, for example, newspaper men seemed to have had little difficulty in finding diverse opinions; and a northern political scientist of my acquaintance has managed to complete a large number of productive interviews with White and Negro Southerners on the touchy subject of integration.

Finally one could argue that even in a society like ours a ruling elite might be so influential over ideas, attitudes, and opinions that a kind of false consensus will exist—not the phony consensus of a terroristic totalitarian dictatorship but the manipulated and superficially self-imposed adherence to the norms and goals of the elite by broad sections of a community. A good deal of Professor Mills' argument can be interpreted in this way, although it is not clear to me whether this is what he means to rest his case on.

Even more than the others this objection points to the need to be circumspect in interpreting the evidence. Yet here, too, it seems to me that the hypothesis cannot be satisfactorily confirmed without something equivalent to the test I have proposed. For once again either the consensus is perpetual and unbreakable, in which case there is no conceivable way of determining who is ruler and who is ruled. Or it is not. But if it is not, then there is some point in the process of forming opinions at which the one group will be seen to initiate and veto, while the rest merely respond. And we can only discover these points by *an examination of a series of concrete cases where key decisions are made:* decisions on taxation and expenditures, subsidies, welfare programs, military policy, and so on.

It would be interesting to know, for example, whether the initiation and veto of alternatives having to do with our missile program would confirm Professor Mills' hypothesis, or indeed any reasonable hypothesis about the existence of a ruling elite. To the superficial observer it would scarcely appear that the military itself is a homogeneous group, to say nothing of their supposed coalition with corporate and political executives. If the military alone or the coalition together is a ruling elite, it is either incredibly incompetent in administering its own fundamental affairs or else it is unconcerned with the success of its policies to a degree that I find astounding.

However I do not mean to examine the evidence here. For the whole point of this paper is that the evidence for a ruling elite, either in the United States or in any specific community, has not yet been properly examined so far as I know. And the evidence has not been properly examined, I have tried to argue, because the examination has not employed satisfactory criteria to determine what constitutes a fair test of the basic hypothesis.

Reputation and Reality in the Study of Community Power

Raymond E. Wolfinger

The general criticisms raised by Dahl in the previous article were subsequently explicated in great detail by two of his students, Nelson Polsby and Raymond Wolfinger. In this selection Raymond Wolfinger objects to the reputational technique as it had been applied in specific studies to that date. The major thrust of his argument is that the technique of employing persons knowledgeable about the town, in order to reveal those with a reputation for power, assumes that appearance and reality are equivalent. His position is that the researcher and the respondent use ambiguous terms such as "power," and that there is no way to validate the latter's opinions of who has influence. Thus a construct of a small elite arrived at in this imprecise fashion is an artifact of bias.

Few books in recent years have had more influence on the study of local politics than Floyd Hunter's *Community Power Structure*.[1] Based on a new research technique which promised to make the study of political influence easier and more systematic, this volume reported that power in "Regional City" (Atlanta) was concentrated in a small, cohesive elite of businessmen. Following the publication of *Community Power Structure* a number of researchers used Hunter's method in other cities and, for the most part, produced similar findings of business dominance.

From Raymond E. Wolfinger, "Reputation and Reality in the Study of Community Power," *American Sociological Review*, XXV (October, 1960) 636–644. Reprinted by permission of the author and publisher.

[1] My thinking on the topics covered in this paper has been greatly influenced by Robert A. Dahl and Nelson W. Polsby. I am indebted to them and to Fred I. Greenstein, Charles E. Lindblom, and Barbara Kaye for their many valuable comments on an earlier draft of this paper. References to New Haven are based on intensive research on that city's politics by Robert A. Dahl, Nelson W. Polsby, and myself. This research is reported in Dahl, *Who Governs?* (New Haven: Yale University Press, 1961); and Wolfinger, *The Politics of Progress* (New Haven: Yale University Press, forthcoming).

The basic assumption underlying this method is that reputations for influence are an index of the distribution of influence. The researcher asks respondents either to rank names on a list or to name individuals who would be most influential in securing the adoption of a project, or both. He assigns power to the leader-nominees according to the number of times they are named by respondents; the highest-ranking nominees are described as the community's "power structure." This technique for describing a local political system is referred to below as the *reputational* or *power-attribution* method.

Several scholars have criticized Hunter's work on various grounds, but there has been no detailed evaluation of the reputational method. Judging by the flow of research making use of this technique, it continues to be highly regarded. The purpose of this paper is to explore the utility of the reputational method for the study of local political systems. This inquiry involves two questions: (1) Are reputations for power an adequate index of the distribution of power? (2) Even if the respondents' perceptions of power relations are accurate, is it useful to describe a political system by presenting rankings of the leading participants according to their power?

It can be argued that the reputational method should be regarded as merely a systematic first step in studying a city's political system rather than a comprehensive technique for discovering the distribution of power. Under this modest construction the researcher would not rely on the method to identify and rank all decision makers but would use it as a guide to knowledgeable persons who would in turn give him leads to other informants until he had a complete picture of the political system under study. Viewed in this unambitious light, the reputational technique is little more than a methodologically elaborate variant of the older procedure of asking insiders—city hall reporters, politicians, and so on—for a quick rundown on the local big shots in order to identify potentially useful interviewees.

The reputational researchers do not make such modest claims for their method, nor do their critics take such a limited view. While I am not aware of any explicit published statement to this effect, the reputational studies give the impression that the technique is regarded as considerably more than a ritualized political introduction. The putative validation of findings yielded by this method, the assumption that a "power structure" consists of those persons most often given high rankings by panels of judges, and a tendency to limit descriptions of decision making to the activities of the top-ranked leaders all point to a belief that this method is a sufficient tool to study the distribution of political power in a community.

THE PROBLEM OF AMBIGUITY

Assuming for the moment that it is worthwhile to rank political actors with respect to their power, is the reputational method adequate for this purpose? There are two major causes of ambiguity inherent in asking respondents to name in rank order the most powerful members of their community: the variability of power from one type of issue to another; and the difficulty of making sure that researcher and respondent share the same definition of power. Each of these problems is examined in turn below, using the familiar concept of power: "A has power over B to the extent that he can get B to do something that B would not otherwise do." The term *scope* is used to refer to those actions by B which are affected by A's exercise of power; for example, the major scope of a school superintendent's power is public education.

In order to compare the power of two individuals one must either assume that power is distributed evenly for all scopes or present a different set of rankings for each scope. Otherwise, if A is judged to be the most powerful man in town on school affairs and B is named the most powerful on urban renewal there is no way to compare their power except by asserting that power in one scope is more "important" than in another. Most of the reputational researchers, by their failure to specify scopes in soliciting reputations for influence, assume that the power of their leader-nominees is equal for all issues; some researchers specifically state that they are concerned with "a general category of community leadership." [2] This is an exceedingly dubious assumption. It is improbable, for instance, that the same people who decide which houses of prostitution are to be protected in return for graft payments also plan the public school curriculum. Moreover, recent research reveals specialized leadership, for example, in studies of Bennington, Vermont, and New Haven.

An individual's political power varies with different issues. Therefore "general power" rankings are misleading. Furthermore, the researcher cannot be sure that his respondent is not tacitly basing his rankings of community leaders on an implicit scope, with the result that an individual may be given a high general power rating because he is perceived to be very influential on a particular issue which is either currently important to the community or salient to the respondent. Data presented in a paper by Robert Agger—the only case, I believe, in which respondents' rankings

---

[2] Schulze and Blumberg, (197), p. 292n. Miller and Hunter also express interest in a "general power structure." See Hunter, Schaffer and Sheps (103), pp. xi-xii; and Miller, (150), p. 10, and (149), p. 300. (Ed. Note: Numbers in brackets refer to citations in the Bibliographic Appendix to this book.)

are presented both for specific issues and general power—suggest that this is more than an academic possibility.[3] Agger reports the number of nominations received by each of eight leader-nominees. Three of these reputed leaders received the bulk of the nominations for "most influential," but the distribution of nominations in the three specialized areas is quite different: "H," who was not named as generally influential by a single respondent, received 47 per cent of all nominations for most influential on "community welfare"; "G" received four per cent of the nominations for general influence and 29 per cent for influence on school affairs; the corresponding figures for "F" were five and 35 per cent. What scopes these respondents had in mind when they made their nominations of general leaders is anybody's guess.

The validity of the reputational method is weakened by the difficulty of determining whether the interviewer and his respondents have the same idea of what the former seeks. The problem of defining political power has vexed generations of social scientists, many of whom have suggested definitions which display considerable conceptual and logical ingenuity. A researcher asking questions based on this complicated concept can either inflict his definition of power on each respondent or use a simplified analogous question. It would require a "man in the street" to be cooperative to the point of masochism to stand still while an interviewer labored through the definitions and qualifications that are found in the literature on power. But the alternative embraced by many researchers has equally great disadvantages because of the ambiguity of their questions. Several researchers have used some variant of the following question: "If a project were before the community that required *decision* by a group of leaders—leaders that nearly everyone would accept —which *ten* on the list of forty would you choose?" This question could ask for popularity, malleability, or willingness to serve on committees.[4] Hunter's "Who is the 'biggest' man in town?" is also susceptible of numerous interpretations.[5]

---

[3] Agger, "Power Attributions . . ." (108). A study soliciting nominations in several specialized areas produced quite different rankings of individuals in each of three scopes, with the exception of one nominee, the local newspaper editor. See A. Alexander Fanelli, (70) pp. 332–338.

[4] Hunter tacitly acknowledges this drawback in mentioning that one very powerful man in Regional City ranked comparatively low on responses to this question because of his reputation for refusing to serve on committees, (102), p. 64. This question assumes that the nature of the "project" under consideration would make no difference in one's nominations.

[5] Hunter, (102), p. 62. Polsby has pointed out the ambiguity of such questions; see "The Sociology . . ." (172), p. 232. The influence of the wording of questions on respondents' answers has long been a serious problem for public opinion researchers and others. Some of the reputational researchers seem not to have been too careful about the phrasing of their questions. It would be interesting to use split-

The ambiguity of such questions is illustrated by a study in which the researchers asked 107 steel union members and officials to identify the "big shots" in town.[6] The respondents named the banker, the Chamber of Commerce, the mayor, other city officials, the gambling syndicate, and the steel company, which dominated the town economically. No respondent mentioned the union or its officers. Hunter and others might take this as evidence of the union's political impotence. But the union obviously was an influential force in local politics. All but three of the respondents said that the police were friendly and partial to them in collective bargaining, the most important issue for most union members; the three exceptions termed the police neutral. In fact, the union leaders had made a deal with the mayor, trading union political support for police favoritism. The police were so friendly that they cooperated in periodic drives in which all non-members were forcibly prevented from entering the steel plant. Most union members did not, however, view police favoritism as a *political* phenomenon. One might also explain their listing of "big shots" as attribution of status rather than power (with the exception, perhaps of the gambling syndicate).

The reputational method appears to be particularly susceptible to ambiguity resulting from respondents' confusion of status and power. This difficulty is amplified by the low esteem in which labor leaders, local politicians, and municipal officials are often held, as well as by their usually lower socio-economic status compared to businessmen and leaders of charitable organizations. In many cities control of political parties and municipal offices has passed from "Anglo-Saxon" businessmen to people of recent immigrant stock and generally lower social status.[7] For example, scarcely any New Haven economic or social leaders participate in party politics, an activity in which the city's populous Irish, Jewish, and Italian groups predominate. In another New England city where the outnumbered high-status Yankees have shifted their attention and aspirations to activities in which money, leisure, and social status count more heavily, "the functions of status allocation and recognition, which were once

---

pair techniques to learn how responses vary with changes in the wording of the basic "Who has the power?" question. See, e.g., Hadley Cantril, *Gauging Public Opinion* (Princeton: Princeton University Press, 1947), Chapters 1 and 2.

[6] Joel Seidman, Jack London and Bernard Karsh, "Political Consciousness in Local Unions," *Public Opinion Quarterly,* 15 (Winter, 1952), pp. 692–702.

[7] James B. McKee has described this process in Lorain, Ohio in "Status and Power in the Industrial Community: A Comment on Drucker's Thesis," (146), pp. 364–370. McKee reports that union leaders do not participate very much in decision-making in private civic welfare activities and that politically powerful members of minority ethnic groups still tend to have rather low social status. See also Peter H. Rossi and Alice S. Rossi, "An Historical Perspective on the Functions of Local Politics," revision of a paper presented at the annual meeting of the American Sociological Society, Detroit, 1956.

performed by public office-holding, have been shifted in this period to . . . the community service organization."

These differences pose a problem for reputational researchers, who often rely on voluntary organizations for initial nominations of leaders. The nominees are then ranked by panels which usually are composed largely of business and professional people. One might expect that as the wealthy become less influential in politics they value political office less highly.[8] In these circumstances, questions which do not distinguish between status and power, and between public and private scopes, are likely to lead researchers to leader-nominees whose power may be exercised chiefly on a country club's admissions committee. Businessmen, when asked questions about "projects," are apt to base their answers on those types of private activity in which they are most active and influential, and which are most salient to them. This may be one reason why the reputational method tends to turn up ruling elites consisting largely of businessmen.

(Ambiguity can be minimized by asking questions about specific scopes and eschewing the "Who's the local big shot?" approach.) This would eliminate situations in which the interviewer assumes that he is getting reports on political power when respondents in fact are ascribing status or merely revealing who pulls the strings in the Rotary Club's program committee. Limiting the questions to specific political issues still will not impose on respondents the same criteria that might lead a social scientist to define a certain event as reflecting a power relationship, but it is probably the best than can be done with this method.

(Specifying scopes minimizes ambiguity and provides a more accurate description of politics by permitting comparisons of influence in different areas. This procedure also gives the respondent a cue to reality and weakens the force of local myths about politics.) A man willing to assert that Yankee bankers run "everything" might make a more cautious reply when asked specifically about the municipal welfare department.

THE PREVALENCE OF MISPERCEPTION

Assuming now that interviewer and respondent have in mind the same phenomenon,(how accurate are the respondent's perceptions?) There is

8 "Far too frequently they [businessmen] also have a strong distaste for politics and politicians—a distaste that can be particularly strong when the politicians happen to be Democrats" (The Editors of Fortune, *The Exploding Metropolis*, New York: Doubleday, Anchor Edition, 1958, p. xvii). Scoble reports that his respondents tended to nominate as leaders those individuals who agreed with them. See Harry M. Scoble, "Yankeetown: Leadership in Three Decision-Making Processes," presented at the annual meeting of the American Political Science Association, St. Louis, 1958, p. 41. Similarly, see Agger and Goldrich, (9), p. 391.

some evidence that these are inaccurate, and to date none of the power attribution studies has been validated on this point by other means.[9]

One of the most striking examples of inaccurate perception appears in a footnote to a paper by Pellegrin and Coates on the influence of absentee-owned corporations in a southern city:

> The typical interviewee [a businessman] in this study described local government officials as relatively powerless figures who do not have the backing of influential groups but secured their positions through the support of working-class voters. Indeed, these officials were more often than not targets of ridicule for those who evaluated their positions in the power structure. . . . The relative lack of integration of Bigtown's interest groups makes it possible for governmental officials to sponsor civic projects which are sometimes successful, in spite of opposition from one or another of the "crowds" [of big business]. Interest groups find it difficult to express publicly opposition to projects which attract widespread support. To do so would be "bad public relations," perhaps unprofitable in the long run.[10]

In the text of this paper the authors emphasize the power of the absentee-owned corporations and report that they can veto any project which they oppose and secure the adoption of any measure they support.[11] Perhaps Pellegrin and Coates were unaware of the implications of the quoted passage, both for their thesis about the distribution of power in "Bigtown" and for the more general assumption that reputations are an adequate index of the actual distribution of power. Whether the passage reveals inaccurate perceptions or an eccentric definition of power, however, it is clear that these respondents' rankings of the community's most powerful men are open to serious question. So many alternate interpretations of such responses are possible that relying on them to define a "power structure" is unwarranted.

[9] Blackwell maintains that studies which Hunter has conducted in other communities have verified the findings of his inquiry in Regional City (34), p. 317. But Hunter's description of the political system in City A is not evidence for the accuracy of his description of City B; and since he has not studied Regional City by means of an alternative procedure, his method has not been validated. Miller reports correlations between choice as a "key influential" and *some* forms of participation in civic groups, but none of these activities has been shown to be an index of political power. See (150), pp. 12, 13. He also asserts that "A valuable test of this technique" of power attribution was conducted by John M. Foskett and Raymond Hohle," (p. 10). See the latter's "The Measurement of Influence in Community Affairs" (96), pp. 148–154. But Foskett and Hohle merely compared the lists of leaders chosen by a number of variants of the reputational method and found a high association between them, which did not test the method by comparing its results with findings produced by another method.

[10] Roland J. Pellegrin and Charles S. Coates, "Absentee-Owned Corporations and Community Power Structure," *American Journal of Sociology*, 61 (March, 1956), p. 414 n.

[11] *Ibid.*, p. 414.

If private citizens are unreliable sources of information, people who are active in public life are not much better informants, either on general or specific questions. Key observes that "Such general conclusions [about the political efficacy of various groups] by politicians and other 'informed' citizens are wrong so much of the time that one becomes skeptical of all such remarks." [12] Rossi reports a striking example of misperception in "Bay City," where Republican politicians explained that their lack of success with various ethnic groups was due to the energetic activities of the local Catholic priests on behalf of the Democratic party. Actually most of the priests were Republicans.

In New Haven a number of prominent citizens active in public affairs could not identify other decision makers in the same policy field. This was most notably revealed in interviews with members of the executive committee of the Citizens Action Commission, a group of about 20 men who direct the Commission's activities in various aspects of civic betterment. This group has been described as the "biggest muscles in town" and includes among others the President of Yale University and the Dean of the Yale Law School, the presidents of the local power and telephone companies, the President of the New York, New Haven and Hartford Railroad, leading bankers and attorneys, the heads of several nationally known industrial firms, the President and Secretary of the Connecticut Labor Council, AFL-CIO, and the Democratic National Committeeman from Connecticut. Although these men meet formally once a month and often get together at other CAC functions, many of them could not identify other committee members. For example, a regular and articulate participant spoke glowingly about the pleasures of his association with the other men on the committee and of his fond image of them all sitting together around the conference table, but except for friends he had known before the CAC was founded, he was unable to identify a single member. Another active participant, describing his fellow committee members, thought that the president of the Labor Council was a realtor employed by the New Haven Redevelopment Agency. Clearly, these respondents' replies to questions about the relative political influence of various New Haven leaders were not very informative.

New Haven politicians were not much better reporters of the distribution of power. Several of them, interviewed on a particular issue, told researchers that a local figure was the "real power" behind the scenes and always had his way; and then, discussing the same measure, added that another politician, opposed to the first, had "rammed it through the board—no one could stand up to him." An enduring item in the political folklore of New Haven is that one political figure or another is nothing but an errand boy for Yale University. As one would expect, this accusa-

[12] V. O. Key, *Southern Politics* (New York: Knopf, 1950), p. 139 n.

tion is most credible to those individuals who are hostile either to Yale or to whichever politician is currently so attacked. Some experienced political figures so devoutly believe this charge that they are impervious to contrary evidence. If people who are professionally involved in community decision making cannot perceive accurately the distribution of political power, how can the rankings of less well-informed respondents be accepted as anything more than a report of public opinion on politics?

The reputational method, then, does not do what it is supposed to do: the ranking of leaders is not a valid representation of the distribution of political power in a given community. But assuming that reputations for power do in fact constitute an adequate index of power, nevertheless the resulting list of powerful individuals would not be useful without additional research which would make the method largely redundant, and even this utility would be very limited.

In compiling a list of leaders ranked according to the degree of power attributed to each of them, the researcher must have some means of limiting its size. Hunter, in selecting the arbitrary number of 40 for his leadership group, assumed what he set out to prove: that no more than 40 people were the rulers of Atlanta, possessed more power than the rest of the population, and comprised its "power structure." He assumed that political power was concentrated in a very small group and concerned himself with identifying its members. Hunter's key question might be paraphrased as follows: "What are the names and occupations of the tiny group of people who run this city?"

Any *a priori* definition of the size of a leadership group carries such an implicit assumption about the distribution of political power. The vital point is the establishment of a cutoff point, a criterion which determines the size of the group. If the criterion is placed too high, it may exclude so many significant actors that only a small part of the total amount of influence exercised in the community is included—the top 40 leaders may be outweighed by the next 200 powerwielders.[13] If too low,

[13] *Cf.* Robert K. Merton, "Patterns of Influence: A Study of Interpersonal Influence and of Communications Behavior in a Local Community," in P. F. Lazarsfeld and F. N. Stanton, editors, *Communications Research, 1948–49* (New York: Harper, 1949) pp. 180–219. Miller defines "power structure" so that it is composed of the most frequently nominated individuals, without knowing whether the "pyramid" of power is shaped so that his *a priori* criterion of nomination will coincide with an actual cut-off point in the distribution of power. Thus he reports that there are 12 "key influentials" and 44 "top influentials" in a city of half a million people, but presents no evidence of their ability to dominate Seattle's political system. See Miller, "Industry and Community . . ." (150), p. 10, and "Decision-making Cliques . . ." (111), pp. 302–303. Other reputational researchers are less explicit about this assumption. In his later article, Miller expresses some doubt about the extent of business dominance in Seattle. These uncertainties are based on interviews with a few participants, however, not on the reputational method; the latter technique turned up a business ruling elite.

it may result in diluting the leadership group with many non-leaders. Clearly the important consideration here is the shape of the influence "pyramid": the more steeply its sides slope, the fewer people in the elite group and the higher the researcher's cut-off point can be. Yet if he knows enough about the community to envision such a pyramid, he already knows much of what the power-attribution method is supposed to tell him, and a great deal more.

There appears to be no way out of this dilemma without making an assumption crucial to the problem. If the researcher's questions do not specify the number of leaders the respondent can nominate and only a few actors are mentioned, he is in effect passing this problem along to his respondents. For while each of the respondents may believe that the person (or persons) he names is the most powerful single individual, nominations of the most influential man in town do not include information about how much power he has compared to other actors. If the researcher decides to establish the cut-off point by a "break" in number of nominations, or by including the nominees who account for a majority of nominations, he is passing the buck to a statistical artifact, for he still has no way of knowing that his criterion corresponds to political reality.

The identification of leaders which the reputational method is supposed to achieve has very limited utility for another reason. A demographic classification of such leaders is not a description of a city's political system because it does not indicate whether they are allies or enemies. To establish the existence of a ruling elite, one must show not only that influence is distributed unequally but also that those who have the most influence are united so as to act in concert rather than in opposition. One cannot conclude that the highest-ranked individuals comprise a ruling group rather than merely an aggregate of leaders without establishing their cohesiveness as well as their power.

Most of the reputational researchers consider this point, but then go on to draw conclusions about the probable decisions of their putative elites by assuming that political preferences can be inferred from socioeconomic status. This inference is questionable on a number of grounds. It assumes that the members of the body politic can be divided into two groups on the basis of a dichotomizing principle (such as relationship to the means of production) which determines all their policy preferences. Thus there will be a "class position" on every issue, with the same people on the same side on all issues. This in turn assumes that economic status is the only variable that determines political preferences. But associations between socioeconomic status and positions on various issues represent correlations, not categoric divisions; there are always sizeable numbers of people on the minority side. Furthermore, persons of different economic status may have similar attitudes on the basis of shared vocational or sectional interests: both the United Mine Workers and coal mine owners worry about competition from other fuels; New England workers and merchants alike are concerned about departing industries. For people in official positions the "norms of the office" represent role demands which often predict behavior more consistently than status. Finally, politicians want to win, to the point at times where they are ideologically indifferent. Even "issue-oriented" politicians accept the need to compromise.

While most political leaders in Bennington were business or professional men, they were split into several durable and bitterly opposed factions on the issues which Scoble studied. In New Haven the six most prominent politicians have the following occupations (or occupational background, in the case of the mayor, a full-time official): attorney (two), undertaker, bond and insurance broker, realtor, and public relations director. The first three are Republicans, the others, Democrats. The two parties are quite differentiated; a change in regime seven years ago brought marked changes in municipal policies. The policies followed by these six men cannot be predicted by reference to their occupations. It should be noted that few of the power-attribution researchers even mention the party identifications of their leader-nominees.

Another weakness of the reputational method is that it assumes and reports a static distribution of power. The three New Haven Democrats mentioned in the preceding paragraph are currently much more powerful than the three Republicans, in large measure because the Democrats are in office. The outcome of elections may be relevant to the distribution of power, a consideration which apparently has escaped the power-attribution researchers and for which their method is illsuited. Changes in the nature and distribution of the sources of power are assumed to occur very slowly, so that the only strategy for a group engaged in political action is to persuade the real elite to go along with it. The model of the political process resulting from the reputational method assumes an equation of potential for power with the realization of that potential. (It may be a misnomer to refer to this as a "process;" actually the reputational researchers appear to assume a kind of equilibrium.) This in turn assumes that all resources will be used to an equal extent and thus that political skill is unimportant. Either elections are of no consequence or one side will win all of them.

It would be interesting to replicate some of the power attribution studies at five-year intervals to learn how persistently the same individuals are nominated at leaders. A study by Donald Olmsted suggests that quite different lists might result.[14] His panel of "knowledgeable citizens" named

[14] "Organizational Leadership and Social Structure in a Small City," *American Sociological Review*, 19 (May, 1954), pp. 273–281.

30 community leaders in 1943 and again in 1949; the names of only nine people were on both lists. One would expect some attrition by death, moving, and so on, but the locale of Olmsted's study did not have an unusually unstable population.

Shifting distribution of power, whether the result of elections or of other factors, presents a problem in political analysis which appears to be unsolvable by the power-attribution method. While some individuals might maintain some or all of their power after a change in regime, others would not, and some relatively powerless persons would be placed high in the "power structure." The inclusion of all political actors within a supposed power elite would be neither surprising nor discriminating. The interesting questions about politics are concerned with the dynamics of policy making and are badly warped in static, reified rankings of individals whose demographic classification is a poor substitute for analysis of goals, strategies, power bases, outcomes, recruitment patterns, and similar questions. When energetic political organization can affect elections and issue outcomes and thus "make new power," [15] description of a dynamic process by a static concept appears to be a mismatch of method and subject matter. The gifts and energies of social scientists can be better used than in this pursuit.

[15] See, e.g., Francis Carney, *The Rise of the Democratic Clubs in California* (New York: Holt), 1959.

The Social Psychology of Reputations for Community Leadership

Howard J. Ehrlich

In the following article Howard J. Ehrlich notes that a reputation for power is a phenomenon that is relevant to the study of community power, even if it is not always an accurate indicator of power itself. He compares the nominations of "influentials," made by a random sample of the adult citizens of Prince George County, Maryland (population 425,000) with the background of the individuals making the nominations and suggests the nature of the biases that are likely to be reflected in assessments of power based on attributed influence. He concludes with a summary of the major propositions that may be derived from the literature on the social psychology of leadership.

This article clarifies some of the problems involved with the reputational approach to community power, and implies some of the factors which one must consider when evaluating the validity of power attributions. Furthermore, it should be recognized that almost all the various ways of studying community power—even those which focus on the disposition of specific issues—rely to some extent on the judgments of the observers (other than the researchers themselves) about the role played by alleged leaders. Ehrlich's contributions may allow us to make more judicious use of such information.

Three procedures are generally used for the identification of community leaders. Leaders may be assessed by criteria of position, by criteria of participation, and by criteria of reputation. Most researchers have relied

Abridged from "The Social Psychology of Reputations for Community Leadership," *The Sociological Quarterly*, VIII (Summer, 1967), pp. 514–530. Reprinted by permission of the author and publisher. The author adds: The materials reported here are derived from a program of research supported by the Community Projects Section of the Mental Health Study Center, National Institute of Mental Health. I am grateful to Mary Lou Bauer for her assistance, and to Patricia M. Schwier, Susan D. Spalter, and David Graeven who served as research assistants. I wish to thank Professor William V. D'Antonio, Carol Ehrlich, and my former colleagues, Dr. Sheila Feld and Dr. Harold F. Goldsmith, for their encouragement and critical aid in preparing this report. An earlier version was presented to the Midwest Sociological Society, April, 1966.

on the latter two procedures and have made assessments exclusively on the basis of participation or on the basis of reputation. In the few studies in which both procedures have been used together, they have appeared to yield listings of community leaders of varying degrees of similarity. D'Antonio and Form, for example, report in their El Paso study that 71 to 93 per cent of the key decision-makers in one or more of the six issues they studied were also reputed leaders. In contrast, Freeman and his associates in their Syracuse study report only a 39 per cent overlap in two independently derived lists of the leading participants and the most frequently nominated leaders.[1] To be sure, the methodologies of the El Paso and Syracuse reports are not directly comparable. However, this is equally true of all of the leadership study comparisons.[2] The problem of establishing empirically meaningful criteria for such comparisons is unresolved.

If the discrepancy between these operations were only in the roster of names produced, the matter, though still challenging, might be relatively unimportant. These leadership rosters, however, form the basis for a network of subsequent research operations that typically lead to statements about the structure of power and decision-making in the local community. Where such statements are based on a single method of research, they appear to lead to systematically biased results. Walton, in a recent review of 41 community studies, found that researchers who use a one-step reputational procedure report observing factional, coalitional, and amorphous power structures with significantly less frequency than do researchers using any other procedure or combination of procedures. Of 27 communities studied by reputational procedures only, 13 were reported as having monolithic power structures. In contrast, only 2 of the 14 communities studied by other and combined techniques displayed monolithic structures. Perhaps more surprising is Walton's finding that a two-step reputational procedure is even more likely to yield observations of

---

[1] Cf. William V. D'Antonio and William H. Form, *Influentials in Two Border Cities* (Notre Dame, Ind.: Univ. of Notre Dame Press, 1965); Linton C. Freeman, Thomas J. Fararo, Warner Bloomberg, Jr., and Morris H. Sunshine, "Locating Leaders in Local Communities." *American Sociological Review*, 28, (1963), 791–98.

[2] See for example, Robert E. Agger, Daniel Goldrich, and Bert E. Swanson, *The Rulers and the Ruled: Political Power and Impotence in American Communities* (New York: Wiley, 1964); L. Vaughn Blankenship, "Community Power and Decision-Making: A Comparative Evaluation of Measurement Techniques," *Social Forces*, 43, (1964) 207–16; M. Kent Jennings, *Community Influentials: The Elites of Atlanta* (New York: Free Press, 1964); Richard Laskin and Serena Phillett, "An Integrative Analysis of Voluntary Associational Leadership and Reputational Influence," *Sociological Inquiry* 35, (1965) 176–85; Robert Presthus, *Men at the Top: A Study in Community Power* (New York: Oxford Univ. Press, 1964); Harry Scoble, "Leadership Hierarchies and Political Issues in a New England Town," in Morris Janowitz (ed.), *Community Political Systems* (Glencoe, Ill.: Free Press, 1961).

monolithic structures of community power than is the (presumably less careful) one-step procedure.[3]

The assessment of community leadership reputations has been almost exclusively used as a procedure for making statements about community power structures, while the more social-psychological dimensions of the reputational procedure have been largely ignored. Rather than look at who gets nominated, we could consider those who make the nominations. Rather than look at the structural implications, we could consider individual attitudinal or behavioral implications. I have said earlier:

> Certainly, we can say that reputations for power are indeed an adequate index of the *perceived* distribution of power in the local community. To ask, then, if this is useful to describe a political system, depends intimately on the purposes at hand. Thus, for example, if we can ascertain that the way in which people perceive the power structure of the local political system affects the way in which they behave towards and in that system, then surely we are dealing with very meaningful and indeed very useful considerations.[4]

In this report I shall examine, first, the socioeconomic characteristics, community involvement, and participation behaviors of persons who can or cannot, with varying degrees of proficiency, nominate community leaders in a mass sociometric survey. Second, I shall explore the sociometric structure of these leader nominations and shall test the post factum hypothesis that demonstrably knowledgeable informants can produce systematically biased leader nominations. Finally, in a substantive appendix, I shall present a codification of the major statements in the research literature on the social psychology of leader reputations. . . .

Reputations for community leadership were assessed through a series of questions in a larger interview dealing with style of life and mental-health–related concerns of county residents. The survey, conducted by the National Opinion Research Center, was based on a multistage, household probability sample of 1,277 county residents, 18 to 59 years of age, who were interviewed in the winter of 1962–63. The leadership questions asked in the survey are reproduced here.

> We'd like to know who the important people in Prince George's County are—the people who are community leaders. You may not know many of their names—many people don't—but one of the things we want to know is how well known they are.

[3] John Walton, "Substance and Artifact: The Current Status of Research on Community Power Structure," *American Journal of Sociology*, 71, (1966), 430–38.

[4] Howard J. Ehrlich, "The Reputational Approach to the Study of Community Power," *American Sociological Review*, 26, (1961), 926–27.

A. Which persons do you think speak for or are the leaders of the *business interests* in the County—people like *bankers, manufacturers* and *real estate men?*

B. Which persons speak for or are the leaders of the *labor unions* in the County?

C. Which persons do you think speak for or are the leaders of the *professional people* in the County—people like *doctors, lawyers, clergymen* and *teachers?*

D. Which persons do you think speak for or are the leaders of the political groups in the County—groups like the *Republican* and *Democratic* parties?

E. Are there any other important people in the County who you think ought to go on a list of community leaders?

The indicators of socioeconomic background selected were age, education, occupational prestige (NORC), family income, and length of residence.[5] Two indicators of community involvement were selected. The first, an index of membership and participation in voluntary associations, is based on a weighting of the cross-tabulation of the number of formal and active memberships reported and coded in the survey. The index ranges from 0 to 8, and the index value for this county sample is 2.92. The index has been demonstrated to yield results directly comparable with the voluntary associations research literature.[6] The second indicator of community involvement consists of responses to questions about four community issues of varying degrees of salience.

THE FINDINGS

The majority of persons in the survey, approximately 51 per cent, could not respond to any of 5 open-ended questions with the name of any person whom they could identify as a community leader. Only 18 per cent were sufficiently knowledgeable to provide 4 or more leader nominations. Among those voting, their leader nominations displayed a relatively high degree of concentration: the survey produced only 705 different names from a roster of 2,299 nominees; and 80 of the leaders cited accounted for a majority of the nominations. The number of leader

[5] The coding units for these variables were primarily prestructured by the survey agent and permitted little manipulation. Related indicators, as well as alternative cutting points where possible, were explored. They displayed few departures from the patterns reported.

[6] Howard J. Ehrlich, "Membership and Participation in Adult Voluntary Associations in Prince George's County, Maryland" (Mental Health Study Center, National Institute of Mental Health, 1966), Part One.

nominations given by respondents displayed a strong, direct, monotonic relationship to indicators of the level of the respondents' socioeconomic background and community involvements.

Three dominant voting orientations appeared to account parsimoniously for the distribution of voting patterns. Half of those voting were able to name a business leader or a political leader but not both. The business-oriented and the politics-oriented respondents each accounted for one-fourth of those voting. Those with a business-political orientation, those who could name both a business and a political leader, comprised 35 per cent of the voters. As in the case of leader nominations, voting orientation displayed a strong, direct, monotonic relationship to indicators of the level of the respondents' socioeconomic background and community involvements. The business-politics–oriented voters ranked first on the criterion variables followed in order by the politics-oriented, the business-oriented, the "other" voter, and the nonvoter. The joint consideration of voting and voting orientation indicated that when voting level was controlled, voting orientations were distributed in a discontinuous relation to the socioeconomic and involvement dimensions. Only for the low voters did voting orientation follow the same relationship with socioeconomic background and community involvement as without the control for voting level. . . .

Those who are knowledgeable about community leaders are not only narrowly distributed in the upper levels of education, occupation, and income; they are older, residentially more stable, and more involved in community affairs. Within this restricted range, voting orientation appears relatively independent of the socioeconomic level and involvement variables. On the other hand, for the less knowledgeable voters, who are distributed in a restricted—but lower—socioeconomic and involvement level, voting orientation does appear to be significantly related to the criterion variables.

Presumably, at a high level of knowledge about community leadership, and despite the fact that high voters are more likely to manifest a business-political orientation, voting orientation is relatively independent of socioeconomic status, stability, and community involvement. At a lower level of knowledge of community leadership voting orientation appears to be distributed by status, stability, and involvement.

Reputational Bias

Mass sociometry, unlike elite sociometry, can not be criticized on the basis of a probable or possible bias in the selection of informants. There can be no doubt that the mass sociometric study of community leadership provides a list of names which nominally and operationally comprise a roster of reputed community leaders.[7] In contrast, the validity claims for leadership rosters derived from elite sociometric studies are more problematic, particularly where researchers attempt to use these rosters as a basis for subsequent community analysis. The bias that frequently —though not always or exclusively—emerges in elite reputational studies may in fact derive from the invalid use of leadership rosters. The findings of this report may help us understand this bias. Particularly, they may help us to understand how the more extensive two-step reputational procedure leads to depictions of monolithic community power structures.

To begin with, we need to note that most reputational studies start with a nonsystematic and casual selection of some knowledgeable elite. This is true in all but 2 of the 27 community studies reviewed by Walton. Typically, I assume, these are informants of relatively high socioeconomic status who are willing to and can spontaneously identify a large number of leaders. If the informant selection were biased, i.e., if the aggregate selection over-represented the business- or the politics-oriented, then it would tend to generate a one-sided list of names.

If we move to the second stage of the reputational procedure, soliciting nominations based on this new (now more biased) listing of reputed leaders, it seems plausible to expect that we should increase the degree of bias in this listing. Thus, our mass sociometric data lead us to the post factum hypothesis that the two-stage reputational study should even more often than the one-stage study produce a monolithic depiction of the community power structure. The confirmation of this hypothesis, independent of retrospectively demonstrating bias in past informant selection, requires two tests. First, we must show that some persons who are "knowledgeables" and hence eligible as informants have, nonetheless, only a segmental knowledge of community leaders. We have accomplished that test here: approximately 28 per cent of the high voters exhibited only segmental knowledge of the county leaders.

The second test requires the demonstration that leaders reputedly influential in a single sector are more likely to nominate persons within their own sector as leaders than they are to nominate persons outside their sector. While this can not be tested with the data of this report, D'Antonio and Form provide supporting evidence from their border cities study. "We found in general that influentials received proportion-

---

[7] The assessment of research operations in a mass sociometric survey appears to be relatively straightforward: (1) Is the sample representative? (2) Is the sociometric question clear and appropriate? (3) Did the respondent understand the question? (4) Was the question answered truthfully? (5) Was the answer registered adequately?

ately more votes from judges within their institutional sector."[8] Presumably, at the first stage of leader nominations, a biased selection of informants could generate a list that would lead the researcher to misidentify the community leadership structure. At the second stage of leader nominations, a biased set of elite informants could result in the further misrepresentation of leaders from those sectors already overrepresented and underrepresented. Thus if bias exists at stage one, it is quite probable that it will be magnified at stage two.

THE SOCIAL PSYCHOLOGY OF LEADER REPUTATIONS

Although the research on leader reputations is relatively limited, a considerable amount of information has been accumulated. The organization of these findings is of methodological importance to the political sociologist and of substantive importance to the social psychologist concerned with social perception. In this appendix I shall try to present these findings in a codified fashion that will emphasize their consistency and interrelatedness as well as their more general implications for political sociology and social psychology.

The Basic Assumptions

1. *The awareness assumption.* An awareness of a community political system, positions of community power, and the existence of community leaders develops previous to a community resident's ability to identify particular leaders.
2. *The power assumption.* All communities are perceived to be controlled through some set of formal and informal arrangements by persons of legal authority, personal influence, or technical competence.
   a) Some formal positions within the community power structure are perceived to hold more power than others.
   b) Some organized arrangements of formal positions within the community power structure are perceived to be more powerful than other arrangements.
   c) Some individuals are perceived to be more powerful than others in the community power structure.
   d) Some organized associations of individuals are perceived to be more powerful than other associations in the community power structure.

[8] William V. D'Antonio and William H. Form, *Influentials in Two Border Cities* (Notre Dame, Ind.: Univ. of Notre Dame Press, 1965), p. 66.

3. *The knowledgeability assumption.* Community residents vary in their perception of community leaders, from residents who perceive a high number of leaders to those who perceive none.
4. *The veridicality assumption.* Leader reputations are based in part on past leader performance and in part on a presumed potential for future performance.

Characteristics of Perceivers

5. *The mass diffusion hypothesis.* Knowledge (the perception) of community leaders is not widely diffused among community residents.
6. *The mass consensus hypothesis.* Among knowledgeable residents (those able to identify community leaders) there is a generally high order of agreement in identifying community leaders.
7. *The mass elite hypothesis.* A resident's socioeconomic position (education, income, occupation, and family cycle) is directly correlated with knowledgeability (the number of leaders he can identify). Residents of high socioeconomic position and those in the middle years of the family cycle are most likely to be knowledgeable about community leaders.
8. *The mass participation hypothesis.* A resident's memberships and participation in voluntary and informal associations are directly correlated with knowledgeability. Residents highly engaged in formal associational and interpersonal networks are most likely to be knowledgeable about community leaders.
9. *The mass stability hypothesis.* Knowledgeability develops with length of community residence (to some limit).
10. *The mass specialization hypothesis.* Knowledgeability tends to be specialized—i.e., confined to a limited set of leaders and leadership sectors (organized arrangements or associations) in the community.
11. *The mass knowledgeability hypothesis.* In their knowledge of leaders and leadership sectors, residents of high knowledgeability are less likely to be specialized, while residents of low knowledgeability are more likely to be specialized.

Characteristics of Reputed Leaders

12. *The leader pool hypothesis.* The greater the potential leader pool, the greater the number of reputed leaders. The size of the potential leader pool will be a direct function of (1) the size of the community, (2) the number of political positions in the community, (3) the economic diversity of the community, (4) the ethnic diversity of the community, and (5) the number of voluntary associations in the community.

13. *The leader elite hypothesis.* Reputed leaders are most likely to possess the social characteristics most valued in the community. (Current studies show that reputed leaders are most likely to be native born, male, white, Protestant, middle-aged, and relatively highly educated.)

14. *The congruency hypothesis.* Reputed leaders and highly knowledgeable residents display a similar profile of socioeconomic characteristics.

15. *The leader specialization hypothesis.* Knowledge of community leaders tends to be specialized among reputed leaders.

16. *The leader consensus hypothesis.* Among reputed leaders there is relatively high agreement in identifying community leaders.

17. *The consensus congruency hypothesis.* Reputed leaders and highly knowledgeable residents tend to agree in identifying community leaders.

The Mechanisms of Leader Visibility

18. *The elite visibility hypothesis.* The ascription or achievement of those characteristics which describe perceived leaders and highly knowledgeable residents should operate to increase a resident's visibility in the community. Thus, visibility should increase (to some limit) with age, residence, socioeconomic position, and membership and participation in informal and voluntary associations—particularly those related to community politics.

19. *The power hypothesis.* The greater the political resources controlled by leaders and leadership sectors, the greater the visibility of leaders in the community.

20. *The specialization hypothesis.* The less the specialization of leaders and leadership sectors, the greater the visibility of leaders in the community.

21. *The stability hypothesis.* The greater the stability of leaders and leadership sectors, the greater the visibility of leaders in the community.

22. *The legitimacy hypothesis.* The past or present occupancy of political office or the assumption of major civic responsibilities increases leader visibility.

23. *The participation hypothesis.* Leader visibility increases the greater the leader participation in community issues which (a) involve the reorganization of traditional community arrangements, or (b) elicit a high degree of controversy, or (c) entail wide community participation.

Power, Pluralism, and Local Politics

Thomas J. Anton

The entire article from which we have excerpted the next selection repre-
sents one of the most thoroughgoing critiques of the pluralist approach to
community studies that is available in the published literature. A lengthy first
section which examines each of the major works in the field has been omitted
here, although students with the time and interest will find it valuable to turn
to the original article. In the following pages Thomas Anton focuses on a
fundamental aspect of the controversy, namely, the basic assumptions about
the nature of "community" and "power" which he argues underlie the pluralist
writings of Dahl and others. This leads him to explore the nature of the
methodological problems which follow from the conceptual framework he
attributes to the pluralists. This critique was followed by a sharp reply from
Dahl and then a rebuttal again from Anton (53, 15), giving the full flavor of
the intellectual process and some of the heat, if not the passion, which often
accompanies it.

EVALUATION OF PLURALIST APPROACH

In view of these striking differences in interpretation, and in view
of pluralist criticisms of the sociological tools of investigation outlined
here, it becomes pertinent to ask whether the claims that have been
made on behalf of pluralism are justified. Exactly how useful is the
pluralist approach in developing empirical generalizations concerning
community power?

Pessimism

Pluralists themselves tend to be rather pessimistic about the usefulness
of their approach for developing generalizations. The whole problem

From Thomas Anton, "Power, Pluralism, and Local Politics," *Administrative Sci-*
ence Quarterly, VII (March, 1963), pp. 448–457.

of power is terribly complex, and since systematic study of the problem is very recent, generalizations are not likely to be produced until some time in the distant future, if at all. Dahl, for example, noting that operational definitions of power are likely to differ widely because of differences in problems attacked, concluded that

> we are not likely to produce—certainly not for some considerable time to come—anything like a single, consistent, coherent "Theory of Power." We are much more likely to produce a variety of theories of limited scope, each of which employs some definition of power that is useful in the context of the particular piece of research or theory but different in important respects from the definitions of other studies. Thus we may never get through the swamp. But it looks as if we might someday get around it.

It must be admitted that this pessimism is well founded, primarily because the pluralist scheme of analysis is ill-suited to drawing significant conclusions about community power. Generalizations—or theories—are usually based upon concepts that define the data and thus determine the kind of generalizations which can be made. Since the link between concepts and theories is so close, it is always necessary to exercise great care in the use of both. If one wishes to derive generalizations about community power one must be sure to use concepts which define community power, so that significant empirical data can be gathered. As Marion Levy has written, "conceptual work in empirical science cannot be carried out in a vacuum. One must always know to some degree for what purpose concepts are to be used."

Now it is a curious thing that the pluralists, who are so anxious to give precise measurement to *community* power, attempt to do so with an analytic scheme that places all its emphasis on *individual* power. If the community is seen as simply a collection of individuals who have differing amounts of power depending on the issue, then to determine the power structure, all that is required—according to the pluralist literature—is the discovery of those individuals who were active in decision making on se-lected key decisions. If the same people are found to make all or most of these key decisions (a finding that no pluralist has yet made), the conclusion is warranted that a power structure exists, and these indi-viduals comprise it. Logically, of course, such a conclusion cannot follow from pluralist assumptions, for the simple reason that examination of selected issues can reveal only the power of selected individuals, not the power of every individual or group of individuals in the community; therefore there is no basis for concluding that the group named as the power structure does in fact have more power than any other possible group.

DEFINITION OF COMMUNITY POWER

While it would appear to be somewhat ridiculous to require investigation of every individual and combination of individuals in a community before coming to any conclusions about power, that is nevertheless the logical outcome of a viewpoint which disclaims the utility of assuming any relationship between power and social structure. "The first, and perhaps most basic presupposition of the pluralist approach," wrote Polsby,

> is that nothing categorical can be assumed about power in any community. It rejects the stratification thesis that *some* group necessarily dominates a community. If anything, there seems to be an unspoken notion among pluralist researchers that at bottom *nobody* dominates in a town so that their first question to a local informant is not likely to be, "Who runs this community?" but rather, "Does anyone at all run this community?"

In a similar vein, Dahl argued that "there is no more *a priori* reason to assume that a ruling elite does exist than to assume that one does not exist." Thus, in the New Haven study, the first decision made by Dahl and his associates was "that no *a priori* assumptions would be entertained about the location in the population of 'real' . . . community decision-makers." But if nothing is assumed about power and if the community is defined as simply a collection of individuals with no permanent relationships to other persons or things, the form of community power structure cannot be determined unless all individuals are examined. As Dahl himself admitted, "unless we use the test [his test for a ruling elite system, described above] on every possible combination of individuals in the community, we cannot be certain that there is not some combination that constitutes a ruling elite."

Fortunately, pluralists have shown themselves willing to sacrifice precise measurement for a more manageable research strategy, which involves (as noted earlier) close examination of selected issues. By careful selection and analysis of a few key community issues, pluralists have argued, inferences can be drawn concerning the whole spectrum of community power, without examining *all* decisions and *all* individuals who could be involved. This is certainly a reasonable position to take, but its utility depends entirely upon the community characteristics of the issues selected for analysis. A community study requires the research worker to select from all the data available to him those data which represent something called the "community." He must, in effect, draw an imaginary circle which separates that which is community from that which is not community. In order to draw this circle, he must have some idea of what he means by community, for unless he has an idea, he will have no criteria for choosing to deal with one kind of data rather than another. And if he is not clear about the bases for his choice of data then he will not understand the meaning of his findings. He may present material which reflects national or regional patterns and refer to it as "community" material. Or, at the other extreme, he may present data reflecting patterns of subcommunity behavior as community behavior. Thus, the researcher may find himself talking not about community, but about something which is more or less than community. Only if the issues selected for examination reflect the community level of generality can any inferences be drawn about community power.[1]

From this point of view, all pluralist conclusions concerning community power must be held suspect, for the pluralist literature does not attempt to come to grips with the notion of community. Instead, such issues as the protection of bawdy houses, the development of an urban renewal program, the control of public education, and the control of individual municipal agencies are all lumped together as though they possessed the same level of significance for the same social group, namely, the community. The criteria which led pluralists to treat such issues as community issues are not readily apparent. In the absence of criteria of this kind to distinguish between "community power" and "power exercised in the community," examination of specific issue-areas will produce little more than information concerning which individuals were involved in making specific policy decisions. Only when such decisions become identified as community decisions will information about them become relevant to the problem of community power.

CONCEPT OF INERTIA

Other aspects of pluralist methodology create similarly important problems. Consider again, for example, the fundamental pluralist notion of "inertia" and the corresponding willingness "to put a high value on overt activity as indicative of involvement in issues." Does the concept "inertia" refer to lack of public involvement and does it apply to all indi-

---

[1] Attempts to define "community" have been summarized by George A. Hillery, Jr., "Definitions of Community: Areas of Agreement," *Rural Sociology,* **20** (1955), 111–123; see especially his bibliography, pp. 120–123. A sampling of more recent attempts to define "community" might include Otis Dudley Duncan and Albert J. Reiss, Jr., *Social Characteristics of Urban and Rural Communities,* 1950 (New York: 1956); Fenton Keyes, "The Correlation of Social Phenomena with Community Size," *Social Forces,* **36** (1958), 311–15; George A. Hillery, Jr., "A Critique of Selected Community Concepts," *Social Forces,* **37** (1959), 237–42; and Harold F. Kaufman, "Toward an Interactional Conception of Community," *Social Forces,* **38** (1959), 8–17.

viduals in the community, except in the development of an issue? If so, then the effect is to deny any public involvement—really to deny power—except in issues which may arise. Surely this cannot be the pluralist intention, for every community has some formal government continually active in public affairs, and such an assumption would deny its existence. On the other hand, if the continuous public activity of the formal government is admitted and considered to show inertia, does not the inertia of an agency active in public affairs imply a structure of power, in the sense of a recurring and repeated pattern of power interaction? Inertia cannot easily be ascribed to some and denied to others, for it is a fundamental concept of human behavior and therefore must apply to all individuals. The notion of inertia, then, forces the pluralist either to deny the existence of government as a wielder of power, or to admit that power is, in fact, a structured and therefore a recurring phenomenon.

PUBLIC AS OPPOSED TO PRIVATE POWER

But the dilemma is never squarely faced. The pluralist can avoid it by the simple expedient of drawing a distinction between public and private power and asserting that he is interested in public power. Yes, all human behavior is conditioned by inertia, but there are some people (government officials) who have a continuing interest and are continually active in public affairs. For these people, inertia simply means continuation of activity which has to do with power. This continuation, however, does not imply structure, because of differences in the scope of power exercised by these public officials. Some, for example, decide school affairs, while others run the water department or decide which houses of prostitution shall be protected. Note, too, that the power of all these people is public, in the sense of being connected with public agencies. Businessmen, farmers, manufacturers, or just plain citizens also have inertia, but their inertia does not involve public agencies and therefore does not involve power. Only when their interests are affected by issues do such people become publicly active as power wielders. Unless these issues somehow involve public officials, however, no power will be involved and therefore it is economical for the pluralist to concentrate on public agencies and officials as the primary focus of inquiry. Thus, Wolfinger chided Hunter for his failure to distinguish "between public and private scopes" of power, and suggested that there is little value in discovering leaders "whose power may be exercised chiefly on a country club's admission committee." Far from denying the power of government agencies, then, pluralists have apparently concluded by *defining* power—and their research interests—in terms of public agencies!

AMBIGUITY OF PLURALIST POSITION

And what a curious twist this is. Under the guise of science we have now been led back to a disciplinary outlook whose inadequacy was the chief *raison d'être* for the increased interest in scientific method in postwar political science. Surely the study of power must involve more than the actions of government agencies. The pluralist approach seems to raise the question of the nature of political science as "science." Perhaps the fact that this is still a question helps to explain some of the deficiencies in that approach. Unlike sociology, political science has not yet reached even a modicum of agreement as to what it is all about and how it should treat terms such as "power."

Ambiguity with regard to the concept of power is a central characteristic of the pluralism discussed here. What, for example, could the pluralist conclude about the community in which no issues ever became subject to public dispute, or in which there was little or no overt political activity? Such communities are hardly atypical. Indeed, one of the most penetrating community studies yet published, *Small Town in Mass Society*, analyzed just such a case. Yet on the basis of what has been presented here the pluralist would be forced to conclude that no power was being exercised in communities of this kind, presumably because everyone was content with the existing state of affairs (or at least not discontented enough to protest). So stated, the pluralist conclusion reveals an interesting conception of power not only as something physical, but also as something usable only in situations of *open conflict*. Since power depends upon the existence of conflict (or issues), there can be no power unless there is recognizable competition between individuals or groups. Thus all that has been learned in the twentieth century about the psychology of mass manipulation or about the persuasive power of such devices as credit, jobs, or social ostracism is ignored by this curiously one-sided notion of power.[2]

It might be suggested, of course, that many of the difficulties which could be expected to arise from this narrow view would normally be avoided, provided that pluralist researchers dug deeply enough, and were intuitive enough, to recognize conflict that was not apparent on the sur-

[2] Unlike political scientists, sociologists have paid a good deal of attention to techniques of social control other than physical violence. For a sampling of some of the best sociological thinking in this area, including contributions by Edward A. Ross, Emile Durkheim, George Herbert Mead, and Jean Piaget, see Lewis A. Coser and Bernard Rosenberg, eds., *Sociological Theory: A Book of Readings* (New York: Macmillan, 1964), pp. 97–122. William H. Whyte, Jr., documents some of the informal pressures used to control the modern middle-class American at work and at play in *The Organization Man* (New York: 1956). For an interesting and important account of the use of the social sciences to control industrial workers, see Loren Baritz, *The Servants of Power* (Middletown, Conn.: 1960).

face of community life. The question is, however, whether pluralism provides any reason for digging below the surface. The answer would appear to be that it does not. Pluralists quite vigorously deny the permanency of power—or to put it differently, that power is structured in any way. Thus if superficial evidence suggests that no power exists in a particular community, pluralist presuppositions warrant the conclusion that any further examination might well turn out to be a waste of time. Such a conclusion would be supported, secondly, by the inertia postulate that the basic reason for lack of public conflict is agreement: If citizens are satisfied enough to be inactive, there must be some minimal agreement on the course of public events.

Beyond this, there is the question of whether persons using pluralist methodology could recognize issues. Issues can be defined either by the observer's commitment to an ideological outlook that defines important problems or by his ability to comprehend fully the issue definitions of the people he studies. The pluralist literature, however, claims no ideology, other than commitment to empirical science—a commitment which emphasizes that which is rather than that which ought to be. And interestingly enough, pluralist ability to get "into the heads" of its subjects appears to be hampered by a similar acceptance of the existing political order. The difference between the two questions that might be asked— "Why don't more people get involved in politics?" and "Why do people become involved in politics?"—can be the difference between a critique and an apology.

None of the preceding criticism should be taken lightly, for pluralism claims greater scientific value than has previously been apparent in studies of community power. Yet this claim rests upon a method of analyzing power that has very limited utility. In studying the legislatures of certain (perhaps most) American states, for example, it would be difficult to avoid coming to ridiculous conclusions if one began with the assumption that only the observable activities of legislators and lobbyists were important. Nor would it be any less difficult to make sense out of totalitarian systems of government if it were initially assumed that lack of protest signified satisfaction. Surely the historic passivity of the Southern Negro, for example, was due to something other than satisfaction with his position in Southern communities. Considerations of this kind suggest that one of the major problems of the pluralist method is that it assumes too much and thereby begs a number of significant questions. Instead of relying on an independently derived formulation of the problem of power to reach empirical conclusions, pluralist assumptions of "inertia" and "satisfaction" are bootlegged into the analysis to explain phenomena (such as nonparticipation) which cannot be explained adequately by the original analytic scheme. The extent to which "inertia" or "satisfaction" may be important in a given community, of course, should be determined empirically. To assume them is to avoid the important question of what specific conditions produce inertia in a given community and the equally important question of how these conditions are brought about. The failure of pluralists to give empirical data for such significant problems suggests an ideological rather than a scientific orientation.

CONCLUSIONS

Enough has been said here to provide some basis for the proposition that the so-called "pluralist alternative" is not as scientifically sound as some of its proponents would have us believe. Political scientists would do well to exercise some caution before rushing to follow this lead in analyzing community power. Yet, for all its defects, this approach is extremely important, precisely because it states a reasoned approach to the study of power and applies it to a level of government that offers many thousands of laboratories in which the approach can be modified, rejected, or confirmed. In the long run, differences of interpretation between sociological and pluralist schools of thought will have to be resolved in these laboratories.

In order for any such resolution to come about, however, it will be necessary to deal with the unsolved problem of defining "community." Neither sociologists nor pluralists have applied themselves very vigorously to this problem; as a result, much of their public dispute has been at cross-purposes.[3] Two further lines of inquiry may prove useful. One would attempt to come to grips with the problem posed by C. Wright Mills by asking the questions: "To what extent is power in American society organized at the local level? What kind of power is in fact exercised by American communities? What kind of power seems to be exercised predominantly by larger social units of one kind or another?" Political scientists will recognize in these questions a problem familiar to them, that of federalism. What is suggested here is a re-examination of this concept using detailed empirical investigations to the fullest extent possible as a supplement to institutional analysis. The second profitable

[3] A major difficulty with Hunter and those who follow him, for example, is the assumption that power is, in fact, organized locally for all purposes and for all things. This may or may not be true in some communities, at some times, and it is always incumbent upon the analyst to demonstrate the extent to which it is or is not true before proceeding to any statements about community power. While such assumptions concerning the location of general power at the community level may well be erroneous, pluralists have not been able to demonstrate it because of their failure to develop any explicit conception of what is meant by community. Thus, pluralists talk about issues, which may or may not be community issues, while the followers of Hunter talk about power, which may or may not be community power.

line of inquiry would attempt a classification of communities according to those characteristics that define them as communities and according to the kinds of power characteristically located at the community level. Some work has begun already in this area, with impressive and potentially fruitful results.

One final word: while it is important to recognize differences in interpretation, it is equally important not to be overcome by them. The final object, after all, is understanding, and no interpretive scheme can properly claim a monopoly here. George Santayana put it:

> No language or logic is right in the sense of being identical with the facts it is used to express, but each may be right by being faithful to these facts, as a translation may be faithful. My endeavor is to think straight in such terms as are offered to me, to clear my mind of cant and free it from the cramp of artificial traditions; but I do not ask anyone to think in my terms if he prefers others. Let him clean better, if he can, the windows of his soul, that the variety and beauty of the prospect may spread more brightly before him.

Locating Leaders in Local Communities:
A Comparison of Some Alternative Approaches

Linton C. Freeman, Thomas J. Fararo,

Warner Bloomberg, Jr., and Morris H. Sunshine

Defense and criticism of research methods must at some point move beyond exhortation and logical exegesis to a comparative analysis of such methods. In the following selection that step is taken in a study of Rochester by Linton Freeman and his associates. The authors directly tested four techniques designed to reveal community leaders and found that each method discovered a different set of "leaders;" no one method furnished the complete picture of the decision-making process in Rochester. Thus in effect, Freeman and his colleagues held constant all factors except the methods for finding leaders, and these varying methods achieved varying results attributable more to the method, it would seem, than to intervening variables.

Most investigators would probably agree that leadership refers to a complex process whereby a relatively small number of individuals in a collectivity behave in such a way that they effect (or effectively prevent) a change in the lives of a relatively large number. But agreement on theoretical details of the leadership process or on how it is to be studied is another matter. Much of the recent literature on community leadership has been critical. Gibb has suggested that there are a great many *kinds* of leadership—many different ways in which changes may be effected. He has proposed that leaders be assigned to various types including "the initiator, energizer, harmonizer, expediter, and the like." Banfield has stressed the importance of the distinction between intended and unintended leadership. And both Dahl and Polsby have called attention to the desirability of considering the *extent* of the effect a given leader has in expediting a particular change and the *range* of changes over which

From Linton C. Freeman, Thomas J. Fararo, Warner Bloomberg, Jr. and Marris H. Sunshine, "Locating Leaders in Local Communities: A Comparison of Some Alternative Approaches," *American Sociological Review*, XXVIII (October, 1963) pp. 791–798.

his effect holds. It seems evident, then, that although these critics might agree with the minimum definition presented above, they would all like to see some additional factors included within its scope.

Polsby has translated the comments of the critics into a set of operational guides for research. He has suggested that a satisfactory study of community leadership must involve a detailed examination of the whole decision-making process as it is exhibited over a range of issues. Here we should have to specify each issue, the persons involved, their intentions, and the extent and nature of their influence if any. Such a program represents an ideal that might be used to think about the process of community leadership. But as a research strategy, this plan raises many problems.

In the first place, both influence and intention are concepts presenting great difficulty in empirical application. Both require that elaborate observational and interviewing procedures be developed, and both raise reliability problems. May we, for example, take a person's word concerning his intentions, or must they be inferred from his behavior? And even when two persons interact and one subsequently changes his stated position in the direction of the views of the other, it is difficult to *prove* that influence has taken place. But even if these questions were eliminated, a practical problem would still remain. To follow the prescriptions listed above would be prohibitively expensive, requiring detailed observation of hundreds (or thousands) of individuals over an extended period. To record all interaction relevant to the decisions under study, it would be necessary to observe each person in a large number of varied situations, many of them quite private. Even then it would be difficult to evaluate the impact of the process of observation itself. Given these considerations, Polsby's ideal has never been reached. All existing studies of community leadership represent some compromise.

Most authors of community leadership studies would probably agree that the critics are on the right track. But most have been willing (or perhaps forced by circumstances) to make one or more basic assumptions in order to achieve a workable research design. Four types of compromise have been common. They will be discussed below.

Perhaps the most realistic of the compromise studies are those based on the assumption that active participation in decision making *is* leadership. Typically, in such studies, one or a series of community decisions are either observed or reconstructed. In so doing, an attempt is made to identify the active participants in the decision-making process. These decision-making studies frequently are restricted to a small number of decisions, and they usually fail to present convincing evidence on the questions of intent and amount of impact. But they do provide a more or less direct index of participation. If they err it is by including individuals who, though present, had little or no impact on the decision. On the face of it this seems preferable to the likelihood of excluding important influentials.

A second compromise approach is to assume that formal authority *is* leadership. Aside from arbitrarily defining which positions are "on top," these studies underestimate the impact of those not in official positions on the outcomes of the decision-making process.

The third approach assumes that leadership is a necessary consequence of social activity. This assumption leads to studies of social participation. Such studies have used everything from rough indexes of memberships in voluntary associations to carefully constructed scales of activity in such associations. In each case it is reasoned that community leadership results from a high degree of voluntary activity in community affairs. The social participation approach is thus the converse of the study of position. While the former stresses activity, the latter is concerned only with formal authority. But to the extent that activity in voluntary associations leads to having an impact upon community change, activists are leaders.

The final approach assumes that leadership is too complex to be indexed directly. Instead of examining leadership as such, proponents of this approach assess reputation for leadership. Their reasoning suggests that all of the more direct approaches neglect one or another key dimensions of the leadership process. They turn, therefore, to informants from the community itself. Often rather elaborate steps have been taken to insure that the informants are indeed informed. For example, positional leaders may be questioned in order to develop a list of reputed leaders or influentials; then the reported influentials are polled to determine the top influentials. In such cases it is reasonable to suppose that the grossly uninformed are ruled out.

Various critics have condemned the indeterminacy and subjectivity of this procedure. But its defenders reason that the reputational approach is the only way to uncover the subtleties of intent, extent of impact, and the like in the leadership process. What, they ask, but a life-long involvement in the activities of a community could possibly yield sophisticated answers to the question "Who are the leaders?" The reputational approach, then, assumes the possibility of locating some individuals who unquestionably meet the criteria of community leadership, and who in turn will be able to name others not so visible to the outside observer.

Currently, the controversy continues. Proponents of one or another of these competing points of view argue for its inherent superiority and the obvious validity of its assumptions. Others take the view that all of these approaches get at leadership. But these are empirical questions; they can be answered only on the basis of comparison, not by faith or by rhetoric.

A number of partial contrasts have been published, but so far no systematic overall comparison of these procedures has been reported. The present report represents such an attempt. An effort is made to determine the degree to which these several procedures agree or disagree in locating community leaders.

The data presented here represent a part of a larger study of leadership in the Syracuse, N.Y. metropolitan area. . . .

DECISION-MAKING

The study of participation in the decision-making process was of central concern in the Syracuse study. The first major task of the project team was to select a set of community problems or issues which would provide a point of entry into a pool (or pools) of participants in the decision-making process. Interviews were conducted with 20 local specialists in community study and with 50 informants representing diverse segments of the city's population. Care was taken to include representatives of each group along the total range of interest and institutional commitment. These 70 interviews provided a list of about 250 community issues. The list was reduced to a set of 39 issues according to the following criteria:

1. Each issue must have been at least temporarily resolved by a decision.
2. The decision must be perceived as important by informants representing diverse segments of the community.
3. The decision must pertain to the development, distribution, and utilization of resources and facilities which have an impact on a large segment of the metropolitan population.
4. The decision must involve alternative lines of action. It must entail a certain degree of choice on the part of participants; and the outcome must not be predetermined.
5. The decision must be administered rather than made by individuals in "the market." For the purpose of this study, an administered decision was defined as one made by individuals holding top positions in organizational structures which empower them to make decisions affecting many people.
6. The decision must involve individuals and groups resident in the Syracuse Metropolitan Area. Decisions made outside the Metropolitan Area (e.g., by the state government), were excluded even though they might affect residents of the Metropolitan Area.
7. The decision must fall within the time period 1955–1960.
8. The set of decisions as a whole must affect the entire range of important institutional sectors, such as governmental, economic, political, educational, religious, ethnic, and the like.

The next step in the research process required the determination of positional leaders or formal authorities for each of the set of 39 issues. The study began with those individuals who were formally responsible for the decisions. The element of arbitrary judgment usually involved in the positional approach was thus avoided. Here, the importance of a position was derived from its role in determining a choice among alternative lines of action rather than of being the consequence of an arbitrary assumption.

The responsible formal authorities were determined on the basis of documents pertinent to the 39 decisions. In addition, several attorneys were consulted to insure that correct determinations were made. The number of authorities responsible for making each of these decisions ranged from two to 57.

The interviews started with authoritative persons. Respondents were presented with a set of 39 cards, each of which identified a decision. They were asked to sort the cards into two piles: (1) "Those in which you participated; that is, where others involved in this decision would recognize you as being involved," and (2) "Those in which you were not a participant." For those issues in which they claimed participation, individuals were then asked to name all the others who were also involved. Here they were instructed to report on the basis of first-hand knowledge of participation rather than on hearsay. Respondents were also given a questionnaire covering their social backgrounds.

When the interviews with authorities were completed, their responses for those decisions on which they possessed authority were tabulated. Then, any person who had been nominated as a participant by two authorities for the same issue was designated as a first zone influential. Two nominations were deemed necessary in order to avoid bias due to accidental contacts, mistakes of memory, or a tendency to mention personal friends. In the final tabulations this same rule of two nominations was applied to authorities also. Therefore, no person is counted as a participant unless he has two nominations by qualified nominators.

As the next step, all first zone influentials were interviewed using exactly the same procedures as those used for authorities. Their responses were tabulated for the decisions in which they had been involved, and any person nominated by one authority and one first zone influential was also classified as a first zone influential and interviewed. Then any person nominated by two first zone influentials was designated a second zone influential—two steps removed from formal authority but still involved. We did not interview beyond these second zone influentials. We might have continued with third and fourth zones and so on; but on the basis of qualitative data gathered during the interviews, we suspected we were moving well into the periphery of impact on the outcome of decision making.

In all, 628 interviews were completed. Of these, 550 qualified as participants. These participants, then, are the leaders as determined by the decision-making phase of the Syracuse study. They were ranked in terms of the number of decisions in which they were involved. For the present analysis the 32 most active participants are considered.

SOCIAL ACTIVITY

Each of the 550 participants uncovered by the decision-making study was asked to complete a questionnaire covering his social background and current activities. These questionnaires were returned by 506 informants. The answers included responses to a set of questions designed to elicit as much information as possible about voluntary association memberships. Specific questions were included to determine memberships in the following areas:

1. Committees formed to deal with community problems.
2. Community service organizations.
3. Business organizations.
4. Professional organizations.
5. Union organizations.
6. Clubs and social organizations.
7. Cultural organizations.
8. Religious organizations.
9. Political parties, organizations and clubs.
10. Veterans' and patriotic organizations.
11. Other clubs and organizations.

Memberships in these organizations were tabulated, and a rough overall index to voluntary activity was calculated by simply summing the number of memberships for each person. The respondents were ranked in terms of number of memberships, and the 32 most active organizational members were included in the present analysis.

REPUTATION

Each questionnaire also invited the respondent to list the most influential leaders in the community. Eight spaces were provided for answers. Nominations were tabulated and, following traditional procedures, the top 41 reputed leaders were listed. The responses of those 41 respondents were then tabulated separately. The top 32 were derived from their rankings. This was done in order to maximize the chances that our nominators would be informed. As it turned out, however, the top 32 nominations of the whole group and the top 32 provided by the top 41 were exactly the same persons and in the same order. For Syracuse these nominations showed remarkable consistency all along the line.

Position

In determining the top positional leaders it seemed desirable to avoid as much as possible making the usual arbitrary assumptions. Traditional usage of the positional approach dictated the determination of the titular heads of the major organizations in business, government, the professions, and the like. Within each of these institutional areas choice could be made in terms of size, but it was difficult to determine how many organizations should be selected in each area.

An empirical resolution for this problem was provided in a recent report by D'Antonio *et al.* These authors provided data on the proportions of reputed leaders representing each of the seven relevant institutional areas in ten previous studies. Since agreement on these relative proportions was reasonably close for the six middle-sized American communities reported, they were used to assign proportions in each institutional area in the present study. The proportions derived from D'Antonio and those used in the present study are reported in Table I. In this case positional leaders are the titular heads of the largest organizations in each of the institutional areas, and each area is represented according to the proportion listed in Table I. Thirty-two organizations were chosen in all. As a check on its validity, the list of organizations was shown to several local experts in community affairs. They were in substantial agreement that the organizations listed seemed consistent with their perceptions of the "top" organizations in Syracuse. The heads of these organizations might be

TABLE I

Percentage of Leaders in Each Institutional Area

Institution	Six Cities	Syracuse
Business	57	59
Government	8	9
Professions	12	13
Education	5	6
Communications	8	6
Labor	4	3
Religion	5	3
Total	99	99

expected to have formal control over much of the institutional system of the community.

These, then, are the raw materials of the current study. An attempt was made to determine the degree to which these several procedures would allocate the same persons to the top leadership category.

RESULTS

The several procedures for determining leaders did not converge on a single set of individuals. Top leaders according to one procedure were not necessarily the same as those indicated by another. An index of agreement for each pair was constructed by calculating the ratio of the actual number of agreements to their total possible number. Results are listed in Table II.

TABLE II

Percentage of Agreement in Determining Leaders by Four Traditional Procedures

Participation			
25	Social activity		
33	25	Reputation	
39	22	74	Position

It is possible that any of the methods used, if modified enough, would have yielded significantly different results.[1] The procedures we followed seem in their essentials to be like those followed in most of the studies so far published. (Those who believe they have altered the use of positions, nominations, memberships, or other indexes in such a way as to obtain a major difference in the output of the technique have only to demonstrate this by empirical comparisons.) Our impression is that most versions of each approach represent only vernier adjustments of the same device and thus can have only marginally differing results.

Table II suggests that there is far from perfect agreement in determining leaders by means of these four methods. In only one case do two of these methods concur in more than 50 per cent of their nominations. Reputation and position seem to be in substantial agreement in locating leaders. To a large degree, therefore, reputed leaders are the titular heads of major community organizations. They are not, however, themselves active as participants in decision making to any great extent.

---

[1] The choice of the top 32 leaders in each category, is, for example, somewhat arbitrary. When another number is used, the *absolute* percentages of agreement vary, but their standings *relative* to one another remain stable.

Reputation for leadership seems to derive primarily from position, not from participation. But it appears unlikely that position itself constitutes a sufficient basis for reputation. The reputations, however, might belong to the organizations and not the individuals. In such a case, when an informant named John Smith as a leader what might have been intended was the fact that the Smith Snippel Company (of which John Smith was president) is influential in community decisions. Smith would thus have been named only because we had asked for a person's name. Our hypothesis, then, is that reputation should correspond with the participation rate of organizations rather than the participation rates of individuals.

On the basis of this hypothesis, the data on participation were retabulated. Each participant was classified according to his organization or place of employment. Then the head of each organization was credited not only with his own participation, but with the sum of the participation of his employees. In this manner an index of organizational participation was constructed and the top 30 organizational leaders were determined. Individuals so nominated were compared with those introduced by the earlier procedures. The results are shown in Table III.

TABLE III

Percentage of Agreement Between Organizational
Participation and Four Traditional Procedures

Traditional Procedure	Percentage of Agreement
Participation	33
Social activity	25
Reputation	67
Position	80

The proportions shown in Table III support our hypothesis. Organizational participation seems to uncover substantially the same leaders as reputation and position. The top reputed leaders, therefore, though not active participants themselves, head up the largest organizations, and the personnel of these organizations have the highest participation rates.

This result accounts for a great deal of participation in community decision making. Since organizational participation provides a workable index, many participants must be employees of large community organizations. But this does not explain the most active class of individual participants—those who were picked up by the individual participation index. These people seem to be virtually full-time participants in community affairs. We know that they are not organizational heads, but we have not determined who they are.

In view of the sheer amount of their participation, the top participants must be professional participants of some sort. And, as a class, professional participants in community affairs should be government officials and employees of full-time professional executives of non-governmental agencies formally and primarily committed to intervention in community affairs. With this as our hypothesis, the individuals nominated as leaders by the four traditional indexes were all classified into either government and professional or non-professional categories. Then percentages of government personnel and professionals were calculated for all four indexes. The results are shown in Table IV.

Again the results support our hypothesis. The most active individual participants are typically government personnel.

TABLE IV

Percentage of Leaders According to Four Traditional Procedures
Who Are Government Officials or Employees or Profession Participants

Traditional Procedure	Percentage of Government Personnel or Professional Participants
Participation	66
Social activity	20
Reputation	20
Position	28

The participation index thus gets at personnel quite different from those selected by reputational or positional indexes, or by social activity. These differing cadres of people seem to represent *different kinds* of leadership behavior with respect to the local community.

SUMMARY AND DISCUSSION OF RESULTS

These results indicate that at least in Syracuse "leadership" is not a homogeneous category. Which "leaders" are uncovered seems in large part to be a function of the mode of study. The several traditional indexes allow us to locate one or another of three basic types of "leaders."

First, there are those who enjoy the reputation for top leadership. These are very frequently the same individuals who are the heads of the largest and most active participating business, industrial, governmental, political, professional, educational, labor and religious organizations in Syracuse. They are uncovered by studies of reputation, position, or organizational participation. In view of their formal command over the institutional structure and the symbolic value of their status as indexed by reputation, these individuals may be called the Institutional Leaders of Syracuse.

These Institutional Leaders, however, are for the most part not active participants in community affairs. There is no evidence that they have any direct impact on most decisions which take place. Their activity may be limited to that of lending prestige to or legitimizing the solutions provided by others. They might conceivably be participating decision makers in secret, but more likely they serve chiefly to provide access to the decision-making structure for their underlings: the Effectors.

The Effectors are located by studying participation. They are the active workers in the actual process of community decision making. Many of the most active Effectors are government personnel and professional participants, and the others are the employees of the large private corporations directed by the Institutional Leaders. In some cases, the Effectors are in touch with their employers, and it seems likely that their activities are frequently guided by what they view as company policy; but, judging from our data, they are often pretty much on their own. At any rate, these men carry most of the burden of effecting community change.

The third type of leader might be called the Activists. There people are active—and often hold office—in voluntary organizations, community service organizations, and clubs. Although they are not involved as often as the Effectors, the Activists do participate in decision making. For the most part they seem to lack the positional stature to be Institutional Leaders. Furthermore, they often work for or direct smaller organizations in the community. They lack the power base provided by association with government or one of the major industrial or business firms. Yet, seemingly by sheer commitment of time and effort to community affairs, these Activists do help shape the future of the community.

In conclusion, the various differing approaches to the study of community leadership seem to uncover different types of leaders. The study of reputation, position or organizational participation seems to get at the Institutional Leaders. Studies of participation in decision making, on the other hand, tap the Effectors of community action. And studies of social activity seem to seek out the Activists who gain entry by dint of sheer commitment, time, and energy.

In part, our results are dependent upon the Syracuse situation. It is likely that 25 years ago, when Syracuse was smaller and less diversified, the Institutional Leaders and the Effectors were the same people. And 25 years from now this description will probably no longer hold. Other communities, in other stages of development and diversification will probably show different patterns. But until more comparative studies are done, conclusions of this kind are virtually guesses.

Men at the Top

Robert V. Presthus

Whereas the preceding study compared different research techniques for finding leaders within one city, Robert Presthus compared the results of using different techniques in two relatively small cities. The selection below reports some of Presthus' comparative findings on the structure of power and on the utility of the reputational versus decision-making techniques for revealing that structure, as well as his thoughts on the relationship of such findings to the study of pluralism. His findings on the measurement techniques are especially well analyzed in terms of the strengths and weaknesses of each. As such, his views represent a sophisticated argument for using at least two measures for the different facets of social reality which they uncover. The reader might contemplate, both carefully and critically, his judgment that, "to some extent, where the sociologists found monopoly and called it elitism, political scientists found oligopoly but defined it in more honorific terms as pluralism."

Our conclusions can be summed up under three broad categories: substantive, methodological, and normative. Wherever possible, major continuities (as well as discontinuities) found in all three spheres will be noted, including similarities between Edgewood and Riverview, and those found between this and earlier community power structure research. Under the normative category we will speculate briefly about the meaning of our findings and the future of pluralism in small communities.

Substantive Continuities

Regarding the structures of power found in the two communities, some 80 citizens (.005 per cent of the total populations) play the central, active role in initiating and directing major community decisions. This is similar to findings in some half-dozen other community studies. Within the power structures reported here there is some specialization. In effect, two discrete decision-making systems were found. One of these is essentially "political," in the narrow sense of the term. It is based upon local electoral support and the co-optation of state and federal offices and resources through political associations resting mainly upon the ability of local politicians to get into office and to deliver majorities to higher level politicians. . . . The second decision-making system is essentially economic, comprising leaders whose power resources rest on high formal positions in industry, finance and business, and superior class status, and who draw essentially upon "private" local resources to carry out their programs. Contrasted with political office, which is the major power base of political elites, economic leaders enjoy greater continuity in the power structure. Their bases of power are likely to be more extensive, constant, and durable than those of their political counterparts.

Economic leaders, in sum, tend to dominate essentially "private" types of decisions that entail the use of nongovernmental resources. Political leaders generally control what we have called "public" issues, i.e. those requiring the expenditure of public funds, legitimation in the form of referenda, negotiations with politicians at higher levels of government, and meeting the conditions prescribed by these centers of power and largesse. There is some evidence that such issues are not very salient for economic leaders. Still, there is some sharing of participation in "public" decisions, resulting from competition and co-operation between the two elites, as well as from the efforts of political leaders to co-opt the superior prestige and status resources of economic leaders, in this way legitimating public decisions by the resulting patina of political nonpartisanship and disinterest.

Such a division of labor is expected, given the political values, resources, and interests possessed by each group. Like the rest of us, active community elites use the resources they have, and their activities are guided by their ideologies and the spheres of interest legitimated by them. A third elite, the specialists, are a residual category of "welfare-oriented" leaders, distinguished from others in the elite structure by their marginal power and prestige. From the community point of view, they probably enjoy considerable prestige, since they are often highly educated, have professional statuses, and play active, highly visible roles in community affairs. However, in a power structure context, they are rarely nominated as "influentials," nor do they characteristically prove to be active in more than one major decision.

By a combined use of reputational, decisional, and *Verstehen* modes of analysis, we found that economic leaders enjoyed somewhat more power than political leaders in Edgewood in contrast to Riverview where political leaders proved to be more powerful than their economic counterparts. But each elite does not simply play the same role in its community, for political leaders exercised *relatively* greater initiative and control in Riverview than did economic leaders in Edgewood. However, in both communities, there was some competition between the two elites, and between them and the specialists. In Edgewood, this competition was generally functional because each group contributed to the solution of local problems. In Riverview, competition was more intense but less utilitarian. With only a few exceptions, economic leaders tended to withdraw. Their inefficacy was partly the result of internecine conflict among them, centered mainly on the divergent policies that characterized an "old economic guard" and a "young Turk" element. Theirs was less an ideological conflict than a strategic one, based upon differing perspectives of the most effective ways of developing the city and halting its gradual decline as a trading center. In Edgewood, by contrast, the economic group was quite cohesive, with the exception of the school bond issue, where some members fought the first issue while others supported it.

Three indicators of individual and organizational participation were used to test the relative degree of pluralism in each community. The evidence indicated that Edgewood decisions ranged along the "middle" of the pluralist continuum, whereas those in Riverview clustered around the "low" side. By these measures, Edgewood citizens were found to be more active in the decisions chosen for analysis. We are unable to conclude from this, however, that decision-making in Edgewood is "pluralistic," if this term is defined to mean a viable competition among many groups and widespread community participation in important decisions. Moreover, if one defines pluralism as the existence of multiple competition among leaders, i.e. little overlapping among the local elites in terms of their participation in major issues, we cannot say that this was the case. The concept of oligopoly seems more germane. In Edgewood, two-fifths of the leaders were active in two or more decisions, each of which was substantively different; in Riverview, it was one-third. Similar degrees of overlapping were found by other researchers in three other communities of roughly the same size. *It appears that there is an inverse association between overlapping (elitism) and size.* For example, in Madison and New Haven (100,000+) overlapping rates were 19 and 6 per cent respectively; in Bennington and Edgewood (10,000+), they were 39 per cent. One may conclude tentatively that size per se is an important variable in determining the degree of pluralism found in local power structures.

Regarding the traditional pluralist expectation [1] that citizens will ex-

---

[1] Obviously, this expectation has been undercut by research in political behavior; nevertheless, a normative residue of pluralism seems to be that everyman can and should have some influence on political affairs.

ercise some direct influence on major decisions through periodic elections, referenda, public meetings, and contributing time and money to campaigns or programs, we found very low rates of participation. This finding is consonant with many others showing that most citizens exercise little direct influence on community affairs. They may exert some indirect influence on specific decisions through periodic elections, etc., but no one has yet demonstrated precisely how this process works. Referenda provide the most used means of participation, ranging from 7 per cent of the adult community in the Riverview hospital issue to 45 per cent in the Edgewood school bond issue which comprised two referenda.

Since most observers agree that very few citizens play a direct role in specific issues, we also tested *organizational* participation as an index of pluralism. The going rationale here is that this medium provides a surrogate for individual participation in a highly organized society. Since pluralism also assumes that a multiplicity of such organizations make their will felt in political decisions, such a test seems equitable and relevant. Here, evidence from a sample of 52 representative voluntary organizations indicates that an average of 40 per cent were concerned in some way with the major decisions. Of this entire group, however, 90 per cent were active in only one decision. In total organizational participation, Edgewood again enjoys some advantage over Riverview: comparative rates of participation are 53 and 28 per cent.

In terms of total individual *memberships* in organizations, the communities are quite similar. However, in such organizations as service clubs, which are especially strategic for community development, Edgewood again has some advantage. It also has a slightly higher proportion of citizens belonging to three or more organizations. Although we find something less than the full-blown picture of membership suggested by de Tocqueville, the Beards, and some contemporary pluralists, membership rates compare favorably with the national averages. . . . Excluding church memberships, some one-third of respondents in both communities belong to three or more organizations: the respective proportions were Edgewood 36 per cent and Riverview 33 per cent. About one-half belong to none or only one organization.

The explanations for these differences are multiple. From the standpoint of both class and industrial resources, Edgewood enjoys considerable advantage. Moreover, these conditions are related to the domination of local decision-making by different elements of the power structure in each community. In Edgewood, economic leaders dominate access to essentially private resources *within* the community. As the new industry decision illustrates, they can mobilize substantial financial resources through their control of local banks. They can pledge the support of their corporations to such programs as the voluntary fund drive for the new hospital. They can delegate active roles to their subordinates, as well as assume an active role themselves. Since they generally have the highest social status and prestige within the community, they can also bring to bear these kinds of resources. In this context, they are "locals," whose span of attention and scope of influence is focused on the immediate community.

On the other hand, political leaders in Riverview have more "cosmopolitan" perspectives. Their peculiar skills and ideology are functionally suited to an environment in which internal community resources of most kinds are generally less promising. As a result, they turn to external, essentially political, power centers for the resources required to handle most local problems. In some cases, such as the housing authority, it may be that the actual need was less relevant than the opportunity to do something positive as an alternative to doing nothing. The community's dependence upon political resources placed a premium on the skills and interests of the mayor and his legal aide, who provided the initiative in four of the five Riverview decisions. *From this, we hypothesize that in communities with limited leadership and economic resources the power structure will be more likely to be dominated by political leaders, whereas in those with more fulsome internal resources it will probably be dominated by economic leaders.*

However, from our evidence, it seems that over an extended period of time economic leaders will probably dispose the most powerful role in community affairs. This is because their characteristic bases of power are relatively more stable than those of political leaders who must often depend upon *office* as the major basis of their power. In addition, economic leaders in both communities typically enjoy higher SES rankings, which means that they possess more of the resources typically required for the exercise of power, including more education and income, higher class and prestige status, and Republican political affiliation. These attributes, combined with their access to the financial and economic resources of local banks and corporations, provide them greater *continuity* of leadership. Even though political leaders also depend upon business as their major source of income, they are more likely than their economic counterparts to be "Main Street" store owners or employees. This latter distinction, however, is more relevant to Edgewood than Riverview, where several of the less powerful economic leaders were also small businessmen.

Another conclusion related to pluralist assumptions may be mentioned. It is often assumed that diversity and constrained conflict are functional attributes of the political system, and no doubt this premise is often well-founded. In essence the idea seems to be that the ventilation of disparate views and the hammering out of consensus culminate in a higher synthesis. In the process governmental power is fragmented and the citizen gains the opportunity for active participation in the policies that affect him. If this thesis were valid for our communities, we should expect that Riverview would prove more viable than Edgewood, as measured by participation in major decisions. It is more diverse in political, ethnic and religious structure, and class distribution. Political values are strongly held and variable; the community includes a small enclave of the New York Liberal party. Edgewood is a more integrated community, in terms of political and class structure, ethnic and religious characteristics. Yet, as we have shown, there tends to be a somewhat higher rate of participation in Edgewood, civic morale (measured by service club memberships and identification with the community) is somewhat higher, and integration and value consensus among the community and its leaders are also somewhat higher. A relatively high degree of social uniformity and value consensus seems to be more functional than great diversity along these lines. *From this evidence, we hypothesize that there is a positive relation between the degree to which a community is socially integrated and the manner in which it solves its problems, i.e. through some citizen participation in crucial local decisions, or through more centralized control and action by a few hyperactive leaders. . . .*

METHODOLOGICAL CONTINUITIES

A major issue in community power research is the relative utility of the reputational and decisional methods of identifying those individuals and groups who dispose power. We began this research assuming that the decisional method would prove to be superior to the older reputational method, which seemed to measure the form rather than the substance of power and to be unduly subject to sociometric bias. Perhaps, too, we felt it was too simple a method. However, given the rudimentary stage of community power research and the tentative state of its methods, we decided to compare the results obtained by each approach.

As our findings were analyzed it became increasingly apparent that both methods had something to contribute. Each had its peculiar weaknesses and strengths. The reputational method tended to isolate those with high "positional" status which gave them a high power *potential*, even though they had not always used this power overtly. It was useful to be made aware of these "behind-the-scenes" leaders, particularly because the resources (both human and financial) of the organizations they controlled were frequently brought into the major decisions. Although such individuals did not always appear on the decisional list, their appearance on the reputational scale directed our attention to the

question of why men who were judged to be powerful by the most sophisticated members of the community failed to manifest their power
overtly, or at least to be identified by the decisional method. We are
satisfied that our analysis of power in Edgewood and Riverview would
have been less penetrating had we accepted uncritically the findings of
the decisional instrument, and relied exclusively upon them.

On the other hand, by asking the question the other way around, we
were able to make judgments about the relative power of some individuals who appeared on the decisional list but were not identified by the
alternative method. For example, some active (i.e. decisional) leaders
played essentially ministerial, implementary, or formal roles in several decisions. When these individuals were not named as powerful by other decision-makers, we were, in effect, given a clue that their high power rating might be an artifact of the decisional method. In several cases, further
analysis showed that these inflated ratings were often a function of official
positions which wired their holders into several decisions, even though
their participation was minimal.

However, the advantages of the decisional method are indicated by
the corroborative evidence provided in the cases just mentioned by the
requirement that all respondents name the two or three "most influential"
decision-makers in each issue in which they participated. By the use of
a rating system which ascribed varying weights for different *intensities*
of participation, we were able further to differentiate between leaders in
terms of their relative power.

More broadly, the decisional method has the advantage of focusing on
behavior, enabling one to differentiate better between overt and potential
power. Even here, however, in the sense that the researcher must always
reconstruct past events and must rely heavily upon the recollections and
judgments of respondents, the method still uses some techniques that are
quite similar to those of the reputational approach. Another serious limitation is that selection of decisions may provide for a built-in tendency
to structure power into certain configurations. In effect, decisions may be
chosen which inadvertently result in overlapping among the leaders or,
on the other hand, in considerable specialization among them. As long
as research resources are limited, so that only a sample of decisions can
be analyzed, this possibility remains. Another problem of the decisional
method is that it tends to overlook the more subtle manifestations of
power whereby certain individuals with impressive resources play a quiet
role in decisions, often through their "leg-men." In such cases, the anom-
alous result follows that the latter are deemed to be overtly, i.e. "really"
powerful, while those who employ, direct, advise, and influence them are
said to be merely "potentially" powerful. This condition raises questions

about the validity of the very distinction between "overt" and "potential" power.

For such reasons, the use of both methods gave us a more systematic differentiation among members of the power structure. From this experience, and the economy of the reputational method, which can easily be incorporated into the study design, it seems desirable to use both the reputational and decisional methods in community power analysis. Here, we share the view of those sociologists who have tested the validity of the reputational method and found it imperfect but effective. It appears to identify over half of the most overtly powerful individuals in the community, as well as certain leaders who are "indirectly" powerful. . . . These leaders, who usually have extensive organizational resources at their command, often play a decisive role in community affairs through their "leg-men" and their ability to commit their prestige and financial resources to various kinds of decisions.

On the other hand, we do not believe that the reputational method should be used independently to identify power. It provides an excellent starting point of analysis, but used alone, it will probably fail to identify individuals whose interest, energy, and sense of community responsibility propel them into decisions despite their comparative lack of rather more concrete and durable attributes of power. Our specialist groups provide several examples of such individuals, who are rarely nominated to the reputational list, but who nevertheless dispose some power in community affairs.

In order to illustrate this point more precisely, the results of the two methods are again compared, with somewhat differing results in the two communities. . . .

The data show that participation and reputed influence are significantly associated in Riverview. Almost two-thirds of the active leaders rank high in reputational power. . . . Generally speaking, "real" power is nicely associated with reputational power.

In Edgewood, the picture is less clear. Almost half of the decision-makers are ranked high on reputed power, but almost 30 per cent of those who were most overtly active are ranked low. These findings probably reflect differences in the two power structures. As noted earlier, in Riverview, power is more concentrated and hence more visible, for there is less difference between overt and reputed power. In Edgewood, power is shared to a great extent, and there are more reputational leaders who have highly visible and important organizational statuses, but do not play an active role personally. These factors may account in part for the greater disparity between overt and reputed power found in Edgewood. . . .

THE FUTURE OF PLURALISM

Comparing our findings with the traditional assumptions of pluralist theory, we do not find the expected measure of individual or organizational participation in major decisions. Multiple group membership, however, compared very favorably with national norms. Edgewood was somewhat advantaged in each of these sectors, but neither community demonstrated what may be called a lively degree of pluralism. This judgment is made in terms of a somewhat traditional definition of pluralism which retains its historic emphasis upon individualism as well as its contemporary assumptions about group membership, competition, and access. We accept the practical modification that in a complex society it is visionary to expect very much individual *qua* individual participation in political affairs. This expectation has been proved untenable in countless studies. However, the alternative propositions that pluralist communities are characterized by multiple memberships and viable competition among groups representing most major interests remain part of contemporary pluralist theory. Against these bench-marks, our findings are not highly supportive.

A final word is needed in the context of the definition of pluralism currently used by some power structure researchers. It will be recalled that pluralism is now said to exist when community decision-making is characterized by competition or specialization among an admittedly small constellation of local elites. If no single elite dominates all types of community decisions, pluralism remains viable. Research findings, however, indicate that in cities of 150,000 and less, the proportion of decisional overlapping among members of the power structure will average about 30 per cent. This figure is found by averaging overlap rates in Madison, Syracuse, New Haven, Green Bay, Racine, Kenosha, Edgewood, Bennington, and Riverview.

From this, we conclude that whereas some specialization of leadership surely occurs, a "significant" amount of overlapping of decisional power is characteristic of members of power elites in cities of these sizes. One explanation is that certain individuals develop local reputations for skill in one or another of the activities typically required in any major decision. Such skills include fund-raising, public relations, "organizing" ability, political contacts, and access to financial resources. As a result, those who possess them tend to be drawn into various decisions, regardless of their substantive nature. Again, the heads of some large corporations designate certain executives to "represent" the organization in community affairs, with similar effects.

In sum, our findings in Edgewood generally support earlier research of sociologists who found a tendency toward elitism in community power structures which were usually dominated by economic elites. In Riverview, the decision structure remains highly concentrated, but political leaders play the major role. Regarding the restriction of active participation to the few, the more recent findings of political scientists are quite similar. Differences regarding the nature of the political system may lie in the interpretation of the data. *To some extent, where the sociologists found monopoly and called it elitism, political scientists found oligopoly but defined it in more honorific terms as pluralism.* This conclusion, as we have tried to show, rests upon a restrictive, although eminently realistic, definition of pluralism, in which its historical emphasis upon individualism and a rough equality of bargaining power among groups has been subjugated to the assumption that pluralism exists if specialization and competition characterize groups of leaders who constitute some one-half of 1 per cent of the community. Certainly this definition meets prevailing conditions of group organization and political access, but it seems to omit some of the conditions and normative by-products traditionally associated with pluralism.

Some of the implications of our power structure findings are disturbing. One of these is the paradox found in Edgewood and Riverview, where an inverse association exists between pluralism and participation. Riverview is a closer approximation to the traditional pluralist model. It has a more diversified socioeconomic structure; far more active political competition; its organizational membership rates are very similar to those of Edgewood; and participation in state and national elections is not greatly different from that in Edgewood while in local elections it is higher. Yet, by the criteria of participation in the major decisions, there is less community interest and activism. Edgewood, on the other hand, is much more integrated socially and politically; its local political system was, until 1961, apparently nonpartisan. There is less controversy and sharp conflict on basic values within the community. Despite these conditions, which oppose those of traditional pluralism, with their assumed advantages, it has been somewhat more effective in meeting change and participation has been higher, as measured by the five major decisions.

Our results suggest that there may be some incompatibility between economic affluence and pluralist democracy. . . . In Edgewood, industrial strength and major control of decisions by economic leaders make possible considerable self-reliance and effective decision-making by those in its power structure; both its political and economic leaders tend to share dominant "free enterprise" values. They believe in doing things by themselves and for themselves, and even when government largesse is accepted, this fact is muted. But decisions are not the result of truly widespread participation (even though participation was more "pluralistic" than in Riverview). There is instead a quiet consensus on most matters, with a belief that leaders know best and will work, as they do, in the community interest. All this results in effective, expeditious decision-making, but it often occurs without the active citizen participation implied by pluralist theory.

The tendency for the major conditions of community decision-making to be set down by higher levels of government and industry is another crucial finding. In this way the periphery of local autonomy is becoming more restricted. Our evidence indicates that participation both within the power structure and the community tends to be positively related to the degree to which decisions involve the use (as well as the rhetoric) of essentially local rather than "external" resources. In both communities, participation was highest in decisions such as schools, hospitals, and new industry, where a good proportion of the resources were of local origin. Essentially external, "political" decisions, such as Riverview's housing authority and the two flood control issues, evoked little participation. From this, we may hypothesize that if the trend toward reducing the scope of local decision-making continues, pluralism at the community level will probably become even less lively. Since integration, easy access to the political apparatus, and "grass-roots" democracy have been historically associated with small communities, it is ironic that the decline of pluralism seems to be occurring precisely at this level. The nation-wide centralization of both political and economic decisions on behalf of greater rationality and control probably includes such among its unanticipated consequences.

A final, somewhat disturbing continuity is that despite high levels of popular education, economic stability, a fair degree of social mobility, a marvelously efficient communication system, and related advantages usually assumed to provide sufficient conditions for democratic pluralism, the vast majority of citizens remains apathetic, uninterested, and inactive in political affairs at the community level. Most political scientists and sociologists who have analyzed community behavior accept this generalization. Some who believe in the cult of expertise or share a Burkian conception of political representation, honor it. But whether this condition is attributed to majority apathy or to minority desires for power, status, and prestige, it remains an awkward reality for those who take democracy seriously.

V

SOME CONTINUING PROBLEMS
IN THE SEARCH FOR POWER

The study of community power is replete with methodological and theoretical problems. In the readings in this section we will explore three of these problems and suggest some considerations which may lead to their resolution.

THE CHARACTER OF THE DECISION-MAKING PROCESS

The first general problem with which we are concerned is the need to take adequate cognizance of the complexity of the decision-making process and the variability of its character from issue to issue. In our view, the identification of leaders and the comparative measurement of their influence would be facilitated if it were more broadly recognized that the decision-making process is multi-stage in character, and if the role of individuals and groups at the various stages of decision-making were more carefully analyzed. In the first article of this subsection Robert Agger, Daniel Goldrich, and Bert Swanson formulate a six step decision-making model which illustrates that influence on policy may often occur at stages of the decision-making process prior to or subsequent to the authoritative consideration of issues and the promulgation of decisions.

Of course, the fact that an individual or a group is active at one of these several stages is not by itself evidence of influence. A person has influence only to the degree that his action, or his anticipated action, affects the substance of the ultimate policy or results in its success or defeat. Moreover, if the role played by an individual is totally defined by others, or if his role could easily have been assigned to someone else, the apparent influence of that person may not be his "own." The second selection by Norton Long suggests, among other things, the utility of specifying the type of role played in the decision-making process by the various participants. For example, Long notes that those who legitimize a decision may have less influence on that decision than those whose role it is to initiate the idea or to bring together those who have either sufficient prestige or formal authority to secure community acceptance.

We are well aware that decision-making itself is often unsystematic and Norton Long's article makes this point most clearly by warning against the error of assuming that policy outcomes always reflect the victory of one set of contending forces over another. The fact that a political or social system may produce a policy output which was not intended seems to have received inadequate attention from most community power analysts. This fact is, of course, another reason to consider carefully the various roles played by presumed or potential decision-makers from the inception of an idea to its implementation or dismissal.

ISSUES AND NON-ISSUES

If one is to determine empirically the distribution of power in any community, it seems essential to investigate, among other things, the specific issues which are raised. There are, however, two fundamental problems in focusing one's research on specific issues and their disposition. The first of these is to ascertain which issues to study and how to weigh their relative importance.

In the lead article of this subsection, Peter Bachrach and Morton Baratz suggest that the importance of a decision is related to the degree to which it represents a challenge to the dominant values or the established "rules of the game" in a given community. The reader may recall that Linton Freeman and his associates suggested some criteria for evaluating the importance of issues in the preceding section. Another approach to assessing the relative importance of decisions is urged by Nelson Polsby in his provocative book, *Community Power and Political Theory* (168). Polsby suggests four criteria:

1. How many people are affected by outcomes.
2. How many different kinds of community resources are distributed by outcomes.
3. How much in amount of resources is distributed by outcomes.
4. How drastically are present community resource distributions altered by outcomes.

A second major difficulty, perhaps the most vexing of all those faced by the student of community power, is closely related to the problem of choosing and weighing issues. Even if researchers are able to analyze carefully all of the important community decisions, there is always the possibility that other "issues" or problems are not being discussed or perceived, or in fact are being directly or indirectly suppressed; these other issues may be more important for an understanding of a community's power structure than those which reach relatively high levels of political "visibility." In the articles in this subsection we thus intend to explore the difficulties posed for the analysis of community power by the "non-issue" or the "non-decision," and to make some modest suggestions for possible approaches to this problem.

Taking some clues from the selection by Bachrach and Baratz, we can identify four types of "non-issues." These types involve matters which are not raised because: (1) certain values and biases are built into the political system and reinforced by individuals and groups so as to protect certain interests; (2) there is an explicit application of influence, i.e., covert power; (3) there is an anticipated response from an opposition which is believed to have power; (4) there is an alienation from the political and social system in general those who desire change.

There appear to be a number of possible ways to deal with the problem of the "non-issue," although none of these possibilities is without serious methodological and conceptual difficulties. Bachrach and Baratz outline a way in which one might begin to assess the role played by individuals in the reinforcement of the values, myths, and "rules of the game" of a given situation from which these individuals benefit. Aaron Wildavsky has suggested that the "non-issue" may be unearthed in part through opinion and attitude surveys (232).

Generally, those who have undertaken to demonstrate empirically the nature of a community's power structure have asked, among other questions, why and how certain decisions take place. It may be that one can make headway in resolving some of the "non-issue" problems described above by asking why certain decisions and actions *do not* occur. In other words, one might formulate a series of hypotheses concerning the circumstances under which certain types of community conflict are likely to occur; where such conflict does not take place, the reason *may be* that conflict has been suppressed by the exercise of influence. Thus, if the community analyst finds an absence of conflict under conditions which in other communities have been associated with conflict, he may not have definite evidence that a "non-issue" situation involving power exists, but he does have some reason and guidelines for exploring that possibility.

One fundamental difficulty with this approach is that our knowledge about the structural and situational correlates of conflict is presently quite limited. Only a handful of comparative studies of community conflict are available. One of the most important of these studies is James S. Coleman's *Community Conflict* (46). Coleman, after examining the literature on community controversy, suggests that conflicts of varying intensity, dealing with various kinds of issues, seem to be associated with certain community characteristics: the community's past history, the homogeneity and stability of the population, the economic structure, the citizens' identification with the community, the organizational density, the rates of participation, and the role of the mass media. This subsection includes a recent article by William A. Gamson which draws heavily on some of Coleman's ideas and seeks to identify certain community characteristics which are associated with particularly hostile conflict. Gamson is concerned with one particular aspect of community conflict, but his research provides a model of comparative analysis which we think is of substantial heuristic value. Especially important, in the light of the suggestions by Bachrach and Baratz that community power research should focus on issues which do or could threaten the status quo, is Gamson's suggestion that hostile conflict and community change appear to be related.

Still another approach to the "non-issue" problem, and especially that aspect of the problem dealing with the possibility of the covert exercise of power, is to ask why various individuals and groups in the community are inactive, although they might be expected to be active participants in decisions relating to certain issues. The first step in this approach is to identify possible sources of power. The reader might develop a list of such sources from the articles in this book, especially those by Weber, Simon, Wildavsky, and Dahl (sections I and IV).

Of course, the possession of power resources does not necessarily mean that an individual is or should be influential, but the nature and extent of his resources suggest his potential influence. Power requires resources, but also depends on the will and ability of the individual who holds the resources, and on the relevance of the resources to the desired objective.

As we have seen, a number of scholars have concluded that there are few exceptions to the general rule that the structure of leadership in a given community varies with the type of issue being studied. Similarly, there is reason to believe that the effectiveness of various power resources also varies with the issue involved. Thus, if one is to pursue the "non-issue" problem by looking for clues in the emergence of or non-emergence of potential decision-makers in conflict situations, it is necessary to establish some expectations about the types of issues in which certain kinds of leaders are likely to be involved.

In the final article in this subsection, Ernest Barth and Stuart Johnson suggest a multi-dimensional method of classifying issues. Their work represents a promising, though empirically untested, beginning to the resolution of this complex problem. The reader may also wish to consider whether the typological outline proposed here might be refined to incorporate notions of the relative importance of various community issues, so that the ultimate typology might facilitate the solution of both of the major difficulties with which the subsection is concerned.

THE ASSESSMENT OF POWER

Power is one of the most important and most ubiquitous concepts with which social scientists deal. And yet, when we seek operational contact with power, it proves a most elusive phenomenon. Thus the third general problem in the study of community power which concerns us in this section is the difficulty of measuring power.

As we have seen, there has been little agreement about the meaning of "power" among students of community influence, except perhaps the minimum agreement that power involves the capacity to bring about or to resist change. But this modest consensus falls far short of being a theoretical statement which can facilitate the explanation and prediction of the outcome of social contests.

In the articles in this subsection we present readings which deal with two questions—what is it that we are looking for when we seek to assess power, and, having found it, how can we measure its component parts? The excerpt from James March's article indicates a number of alternative concepts of social power which are found in the research literature. Obviously, the concept employed to define power should affect the way in which we measure it. While March does not propose a single theory of power—in fact, he is rather pessimistic that such a theory is possible at this time—his models of power may bring us closer to that objective.

Having determined what it is that we wish to assess, how should the assessment proceed? The second selection in this subsection offers some criteria for assessing the relative power of participants in the decision-making process. Refining Robert Dahl's seminal article on "The Concept of Power" (50), the economist John Harsanyi develops a framework for analyzing the components of power relations. His focus is upon the need to examine the comparative "costs" incurred by individuals or groups when they seek to use their power resources. "Costs" are a function of the situation, including the motives and resources of all actors involved.

It seems to us that these two pieces are illustrative not merely of the creative insights which complex intellectual problems produce, but of the increasingly rigorous demands of methodology and conceptualization which underlie current efforts to develop more sophisticated predictions about the results of decision-making. A number of authors, including March and Harsanyi, have produced complex mathematical models of power relationships, which, in their use of calculus and symbolic notation, highlight the changes from early work in this field (cf. 141, 92, 93).

Our emphasis on the difficulty of measuring power should not imply that such measurement can be, or needs to be, quantified with great precision. However, with the help of ideas such as those offered below, it is conceivable that we can substantially improve our assessment of the distribution of power in communities.

The articles in this section will not provide complete nor perhaps even partial answers to the problems we have stressed, but it is hoped that they will clarify the difficulties and suggest further areas of inquiry and research. It is the reader's task to move us toward a more effective way of analyzing the structure of community power.

A Political Decision-Making Model

Robert E. Agger

Daniel Goldrich

Bert E. Swanson

In this selection Robert Agger and his associates develop a multi-phase model of the process of political decision-making. They show the relationship between these phases and point to a number of considerations which should concern those interested in community power.

Of particular importance, because it is so often overlooked by community power analysts, is the authors' emphasis on the consequence of the "implementation phase" of policy-making, and the discretion—i.e., power—enjoyed by professional civil servants at this and other stages of the decision-making process.

Political decision-making concerns the actions of men in the process of making choices. A process is a series of related events or acts over a period of time. Each act in a decision-making series of acts may itself be a choice or a decision. In order to understand this complex of decisions within decisions, it is useful to conceive of decision-making processes as consisting of six stages and one event:

(1) Policy formulation

(2) Policy deliberation

(3) Organization of political support

(4) Authoritative consideration

Event: Decisional outcome

(5) Promulgation of the decisional outcome

(6) Policy effectuation

The political decision-making process is political only in the sense that those engaged in action at any stage are acting consciously, in

From Robert E. Agger, Daniel Goldrich, and Bert E. Swanson, *The Rulers and the Ruled* (New York: John Wiley & Sons, Inc., 1964), pp. 40–51.

some measure, in reference to the scope of government. Any decision-making process, whether intrapersonal or interpersonal, and whether in a family, job, or other institutional setting, may be thought of as involving such stages.

Policy formulation occurs when someone thinks that a problem can be alleviated, solved, or prevented by a shift in the scope of government. The problem—or unsatisfied need—may or may not be perceived by others as a problem or as being appropriate for local government action. Even though there may be widespread satisfaction with many policy areas, the complexities of and the continuous changes in modern life make it likely that problems will arise somewhere to stimulate policy formulation directed toward a shift in the current scope of local government. The formulator, and those participating in any of the stages of political decision-making, may be a private citizen or a government official.

A policy formulation may originate outside the particular polity. For example, as a general policy, municipal ownership of facilities to distribute electric power was first formulated outside one of our communities; a general desegregation policy was first formulated outside another. But whether someone "borrows" a policy formulation from outside the community or whether a policy is of local origin, it must at some time become a preference of a person within the polity in order to become part of a community political decision-making process. A policy preference that is not deliberated once it is formed is a political decision-making process that has been started but is stillborn in the mind of the potential political participant. Policy formulation is a stage that is necessary but not sufficient to sustain the existence of a political decision-making process.

Policy deliberation is the stage following policy formulation. It may take the political-action form of talking, writing, listening, or reading. When a policy formulation—a policy preference for a shift in the net or internal scope of government—is transmitted by one actor to another, and interpersonal deliberation of the policy formulation occurs, a political demand has been made in the polity. It is at this point that the consideration of other policies may generate counter-demands.

Overt action in this context does not necessarily mean publicized action. Indeed, the action may take place behind closed doors, and the most aggressive newspaper reporter or political researcher may never hear of it. What makes research on political relations possible is that, although such actions may be known only to a few people, a sufficient number of those actions may be identified to enable researchers to construct a relatively valid picture of political decision-making processes.

Policy deliberation therefore may be open or secret: it may be restricted to smoke-filled rooms; it may take place at public meetings of the City Council; or it may be a topic of conversation on street corners or in private clubs. As with policy formulation, it is a stage that may be pre-empted either by public officials or by private citizens; or it may be a joint function. Wherever it occurs and whoever participates, this necessary stage is sufficient to allow a political decision-making process to be considered extant.

The decision-making process is considered arrested if a policy proposal is formulated and deliberated but does not advance beyond policy deliberation to the organization-of-political-support stage. Political demands may remain in this stage of decision-making. A decision-making process may be arrested at this point because those who started it believe that organization in behalf of their demands would provoke counter organization and defeat; or they may even fear severe, illegitimate sanctions if they were to organize. Demands of this sort may be suppressed or repressed as a result of correct or incorrect estimates of others' policy preferences, or of accurate or unwarranted fears that opponents will apply severe, illegitimate sanctions if they push their demands. In any event, political decision-making processes may die in this stage.

Organization of political support refers to such actions as holding and attending meetings to plan political strategy, producing and distributing information, and otherwise mobilizing support for or against demands for shifts in the scope of government. In most communities there are occasions in political life when leaflets are printed, handbills and petitions circulated, mimeograph machines run, and doorbells rung; paid political advertisements are published or broadcast and notices posted. These activities are considered the hallmarks of big-city machine politics. But in the four research communities they all were used to some extent by individuals other than party leaders, precinct committeemen, and their partisan coteries.

The organization of political support does not always require the use of these methods. Necessary political support might be mobilized by a telephone call from a single policy formulator or a few words spoken to one or two officials. On the other hand, a political decision-making process may involve extensive appeals using the highly refined techniques of mass-communications propaganda and public relations.

The decisional process has become a political issue when a demand reaches the stage of organizing political support, and two or more groups oppose each other on an aspect of policy formulation. Issues may be characterized according to the number and the emotional intensity of the individuals who have become actively involved in the issue, the extent to which issues are open or covert, and the extent to which participants view policy questions as involving basic ideological principles.

At times, certain patterns of governmental functioning may become accepted as customary, and demands for change may then take on a moralistic quality. A person's basic political beliefs—the political doctrines or ideology to which he subscribes—his way of life, or his personal integrity may seem to be at stake. It must be remembered that not all political decision-making processes need be issues; the organization of political support may be characterized by consensus rather than conflict. We will examine empirically the role of ideology in the emergence or avoidance of issues in decision-making later in the book.

Authoritative consideration is the next stage of decision-making. A variety of techniques may be used to make decisional choices or to select one of a set of optional courses as the decisional outcome. A demand may be voted upon directly by the citizens; proposed constitutional changes and local charter amendments are decided in this way, as are measures that involve the issuance of special bonds and the levying of special taxes. Other major policy questions also may be decided by citizen votes. The initiative and referendum are two electoral devices designed to give the citizenry a direct method for authoritatively approving or rejecting a policy.

On the other hand, a policy may be selected from several choices by formal or informal balloting in smaller groups of active participants: a city council may vote on a policy proposal without submitting it to the electorate. A small group of private citizens may even make the final decision either by voting down a policy proposal without giving officials the option of voting on it, or by choosing an alternative that is the authoritative decisional outcome, in fact if not in theory. There are occasions when government officials appear to act as independent lawmakers but are really the agents of private citizens.

To control a decision-making process a group of private citizens must control (1) the policy-formulation stage, (2) the policy-deliberation stage, (3) the organizing-political-support stage, or all of these stages. If a policy proposal that is unacceptable to a group of influential private citizens manages to reach officials, the officials may allow these influential private citizens to select the policy and may not exercise their constitutional authority; or the officials may share in the selection of policies with nonofficials. Constitutional, formal authority to choose among several outcomes in decision-making does not mean that the authorities will or can so choose. Even the political status associated with constitutional authority may prove a narrow base for the exercise of political influence, compared to the political status of certain private citizens.

A new policy that effects a shift in the scope of government must be transmitted to an appropriate local government agency for official action, if that shift is to become part of the formal, authoritative code of the polity. If the formulators of a particular policy are themselves government officials, they still must transmit the policy—that is, place the policy on the official agenda for formal consideration—in order for it to become part of the decisions of record, the laws, ordinances, or administrative regulations of government.

But what of a policy proposal that is blocked, vetoed, or otherwise defeated before it is transmitted to governmental authorities? Assume that a private citizen or an official makes a policy suggestion or demand to other private citizens or, informally, to other officials. Then suppose that the proposed policy change is rejected, no action is taken, and the existing rule remains unchanged, either through the action of these private citizens or through informal action by the officials. Although the suggested policy was never transmitted formally to a local agency, political decision-making has occurred: the actual political decision has been to affirm the existing policy. Political decision-making does not mean that existing rules and regulations must be revised or that political decisions may not be made outside the locus of an official government agency.

The objective of demands for shifts in the scope of government may be to see a change in the way government operates without a change in the law or a decision to maintain an existing law. Laws or ordinances, administrative regulations, and judicial decisions, much like constitutions or charters, are often open to a variety of interpretations. Thus, a demand for a shift in the scope of government can be a demand for altered patterns of action by government officials without a formal change in the law or ordinance, administrative regulation, or judicial decision. Inducing government officials to act informally in appropriate ways may be a wiser course of action than attempting to obtain an authoritative modification in the scope of government. Therefore, political decision-making may take place either outside the halls of government or informally within the government, with neither fanfare nor public proclamations.

So far, the word "authoritative" has been used in two distinct but related ways; one is a special case of the other. We [have] said that government has "authoritative supremacy, a monopoly of legitimate force." In the phrases *authoritative rule, authoritative code of the polity,* and *constitutional authority,* the word *authoritative* refers to the existence of a governmental policy, that is, of a rule regarding the way men should behave toward each other. The violation of such a policy can be expected to lead to punishments deriving from the monopoly of force possessed by all governments.

In this view, government exists and is "legitimate," even though its citizens despise it, so long as the citizens do not revolt and as long as they expect that force will probably be used to punish violators of policy. If such expectations do not exist, or if the expectations refer not to a legitimate government but to contending groups whose policy views conflict, so that any action might be met by punishment, government has broken down, and anarchy temporarily reigns. Constitutions, written or unwritten, and their subsidiary laws and customs are the plan of government as an institution in which those who govern have effective authority derived from their ability to sanction, using force if necessary. These officials may not express themselves before others do, but theirs is the last voice heard before sanctions are used in the pursuit of social control and public order. By the decision-making stage of *authoritative consideration*—the second sense of the word *authoritative*—we mean the stage of action by the political participants who have the final voice. These participants have the last word in selecting one or another of two or more outcomes as the policy that defines the scope of government for a succeeding time period.

All decision-making processes have *decisional outcomes*. If a particular aspect of the scope of government has been questioned and a decisional process has developed, regardless of the degree of consensus or conflict, the process will influence events thereafter, even though it is no longer extant. A decisional outcome is assessed by comparing the scope of government that existed and was questioned with the scope that exists at the point in time selected for identifying the outcome. This assessment may be done on the basis of a simple scale showing whether there has been change or not, or on the basis of a more complex set of parameters.

A decisional outcome involves purposeful behavior by participants, but does not require particular forms of choice-making. For example, it does not require a formal balloting procedure by either the electorate or their governmental representatives. The "authorities" in the second sense of the term *authoritative* are not necessarily government officials or the electorate acting as officials, as in the case of the "authorities" in the first sense. This is because authoritative consideration in a decision-making process is that stage wherein the participants select one or another of two or more ways in which local government is to function henceforth. Thus, participants in an authoritative consideration stage may be government officials, private citizens, or both. There may be no opportunity for government officials to reject the choice of private citizens of a particular decisional outcome, just as there may be no occasion for any but government officials to participate in selecting one of several outcomes. Private citizens may select an outcome that maintains the scope of government as is, thus obviating any need for a new law or ordinance. But whether a decisional outcome maintains or shifts the scope of government, the question of whether the participants are officials or citizens should be answered by empirical investigation rather than by definition.

An analyst must select a point in time to assess what outcomes have occurred in political decision-making. This point will be discussed further in connection with the concepts of political power and community power structures. The analyst might find that the stage of authoritative consideration has not been reached in one or another decision-making process. Thus, there may be decisional outcomes without authoritative consideration in a decision-making process because demands may not have reached the men who could act to shift the scope of government. When a change in a specific scope of government has become the subject of political demands in a decisional process, the analyst must determine whether the maintenance of the specific scope of government resulted from purposeful resistance by people capable of shifting the scope or from lack of access to people with such capabilities.[1] "Access" refers to the ability to reach the authorities, the men who can choose one or another pattern of local-government functioning as the decisional outcome in a decisional process. If there have been no demands for a shift in the scope of government, there has been no decisional process and, consequently, no authoritative consideration.[2] If demands have resulted in a shift in the scope of government, there has been authoritative consideration, even if a consensus has existed.

An authoritative-consideration stage may exist in a wide range of forms: it may be a distinct stage which succeeds the prior stages and has different participants from those in the prior stages; it may be a stage that partially overlaps earlier stages with some overlapping of personnel; or it may be a stage that is indistinguishable from other stages either temporally or by its participants. Decisional processes range from those with relatively well-developed and distinct stages to those with a single, composite stage that empirically encompasses the four analytic stages. In the decisional process that has a single, composite stage only one set of people—or one person in an instance of complete one-man rule—formulates policy, deliberates, organizes political support, and authoritatively considers the proposed shift in the scope of government at any one time. These participants may decide to adopt or reject a given policy formulation, thereby shifting or maintaining a particular scope of government. In relatively developed and distinct decisional stages, the participants in one stage may or may not be the same as the participants in other stages. Political role specialization may develop in reference to these stages, so that in one community, or in one policy area within a community, some men—"idea men"—specialize in policy formulation, others specialize in deliberative activities, others in the organization of political support, and

---

[1] Acts intended to influence others by creating or reinforcing satisfaction with an existing scope of government are not treated as demands and, hence, are not by themselves components of decision-making processes. On the other hand, such demands may be seen as part of a special category of "general" decision-making processes.

[2] An analyst, alternatively, may maintain that neither political power nor a political decision-making process exists until an authoritative-consideration stage has been reached.

still others may limit their participation to a final authoritative-consideration stage. Subspecialization in political roles within stages is also possible. For example, some people may specialize in doorbell-ringing and precinct work, others in pamphleteering, and still others in financing during the organization-of-political-support stage. However, political roles in the decisional stages may be more general in other communities or in other decisional processes.

Promulgation of the decisional outcome is also a stage not necessarily reached in a particular decision-making process. If the participants think that an existing policy is the best policy and that it should not be modified, there may be no occasion for an authoritative proclamation of an outcome. If a shift in the scope of government takes place without a formal, public pronouncement, this stage may not be present. But another way of looking at it is that this stage is manifested in the affirmation of an existing policy or in a quiet, covert change of policy. In any event, the present analysis of the decision-making process is most concerned with the four prior stages.

Policy effectuation is the last stage in this model of a political decision-making process. Administrative rather than legislative officials are ordinarily, but not always, the authorities at this stage. The courts may also play important roles in interpreting and shaping a general-policy decision. Private citizens also may join with, or even dominate, public administrators in this stage of political decision-making.

Policy effectuation is included as a stage in the decision-making process not only because a decisional outcome must be applied to be "final" or because its application may substantially change the decisional outcome from what had been intended. It is included primarily because policy effectuation may generate new policy formulations. For example, it may result in reappraisal of the policy, thereby initiating another cycle in the decision-making process. In this sense even policy effectuation is not a final or terminal stage of decision-making.

For a long time the functions of public administrators were regarded by political scientists as distinct from the functions of politicians. Politicians made the general rules in politics, while administrators applied these general rules to specific cases. Recently, the conception of politics and administration as inextricably intertwined has become accepted. In our view a useful distinction ought still to be made between administrative and political decision-making. This distinction does not preclude administrators from active involvement in political decision-making, nor politicians from active participation in administrative decision-making.

Demands that local government shift its scope may be administrative or political. Decisional processes may be similarly categorized. These are terms for polar opposites on a continuum and are therefore matters of degree rather than of kind. An *administrative* demand or decision-making process is regarded by its maker or participants as involving relatively routine implementations of a prior, more generally applicable decision; it implicates relatively minor values of a relatively few people at any one time and has "technical" criteria available to guide the technically trained expert in selecting one or another outcome as *the* decision. A *political* demand or decision-making process is thought to involve either an unusual review of an existing decision or an entirely new decision; it implicates relatively major values of a relatively large number of people and has value judgments or preferences as the major factors in determining selection by "policy-makers" of one or another outcome as *the* decision.[3]

The administrator thus is "in" politics by definition, but whether he is involved in political or administrative decision-making, or both, is an open, empirical question. The politician is also "in" politics, and he may be involved as a participant in the making of administrative as well as political decisions.

The roles played by bureaucrats—"administrators"—in the political system tend to be shaped by the organization of each government and by the constitutional doctrines and practices in each polity. However, a casual examination of political systems at the local-community or nation-state level suggests that official and informal organizations of political systems may diverge as much from one another as do official and informal internal structures of administrative agencies.

Several important consequences follow from these distinctions between administrative and political decisions, based as they are on the psychology of participants. One is that a particular decisional process may be political in one community and administrative in another. Or a decisional process may in time move from the political to the administrative category and back within a single community. Civil servants, bureaucrats, or public administrators may be active participants in political decision-making under some conditions and active participants in administrative decision-making under others. . . .

Summarizing the features of the model of political decision-making,

[3] Under many conditions of modern political life, the constituent variables may cluster together. The degree to which decisional processes are regarded by participants as (variable 1) routine, as (variable 2) implementations of earlier decisions, as (variable 3) implicating relatively minor values, as (variable 4) directly affecting relatively few people, as (variable 5) subject primarily to technical criteria of choice among alternatives, and as (variable 6) properly "decided" by experts generally may be seen as congruent. However, as one example of another possible pattern, some decisional processes may be regarded as relatively routine but involving major values of many people. It might be fruitful to develop more complex multi-dimensional schemes for the classification of decisional processes rather than simply viewing them as on a single administrative-political dimension.

we can say: a decision-making process exists when a political demand is made. A demand is a communicated policy formulation that envisages a shift in the scope of government. The decision-making process may become arrested at this point because those considering the demand are pessimistic about attaining the desired decisional outcome, because they fear the consequences that might ensue if they press their demands, because they are insufficiently motivated, or for other reasons. If counterdemands and counterorganization develop along with political support in behalf of demands, the process has become a political issue.

Decisional outcomes may result from arrested processes, from unopposed demands, from the resolution of a political issue, or as a consequence of effectively opposed and defeated demands which have not become issues. The decisional outcome may or may not be publicly promulgated. A political decision-making process may generate new policy formulations and demands or lead to new policy effectuation—administrative decision-making—that may then generate new political decision-making processes. In order to determine the outcomes of decisional processes, an analyst must specify the point in time at which he is interested in evaluating the outcomes. This will be discussed later, since it is crucial in determining who has had the political power that accrues to those who contribute to decisional outcomes.

Government officials may or may not be the only political actors at any stage of a decision-making process. Theoretically, they may monopolize political action or they may never enter the political scene actively. However, in most American communities they probably do engage in political action and share power with private citizens. But this is something for empirical determination rather than assumption. Since decision-making is not necessarily monopolized by officials, observations must be made to assess the extent to which citizens of a community participate and have power in the making of political decisions. . . .

The Local Community as an Ecology of Games

Norton E. Long

This article by Norton Long is extraordinarily rich with insights into the nature of decision-making in urban areas. Some of his notions are particularly relevant to the theme of this subsection, the decision-making process. For example, Long argues that many community "decisions" are actually the somewhat accidental result of the unplanned and uncoordinated activity of various individuals and groups, with a final outcome intended by no one. He also points to the importance of "civic staff men" as integrators who mobilize or put together the influence of others to secure action on community projects (see also 191).

Perhaps the most influential theme in this article has been the idea that game theory could be applied with both propriety and utility in understanding the nature of community decision-making. Students of community power might particularly note Long's emphasis on the functional interdependence of various games. One other important idea to which we draw particular attention is Long's use of role theory—he observes that the allocation of values which results from the decision-making process is, in important ways, a function of the expectations and self-images of decision makers.

The local community whether viewed as a polity, an economy, or a society presents itself as an order in which expectations are met and functions performed. In some cases, as in a new, company-planned mining town, the order is the willed product of centralized control, but for the most part the order is the product of a history rather than the imposed effect of any central nervous system of the community. For historic reasons we readily conceive the massive task of feeding New York to be achieved through the unplanned, historically developed cooperation of thousands of actors largely unconscious of their collaboration to this individually unsought end. The efficiency of this system is attested to by

Reprinted from "The Local Community as an Ecology of Games," by Norton E. Long, *American Journal of Sociology*, LXIII (November, 1958), 251–261, by permission of The University of Chicago Press. Copyright 1958 by the University of Chicago.

the extraordinary difficulties of the War Production Board and Service of Supply in accomplishing similar logistical objectives through an explicit system of orders and directives. Insofar as conscious rationality plays a role, it is a function of the parts rather than the whole. Particular structures working for their own ends within the whole may provide their members with goals, strategies, and rules that support rational action. The results of the interaction of the rational strivings after particular ends are in part collectively functional if unplanned. All this is the well-worn doctrine of Adam Smith, though one need accept no more of the doctrine of beneficence than that an unplanned economy can function.

While such a view is accepted for the economy, it is generally rejected for the polity. Without a sovereign, Leviathan is generally supposed to disintegrate and fall apart. Even if Locke's more hopeful view of the naturalness of the social order is taken, the polity seems more of a contrived artifact than the economy. Furthermore, there is both the hangover of Austinian sovereignty and the Greek view of ethical primacy to make political institutions seem different in kind and ultimately inclusive in purpose and for this reason to give them an over-all social directive end. To see political institutions as the same kind of thing as other institutions in society rather than as different, superior, and inclusive (both in the sense of being sovereign and ethically more significant) is a form of relativistic pluralism that is difficult to entertain. At the local level, however, it is easier to look at the municipal government, its departments, and the agencies of state and national government as so many institutions, resembling banks, newspapers, trade unions, chambers of commerce, churches, etc., occupying a territorial field and interacting with one another. This interaction can be conceptualized as a system without reducing the interacting institutions and individuals to membership in any single comprehensive group. It is psychologically tempting to envision the local territorial system as a group with a governing "they." This is certainly an existential possibility and one to be investigated. However, frequently, it seems likely, systems are confused with groups, and our primitive need to explain thunder with a theology or a demonology results in the hypostatizing of an angelic or demonic hierarchy. The executive committee of the bourgeoisie and the power elite make the world more comfortable for modern social scientists as the Olympians, did for the ancients. At least the latter-day hypothesis, being terrestrial, is in principle researchable, though in practice its metaphysical statement may render it equally immune to mundane inquiry.

Observation of certain local communities makes it appear that inclusive over-all organization for many purposes is weak or non-existent. Much of what occurs seems to just happen with accidental trends becoming cumulative over time and producing results intended by nobody.

A great deal of the communities' activities consist of undirected co-operation of particular social structures, each seeking particular goals and, in doing so, meshing with others. While much of this might be explained in Adam Smith's terms, much of it could not be explained with a rational, atomistic model of calculating individuals. For certain purposes the individual is a useful way of looking at people; for many others the role-playing member of a particular group is more helpful. Here we deal with the essence of predictability in social affairs. If we know the game being played is baseball and that X is a third baseman, by knowing his position and the game being played we can tell more about X's activities on the field than we could if we examined X as a psychologist or a psychiatrist. If such were not the case X would belong in the mental ward rather than in a ball park. The behavior of X is not some disembodied rationality but, rather, behavior within an organized group activity that has goals, norms, strategies, and roles that give the very field and ground for rationality. Baseball structures the situation.

It is the contention of this paper that the structured group activities that coexist in a particular territorial system can be looked at as games. These games provide the players with a set of goals that give them a sense of success or failure. They provide them determinate roles and calculable strategies and tactics. In addition, they provide the players with an elite and general public that is in varying degrees able to tell the score. There is a good deal of evidence to be found in common parlance that many participants in contemporary group structures regard their occupations as at least analogous to games. And, at least in the American culture, and not only since Eisenhower, the conception of being on a "team" has been fairly widespread.

Unfortunately, the effectiveness of the term "game" for the purpose of this paper is vitiated by, first, the general sense that games are trivial occupations and, second, by the pre-emption of the term for the application of a calculus of probability to choice or decision in a determinate game situation. Far from regarding games as trivial, the writer's position would be that man is both a game-playing and a game-creating animal, that his capacity to create and play games and take them deadly seriously is of the essence, and that it is through games or activities analogous to game-playing that he achieves a satisfactory sense of significance and a meaningful role.

While the calculability of the game situation is important, of equal or greater importance is the capacity of the game to provide a sense of purpose and a role. The organizations of society and polity produce satisfactions with both their products and their processes. The two are not unrelated, but, while the production of the product may in the larger sense enable players and onlookers to keep score, the satisfaction in the process is the satisfaction of playing the game and the sense in which any activity can be grasped as a game.

Looked at this way, in the territorial system there is a political game, a banking game, a contracting game, a newspaper game, a civic organization game, an ecclesiastical game, and many others. Within each game there is a well-established set of goals whose achievement indicates success or failure for the participants, a set of socialized roles making participant behavior highly predictable, a set of strategies and tactics handed down through experience and occasionally subject to improvement and change, an elite public whose approbation is appreciated, and finally, a general public which has some appreciation for the standing of the players. Within the game the players can be rational in the varying degrees that the structure permits. At the very least, they know how to behave, and they know the score.

Individuals may play in a number of games, but, for the most part, their major preoccupation is with one, and their sense of major achievement is through success in one. Transfer from one game to another is, of course, possible, and the simultaneous playing of roles in two or more games is an important manner of linking separate games.

Sharing a common territorial field and collaborating for different and particular ends in the achievement of over-all social functions, the players in one game make use of the players in another and are, in turn, made use of by them. Thus the banker makes use of the newspaperman, the politician, the contractor, the ecclesiastic, the labor leader, the civic leader—all to further his success in the banking game—but, reciprocally, he is used to further the others' success in the newspaper, political, contracting, ecclesiastical, labor, and civic games. Each is a piece in the chess game of the other, sometimes a willing piece, but, to the extent that the games are different, with a different end in view.

Thus, a particular highway grid may be the result of a bureaucratic department of public works game in which are combined, though separate, a professional highway engineer game with its purposes and critical elite onlookers; a departmental bureaucracy; a set of contending politicians seeking to use the highways for political capital, patronage, and the like; a banking game concerned with bonds, taxes, and the effect of the highways on real estate; newspapermen interested in headlines, scoops, and the effect of highways on the papers' circulation; contractors eager to make money by building roads; ecclesiastics concerned with the effect of highways on their parishes and on the fortunes of the contractors who support their churchly ambitions; labor leaders interested in union contracts and their status as community influentials with a right to be consulted; and civic leaders who must justify the contributions of their bureaus of municipal research or chambers of commerce to the social activity. Each game is in play in the complicated pulling and hauling of siting and constructing the highway grid. A wide variety of purposes is subserved by the activity, and no single over-all directive authority controls it. However, the interrelation of the groups in constructing a highway has been developed over time, and there are general expectations as to the interaction. There are also generalized expectations as to how politicians, contractors, newspapermen, bankers, and the like will utilize the highway situation in playing their particular games. In fact, the knowledge that a banker will play like a banker and a newspaperman like a newspaperman is an important part of what makes the situation calculable and permits the players to estimate its possibilities for their own action in their particular game.

While it might seem that the engineers of the department of public works were the appropriate protagonists for the highway grid, as a general activity it presents opportunities and threats to a wide range of other players who see in the situation consequences and possibilities undreamed of by the engineers. Some general public expectation of the limits of the conduct of the players and of a desirable outcome does provide bounds to the scramble. This public expectation is, of course, made active through the interested solicitation of newspapers, politicians, civic leaders, and others who see in it material for accomplishing their particular purposes and whose structured roles in fact require the mobilization of broad publics. In a sense the group struggle that Arthur Bentley described in his *Process of Government* is a drama that local publics have been taught to view with a not uncritical taste. The instruction of this taste has been the vocation and business of some of the contending parties. The existence of some kind of over-all public puts general restraints on gamesmanship beyond the norms of the particular games. However, for the players these are to all intents as much a part of the "facts of life" of the game as the sun and the wind.

It is perhaps the existence of some kind of a general public, however rudimentary, that most clearly differentiates the local territorial system from a natural ecology. The five-acre woodlot in which the owls and the field mice, the oaks and the acorns, and other flora and fauna have evolved a balanced system has no public opinion, however rudimentary. The co-operation is an unconscious affair. For much of what goes on in the local territorial system co-operation is equally unconscious and perhaps, but for the occasional social scientist, unnoticed. This unconscious co-operation, however, like that of the five-acre woodlot, produces results. The ecology of games in the local territorial system accomplishes unplanned but largely functional results. The games and their players mesh in their particular pursuits to bring about over-all results; the territorial system is fed and ordered. Its inhabitants are rational within limited areas and, pursuing the ends of these areas, accomplish socially functional ends.

While the historical development of largely unconscious co-operation between the special games in the territorial system get certain routine, over-all functions performed, the problem of novelty and breakdown must be dealt with. Here it would seem that, as in the natural ecology, random adjustment and piecemeal innovation are the normal methods of response. The need or cramp in the system presents itself to the players of the games as an opportunity for them to exploit or a menace to be overcome. Thus a transportation crisis in, say, the threatened abandonment of commuter trains by a railroad will bring forth the players of a wide range of games who will see in the situation opportunity for gain or loss in the outcome. While overall considerations will appear in the discussion, the frame of reference and the interpretation of the event will be largely determined by the game the interested parties are principally involved in. Thus a telephone executive who is president of the local chamber of commerce will be playing a civic association, general business game with concern for the principal dues-payers of the chamber but with a constant awareness of how his handling of this crisis will advance him in his particular league. The politicians, who might be expected to be protagonists of the general interest, may indeed be so, but the sphere of their activity and the glasses through which they see the problem will be determined in great part by the way they see the issue affecting their political game. The generality of this game is to a great extent that of the politician's calculus of votes and interests important to his and his side's success. To be sure, some of what Walter Lippmann has called "the public philosophy" affects both politicians and other game-players. This indicates the existence of roles and norms of a larger, vaguer game with a relevant audience that has some sense of cricket. This potentially mobilizable audience is not utterly without importance, but it provides no sure or adequate basis for support in the particular game that the politician or anyone else is playing. Instead of a set of norms to structure enduring role-playing, this audience provides a cross-pressure for momentary aberrancy from gamesmanship or constitutes just another hazard to be calculated in one's play.

In many cases the territorial system is impressive in the degree of intensity of its particular games, its banks, its newspapers, its downtown stores, its manufacturing companies, its contractors, its churches, its politicians, and its other differentiated, structured, goal-oriented activities. Games go on within the territory, occasionally extending beyond it, though centered in it. But, while the particular games show clarity of goals and intensity, few, if any, treat the territory as their proper object. The protagonists of things in particular are well organized and know what they are about; the protagonists of things in general are few, vague, and weak. Immense staff work will go into the development of a Lincoln Square project, but the twenty-two counties of metropolitan New York have few spokesmen for their over-all common interest and not enough staff work to give these spokesmen more substance than that required for a "do-gooding" newspaper editorial. The Port of New York Authority exhibits a disciplined self-interest and a vigorous drive along the lines of its developed historic role. However, the attitude of the Port Authority toward the general problems of the metropolitan area is scarcely different than that of any private corporation. It confines its corporate good citizenship to the contribution of funds for surveys and studies and avoids acceptance of broader responsibility. In fact, spokesmen for the Port vigorously reject the need for any superior level of structured representation of metropolitan interests. The common interest, if such there be, is to be realized through institutional interactions rather than through the self-conscious rationality of a determinate group charged with its formulation and attainment. Apart from the newspaper editorial, the occasional politician, and a few civic leaders the general business of the metropolitan area is scarcely anybody's business, and, except for a few, those who concern themselves with the general problems are pursuing hobbies and causes rather than their own business.

The lack of over-all institutions in the territorial system and the weakness of those that exist insure that co-ordination is largely ecological rather than a matter of conscious rational contriving. In the metropolitan area in most cases there are no over-all economic or social institutions. People are playing particular games, and their playgrounds are less or more than the metropolitan area. But even in a city where the municipal corporation provides an apparent over-all government, the appearance is deceptive. The politicians who hold the offices do not regard themselves as governors of the municipal territory but largely as mediators or players in a particular game that makes use of the outer inhabitants. Their roles, as they conceive them, do not approach those of the directors of a TVA developing a territory. The ideology of local government is a highly limited affair in which the office-holders respond to demands and mediate conflicts. They play politics, and politics is vastly different from government if the latter is conceived as the rational, responsible ordering of the community. In part, this is due to the general belief that little government is necessary or that government is a congery of services only different from others because it is paid for by taxes and provided for by civil servants. In part, the separation of economics from politics eviscerates the formal theory of government of most of the substance of social action. Intervention in the really important economic order is by way of piecemeal exception and in deviation from the supposed norm of the separation of politics and economics. This ideal of separation has blocked the development of a theory of significant government action and reduced the politician to the role of registerer of pressure rather than responsible governor of a local political economy. The politics of the community becomes a different affair from its government, and its government is so structured as to provide the effective actors in it neither a sense of general responsibility nor the roles calling for such behavior.

The community vaguely senses that there ought to be a government. This is evidenced in the nomination by newspapers and others of particular individuals as members of a top leadership, a "they" who are periodically called upon to solve community problems and meet community crises. Significantly, the "they" usually are made up of people holding private, not public, office. The pluralism of the society has separated political, ecclesiastical, economic, and social hierarchies from one another so that the ancient union of lords spiritual and temporal is disrupted. In consequence, there is a marked distinction between the status of the holders of political office and the status of the "they" of the newspapers and the power elite of a C. Wright Mills or a Floyd Hunter. The politicians have the formal government office that might give them responsible governing roles. However, their lack of status makes it both absurd and presumptuous that they should take themselves so seriously. Who are they to act as lords of creation? Public expectation neither empowers nor demands that they should assume any such confident pose as top community leaders. The latter position is reserved for a rather varying group (in some communities well defined and clear-cut, in others vague and amorphous) of holders for the most part of positions of private power, economic, social, and ecclesiastical. This group, regarded as the top leadership of the community, and analogous to the top management of a corporation, provides both a sense that there are gods in the heavens whose will, if they exercise it, will take care of the community's problems and a set of demons whose misrule accounts for the evil in the world. The "they" fill an office left vacant by the dethronement of absolutism and aristocracy. Unlike the politicians in that "they" are only partially visible and of untested powers, the top leadership provides a convenient rationale for explaining what goes on or does not go on in the community. It is comforting to think that the executive committee of the bourgeoisie is exploiting the community or that the beneficent social and economic leaders are wearying themselves and their digestions with civic luncheons in order to bring parking to a congested city. . . .

The community needs to believe that there are spiritual fathers, bad or good, who can deal with the dark: in the Middle Ages the peasants combated a plague of locusts by a high Mass and a procession of the clergy who damned the grasshoppers with bell, book, and candle. The Hopi Indians do a rain dance to overcome a drought. The harassed citizens of the American city mobilize their influentials at a civic luncheon to perform the equivalent and exorcise slums, smog, or unemployment. We smile at the medievals and the Hopi, but our own practices may be equally magical. . . .

While ritual activities are tranquilizing anxieties, the process of experimentation and adaptation in the social ecology goes on. The piecemeal responses of the players and the games to the challenges presented by crises provide the social counterpart to the process of evolution and natural selection. However, unlike the random mutation of the animal kingdom, much of the behavior of the players responding within the perspectives of their games is self-conscious and rational, given their ends in view. It is from the over-all perspective of the unintended contribution of their actions to the forming of a new or the restoration of the old ecological balance of the social system that their actions appear almost as random and lacking in purposive plan as the adaptive behavior of the natural ecology.

Within the general area of unplanned, unconscious social process technological areas emerge that are so structured as to promote rational, goal-oriented behavior and meaningful experience rather than mere happenstance. In these areas group activity may result in cumulative knowledge and self-corrective behavior. Thus problem-solving in the field of public health and sanitation may be at a stage far removed from the older dependence on piecemeal adjustment and random functional innovation. In this sense there are areas in which society, as Julian Huxley suggests in his *The Meaning of Evolution,* has gone beyond evolution. However, these are as yet isolated areas in a world still swayed by magic and, for the most part, carried forward by the logic of unplanned, undirected historical process.

It is not surprising that the members of the "top leadership" of the territorial system should seem to be largely confined to ritual and ceremonial roles. "Top leadership" is usually conceived in terms of status position rather than specifiable roles in social action. The role of a top leader is ill defined and to a large degree unstructured. It is in most cases a secondary role derived from a primary role as corporation executive, wealthy man, powerful ecclesiastic, holder of high social position, and the like. The top-leadership role is derivative from the other and is in most cases a result rather than a cause of status. The primary job is bank president, or president of Standard Oil; as such, one is naturally picked, nominated, and recognized as a member of the top leadership. One seldom forgets that one's primary role, obligation, and source of rational conduct is in terms of one's business. . . .

A fair gauge of the significance of top-leadership roles is the time put into them by the players and the institutionalized support represented by staff. Again and again the interviewer is told that the president of such-and-such an organization is doing a terrific job and literally knocking himself out for such-and-such a program. On investigation a "terrific job" turns out to be a few telephone calls and, possibly, three luncheons a month. The standard of "terrific job" obviously varies widely from what would be required in the business role. . . .

A wide variety of civic undertakings need to organize top prestige support both to finance and to legitimate their activities. The staff man of a bureau of municipal research or the Red Feather Agency cannot proceed on his own; he must have the legitimatizing sponsorship of top influentials. His task may be self-assigned, his perception of the problem and its solution may be his own, but he cannot gain acceptance without mobilizing the influentials. For the success of his game he must assist in creating the game of top leadership. The staff man in the civic field is the typical protagonist of things in general—a kind of entrepreneur of ideas. He fulfills the same role in his area as the stock promoter of the twenties or the Zeckendorfs of urban redevelopment. Lacking both status and a confining organizational basis, he has a socially valuable mobility between the specialized games and hierarchies in the territorial system. His success in the negotiation of a port authority not only provides a plus for his taxpayers federation or his world trade council but may provide a secure and lucrative job for himself.

Civic staff men, ranging from chamber of commerce personnel to college professors and newspapermen, are in varying degrees interchangeable and provide an important network of communication. The staff men in the civic agencies play similar roles to the Cohens and Corcorans in Washington. In each case a set of telephone numbers provides special information and an effective lower-echelon interaction. Consensus among interested professionals at the lower level can result in action programs from below that are bucked up to the prestige level of legitimatization. As the Cohens and Corcorans played perhaps the most general and inclusive game in the Washington bureaucracy, so their counterparts in the local territorial system are engaged in the most general action game in their area. Just as the Cohens and Corcorans had to mobilize an effective concentration of top brass to move a program into the action stage, so their counterparts have to mobilize concentrations of power sufficient for their purposes on the local scene. . . .

The attempt to transform the metropolitan appearance of disorder into a tidy territory is a built-in predisposition for the self-constituted staff of the embryonic top metropolitan management. The major disorder that has to be overcome before all others is the lack of order and organization among the "power elite." As in the case of the social workers, there is a thrust from below to organize a "power elite" as a necessary instrument to accomplish the purposes of civic staff men. This is in many ways nothing but a part of the general groping after a territorial government capable of dealing with a range of problems that the existing feudal disintegration of power cannot. The nomination of a top leadership by newspapers and public and the attempt to create such a leadership in fact by civic technicians are due to a recognition that there is a need for a leadership with the status capacity, and role to attend to the general problems of the territory and give substance to a public philosophy. This involves major changes in the script of the top-leadership game and the self-image of its participants. In fact, the insecurity and the situational limitations of their positions in corporations or other institutions that provide the primary roles for top leaders make it difficult to give more substance to what has been a secondary role. Many members of present top leaderships are genuinely reluctant, fearful, and even morally shocked at their positions' becoming that of a recognized territorial government. While there is a general supposition that power is almost instinctively craved, there seems considerable evidence that at least in many of our territorial cultures responsibility is not. Machiavellian *virtu* is an even scarcer commodity among the merchant princes of the present than among their Renaissance predecessors. In addition, the educational systems of school and business do not provide top leaders with the inspiration or the know-how to do more than raise funds and man committees. Politics is frequently regarded with the same disgust as military service by the ancient educated Chinese.

It is possible to translate a check pretty directly into effective power in a chamber of commerce or a welfare agency. However, to translate economic power into more general social or political power, there must be an organized purchasable structure. Where such structures exist, they may be controlled or, as in the case of *condottieri*, gangsters, and politicians, their hire may be uncertain, and the hired force retains its independence. Where businessmen are unwilling or unable to organize their own political machines, they must pay those who do. Sometimes the paymaster rules; at other times he bargains with equals or superiors. . . .

A final game that does in a significant way integrate all the games in the territorial system is the social game. Success in each of the games can in varying degrees be cashed in for social acceptance. The custodians of the symbols of top social standing provide goals that in a sense give all the individual games some common denominator of achievement. While the holders of top social prestige do not necessarily hold either top political or economic power, they do provide meaningful goals for the rest. One of the most serious criticisms of a Yankee aristocracy made by a Catholic bishop was that, in losing faith in their own social values, they were undermining the faith in the whole system of final clubs. It would be a cruel joke if, just as the hard-working upwardly mobile had worked their way to entrance, the progeny of the founders lost interest. The decay of the Union League Club in *By Love Possessed* is a tragedy for more than its members. A common game shared even by the excluded spectators gave a purpose that was functional in its time and must be replaced—hopefully, by a better one. A major motivation for seeking membership in and playing the top-leadership game is the value of the status it confers as a counter in the social game.

Neither the civic leadership game nor the social game makes the territorial ecology over into a structured government. They do, however, provide important ways of linking the individual games and make possible cooperative action on projects. Finally, the social game, in Ruth Benedict's sense, in a general way patterns the culture of the territorial ecology and gives all the players a set of vaguely shared aspirations and common goals.

Two Faces of Power

Peter Bachrach

Morton S. Baratz

While Peter Bachrach and Morton Baratz focus their attack in this article on pluralist studies of community power, especially on the work of Robert Dahl, their central argument is applicable to almost all studies of community influence.

The thrust of their argument is that power has "two faces"—one manifest in the outcome of the overt decision-making process, the other manifest in the capacity of individuals and groups to prevent issues or contests from arising which could threaten their interests. In making their case Bachrach and Baratz point to the importance of establishing criteria with which to judge the relative importance of various decisions.

In their concluding paragraphs the authors suggest the broad outlines of an approach for resolving the difficulties they have raised. The student might critically examine these proposals with the goal of formulating some tentative ideas about problems and methods of operationalizing them in field research.

I

Against the elitist approach to power several criticisms may be, and have been levelled.[1] One has to do with its basic premise that in every human institution there is an ordered system of power, a "power structure" which is an integral part and the mirror image of the organization's stratification. This postulate the pluralists emphatically—and, to our mind, correctly—reject, on the ground that

> nothing categorical can be assumed about power in any community. . . .
> If anything, there seems to be an unspoken notion among pluralist researchers that at bottom *nobody* dominates in a town, so that their first

From Peter Bachrach and Morton Baratz, "The Two Faces of Power," *American Political Science Review*, LVII (December, 1962), 947–952.

[1] See especially N. W. Polsby, (150) p. 476.

question is not likely to be, "Who runs this community?," but rather, "Does anyone at all run this community?" The first query is somewhat like, "Have you stopped beating your wife?," in that virtually any response short of total unwillingness to answer will supply the researchers with a "power elite" along the lines presupposed by the stratification theory.[2]

Equally objectionable to the pluralists—and to us—is the sociologists' hypothesis that the power structure tends to be stable over time.

Pluralists hold that power may be tied to issues, and issues can be fleeting or persistent, provoking coalitions among interested groups and citizens, ranging in their duration from momentary to semi-permanent. . . . To presume that the set of coalitions which exists in the community at any given time is a timelessly stable aspect of social structure is to introduce systematic inaccuracies into one's description of social reality.[3]

A third criticism of the elitist model is that it wrongly equates reputed with actual power:

If a man's major life work is banking, the pluralist presumes he will spend his time at the bank, and not in manipulating community decisions. This presumption holds until the banker's activities and participations indicate otherwise. . . . If we presume that the banker is "really" engaged in running the community, there is practically no way of disconfirming this notion, even if it is totally erroneous. On the other hand, it is easy to spot the banker who really *does* run community affairs when we presume he does not, because his activities will make this fact apparent.[4]

This is not an exhaustive bill of particulars; there are flaws other than these in the sociological model and methodology [5] including some which the pluralists themselves have not noticed. But to go into this would not materially serve our current purposes. Suffice it simply to observe that whatever the merits of their own approach to power, the pluralists have effectively exposed the main weaknesses of the elitist model.

As the foregoing quotations make clear, the pluralists concentrate their attention, not upon the sources of power, but its exercise. Power to them means "participation in decision-making" [6] and can be analyzed

---

[2] *Ibid.*, pp. 478–79.

[3] *Ibid.*

[4] *Ibid.*, pp. 480–81.

[5] See especially Robert A. Dahl, "A Critique of the Ruling-Elite Model," *American Political Science Review*, 52 (June, 1958), 463–69; and Lawrence J. R. Herson, "In the Footsteps of Community Power," *American Political Science Review*, 55 (December, 1961), 817–31.

[6] This definition originated with Harold D. Lasswell and Abraham Kaplan, *Power and Society* (New Haven: 1950), p. 75.

only after "careful examination of a series of concrete decisions." [7] As a result, the pluralist researcher is uninterested in the reputedly powerful. His concerns instead are to (a) select for study a number of "key" as opposed to "routine" political decisions, (b) identify the people who took an active part in the decision-making process, (c) obtain a full account of their actual behavior while the policy conflict was being resolved, and (d) determine and analyze the specific outcome of the conflict.

The advantages of this approach, relative to the elitist alternative, need no further exposition. The same may not be said, however, about its defects—two of which seem to us to be of fundamental importance. One is that the model takes no account of the fact that power may be, and often is, exercised by confining the scope of decision-making to relatively "safe" issues. The other is that the model provides no *objective* criteria for distinguishing between "important" and "unimportant" issues arising in the political arena.

II

There is no gainsaying that an analysis grounded entirely upon what is specific and visible to the outside observer is more "scientific" than one based upon pure speculation. To put it another way,

> If we can get our social life stated in terms of activity, and of nothing else, we have not indeed succeeded in measuring it, but we have at least reached a foundation upon which a coherent system of measurements can be built up. . . . We shall cease to be blocked by the intervention of unmeasurable elements, which claim to be themselves the real causes of all that is happening, and which by their spook-like arbitrariness make impossible any progress toward dependable knowledge.[8]

The question is, however, how can one be certain in any given situation that the "unmeasurable elements" are inconsequential, are not of decisive importance? Cast in slightly different terms, can a sound concept of power be predicated on the assumption that power is totally embodied and fully reflected in "concrete decisions" or in activity bearing directly upon their making?

We think not. Of course power is exercised when A participates in the making of decisions that affect B. But power is also exercised when A devotes his energies to creating or reinforcing social and political values and institutional practices that limit the scope of the political process to public

[7] Robert A. Dahl, "A Critique of the Ruling-Elite Model," *loc. cit.*, p. 466.
[8] Arthur Bentley, *The Process of Government* (Chicago: 1908), p. 202, quoted in Polsby, (150), p. 481 n.

consideration of only those issues which are comparatively innocuous to A. To the extent that A succeeds in doing this, B is prevented, for all practical purposes, from bringing to the fore any issues that might in their resolution be seriously detrimental to A's set of preferences.[9]

Situations of this kind are common. Consider, for example, the case—surely not unfamiliar to this audience—of the discontented faculty member in an academic institution headed by a tradition-bound executive. Aggrieved about a long-standing policy around which a strong vested interest has developed, the professor resolves in the privacy of his office to launch an attack upon the policy at the next faculty meeting. But, when the moment of truth is at hand, he sits frozen in silence. Why? Among the many possible reasons, one or more of these could have been of crucial importance: (a) the professor was fearful that his intended action would be interpreted as an expression of his disloyalty to the institution; or (b) he decided that, given the beliefs and attitudes of his colleagues on the faculty, he would almost certainly constitute on this issue a minority of one; or (c) he concluded that, given the nature of the law-making process in the institution, his proposed remedies would be pigeonholed permanently. But whatever the case, the central point to be made is the same: to the extent that a person or group—consciously or unconsciously—creates or reinforces barriers to the public airing of policy conflicts, that person or group has power. Or, as Professor Schattschneider has so admirably put it:

> All forms of political organization have a bias in favor of the exploitation of some kinds of conflict and the suppression of others because *organization is the mobilization of bias*. Some issues are organized into politics while others are organized out.[10]

Is such bias not relevant to the study of power? Should not the student be continuously alert to its possible existence in the human institution that he studies, and be ever prepared to examine the forces which brought it into being and sustain it? Can he safely ignore the possibility, for instance, that an individual or group in a community participates more vigorously in supporting the *nondecision-making* process than in partici-

---

[9] As is perhaps self-evident, there are similarities in both faces of power. In each, A participates in decisions and thereby adversely affects B. But there is an important difference between the two: in the one case, A openly participates; in the other, he participates only in the sense that he works to sustain those values and rules of procedure that help him keep certain issues out of the public domain. True enough, participation of the second kind may at times be overt; that is the case, for instance, in cloture fights in the Congress. But the point is that it need not be. In fact, when the maneuver is most successfully executed, it neither involves nor can be identified with decisions arrived at on specific issues.

[10] E. E. Schattschneider, *The Semi-Sovereign People* (New York: 1960), p. 71.

pating in actual decisions within the process? Stated differently, can the researcher overlook the chance that some person or association could limit decision-making to relatively non-controversial matters, by influencing community values and political procedures and rituals, notwithstanding that there are in the community serious but latent power conflicts? [11] To do so is, in our judgment, to overlook the less apparent, but nonetheless extremely important, face of power.

III

In his critique of the "ruling-elite model," Professor Dahl argues that "the hypothesis of the existence of a ruling elite can be strictly tested only if . . . [t] here is a fair sample of cases involving key political decisions in which the preferences of the hypothetical ruling elite run counter to those of any other likely group that might be suggested." [12] With this assertion we have two complaints. One we have already discussed, viz., in erroneously assuming that power is solely reflected in concrete decisions, Dahl thereby excludes the possibility that in the community in question there is a group capable of preventing contests from arising on issues of importance to it. Beyond that, however, by ignoring the less apparent face of power Dahl and those who accept his pluralist approach are unable adequately to differentiate between a "key" and a "routine" political decision.

Nelson Polsby, for example, proposes that "by pre-selecting as issues for study those which are generally agreed to be significant, pluralist researchers can test stratification theory." [13] He is silent, however, on how the researcher is to determine *what* issues are "generally agreed to be significant," and on how the researcher is to appraise the reliability of the agreement. In fact, Polsby is guilty here of the same fault he himself has found with elitist methodology: by presupposing that in any community

---

[11] Dahl *partially* concedes this point when he observes ("A Critique of the Ruling-Elite Model," pp. 468–69) that "one could argue that even in a society like ours a ruling elite might be so influential over ideas, attitudes, and opinions that a kind of false consensus will exist—not the phony consensus of a terroristic totalitarian dictatorship but the manipulated and superficially self-imposed adherence to the norms and goals of the elite by broad sections of a community. . . . This objection points to the need to be circumspect in interpreting the evidence." But that he largely misses our point is clear from the succeeding sentence: "Yet here, too, it seems to me that the hypothesis cannot be satisfactorily confirmed without something equivalent to the test I have proposed," and that is "by an examination of a series of concrete cases where key decisions are made. . . ."

[12] *Ibid.*, p. 466.

[13] *Ibid.*, p. 478.

there are significant issues in the political arena, he takes for granted the very question which is in doubt. He accepts as issues what are reputed to be issues. As a result, his findings are fore-ordained. For even if there is no "truly" significant issue in the community under study, there is every likelihood that Polsby (or any like-minded researcher) will find one or some and, after careful study, reach the appropriate pluralistic conclusions.[14]

Dahl's definition of "key political issues" in his essay on the ruling-elite model is open to the same criticism. He states that it is "a necessary although possibly not a sufficient condition that the [key] issue should involve actual disagreement in preferences among two or more groups."[15] In our view, this is an inadequate characterization of a "key political issue," simply because groups can have disagreements in preferences on unimportant as well as on important issues. Elite preferences which border on the indifferent are certainly not significant in determining whether a monolithic or polylithic distribution of power prevails in a given community. Using Dahl's definition of "key political issues," the researcher would have little difficulty in finding such in practically any community; and it would not be surprising then if he ultimately concluded that power in the community was widely diffused.

The distinction between important and unimportant issues, we believe, cannot be made intelligently in the absence of an analysis of the "mobilization of bias" in the community; of the dominant values and the political myths, rituals, and institutions which tend to favor the vested interests of one or more groups, relative to others. Armed with this knowledge, one could conclude that any challenge to the predominant values or to the established "rules of the game" would constitute an "important" issue; all else, unimportant. To be sure, judgments of this kind cannot be entirely objective. But to avoid making them in a study of power is both to neglect a highly significant aspect of power and thereby to undermine the only sound basis for discriminating between "key" and "routine" decisions. In effect, we contend, the pluralists have made each of these mistakes; that is to say, they have done just that for which Kaufman and Jones so severely taxed Floyd Hunter: they have begun "their structure at the mezzanine without showing us a lobby or foundation,"[16] i.e., they have begun by studying the issues rather than the values and biases that are built into the political system and that, for the student of power, give real meaning to those issues which do enter the political arena.

[14] As he points out, the expectations of the pluralist researchers "have seldom been disappointed." *Ibid.*, p. 477.

[15] *Ibid.*, p. 467.

[16] Herbert Kaufman and Victor Jones, "The Mystery of Power," *Public Administration Review*, 14 (Summer 1954), 207.

IV

There is no better fulcrum for our critique of the pluralist model than Dahl's recent study of power in New Haven.[17]

At the outset it may be observed that Dahl does not attempt in this work to define his concept, "key political decision." In asking whether the "Notables" of New Haven are "influential overtly or covertly in the making of government decisions," he simply states that he will examine "three different 'issue-areas' in which important public decisions are made: nominations by the two political parties, urban redevelopment, and public education." These choices are justified on the grounds that "nominations determine which persons will hold public office. The New Haven redevelopment program measured by its cost—present and potential—is the largest in the country. Public education, aside from its intrinsic importance, is the costliest item in the city's budget." Therefore, Dahl concludes, "It is reasonable to expect . . . that the relative influence over public officials wielded by the . . . Notables would be revealed by an examination of their participation in these three areas of activity." [18]

The difficulty with this latter statement is that it is evident from Dahl's own account that the Notables are in fact uninterested in two of the three "key" decisions he has chosen. In regard to the public school issue, for example, Dahl points out that many of the Notables live in the suburbs and that those who do live in New Haven choose in the main to send their children to private schools. "As a consequence," he writes, "their interest in the public schools is ordinarily rather slight." [19] Nominations by the two political parties as an important "issue-area," is somewhat analogous to the public schools, in that the apparent lack of interest among the Notables in this issue is partially accounted for by their suburban residence—because of which they are disqualified from holding public office in New Haven. Indeed, Dahl himself concedes that with respect to both these issues the Notables are largely indifferent: "Business leaders might ignore the public schools or the political parties without any sharp awareness that their indifference would hurt their pocketbooks . . ." He goes on, however, to say that

> the prospect of profound changes [as a result of the urban-redevelopment program] in ownership, physical layout, and usage of property in the downtown area and the effects of these changes on the commercial and industrial prosperity of New Haven were all related in an obvious way to the daily concerns of businessmen.[20]

[17] Robert A. Dahl, *Who Governs?* (New Haven: 1961).
[18] *Ibid.*, p. 64.
[19] *Ibid.*, p. 70.
[20] *Ibid.*, p. 467.

Thus, if one believes—as Professor Dahl did when he wrote his critique of the ruling-elite model—that an issue, to be considered as important, "should involve actual disagreement in preferences among two or more groups,"[21] then clearly he has now for all practical purposes written off public education and party nominations as key "issue-areas." But this point aside, it appears somewhat dubious at best that "the relative influence over public officials wielded by the Social Notables" can be revealed by an examination of their nonparticipation in areas in which they were not interested.

Furthermore, we would not rule out the possibility that even on those issues to which they appear indifferent, the Notables may have a significant degree of *indirect* influence. We would suggest, for example, that although they send their children to private schools, the Notables do recognize that public school expenditures have a direct bearing upon their own tax liabilities. This being so, and given their strong representation on the New Haven Board of Finance,[22] the expectation must be that it is in their direct interest to play an active role in fiscal policy-making, in the establishment of the educational budget in particular. But as to this, Dahl is silent: he inquires not at all into either the decisions made by the Board of Finance with respect to education nor into their impact upon the public school.[23] Let it be understood clearly that in making these points we are not attempting to refute Dahl's contention that the Notables lack power in New Haven. What we *are* saying, however, is that this conclusion is not adequately supported by his analysis of the "issue-areas" of public education and party nominations.

The same may not be said of redevelopment. This issue is by any reasonable standard important for purposes of determining whether New Haven is ruled by "the hidden hand of an economic elite."[24] For the Economic Notables have taken an active interest in the program and, beyond that, the socio-economic implications of it are not necessarily in harmony with the basic interests and values of businesses and businessmen.

[21] *Ibid.*, p. 467.
[22] *Who Governs?*, p. 82. Dahl points out that the main policy thrusts of the Economic Notables is to oppose tax increases; this leads them to oppose expenditures for anything more than minimal traditional city services. In this effort their two most effective weapons ordinarily are the mayor and the Board of Finance. The policies of the Notables are most easily achieved under a strong mayor if his policies coincide with theirs or under a weak mayor if they have the support of the Board of Finance. . . . New Haven mayors have continued to find it expedient to create confidence in their final policies among businessmen by appointing them to the Board." (pp. 81–2)
[23] Dahl does discuss in general terms (pp. 79–84) changes in the level of tax rates and assessments in past years, but not actual decisions of the Board of Finance or their effects on the public school system.
[24] *Ibid.*, p. 124.

In an effort to assure that the redevelopment program would be acceptable to what he dubbed "the biggest muscles" in New Haven, Mayor Lee created the Citizens Action Commission (CAC) and appointed to it primarily representatives of the economic elite. It was given the function of overseeing the work of the mayor and other officials involved in redevelopment, and, as well, the responsibility for organizing and encouraging citizens' participation in the program through an extensive committee system.

In order to weigh the relative influence of the mayor, other key officials, and the members of the CAC, Dahl reconstructs "all the *important* decisions on redevelopment and renewal between 1950–58 . . . [to] determine which individuals most often initiated the proposals that were finally adopted or most often successfully vetoed the proposals of the others." [25] The results of this test indicate that the mayor and his development administrator were by far the most influential, and that the "muscles" on the Commission, excepting in a few trivial instances, "never directly initiated, opposed, vetoed, or altered any proposal brought before them. . . ." [26]

This finding is, in our view, unreliable, not so much because Dahl was compelled to make a subjective selection of what constituted *important* decisions within what he felt to be an *important* "issue-area," as because the finding was based upon an excessively narrow test of influence. To measure relative influence solely in terms of the ability to initiate and veto proposals is to ignore the possible exercise of influence or power in limiting the scope of initiation. How, that is to say, can a judgment be made as to the relative influence of Mayor Lee and the CAC without knowing (through prior study of the political and social views of all concerned) the proposals that Lee did *not* make because he anticipated that they would provoke strenuous opposition and, perhaps, sanctions on the part of the CAC? [27]

---

[25] *Ibid.* "A rough test of a person's overt or covert influence," Dahl states in the first section of the book, "is the frequency with which he successfully initiates an important policy over the opposition of others, or vetoes policies initiated by others, or initiates a policy where no opposition appears." *Ibid.*, p. 66.

[26] *Ibid.*, p. 121.

[27] Dahl is, of course, aware of the "law of anticipated reactions." In the case of the mayor's relationship with the CAC, Dahl notes that Lee was "particularly skillful in estimating what the CAC could be expected to support or reject." (p. 137). However, Dahl was not interested in analyzing or appraising to what-extent the CAC limited Lee's freedom of action. Because of his restricted concept of power, Dahl did not consider that the CAC might in this respect have exercised power. That the CAC did not initiate or veto actual proposals by the mayor was to Dahl evidence enough that the CAC was virtually powerless; it might as plausibly be evidence that the CAC was (in itself or in what it represented) so powerful that Lee ventured nothing it would find worth quarreling with.

In sum, since he does not recognize *both* faces of power, Dahl is in no position to evaluate the relative influence or power of the initiator and decision-maker, on the one hand, and of those persons, on the other, who may have been indirectly instrumental in preventing potentially dangerous issues from being raised.[28] As a result, he unduly emphasizes the importance of initiating, deciding, and vetoing, and in the process casts the pluralist conclusions of his study into serious doubt.

V

We have contended in this paper that a fresh approach to the study of power is called for, an approach based upon a recognition of the two faces of power. Under this approach the researcher would begin—not, as does the sociologist who asks, "Who rules?" nor as does the pluralist who asks, "Does anyone have power?"—but by investigating the particular "mobilization of bias" in the institution under scrutiny. Then, having analyzed the dominant values, the myths and the established political procedures and rules of the game, he would make a careful inquiry into which persons or groups, if any, gain from the existing bias and which, if any, are handicapped by it. Next, he would investigate the dynamics of *nondecision-making;* that is, he would examine the extent to which and the manner in which the *status quo* oriented persons and groups influence those community values and those political institutions (as, *e.g.,* the unanimity "rule" of New York City's Board of Estimate[29]) which tend to limit the scope of actual decision-making to "safe" issues. Finally, using his knowledge of the restrictive face of power as a foundation for analysis and as a standard for distinguishing between "key" and "routine"

---

[28] The fact that the initiator of decisions also refrains—because he anticipates adverse reactions—from initiating other proposals does not obviously lessen the power of the agent who limited his initiative powers. Dahl missed this point: "It is," he writes, "all the more improbable, then, that a secret cabal of Notables dominates the public life of New Haven through means so clandestine that not one of the fifty prominent citizens interviewed in the course of this study—citizens who had participated extensively in various decisions—hinted at the existence of such a cabal . . ." (p. 185).

In conceiving of elite domination exclusively in the form of a conscious cabal exercising the power of decision-making and vetoing, he overlooks a more subtle form of domination; one in which those who actually dominate are not conscious of it themselves, simply because their position of dominance has never seriously been challenged.

[29] Sayre and Kaufman, *op. cit.,* p. 640. For perceptive study of the "mobilization of bias" in a rural American community, see Arthur Vidich and Joseph Bensman, *Small Town in Mass Society* (Princeton: 1958).

political decisions, the researcher would, after the manner of the pluralists, analyze participation in decision-making of concrete issues.*

We reject in advance as unimpressive the possible criticism that this approach to the study of power is likely to prove fruitless because it goes beyond an investigation of what is objectively measurable. In reacting against the subjective aspects of the sociological model of power, the pluralists have, we believe, made the mistake of discarding "unmeasurable elements" as unreal. It is ironical that, by so doing, they have exposed themselves to the same fundamental criticism they have so forcefully levelled against the elitists: their approach to and assumptions about power predetermine their findings and conclusions.

---

* Ed. Note: The student should not misunderstand the authors' position here to mean that determining the distribution of values or benefits in a social or political system will allow one to know the distribution of power. The temptation to equate the possession of values and benefits with influence is strong, but should be resisted. The reasons for this have been cataloged by Nelson Polsby: "(1) value distributions occur without explicit decisions taking place, hence may tell us nothing about decision-making; (2) values within the community may be distributed in important ways as a by-product of decisions and "non-decisions made outside the community; (3) there are many irrationalities in decision-making, which may lead to the distribution of values in unpredictable, unintended ways; (4) the powerful may intentionally distribute values to the non-powerful."

Rancorous Conflict in Community Politics

William A. Gamson

The following article reports a study of conflict in eighteen New England communities. Nine communities in which community conflicts are often rancorous or hostile are compared with an equal number of communities in which rancorous conflict is rare. In all, William Gamson studied 54 different issues, including the flouridation of water systems (which arose in all 18 cities), as well as education, zoning, and community development.

The author seeks to identify factors which might explain the different ways the communities handle conflict. He does not explicitly consider the relationship between the nature of conflict and the patterns of community influence, but, as we suggested in the section introduction, work of this sort may provide the groundwork upon which such relationships can be formulated.

Community issues differ in many respects. Some involve vitriolic exchanges of threats and denunciations while others run their course through routine hearings and are resolved before unfilled council chambers. The same issue—for example, fluoridation—may run its course in undramatic fashion in one town, but prove to be the trigger for an explosive confrontation in another town with seemingly similar characteristics. This paper addresses itself to the structural differences between those communities in which such outbursts occur and those in which they do not.

In particular, two ways of carrying on conflict in the local community are contrasted. In *conventional conflicts*, established means of political expression are used to influence the outcome of issues. Opponents regard each other as mistaken or as pursuing different but legitimate goals, but not as the representatives of evil forces. Such tactics as threats of punishment, personal vilification, and deliberate, conscious deceptions are not involved. In contrast to conventional conflicts, *rancorous conflicts* are characterized by the belief that norms about the waging of political con-

From William A. Gamson, "Rancorous Conflict in Community Politics," *American Sociological Review*, XXXI (January, 1966), 71–81.

flict in American communities have been violated. In such conflicts, actions occur which produce a shared belief that tactics used to influence the outcome are "dirty," "underhanded," "vicious" and so forth.

Some communities are much more prone than others to rancorous conflicts. The differences between rancorous and conventional communities can be organized under three general headings: structural conduciveness, structural strain, and structural integration.[1] *Conduciveness* refers to the extent to which structural characteristics in the community permit or encourage rancorous conflicts. *Strain* refers to the extent to which structural characteristics generate discontent or dissatisfaction among the community members. *Integration* refers to the extent to which structural characteristics prevent or inhibit rancorous conflict. Although integration is just the other side of conduciveness, each refers to different structural elements. In other words, we do not consider the absence of integration as an element of conduciveness or the presence of integration as the absence of conduciveness.

The three categories of determinant are highly related to each other. High conduciveness will not produce rancorous conflict if unaccompanied by strain nor if, although accompanied by strain, structural integration is great. High strain will not produce rancorous conflict unless the social structure is conducive to conflict and structural integration is inadequate. The absence of structural integration will not produce rancorous conflict if there is little strain or conduciveness. In other words, we should expect rancorous conflicts *to occur most frequently in those communities characterized by high conduciveness, high strain, and low integration.*

Structural Conduciveness. Such highly general categories as conduciveness, strain, and integration need specification if they are to be measured. With respect to conduciveness, we will focus on two aspects of community social structure: the degree to which it encourages widespread citizen participation and the degree to which it offers highly visible targets for the expression of rancor.

Participative Political Structure. The more the political structure permits or encourages widespread citizen participation, the greater is the conduciveness to rancorous conflict. Since it is typically argued that such conflict is encouraged by the *closing* of channels of legitimate political

---

[1] I draw here on Neil J. Smelser, *Theory of Collective Behavior,* (New York: The Free Press of Glencoe, 1963). He organizes his discussion of the determinants of collective behavior under six categories. Three of them are covered here with slight differences in terminology and formulation. The other three—the growth and spread of a generalized belief, precipitating factors, and mobilization of participants for action—are not included because our objective is to understand the structural differences between communities rather than the outbreak of a given episode at a particular time in a community. The discussion which follows also draws heavily on James S. Coleman, *Community Conflct,* (New York: The Free Press of Glencoe, 1957).

expression, this hypothesis needs defense. The argument for the proposition may take a weak or a strong form. In the weak form, a distinction is made between the intensity and the frequency of rancorous conflict. In high participation communities, it is argued, the political system offers not only an instrumental channel but an expressive one as well. Mild discontent which might otherwise find no outlet or a non-political one is encouraged to find political expression. In finding frequent release in this fashion, such discontent does not build up an explosive potential. Although rancorous conflicts may occur less frequently in communities with a non-participative political structure, they have more intensity when they do occur.

The stronger form of the argument is a denial of the counter-proposition that the blocking of channels of political expression encourages rancorous conflict. This argument challenges the assumption that there is a reservoir of discontent which will either find controlled outlet in legitimate political expression or will accumulate until the dam bursts. Instead, it is assumed that the relief or exacerbation of discontent depends on the nature of the resultant decisions made and not on the catharsis which comes from political expression. If the political system allows for high political participation but does not deal successfully with the sources of dissatisfaction, then rancorous conflicts are *more* likely to occur because strain is combined with high conduciveness. Only when political participation is combined with the influence which can alleviate the source of discontent do rancorous conflicts become less likely. This argument does not imply that high citizen participation is necessarily conducive to rancorous conflict (and hence is bad), but merely that participation does not automatically remove strain.

Given the truth of this proposition, then it is false that such actions as civil rights demonstrations must lessen the probability of other less orderly expressions. As long as the underlying sources of strain are not dealt with, such participation simply increases structural conduciveness and thus makes other expressions more likely. Of course, if the action also helps to remove the strain, for example, by aiding the passage of remedial legislation, then the *net* effect may be to reduce the probability of other less orderly expressions.

A study of fluoridation by Crain, Katz, and Rosenthal contains some suggestive results concerning this hypothesis.[2] They find that the participative nature of the political structure affects both the degree of controversy about fluoridation and the likelihood of its adoption. "Governments which do not place 'obstacles' such as political parties between the

---

[2] Robert L. Crain, Elihu Katz, and Donald B. Rosenthal, *The Fluoridation Decision: Community Structure and Innovation*, forthcoming.

citizen and the decision-makers experience the pattern of a large number of referenda and high controversy [as well as high rejection]." Fluoridation is at least more likely to provoke strong controversy where participative political structures provide conduciveness.[3]

Solidary Groups. The greater the clarity of solidary groups within a social structure, the greater is the conduciveness to rancorous conflict. Communities differ in the extent to which they contain sub-groups with: (1) feelings of membership or identification with a group or collectivity; (2) feelings of common interest with respect to political decisions; (3) a common style of life, norms, and values; (4) a high rate of interaction among themselves. The degree of solidarity of a sub-group is its magnitude on the above characteristics; the clarity of solidary group structure is the extent to which there exist community sub-groups of high solidarity.

Clearly identifiable solidary groups are conducive to rancorous conflict because they provide readily identifiable targets for hostility. Such subdivisions of the community do not in themselves signify cleavage. Nevertheless, any clear-cut basis of differentiation among the citizens of a town may provide a structural basis for the development of inter-group hostility if there also exist strains and low integration among solidary groups.

Structural Strain. Any part of the social structure may produce strains which are relevant for rancorous conflict in the community. Many strains originate outside of the community but have ramifications for the social and political life of the town. There are undoubtedly strains deriving from fear of nuclear war, increasing bureaucratization, depersonalization, commercialism, manipulation, and so forth. Such strains may make their own contributions to rancorous conflicts in the community,[4] but they are felt by all communities, rancorous as well as conventional. Therefore, we must turn to strains which can differentiate our communities in order to explain why some are prone to rancorous conflict and others are not.

There are many possibilities. Although the specification of such strains requires detailed knowledge of the particular communities in question, it seems likely that they are connected with change. The change might include, for example, rapid economic growth or decline, heavy in-migra-

---

[3] The volatile nature of California politics may be due (among other things) to the structural conduciveness stemming from a long tradition of initiative and referendum.

[4] A good deal of recent work on such strains has used the rubric of "alienation." See, for example, John E. Horton and Wayne E. Thompson, "Powerlessness and Political Negativism: A Study of Defeated Local Referendums," *American Journal of Sociology*, 68 (March, 1962), 485–93; Kenneth Keniston, "Alienation and the Decline of Utopia," *American Scholar*, 29 (Spring, 1960), 161–200; and William A. Gamson, "The Fluoridation Dialogue: Is it an Ideological Conflict?" *Public Opinion Quarterly*, 25 (Winter, 1961), 526–37.

tion or out-migration, or shifts in the distribution of power in the community. For two reasons I have chosen to focus on strains emanating from a shift in political control: (1) the existence or non-existence of a shift in control sharply differentiates the communities studied here; (2) a shift in political control is likely to be a reflection of other strains as well as a creator of strains in its own right.

Shifts in political control are a source of structural strain which contribute to rancorous conflict. I have in mind here something broader than the circulation of elites. In particular, two kinds of shift will be considered. They have in common the existence of a relatively homogeneous group whose leaders find that they face competition in areas of decision-making where they did not before, or that they are competing less successfully than before. In one type of community, there are clear solidary groups with one gaining or losing political power relative to others. In a second type of community, a homogeneous native population has been, or threatens to be, supplanted by a large, heterogeneous, and politically active group of newcomers.

Structural Integration. Strain and conduciveness deal with those characteristics of social structure that promote or encourage rancorous conflict. We now turn our attention to those features which tend to control or inhibit such expressions. Basically, we expect rancorous and conventional communities to differ in the extent to which potential antagonists are bound together. In particular, we examine the connections which exist between those with different opinions on community issues. Are proponents and opponents bound by associational ties, by friendship, or by shared backgrounds? If they are not, then we should expect a given amount of strain and conduciveness to be more likely to produce rancorous conflict. We will consider three kinds of tie here.

Organizational Ties. The greater the degree of common organizational membership among proponents and opponents, the greater the resistance to rancorous conflict. If the organizational life of a community puts potential antagonists together in a variety of meetings over a variety of issues, they are likely to find occasions for agreement, to develop bonds of friendship, a sense of joint accomplishment, and other integrative ties. When a disagreement occurs, it should be less likely to produce the kind of break in a relationship which rancorous conflict represents.

Interpersonal Ties. The greater the degree of friendship among proponents and opponents, the greater the resistance to rancorous conflict. If potential antagonists know each other well socially, such friendship bonds should help to provide that degree of trust and belief in good faith which inhibit rancorous conflicts.

Shared Background. The more proponents and opponents tend to be of different length of residence, nationality background, education, and religion, the less the resistance to rancorous conflict. These four bases of differentiation were chosen because they seemed particularly likely to be correlated with partisan divisions in the set of New England communities we studied. Since these are the bases of differentiation that presumably underlie solidary groups, this hypothesis might appear to be simply another statement of the earlier one on structural conduciveness. We argued above that the existence of clear sub-groups was conducive to rancorous conflict but that they did not, in themselves, signify cleavage. It is possible to have solidary groups which cross-cut issues, thus giving proponents and opponents an important common group membership. It is also possible to find the opposite—that proponents and opponents have different background characteristics but lack any feeling of membership or identification with distinct community sub-groups. Even where clear solidary groups are not present, the absence of these integrative bonds should make such communities more vulnerable to rancorous conflict. Finally, it is possible to have full fledged cleavages in which clearly defined solidary groups exist and do correspond to divisions on issues. This condition combines conduciveness with lack of integration; when strain is added, we should particularly expect rancorous conflict.

STUDY DESIGN

The data to be presented here are drawn from a study of fifty-four issues in eighteen New England communities. The towns ranged in size from 2,000 to 100,000, with a median of approximately 10,000. Seven of the communities were essentially suburbs of Boston, three were resort towns, and the remaining eight were more or less independent cities with some industrial base of their own. All but two of the communities were in Maine or Massachusetts.

Material on these communities was gathered through interviews with 426 informants, an average of twenty-four per town, supplemented by information from a variety of documents. Interviewing was done by teams of three or four individuals who stayed in each community for several days. Three issues were studied in each town, one of which, fluoridation, was common to all eighteen. The presence of a decision on fluoridation was, in fact, the basis of selection of these communities; the eighteen comprise all those New England communities which made a fluoridation decision during an eighteen-month period of data collection.

Before any interviews began, each town was investigated through such sources as the local newspaper, formal statistical data from the state and federal censuses, city planning reports, annual town reports, and various state manuals. The persons interviewed fell into two categories: active partisans on both sides of each of the three issues; and people named by these "issue leaders" as influential in the community, i.e., as "reputational leaders." . . .

RESULTS

As Table I indicates, shifts in political control are clearly related to rancorous conflict in this particular set of New England communities. Only one of the nine conventional towns is undergoing political change while two-thirds of the rancorous towns are undergoing such change. Are these rancorous towns also higher on our measures of conduciveness and lower on integration than the conventional towns?

There is a limit to how far one can examine interrelationships among variables with only eighteen communities. Nevertheless, some attempt at this is necessary even at the risk of breaking these eighteen cases down into meaninglessly small cells. Eighteen may be a small number, but it is a great deal larger than the case study or comparison of two or three communities which is typical of the literature on community politics.

TABLE I

Rancorous Conflict and Political Instability

	Rancorous	Conventional
Undergoing political change	6	1
Politically stable	3	8
	—	—
N	9	9

P < .05 (Fisher's Exact Test).

There is little overall relationship between the measures of conduciveness used here—participative political structure and presence of clear solidary groups—and the presence of rancorous conflict. As Table II indicates, communities without town meetings are about as likely to have rancorous conflicts as those with them. Solidary groups are present about as often in rancorous as in conventional ones. These results are not, in themselves, negative evidence since we would not expect higher conduciveness alone (without evidence of strain) to produce differences between the two kinds of community. However, there is little suggestion in these data that, for those seven towns with political instability, the presence of town meetings or solidary groups increases the likelihood of rancorous conflict. It is true that four out of five politically unstable communities which have town meetings are rancorous, but then both of the unstable towns without town meetings are rancorous also. Three out of four of the unstable towns with solidary groups are rancorous but all three of the unstable towns without such groups are rancorous. Put another way, the one exception among the seven politically unstable communities is *not* lower on our measures of conduciveness; it has both solidary groups and town meetings to accompany its political strain but still it is not rancorous. For the measures used here the evidence on the conduciveness hypotheses must be considered inconclusive at best.

There is no overall relationship between rancorous conflict and the extent to which some organization provides a central focus for those involved in community affairs. However, if we focus specifically on the

TABLE II

Rancorous Conflict and Structural Conduciveness

	Rancorous	Conventional
Has town meeting form of government	6	5
Does not have town meeting form of government	3	4
N	$\overline{9}$	$\overline{9}$
Solidary groups present	4	5
Solidary groups absent	5	4
N	$\overline{9}$	$\overline{9}$

seven politically unstable towns, there is some indication that this variable does have an effect. Using as our measure the ratio of the largest number of respondent memberships in any single organization to the total number of respondents in a town, we find that the six politically unstable rancorous communities have an average ratio of 0.32 as against 0.41 for the eleven towns without political strain ($p<0.05$); the one conventional town among the politically unstable has a ratio of 0.45, well above average on this measure of integration.

The average degree of acquaintance among opponents is substantially lower in rancorous than in conventional towns—2.89 vs. 2.39 ($p<0.05$, using a one tailed test).[5] Among the politically unstable towns, the

[5] A lower score indicates closer friendships.

TABLE III

Rancorous Conflict and Cleavage

	Rancorous	Conventional
All Towns		
CC of .5 or higher on at least one issue *	6	2
CC of less than .5 on all issues	3	7
	—	—
N	9	9
Politically Unstable Towns		
CC of .5 or higher	5	0
CC of less than .5	1	1
Politically Stable Towns		
CC of .5 or higher	1	2
CC of less than .5	2	6
	—	—
N	9	9

* (Or, 50% or less cross-cutting on at least one issue.) CC stands for Coefficient of Cleavage.

relationship is even stronger; the average is 2.97 for the six rancorous towns and the score is 1.50 for the conventional town, ranking it first among the set of 18 in friendship among opponents.

The Coefficient of Cleavage, our last measure of integration or lack of integration, shows similar results.* As Table III indicates, six of eight towns which have at least one issue with a high degree of cleavage between proponents and opponents are rancorous. Five of the six politically unstable and rancorous towns have such sharp differences between proponents and opponents but only three of the other twelve.

Summary. In the towns studied here there were four exceptions to the relationship between political instability and the appearance of rancor-

---

* Ed. note: The "Coefficient of Cleavage" is a function of an issue position held by those surveyed in each community compared to their length of residence, nationality background, religion and education. It is meant to reflect the total cleavage in the community on any given issue. Gamson gives this example: "if there are 10 Protestants and 10 Catholics among 12 proponents and 8 opponents on fluoridation, we would expect by chance to get six Protestant proponents. However, we could get as many as 10 or as few as 2. Thus, the denominator of the coefficient of cleavage (CC) would be: 10 (Maximum frequency)—6 (Expected frequency) = 4. If there were actually nine Protestant proponents, the numerator of the CC would be: 9 (Actual frequency)—6 (Expected frequency) = 3, and the CC would be ¾ = 0.75. The direction of relationship has no significance here. To avoid artificial results due to discontinuity and to simplify calculation, the expected frequencies were always rounded to the nearest integer."

ous conflict. One of these, a town which is politically changing but is not rancorous, scores high on all our measures of integration. But there are also three towns without the kind of political strain measured here which are rancorous. One of these three is the only town among the eighteen which is experiencing severe economic strain. Seven years earlier, a major mill closed and the unemployment rate remained quite high. Numerous stores were empty on Main Street and many of those who were able to leave had already done so. The two other exceptions are not so easily explained. Not only are they not undergoing any political or other obvious strain but they score high on our measures of integration as well. One can, of course, always find some sort of strain in any town but in the absence of special evidence to suggest such strains, rancorous conflict in these two communities must be regarded as unexplained by the hypotheses presented here.

There are two final variables which while they play no role in the hypotheses, might well be affecting the results. The first of these—the type of community—has no relationship to rancorous conflict for this set of towns; four of the nine rancorous communities and four of the nine conventional ones are independent towns rather than suburbs or resorts. Size of town, the second control variable, also has no overall relationship to rancorous conflict; five of the nine largest and four of the nine smallest towns are rancorous. Nevertheless it turns out that all of the exceptions fall among those with population under 5000. As Table IV indicates, there is a perfect relationship between political instability and rancorous conflict for communities over 5000.

DISCUSSION

It is important to specify some content for such general classes of variable as structural strain, conduciveness, and integration. I have tried to do this here by explaining rancorous conflict in terms of the strain which political change provides or reflects, the conduciveness which a participative structure and solidary groups provide, and the integrative ties which a common organizational focus, friendships, and common bonds of nationality, religion, education and length of residence provide. . . .

This paper has a purpose more general than understanding modes of community conflict. Both the specific variables used and the general strategy of political analysis are relevant to a wide variety of political expression. The politics of fluoridation is not so far removed from battles over open-occupancy housing or school Bible readings. The present explanation of rancorous conflict in small communities is not very different

TABLE IV

Rancorous Conflict and Political Instability Controlled
for Size of Town

	Rancorous	Conventional
Towns over 5000		
Undergoing political change	6	0
Politically stable	0	5
Towns under 5000		
Undergoing political change	0	1
Politically stable	3	3
	—	—
(N)	9	9

in kind from the explanation we would use in contrasting countries with or without revolutionary movements. Of course, the content of such general classes of variable as structural conduciveness, strain, and integration may vary in different social-organizational settings. However, if one can establish that a participative political structure promotes conduciveness to rancorous conflict in one setting, it becomes a more plausible hypothesis for other settings. For example, this may explain why apparent improvements or efforts to remove strains may be accompanied by increases in rancorous conflict. Such changes may have their initial or most radical effects on conduciveness or on sources of structural integration or control and only secondary effects on the removal of sources of discontent. The study of such limited phenomena as rancorous conflicts in communities may teach us something more general about social movements and social change.

Because of the negative connotations of a term like "rancorous conflict," some final observations about the towns studied here are worth making. Many of the conventional communities are rather dull and stagnant, while some of the rancorous ones are among the most vital. Some of the conventional towns not only have an absence of rancorous conflict but a general absence of change; the rancorous towns have the strains that accompany change but some of them also have the advantages of stimulation and growth. The absence of rancorous conflict is no necessary sign of an "ideal" community.

Community Power and a Typology of Social Issues

Ernest A. T. Barth

Stuart D. Johnson

The authors of this article seek to formulate a multi-dimensional scheme for classifying social issues which will be related to alternative patterns of community power. As we have seen throughout this book, the issues one studies may shape one's perspective of the distribution of influence. Barth and Johnson speculate on the relationship between different types of issues, different kinds of leaders, and different patterns of decision-making. They readily acknowledge that their typology is only a tentative framework, and they make some useful suggestions about steps to be taken to improve their outline. One step which they do not mention is to specify the relationships among their five dimensions.

In a recent critical analysis of the research approaches to the study of community decision making, Peter Rossi identified three major research gaps.[1] The first of these pertained to the fact that "none of the studies reviewed have considered the full range of issues which come before a particular decision maker."[2] The second is concerned with the fact that, "the issues which have been subjected to study have been on the more dramatic side, perhaps more properly labeled 'controversies'." This constitutes a research gap in the thinking of Rossi because "by and large we can expect that most issues up for decision are settled without becoming controversies."[3] The third major gap in present research involves Rossi's belief that, "Research on decision making should be extensive

From Ernest A. T. Barth and Stuart D. Johnson, "Community Power and a Typology of Social Issues," *Social Forces*, XXXVIII (October, 1959) 29–32. Reprinted by permission of the authors and publisher.

[1] The authors wish to thank the Research Fund of the Graduate School of the University of Washington for the financial support which has made it possible for them to carry on research in this area.

[2] Peter H. Rossi, "Community Decision Making," *Administrative Science Quarterly,* I (March, 1957), 438–39.

[3] *Ibid.*, p. 441.

rather than intensive and comparative rather than the case study technique." He amplifies this point by saying, "three levels of comparison would be made: decision makers of different types, operating within different community and institutional settings, should be compared as they come to the settlement of a *range of issues*. This approach implies a sampling of decision makers, of issues, and of communities." [4]

It is the purpose of this paper to point out the importance of concern with the *type of issue* under consideration by decision makers and to suggest the basis for a typology of issues. [5]

The primary focus of recent research on community decision making has been on the identification of decision makers and the description of their background characteristics and interpersonal relations within a given community context. Relatively little attention has been given to the systematic analysis of the conditions under which influencing behavior occurs. [6] As Rossi has indicated, one set of such conditions involves issue content, and, in the thinking of the present authors, this condition has been greatly neglected.

Failure to consider the impact of issue content on the selection of influentials has led to problems in building models adequate to describe structures of community influence. For example, Hunter, in his study of power in "Regional City," allowed his sample of community leaders to designate the issues which they thought were of major concern to the community. [7] He then discovered that these leaders held a central place in the decision-making processes centering on issues which they had described. One might ask whether the almost monolithic structure of leadership which he found in that community was not, in fact, an artifact resulting from his methodology. Might not it be argued that, had he set out to discover the patterns of power organization operating around a *range* of issues, he might have found a somewhat different and less solidary power structure? It might be further argued that if different types of issues in a community tend to be selective of different types of leaders, then the task which Hunter set before his respondents (i.e., that of choosing "the biggest man in the community," or of selecting the "ten leaders who nearly everyone would accept."), is an almost impossible task. His respondents might legitimately have asked, "Biggest man with respect to what type of activities?"

A second problem which is central to the understanding of the in-

---

[4] *Ibid.*, pp. 438–39.
[5] For a further discussion of this point see Nelson W. Polsby, "The Sociology of Community Power: A Reassessment," *Social Forces*, 37 (March, 1959), 232–36.
[6] Rossi, *op. cit.*, p. 438.
[7] Floyd Hunter, *Community Power Structure: A Study of Decision Makers* (Chapel Hill: The University of North Carolina Press, 1954).

fluencing process relates to observations that not all issues come to the attention of the most influential decision makers. If one distinguishes between the "top level" leadership and the "understructure" leadership, as did Hunter,[8] it becomes evident that some issues never come before the former group, while other issues achieve major importance to them.

A third consideration in the study of influence systems derives from attempts to compare influence systems, along with the processes which characterize them, in different community settings. For example, in attempting to characterize the structure of relations among the top leaders of "Pacific City," Miller developed the concepts of "top influentials" and "key influentials" who were viewed as interacting in accordance with what he termed a "fluid coalition" model.[9] This model is distinct from the "monolithic power structure" model which Hunter felt described the structure of power relations in "Regional City."

Since the present authors find little reason to question the major findings and conclusions of either Miller or Hunter, aside from the methodological perspective mentioned above, it seems reasonable to assume that the structure of the influence system and the kinds of participants in decision-making processes vary with the types of issues facing a community at any given time. For example, the range of issues will be very different for a metropolitan center as compared to an open-country community; for a southern, as compared with a northern or western community; and for a college town as compared to an industrial center. For the reasons cited above, it appears then, that there is a pressing need for research leading to the development of a typology of issues.

BASIS FOR AN EMPIRICAL TYPOLOGY OF ISSUES

In a pilot project the authors attempted to derive a typology of community issues based upon industrial categories. In analyzing questionnaire data from a sample of community residents, issues were classed together when they appeared to deal with subject matter falling into given institutional sectors of community life such as economic issues, political issues, and educational issues. It quickly became apparent that classification was arbitrary, some issues falling under two or more headings, and similar patterns of influencing behavior appeared in different institutional settings. Therefore, on the basis of this experience, it was concluded that such a classification of issue content would not produce a fruitful typology.

[8] *Ibid.*, p. 57.
[9] Delbert C. Miller, "The Prediction of Issue Outcome in Community Decision Making," *Research Studies of the State College of Washington,* XXV, No. 2 (June, 1957).

The pilot study did provide us with the following conclusions. In developing a typology of issues it is of primary importance to view the dimensions along which community issues are to be typed in terms of two major requirements. First, to be of maximum value, the dimensions must be generic to all issues. Second, variations in each dimension must be theoretically relatable to variations in patterns of influencing behavior. Thus, they must not only meet the test of logical inclusiveness, but they must also meet the empirical test of being "tied" to observable leadership behavior. Our concern in the present analysis is with the following three aspects of influencing behavior:

(1) the types of community structures involved in the flow of influence with respect to a range of issues;

(2) the direction of the flow of influence on any issue;

(3) the direction of the flow of communications around a range of issues.

Reanalysis of the pilot study data led to the development of the following five dimensions. Each meets the specifications mentioned above in that each is generic to all community issues, and each is relatable to the structure of influencing behavior. For these reasons it is suggested that they will profitably serve as a basis for the development of a typology of community issues. It should be noted, however, that each dimension is treated from the point of view of the actors in the community—in this case from the point of view of community leaders. It is their perception of community issues that modifies the type of action which they attempt to undertake with respect to the different kinds of issues.

Unique—Recurrent Dimension

It may be predicted that differentiated social organizations tend to evolve out of a community's recurrent experiences with a given type of community issue. Thus, the problem of dealing with recurrent issues, when they arise in a community, would in all likelihood be handled by constituted community agencies having access to regularly allocated resources. On the other hand, in the case of a unique issue (one which community leaders feel has not been previously experienced), no such structure or procedure would necessarily be available to members of the community. Therefore, when decisions must be made on such issues, leadership tends to be emergent, and resources would have to be developed. Such leadership would probably be less subject to formal community social controls. In addition, such leaders would also be more likely to have less restricted access to the *means* of power, such as money and the control of jobs, than in the case of a regularly organized community agency dealing administratively with a recurrent issue.

Salient—Nonsalient to Leadership

Community issues vary along a continuum from some that are central to the interests of community leaders and the organizational structures in which they hold positions, to some that are peripheral to their interests and of little concern to them. When an issue is of great importance to community leaders, but perceived to be of little importance to the general public of a community, action taken on that issue may be unpublicized and directed through informal influence structures. If, however, leaders feel that a "public relations program—" is required, communications regarding the issue will generally flow from leaders to community members, frequently through the mass media. On the other hand, community leaders may be "forced to act" on some issues that are of little relevance to their personal interests when public pressures are brought to bear upon them. Under such circumstances, they may be *reacting* to the upward flow of communications exercised through formal mechanisms of the community such as political parties or the hierarchies of public offices.

Salient—Nonsalient to Community Publics

This dimension refers to the degree of prominence, or importance, which leaders feel the various community publics attach to specific issues. Issues of low salience to community leaders, which are perceived as being of low salience to the general public, are likely to be handled by professional community organizers or lower echelon power figures. In such cases, the flow of influence and communications would be predominantly from decision makers to followers. When an issue is thought to be highly salient to the public, the potential decision makers are likely to be concerned with the "public relations" of any decision. Under such conditions one might expect that the flow of communications and influence would be generally upward, from public to "decision makers." [10]

[10] There appear to be two polar views of the community leadership or influencing process. In one, the leader, or decision maker, is seen as making decisions in a rather arbitrary fashion and then implementing them by manipulating the means of power at his command. The other view sees the decision maker in the *process* of decision making. It views him from the time he discovers the need for action on any particular issue until he takes action on that issue. This latter view focuses on the communications behavior of leaders. It stresses the fact that leaders are in constant communication with relevant (or interested) publics for any issue. Such an approach makes it problematic as to whether the leader is exercising individual initiative in announcing a decision, or whether he is simply expressing an already formed, but latent (uncrystallized) community consensus on that issue. It appears to the authors that both types of processes operate. The problem at present is to discover the conditions under which one takes precedence over the other.

Effective Action Possible—Effective Action Impossible

Some issues might be highly salient to the members of a community, or a segment thereof, and at the same time be perceived as necessitating impossible decisions or requiring inaccessible resources. For example, many southern communities have felt a strong need to improve the level of education offered to the local children. However, often they have had to face the fact that money was not available for new buildings, libraries, and other facilities. In addition, they realized that it was difficult to attract well qualified teachers with the low salaries which could be offered. For this type of issue, the only type of action which is undertaken involves the development of "tension-reducing mechanisms," or, perhaps, merely the manipulation of symbols.

Local—Cosmopolitan Dimension

When the leaders of a local community perceive an issue as concerning programs and problems dealt with by other organizations in the state or nation, they tend to look, in many cases, to higher levels of organization for guides and direction in program development. If, however, an issue is perceived as purely local in its implications, then it is probable that the range of alternative courses of action will be seen as less limited, and the need for recourse to "experts" from outside the community will be lessened.

DIRECTIONS FOR FUTURE RESEARCH

If this five-dimensional basis for a typology of community issues is to be fruitfully applied to the study of community power and influence, then the following steps will seemingly have to be undertaken.

1. An instrument will have to be developed for the purpose of measuring and locating specific issues along these dimensions.

2. A set of issues, representative of the variety of issues facing a given community will have to be obtained from community leaders, and the leaders will have to describe each issue in terms of the instrument referred to in step 1. Information will also be required regarding the patterns of influence and communications associated with each issue.

3. An empirical typology of community issues will have to be developed from the data on community issues.

4. Finally, the resulting typology of issues will have to be related to the patterns of influence and communications behavior. At this point one would expect to find identifiable patterns of influence and commu-

nications flow associated with each type of issue. It would also be expected that specific types of community structures would be regularly involved in the decision-making process for the different types of issues.

At the present stage of our thinking, it has appeared meaningful to conceive of issues as flowing through a life cycle approximating the public opinion life cycle suggested by Foote and Hart.[11] Thus, an issue would be visualized as "living through" five phases: (a) the phase of emergence of the problem; (b) the proposal phase; (c) the policy-making phase; (d) the program phase; and finally, (e) the appraisal phase. It is expected that different types of issues will exhibit varying patterns of influence and communications flow for the several stages of issue life cycle. Therefore, this factor would have to be controlled in selecting a sample of issues for study.

A classification of community issues based on the dimensions proposed in this paper will make it possible to control one of the major variables in the study of influence systems. In this manner it should be possible to clarify some of the problems characteristic of attempts to identify the structure of influence systems. In addition, it should clear the way for comparative research on influence systems in different community contexts.

[11] Nelson N. Foote and Clyde W. Hart, "Public Opinion and Collective Behavior," *Group Relations at the Crossroads*, Sherif and Wilson, eds. (New York: Harper and Brothers, 1953), pp. 308–31.

The Power of Power

James G. March

This article formulates several models of power relations and explores the problems involved in using each of these to analyze systems of social choice. It represents an important step toward the development of empirical theories of community power.

Another value of these models of social power is that each suggests an alternative pattern in the distribution of community power. When formulating study designs, researchers would do well to keep these models in mind to ensure that their methods of inquiry do not preclude the discovery of any of these alternatives. Similarly, the models suggest what things one may want to look for when evidence developed in the process of research suggests that the dominant pattern of power in a community resembles one model more than another.

Students with a mathematical background will find their understanding of March's ideas enhanced by turning to the original article with its mathematical formulation of the models.

INTRODUCTION

Power is a major explanatory concept in the study of social choice. It is used in studies of relations among nations, of community decision making, of business behavior, and of small-group discussion. Partly because it conveys simultaneously overtones of the cynicism of *Realpolitik,* the glories of classical mechanics, the realism of elite sociology, and the comforts of anthropocentric theology, *power* provides a prime focus for disputation and exhortation in several social sciences.

Within this galaxy of nuances, I propose to consider a narrowly technical question: To what extent is one specific concept of power useful in the empirical analysis of mechanisms for social choice? The narrowness of

Abridged from "The Power of Power" by James G. March in *Varieties of Political Theories,* David Easton, ed., © 1966. By permission of Prentice-Hall, Inc., Englewood Cliffs, N.J.

the question is threefold. First, only theories that focus on mechanisms of choice are considered. Second, only considerations of utility for the development or testing of empirically verifiable theories are allowed. Third, only one concept of power—or one class of concepts—is treated. The question is technical in the sense that it has primary relevance for the drudgery of constructing a predictive theory; the immediate implications for general theories of society, for the layman confronted with his own complex environment, or for the casual student, are probably meager. They certainly are not developed here.

By a mechanism for social choice, I mean nothing more mysterious than a committee, jury, legislature, commission, bureaucracy, court, market, firm, family, gang, mob, and various combinations of these into economic, political, and social systems. Despite their great variety, each of these institutions can be interpreted as a mechanism for amalgamating the behavior (preferences, actions, decisions) of subunits into the behavior of the larger institution; thus, each acts as a mechanism for social choice. The considerations involved in evaluating the usefulness of power as a concept are the same for all the mechanisms cited above, although it is patently not necessarily true that the conclusions need be the same.

By an empirically verifiable theory, I mean a theory covered by the standard dicta about prediction and confirmation. We will ask under what circumstances the use of *power* contributes to the predictive power of the theory.

The specific concept of power I have in mind is the concept used in theories having the following general assumptions:

1. The choice mechanism involves certain basic components (individuals, groups, roles, behaviors, labels, etc.).
2. Some amount of power is associated with each of these components.
3. The responsiveness (as measured by some direct empirical observation) of the mechanism to each individual component is monotone increasing with the power associated with the individual component.

There are a number of variations on this general theme, each with idiosyncratic problems; but within a well-defined (and relatively large) class of uses of the concept of power, power plays the same basic role. It is a major intervening variable between an initial condition, defined largely in terms of the individual components of the system, and a terminal state, defined largely in terms of the system as a whole. . . .

I wish to examine six different classes of models of social choice that are generally consistent with what at least one substantial group of students means by *social power*. In this examination, I will ask what empirical and technical problems there are in the use of the concept of power and in the use of alternative concepts, and under what circumstances the concept of power does, or can, contribute to the effective prediction of social choice. . . .

Six Models of Social Choice and the Concept of Power

I wish to explore the utility of the concept of power in the analysis of systems for social choice. The utility depends first, on the true characteristics of the system under investigation. The concept of power must be embedded in a model and the validity of the model is a prerequisite to the utility of the concept. Second, the utility depends on the technical problems of observation, estimation, and validation in using the concept in an empirically reasonable model.

Consider six types of models of social choice. . . .

1. Chance models, in which we assume that choice is a chance event, quite independent of power.

2. Basic force models, in which we assume that the components of the system exert all their power on the system with choice being a direct resultant of those powers.

3. Force activation models, in which we assume that not all the power of every component is exerted at all times.

4. Force-conditioning models, in which we assume that the power of the components is modified as a result of the outcome of past choices.

5. Force depletion models, in which we assume that the power of the components is modified as a result of the exertion of power on past choices.

6. Process models, in which we assume that choice is substantially independent of power but not a chance event. . . .

Chance Models

Let us assume that there are no attributes of human beings affecting the output of a social-choice mechanism. Further, let us assume that the only factors influencing the output are chance factors, constrained perhaps by some initial conditions. . . .

What are the implications of such models? . . .

. . . All of the chance models generate power distributions. They are spurious distributions in the sense that power, as we usually mean it, had nothing to do with what happened. But we can still apply our measures of power to the systems involved. After observing such a system, one can make statements about the distribution of power in the system and describe how power was exercised. Despite these facts, I think that most students of power would agree that if a specific social-choice system is in fact a chance mechanism, the concept of power is not a valuable concept for that system.

To what extent is it possible to reject the chance models in studies of social choice? Although there are some serious problems in answering that question, I think we would probably reject a pure-chance model as a reasonable model. I say this with some trepidation because studies of power have generally not considered such alternative models, and many features of many studies are certainly consistent with a chance interpretation. The answer depends on an evaluation of four properties of the chance models that are potentially inconsistent with data either from field studies or from the laboratory.

First, we ask whether power is stable over time. With most of the chance models, knowing who won in the past or who had a reputation for winning in the past would not help us to predict who would win in the future. Hence, if we can predict the outcome of future social choices by weighting current positions with weights derived from past observations or from a priori considerations, we will have some justification for rejecting the chance model. Some efforts have been made in this direction, but with mixed results. Even conceding the clarity of the tests and the purity of the procedures and assuming that the results were all in the predicted direction, the argument for the various power models against a chance model would be meager. The "powerful" would win about half the time even under the chance hypothesis.

Second, we ask whether power is stable over subject matter. Under the chance models, persons who win in one subject-matter area would be no more likely to win in another area than would people who lost in the first area. Thus, if we find a greater-than-chance overlap from one area to another, we would be inclined to reject the chance model. The evidence on this point is conflicting. As was noted earlier, some studies suggest considerable specialization of power, while others do not. On balance, I find it difficult to reject the chance model on the basis of these results; although it is clear that there are a number of alternative explanations for the lack of stability, nonchance explanations are generally preferred by persons who have observed subject-matter instability.

Third, we ask whether power is correlated with other personal attributes. Under the chance model, power is independent of other attributes. Although it might occasionally be correlated with a specific set of attributes by chance, a consistent correlation would cast doubt on the chance hypothesis. It would have to be saved by some assumption about the inadequacy (that is, irrelevance) of the power measure or by assuming that the covariation results from an effect of power on the correlated attribute. Without any exception of which I am aware, the studies do show a greater-than-chance relation between power and such personal attributes as economic status, political office, and ethnic group. We cannot account under the simple chance model for the consistent underrepresentation of the poor, the unelected, and the Negro.

And fourth, we ask whether power is *susceptible to experimental manipulation*. If the chance model were correct, we could not systematically produce variations in who wins by manipulating power. Here the experimental evidence is fairly clear. It is possible to manipulate the results of choice mechanisms by manipulating personal attributes or personal reputations. Although we may still want to argue that the motivational or institutional setting of real-world choice systems is conspicuously different from the standard experimental situation, we cannot sustain a strictly chance interpretation of the experimental results.

Chance models are extremely naïve; they are the weakest test we can imagine. Yet we have had some difficulty in rejecting them, and in some situations it is not clear that we can reject them. Possibly much of what happens in the world is by chance. If so, it will be a simple world to deal with. Possibly, however, our difficulty is not with the amount of order in the world, but with the concept of power. Before we can render any kind of judgment on that issue, we need to consider some models that might be considered more reasonable by people working in the field.

Basic Force Models

Suppose we assume that power is real and controlling, and start with a set of models that are closely linked with classical mechanics although the detailed form is somewhat different from mechanics. In purest form, the simple force models can be represented in terms of functions that make the resultant social choice a weighted average of the individual initial positions—the weights being the power attached to the various individuals. . . .

Consider the basic characteristics of the simple force models:

1. There are a fixed number of known power sources.
2. At any point in time, each of these sources can be characterized as affecting the social choice by exerting force in terms of two dimensions, magnitude (power) and direction (initial position or behavior).
3. Any given source has a single, exogenously determined power. That is, power is constant (over a reasonable time period and subject-matter domain of observation) and always fully exercised.
4. The result (social choice) is some sum of the individual magnitudes and directions.

Insofar as the determinate models are concerned, both experimental and field observations make it clear that the models are not accurate portrayals of social choice. In order for the models to be accepted, the total power resources of each individual (as defined in the models) must be stable. As far as I know, no one has ever reported data suggesting that such resources are stable in a determinate model. The closest thing to such stability occurs in some experimental groups where the choices consistently come close to the mean, and in some highly formal voting schemes. In such cases, the power indices are occasionally close to stable at a position of equal power. Nevertheless, few students of power have claimed stability of the power indices.

When we move to the probabilistic case—or if we add an error term to the determinate models—the situation becomes more ambiguous. Since it has already been observed that rejection of a purely chance model is not too easy with the available data, the argument can be extended to models that assume significant error terms, or to models in which the number of observations is small enough to introduce significant sampling variation in the estimate of underlying probabilities. . . .

The basis for rejecting the simple force models (aside from the necessity of making them untidy with error terms) is twofold:

(1) There seems to be general consensus that either potential power is different from actually exerted power or that actually exerted power is variable. . . .

(2) There appears to be ample evidence that power is not strictly exogenous to the exercise of power and the results of that exercise. . . .

These objections to the simple force model are general; we now need to turn to models that attempt to deal with endogenous shifts in power and with the problem of power activation or exercise. As we shall see, such models have been little tested and pose some serious problems for evaluation on the basis of existing data. We will consider three classes of models, all of which are elaborations of the simple force models. The first class can be viewed as *activation models*. They assume that power is a potential and that the exercise of power involves some mechanism of activation. The second class can be described as *conditioning models*. They assume that power is partly endogenous—specifically that apparent power leads to actual power. The third class can be classified as *depletion models*. They assume that power is a stock, and that exercise of power leads to a depletion of the stock.

Force Activation Models

The basic force models accept the postulate that all power is exerted all of the time. In fact, few observers of social-choice systems believe this to be true, either for experimental groups or for natural social systems. . . . It is frequently suggested that power must be made relative to a specific set of actions or domain of joint decisions. . . .

We often assume that the participants in the system can vary their exercised power from zero to the total of their power resource. . . .

Consider the problem of relating the activation models to observations of reality. Let us assume initially that potential power is constant over all choices. We assume that there is something called *potential power* that is associated with a component of the choice system and that this power resource does not depend on the choice. In effect, this assumes that [potential power] is also constant over time, for we will require a time series of observations in order to make our estimates. We will relax this assumption in subsequent classes of models, but the constancy assumption is characteristic of most activation models.

Given the assumption of fixed potential power we have two major alternatives. First, we can attempt to determine the degree of activation for each component and each choice and use that information to estimate the potential power for each component. If we can determine by direct observation either the level of power utilization or the distribution of power utilization (or if we can identify a procedure for fixing the extent of utilization), we can estimate the potential power by a simple modification of our basic force models. . . .

The second major alternative, given the assumption of constant potential power, is also to assume a constant utilization of power over all choices. Under such circumstances, the power exerted by any individual is a constant over all situations. If both utilization and potential power are constant, we are back to the simple force model. . . . Under such circumstances, the introduction of the concepts of power utilization and power potential is unnecessary and we can deal directly with power exercised as the core variable.

The force activation model has been compared with empirical data to a limited extent. Hanson and Miller undertook to determine independently the potential power and power utilization of community members and to predict from those measures the outcome of social choices. Potential power was determined by a priori theory; utilization was determined by inviews and observation. The results were consistent not only with the force activation model but also with a number of other models. . . . Dahl used a force activation model as a definition of power in his study of New Haven. That is, he assumed the constancy of the power exerted within subject-matter partitions in order to estimate power. On the basis of other observations, Dahl, Polsby, and Wolfinger seem to have concluded that it is meaningful to separate the two elements for certain special purposes (thus the classification as a force activation model rather than a simple force model). A New Haven test of the model, however, requires a subsequent observation of the stability of the indices.

It is clear from a consideration both of the formal properties of activation models and of the problems observers have had with such models that they suffer from their excessive a posteriori explanatory power. If we observe that power exists and is stable and if we observe that sometimes weak people seem to triumph over strong people, we are tempted to rely on an activation hypothesis to explain the discrepancy. But if we then try to use the activation hypothesis to predict the results of social-choice procedures, we discover that the data requirements of "plausible" activation models are quite substantial. As a result, we retreat to what are essentially degenerate forms of the activation model—retaining some of the form but little of the substance. This puts us back where we started, looking for some device to explain our failures in prediction. Unfortunately, the next two types of models simply complicate life further rather than relieve it.

Force-Conditioning Models

The conditioning models take as given either the basic force model or the force activation model. The only modification is to replace a constant power resource with a variable power resource. The basic mechanisms are simple: (1) People have power because they are believed to have power. (2) People are believed to have power because they have been observed to have power. It is possible, of course, to have models in which one or the other of these mechanisms is not present. If we assume the first but not the second, we have a standard experimental paradigm. If we assume the second but not the first, we have an assortment of prestige learning models. . . .

Models of this general class have not been explored in the power literature. Experimental studies have demonstrated the realism of each of the two mechanisms—success improves reputation, reputation improves success. As a result, conditioning models cannot be rejected out of hand. Moreover, they lead directly to some interesting and relevant predictions.

In most of the literature on the measurement of power, there are two nagging problems—the problem of the chameleon who frequently jumps in and agrees with an already decided issue and the satellite who, though he himself has little power, is highly correlated with a high-power person. Since these problems must be at least as compelling for the individual citizen as they are for the professional observer, they have served as a basis for a number of strong attacks on the reputational approach to the attribution of power. But the problem changes somewhat if we assume that reputations affect outcomes. Now the chameleon and the satellite are not measurement problems but important phenomena. The models will predict that an association with power will lead to power. Whether the association is by chance or by deliberate limitation, the results are substantially the same.

To the best of my knowledge, no formal efforts have been made to test either the satellite prediction in a real-world situation, or to test some of its corollaries, which include:

1. Informal power is unstable. Let the kingmaker beware of the king.
2. Unexercised power disappears. Peace is the enemy of victory.
3. Undifferentiated power diffuses. Beware of your allies lest they become your equals.

Moreover, it is really not possible to re-evaluate existing data to examine the plausibility of conditioning models. Virtually all of the studies are cross-sectional rather than longitudinal. The data requirements of the conditioning models are longitudinal. They are also substantially more severe than for the basic force models. . . . In order to have much chance of using the model (or variants on it), we will probably need to have data on variables in addition to simply social choice and individual attitudes or behavior. For example, we will probably need reputational data. We will need data that is subscripted with respect to time. We will probably have to make some additional simplifying assumptions, particularly if we want to allow for probabilistic elements in the model or introduce error terms. I do not think these are necessarily insuperable problems but I think we should recognize that even simple conditioning models of this type will require more and different data than we have been accustomed to gather.

Force Depletion Models

Within the conditioning models, success breeds success. But there is another class of plausible models in which success breeds failure. As in the conditioning models, we assume that power varies over time. As in the force activation models, we assume that not all power is exercised at every point in time. . . . We consider power to be a resource. The exercise of power depletes that resource. Subject to additions to the power supply, the more power a particular component in the system exercises, the less power there is available for that component to use. . . .

Under this scheme, it is quite possible for power to shift as a result of variations in the rates of power utilization. So long as additions to the power supply are independent of the exercise of power, the use of power today means that we will have less to use tomorrow. We can show various conditions for convergence and divergence of power resources or exercised power. We can also generate a set of aphorisms parallel to—but somewhat at variance with—the conditioning model aphorisms:

1. Formal power is unstable. Let' the king beware of the kingmaker.
2. Exercised power is lost. Wars are won by neutrals.
3. Differentiation wastes power. Maintain the alliance as long as possible.

As far as I know, no one has attempted to apply such a model to power situations, although there are some suggestions of its reasonableness (at least as a partial model). . . .

Even if power resources are exogenous, the problems of testing a simple depletion model are more severe than the problems of testing the basic activation model. As in the case of the conditioning model, we require longitudinal data. Thus, if we can assume that power resources or increments to power resources are a function of social or economic status, skill in performing some task, or physical attributes (e.g., strength), the model probably can be made manageable if the simplifying assumptions made for force activation models are sensible. On the other hand, if we combine the depletion model with a conditioning model—as I think we probably ought to—we will have complicated the basic force model to such a point that it will be difficult indeed to be sanguine about testing.

One way of moderating the test requirements is to use experimental manipulation to control some variables, and experimental observation to measure others. If we can control the resources available and directly measure the extent to which power is exercised, we can develop depletion and depletion-conditioning models to use in experimental situations.

If, however, we want to apply any of the more elaborate force models to a natural system, or if we want to develop natural-system predictions from our experimental studies, we will need far more data than recent research provides. Perhaps a model that includes considerations of activation, conditioning, and power depletion can be made empirically manageable, but such a model (and associated observations) would be a major technical achievement. We are not within shouting distance of it now.

Once we do get such a model, we may well find that it simply does not fit and that a new elaboration is necessary. From a simple concept of power in a simple force model, we have moved to a concept of power that is further and further removed from the basic intuitive notions captured by the simple model, and to models in which simple observations of power are less and less useful. It is only a short step from this point to a set of models that are conceptually remote from the original conception of a social-choice system.

Process Models

Suppose that the choice system we are studying is not random. Suppose further that power really is a significant phenomenon in the sense that it can be manipulated systematically in the laboratory and can be used to explain choice in certain social-choice systems. I think that both those suppositions are reasonable. But let us further suppose that there is a class of social-choice systems in which power is insignificant. Unless we treat *power* as true by definition, I think that supposition is reasonable. If we treat *power* as a definition, I think it is reasonable to suppose there is a class of social-choice systems in which power measurement will be unstable and useless.

Consider the following process models of social choice as representative of this class:

An exchange model. We assume that the individual components in the system prefer certain of the alternative social choices, and that the system has a formal criterion for making the final choices (e.g., majority vote, unanimity, clearing the market). We also assume that there is some medium of exchange by which individual components seek to arrange agreements (e.g., exchanges of money or votes) that are of advantage to themselves. These agreements, plus the formal criterion for choice, determine the social decision. . . .

A problem-solving model. We assume that each of the individual components in the system has certain information and skills relevant to a problem of social choice, and that the system has a criterion for solution. We postulate some kind of process by which the system calls forth and organizes the information and skills so as systematically to reduce the difference between its present position and a solution. . . .

A communication-diffusion model. We assume that the components in the system are connected by some formal or informal communication system by which information is diffused through the system. We postulate some process by which the information is sent and behavior modified, one component at a time, until a social position is reached. . . .

A decision-making model. We assume that the components in the system have preferences with respect to social choices, and that the system has a procedure for rendering choices. The system and the components operate under two limitations:

1. Overload: They have more demands on their attention than they can meet in the time available.
2. Undercomprehension: The world they face is much more complicated than they can handle. . . .

I am impressed by the extent to which models of this class seem to be generally consistent with the reports of recent (and some not so recent) students of political systems and other relatively large (in terms of number of people involved) systems of social choice. . . .

Such descriptions of social choice have two general implications. On the one hand, if a system has the properties suggested by such students as Coleman, Long, Riesman, Lindblom, and Dahl, power will be a substantially useless concept. In such systems, the measurement of power is feasible, but it is not valuable in calculating predictions. The measurement of power is useful primarily in systems that conform to some variant of the force models. In some complex process systems we may be able to identify subsystems that conform to the force model, and thus be able to interpret the larger system in terms of a force activation model for some purposes. But I think the flavor of the observations I have cited is that even such interpretations may be less common-sensible than we previously believed.

On the other hand, the process models—and particularly the decision-making process models—look technically more difficult with regard to estimation and testing than the more complex modifications of the force model. We want to include many more discrete and nominal variables, many more discontinuous functions, and many more rare combinations of events. Although some progress has been made in dealing with the problems, and some predictive power has been obtained without involving the force model, the pitfalls of process models are still substantially uncharted.

THE POWER OF POWER

. . . Although *power* and *influence* are useful concepts for many kinds of situations, they have not greatly helped us to understand many of the natural social-choice mechanisms to which they have traditionally been applied.

The extent to which we have used the concept of power fruitlessly is symptomatic of three unfortunate temptations associated with power:

Temptation No 1: The obviousness of power. To almost anyone living in contemporary society, power is patently real. . . .

Because of this ubiquity of power, we are inclined to assume that it is real and meaningful. . . . We run the risk of treating the social validation of power as more compelling than it is simply because the social conditioning to a simple force model is so pervasive.

Temptation No. 2: The importance of measurement. The first corollary of the obviousness of power is the importance of the measurement problem. . . . Since we have a persistent problem discovering a measurement procedure that consistently yields results which are consistent with the model, we assert a measurement problem and a problem of the concept of power. We clarify and reclarify the concept, and we define and redefine the measures. . . .

We should consider whether subsuming all our problems under the rubric of conceptual and measurement problems may be too tempting. I think we too often ask *how* to measure power when we should ask *whether* to measure power. The measurement problem and the model problem have to be solved simultaneously.

Temptation No. 3: The residual variance. The second corollary of the obviousness of power is the use of *power* as a residual category for explanation. We always have some unexplained variance in our data—results that simply cannot be explained within the theory. It is always tempting to give that residual variance some name. . . . But where the unexplained variance is rather large, as it often is when we consider social-choice systems, we can easily fool ourselves into believing that we know something simply because we have a name for our errors. In general, I think we can roughly determine the index of the temptation to label errors by computing the ratio of uses of the variable for prediction to the uses for a posteriori explanation. On that calculation, I think power exhibits a rather low ratio, even lower than such other problem areas as personality and culture. Having been trapped in each of these cul-de-sacs at one time or another, I am both embarrassed by the inelegance of the temptations involved and impressed by their strength. We persist in using the simple force model in a variety of situations in which it is quite inconsistent with observations. As a result, we bury the examination of alternative models of social choice under a barrage of measurement questions.

I have tried to suggest that the power of power depends on the extent to which a predictive model requires and can make effective use of such a concept. Thus, it depends on the kind of system we are confronting, the amount and kinds of data we are willing or able to collect, and the kinds of estimation and validation procedures we have available to us. Given our present empirical and test technology, power is probably a useful concept for many short-run situations involving the direct confrontations of committed and activated participants. Such situations can be found in natural settings, but they are more frequent in the laboratory. Power is probably not a useful concept for many long-run situations involving problems of component-overload and undercomprehension. Such situations can be found in the laboratory but are more common in natural settings. Power may become more useful as a concept if we can develop analytic and empirical procedures for coping with the more complicated forms of force models, involving activation, conditioning, and depletion of power.

Thus, the answer to the original question is tentative and mixed. Provided some rather restrictive assumptions are met, the concept of power and a simple force model represent a reasonable approach to the study of social choice. Provided some rather substantial estimation and analysis problems can be solved, the concept of power and more elaborate force models represent a reasonable approach. On the whole, however, power is a disappointing concept. It gives us surprisingly little purchase in reasonable models of complex systems of social choice.

The Measurement of Social Power and Opportunity Costs

John C. Harsanyi

The central theme of this article by John Harsanyi is that the analysis of influence must contemplate the interplay of both the costs and benefits of exercising power. He further argues that the power of an individual cannot be assessed outside the context of the situation or outcome he wishes to influence. If Harsanyi is correct, it follows that the power of a group or an individual will vary from issue to issue and over time.

Harsanyi identifies a number of the components of power which it is necessary to take into account if we are to improve our capacity to assess an individual's or a group's share in the distribution of community power. In view of the often conflicting views of community power held by political scientists and sociologists, the reader may wish to give particular attention to the importance of evaluating an individual's "scope of power," i.e., the various issues on which a holder of power resources can effectively exert his influence. While, as Robert Presthus has observed, there are probably no purely private or public issues in community politics, nevertheless the way in which values in communities are allocated might be clarified if more attention were given to specifying an individual's "scope of power" and if more distinctions were made between matters which are essentially public and those which are private.

The analysis of power measurement is here set in the context of a two-person "bargaining game." Of course, community decisions invariably involve more complex interactions between individuals and groups. However, the difficulty of measuring power in simple interrelationships must be understood and dealt with before we can successfully tackle more complicated problems. Moreover, the arguments below can be extrapolated to multi-person situations, as Harsanyi has shown in another article (92).

INTRODUCTION

Recent papers by Simon (1957), by March (1955, 1957), and by Dahl (1957) have suggested measuring person A's power over person B in

From John C. Harsanyi, "The Measurement of Social Power, Opportunity Costs, and the Theory of Two Person Bargaining Games," *Behavioral Science* VII (January, 1962), 67–75.

terms of its actual or potential *effects*, that is, in terms of the changes that A causes or can cause in B's behavior. [1] As Dahl puts it, A has power over B to the extent to which "he can get B to do something that B would not otherwise do" (1957, p. 203).

As Simon and March have obtained very similar results, I shall restrict myself largely to summarizing Dahl's main conclusions. Dahl distinguishes the following constituents of the power relation:

(a) the *base* of power, i.e., the resources (economic assets, constitutional prerogatives, military forces, popular prestige, etc.) that A can use to influence B's behavior;

(b) the *means* of power, i.e., the specific actions (promises, threats, public appeals, etc.) by which A can make actual use of these resources to influence B's behavior;

(c) the *scope* of power, i.e., the set of specific actions that A, by using his means of power, can get B to perform; and finally

(d) the *amount* of power, i.e., the net increase in the probability of B's actually performing some specific action X, due to A's using his means of power against B (1957, pp. 203–205).

If A has power over several individuals, Dahl adds a fifth constituent:

(e) the set of individuals over whom A has power—this we shall call the *extension* of A's power.

Dahl points out that the power of two individuals can be compared in any of these five dimensions. Other things being equal, an individual's power is greater: (a) the greater his power base, (b) the more means of power available to him, and the greater (c) the scope, (d) the amount, and (e) the extension of his power. But Dahl proposes to use only the last three variables for the formal definition and measurement of social power. He argues that what we primarily mean by great social power is an ability to influence many people (extension) in many respects (scope) and with a high probability (amount of power). In contrast, a large power base or numerous means of power are not direct measures of the extent of the influence or power that one person can exert over other persons; they are only instruments by which great power can be achieved and maintained, and are indicators from which we can normally *infer* the likely possession of great power by an individual.

Among the three variables of scope, amount, and extension, amount of power is the crucial one, in terms of which the other two can be defined. For the scope of A's power over B is simply the set of specific ac-

[1] I am indebted to Professor Jacob Marschak, of U.C.L.A., and to Professors Herbert A. Simon and James G. March, of Carnegie Institute of Technology, for helpful discussions on this and related topics.

tions X with respect to which A has a nonzero amount of power over B, i.e., the set of those actions X for which A can achieve a nonzero increase in the probability of these actions actually being performed by B. Similarly, the extension of A's power is the set of specific individuals over whom A has power of nonzero scope and amount.

While the amount of power is a difference of two probabilities, and therefore is directly given as a *real number* [2] all other dimensions of power are directly given as lists of specific objects (e.g., a list of specific resources, a list of specific actions by A or by B, or a list of specific individuals over whom A has power). But Dahl and March suggest that at least in certain situations it will be worthwhile to develop straight numerical measures for them by appropriate aggregating procedures—essentially by counting the number of comparable items in a given list, and possibly by assigning different weights to items of unequal importance (e.g., we may give more "marks" for power over an important individual than for power over a less important one) (March, 1957, pp. 213–220). In other cases we may divide up a given list into several sublists and may assign a separate numerical measure to each of them, without necessarily aggregating all these numbers into a single figure. That is, we may characterize a given dimension of power not by a single number, but rather by a set of several numbers, i.e., a vector. (For instance, we may describe the extension of President de Gaulle's power by listing the numbers [or percentages] of deputies, of army officers of various ranks, of electors, etc., who support him, without trying to combine all these figures into one index number.)

Two Additional Dimensions of Social Power

A quantitative characterization of a power relation, however, in my view must include two more variables not mentioned in Dahl's list:

(f) the opportunity costs to A of attempting to influence B's behavior, i.e., the opportunity costs of using his power over B (and of acquiring this power over B in the first place if A does not yet possess the required power), which we shall call the *costs* of A's power over B; and

(g) the opportunity costs to B of refusing to do what A wants him to do, i.e., of refusing to yield to A's attempt to influence his behavior.

[2] But as the probability that B will actually perform a specific action X suggested by A will in general be different for different actions X and for different individuals B, the total amount of A's power (or even the amount of A's power over a given individual B) will also have to be described by a vector rather than by a single number, except if some sort of aggregation procedure is used.

As these opportunity costs measure the strength of B's incentives for yielding to A's influence, we shall call them the *strength* of A's power over B.[3]

More precisely, the *costs* of A's power over B will be defined as the *expected value* (actuarial value) of the costs of his attempt to influence B. It will be a weighted average of the net total costs that A would incur if his attempt were successful (e.g., the costs of rewarding B), and of the net total costs that A would incur if his attempt were unsuccessful (e.g., the costs of punishing B).

Other things being equal, A's power over B is greater the smaller the cost of A's power and the greater the strength of A's power.

Both of these two cost variables may be expressed either in physical units (e.g., it may cost A so many bottles of beer or so many working hours to get B to adopt a given policy X; and again it may cost B so many bottles of beer or so many years' imprisonment if he does not adopt policy X), in monetary units (e.g., A's or B's relevant costs may amount to so many actual dollars, or at least may be equivalent to a loss of so many dollars for him), or in utility units. (In view of the theoretical problems connected with interpersonal comparisons of utility, and of the difficulties associated with utility measurement even for one individual, in practice the costs and the strength of power will usually be expressed in physical or in monetary units. But for the purposes of theoretical analysis the use of utility costs sometimes has important advantages, as we shall see.)

Unlike the power base and the means of power, which need not be included in the definition of the power relation, both the costs of power and the strength of power are essential ingredients of the definition of power. A's power over B should be defined not merely as an ability by A to get B to do X with a certain probability p, but rather as an ability by A to achieve this at a certain total cost u to himself, by convincing B that B would have to bear the total cost v if he did not do X.

THE COSTS OF POWER

One of the main purposes for which social scientists use the concept of A's power over B is for the description of the policy possibilities open to A. If we want to know the situation (or environment) which A faces as a decision-maker, we must know whether he can or cannot get B to perform a certain action X, and more specifically how sure he can be (in a probability sense) that B will actually perform this action. But a realis-

[3] Of course, instead of taking the opportunity costs (i.e. the net disadvantages) associated for B with noncompliance, we could just as well take the net advantages for him with compliance—they both amount to the same thing.

tic description of A's policy possibilities must include not only A's ability or inability to get B to perform a certain action X, but also the *costs* that A has to bear in order to achieve this result. If two individuals are in a position to exert the same influence over other individuals, but if one can achieve this influence only at the cost of great efforts and/or financial or other sacrifices, while the other can achieve it free of any such costs, we cannot say in any useful sense that their power is equally great. Any meaningful comparison must be in terms of the influence that two individuals can achieve at comparable costs, or in terms of the costs they have to bear in order to achieve comparable degrees of influence.

For instance, it is misleading to say that two political candidates have the same power over two comparable constituencies if one needs much more electioneering effort and expenditure to achieve a given majority, even if in the end both achieve the same majorities; or that two businessmen have the same power over the city government if one can achieve favorable treatment by city officials only at the price of large donations to party funds, while the other can get the same favorable treatment just for the asking.

Of course, a power concept which disregards the costs of power is most inaccurate when the costs of using a given power become very high or even prohibitive. For instance, suppose that an army commander becomes a prisoner of enemy troops, who try to force him at gun point to give a radio order to his army units to withdraw from a certain area. He may very well have the power to give a contrary order, both in the sense of having the physical ability to do so and in the sense of there being a very good chance of his order being actually obeyed by his army units—but he can use his power only at the cost of his life. Though the scope, the amount, and the extension of his power over his soldiers would still be very great, it would clearly be very misleading in this situation to call him a powerful individual in the same sense as before his capture.

More generally, measurement of power merely in terms of its scope, amount, and extension tends to give counterintuitive results when the possessor of power has little or no real opportunity to actually use his power. For example, take the case of a secretary who has to compile various reports for her employer, according to very specific instructions which leave her little actual choice as to how to prepare them. Suppose that her employer then uses these reports as a basis for very important decisions.[4] Physically she could exert considerable influence on her employer's policies by omitting certain pieces of information from her reports, or including misleading information. In this sense, the scope and the amount

---

[4] I owe this example to Professor Jacob Marschak.

of her power over her employer is considerable. But normally she will have little opportunity for using this power, and social scientists would hardly wish to describe her as a powerful individual, as they would have to do if they used Dahl's power concept without modification.

In terms of our own power concept, however, the secretary in question has little real power if all dimensions of her power are taken into account. Though she does have power of great scope and great amount over her employer, this fact is normally more than offset by the very high costs of using her power. If she intentionally submits misleading reports she probably will be found out very soon and will be dismissed and/or punished in other ways. Moreover, if she is a loyal employee such flagrant violation of her instructions would in itself involve very high disutility costs to her.

To conclude, a realistic quantitative description of A's power over B must include, as an essential dimension of this power relation, the costs to A of attempting to influence B's behavior.

THE STRENGTH OF POWER

While the costs of power must be included in the definition of our power concept in order to ensure its descriptive validity, the variable of *strength* of power must be included to ensure the usefulness of our power concept for explanatory purposes.

As March (1955, pp. 431–432) has pointed out about the concept of influence, one of the main analytical tasks of such concepts as influence or power (which essentially is an ability to exert influence) is to serve as *intervening variables* in the analysis of individual or social decision-making. Therefore we need a power or influence concept which enables us in the relevant cases to explain a decision by a given private individual or by an official of a social organization, in terms of the power or influence that another individual or some social group has over him. But fundamentally, the analysis of any human decision must be in terms of the variables on the basis of which the decision-maker concerned actually makes his decision—that is, in terms of the advantages and disadvantages he associates with alternative policies available to him. In order to explain why B adopts a certain policy X in accordance with A's wishes, we must know what *difference it makes* for B whether A is his friend or his enemy —or more generally, we must know the *opportunity costs* to B of not adopting policy X. Hence, if our power concept is to serve us as an explanatory intervening variable in the analysis of B's decision to comply with A's wishes, our power concept must include as one of its essential dimensions the opportunity costs to *B* of noncompliance, which measure the strength of *B*'s incentives to compliance and which we have called the strength of *A*'s power over *B*.

For instance, if we want to explain the decision of Senator Knowland to support a certain bill of the Eisenhower administration we must find out, among other things, which particular individuals or social groups influenced his decision, and to what extent. Now suppose that we have strong reasons to assume that it was President Eisenhower's personal intervention which made Senator Knowland change his mind and decide to support the bill in question. Then we still have to explain *how* the variables governing the Senator's decision were actually affected by the President's intervention. Did the President make a promise to him, i.e., did he attach new *advantages*, from the Senator's point of view, to the policy of supporting the bill? Or did the President make a threat, i.e., did he attach new *disadvantages* to the policy of opposing the bill? Or did the President supply new information, pointing out certain already *existing* advantages and/or disadvantages associated with these two policies, which the Senator had been insufficiently aware of before? In any case we must explain how the President's intervention increased the opportunity costs that Senator Knowland came to associate with opposing the bill.

If we cannot supply this information, then the mere existence of an influence or power relationship between President Eisenhower and Senator Knowland will not *explain* the latter's decision to support the bill. It will only pose a *problem* concerning this decision. (Why on earth did he comply with the President's request to support the bill, when it is known that he had many reasons to oppose it, and did actually oppose it for a while?)

There seem to be four main ways by which a given actor *A* can manipulate the incentives or opportunity costs of another actor *B*:

1. *A* may provide certain *new* advantages or disadvantages for *B*, subject to *no condition*. For instance, he may provide certain facilities for *B* which make it easier or less expensive for *B* to follow certain particular policy objectives desirable to *A*. (For example, country *A* may be able to induce country *B* to attack some third country *C*, simply by supplying arms to *B*, even if *A* supplies these arms "without any strings attached"—and in particular without making it a condition of her arms deliveries that *B* will actually attack *C*.) Or *A* may withdraw from *B* certain facilities that could help *B* in attaining policy objectives undesirable to *A*. More generally, *A* may provide for *B* goods or services complementary to some particular policy goal *X*, or competitive to policy goals alternative to *X*, so as to increase for *B* the net utility of *X*, or to decrease the net utility of its alternatives;

or *A* may achieve similar results by depriving *B* of goods or services either competitive to *X* or complementary to its alternatives.[5]

2. *A* may set up *rewards* and *punishments*, i.e. *new* advantages and disadvantages subject to certain *conditions* as to *B*'s future behavior.

3. *A* may supply *information* (or misinformation) on (allegedly) already *existing* advantages and/or disadvantages connected with various alternative policies open to *B*.

4. *A* may rely on his legitimate *authority* over *B*, or on *B*'s personal *affection* for *A*, which makes *B* attach *direct disutility* to the very act of disobeying *A*.

Of course, in a situation where *A* has certain power over *B*, either party can be mistaken about the true opportunity costs to him of various alternatives. Therefore both in discussing the costs of *A*'s power over *B*, and in discussing the strength of his power, we must distinguish between *objective* costs and *perceived* costs—between what these costs actually are and what the individual bearing these costs thinks them to be. For the purpose of a formal definition of the power relation, the costs of *A*'s power over *B* have to be stated as the *objective* costs that an attempt to influence *B* would actually entail upon *A*, while the *strength* of *A*'s power over *B* has to be stated in terms of the costs of noncompliance as *perceived* by *B* himself. The reason is that the costs of *A*'s power serve to describe the objective policy possibilities open to *A*, whereas the strength of *A*'s power serves to explain *B*'s subjective motivation for compliant behavior. (Of course, a full description of a given power situation would require listing both objective and perceived costs for both participants.)

THE STRENGTH OF POWER,
AND THE AMOUNT OF POWER IN DAHL'S SENSE

Clearly, in general the greater the *strength* of *A*'s power over *B*, the greater will be *A*'s *amount* of power over *B* with respect to action *X*. The relationship between these two variables will take a particularly simple mathematical form if the strength of *A*'s power is measured in *utility* terms, i.e., in terms of the disutility costs to *B* of noncompliance.[6]

[5] Case 1 is discussed in somewhat greater détail because power based on providing services or disservices without any conditions attached is often overlooked in the literature. For our purposes, the distinction between unconditional advantages or disadvantages on the one hand, and conditional rewards or punishments on the other hand, is important because the latter lend themselves to *bargaining* much more easily than the former do.

[6] To simplify our analysis, in what follows we shall be concerned only with the case where *A* is able to influence *B* in the intended direction, i.e., has a nonnegative amount of power over him. (*A* can have a negative amount of power over *B* only if he seriously misjudges the situation, because otherwise he can always make the amount of his power at worst *zero*, by simply refraining from intervention.)

We shall use the following model. A wants B to perform action X. But B associates disutility x with doing X. Nevertheless B would perform X with probability p_1 (i.e., would adopt the mixed strategy $s[p_1]$ assigning probability p_1 to doing X and probability $[1 - p_1]$ to not doing X), even in the absence of A's intervention.[7] B would adopt this strategy because if he completely refused to do X (i.e., if he adopted the mixed strategy $s[0]$) he would obtain only the utility payoff u_0 —; while if he did X with probability p_1 (i.e., if he adopted strategy $s[p_1]$), then he would obtain the higher utility payoff u_1, making his total expected utility $u_1 - p_1 x > u_0$.

Now A intervenes and persuades B that B will obtain the still higher utility payoff u_2 if he agrees to do action X with a certain probability $p_2 > p_1$ (i.e., if he adopts strategy $s[p_2]$), making his total expected utility $u_2 - p_2 x$. In view of this, B does adopt strategy $s[p_2]$.

Under these assumptions, obviously the *amount* of A's power over B will be the difference $\triangle p = p_2 - p_1$, while the *strength* of A's power over B will be the difference $u_2 - u_1$. As $p_2 \leqslant 1$, we must have $\triangle p \leqslant 1 - p_1$. Moreover, by assumption (cf. Footnote 7); $\triangle p \geqslant 0$.

If B tries to maximize his expected utility, then he will adopt strategy $s[p_2]$ only if

$$u_2 - p_2 x \geqslant u_1 - p_1 x, \tag{1}$$

that is, if

$$\triangle p = p_2 - p_1 \geqslant \frac{u_2 - u_1}{x} = \frac{\triangle u}{x} \tag{2}$$

This gives us:

Theorem I. The maximum *amount* of power that A can achieve over B with respect to action X tends to be equal to the *strength* of A's power over B (as expressed in utility units) divided by the disutility to B of doing action X—except that this maximum amount of power cannot be more than the amount of power corresponding to B's doing action X with probability *one*.

The strength of A's power over B divided by the disutility to B of doing X may be called the *relative strength* of A's power over B. Accordingly, we obtain:

Theorem I'. The maximum *amount* of power that A can achieve over B with respect to action X tends to be equal to the *relative strength* of A's power over B with respect to action X (except that, again, this maximum amount of power cannot be more than the amount of power corresponding to B's doing action X with probability one).

---

[7] We follow Dahl in considering the more general case where B would do action X with some probability p_1 (which of course may be zero), even in the absence of A's intervention.

Of course, in the real world we seldom observe B to use a randomized mixed strategy of form $s[p]$, in a literal sense. What we do find is that, if we watch B's behavior over a series of comparable occasions, he will comply with A's wishes in some proportion p of all occasions and will fail to comply in the remaining proportion $(1-p)$ of the occasions. Moreover, the disutility to B of compliant behavior will vary from one occasion to another. Hence if B wants to comply with A's wishes in pn cases out of n then, other things being equal, he will tend to select those pn cases where compliance is associated with the smallest disutility to him. For example, suppose that a U.S. senator, with political attitudes rather different from the administration's, decides to vote for the president's legislative program often enough to avoid at least an open break with the administration. Then he is likely to select for his support those administration bills which are least distasteful to him and to his constituents. This means that the total disutility to B of a given strategy $s[p]$ (which now has to be defined as a strategy involving compliance in *proportion p of all cases*) will tend to increase somewhat more than proportionally as p increases, because should B decide to increase the frequency of his compliant behavior he would have to include a higher fraction of "difficult" cases.

Accordingly, if we restate our model in terms of empirical *frequencies*, rather than theoretical *probabilities*, we must expect that the maximum *amount* of power that A can achieve over B will increase somewhat less than in proportion to increments in the *strength* of A's power over B (measuring this strength now in terms of the *average* utility value of B's incentives for compliance over all occasions). But our Theorem I is likely to retain at least its approximate validity in most empirical situations.[8]

POWER IN A SCHEDULE SENSE

We have just seen that the greater the strength of a person's power over other persons the greater the amount of his power over them tends to be. But likewise, the greater the strength of a person's power over other people, the greater both the scope and the extension of his power

[8] More exactly, in most unilateral power situations. The distinction between unilateral and bilateral power situations will be discussed below.

Note that in empirical applications based on a *frequency* interpretation, a further complication may arise owing to the fact that the utilities to A, and the disutilities to B, of a set of several compliant actions $X_1, \ldots, X_k$ by B may *not* be simply *additive* (as they may have the nature of complementary or of competitive "goods" from A's point of view, and/or the nature of complementary or of competitive "evils" from B's point of view).

over these people. That is, the stronger incentives he can provide for compliance, the larger the number of specific actions he can get other people to perform for him will be, and the larger the number of individuals he can get to perform these actions.

But while the scope, the amount, and the extension of his power are all functions of the *strength* of his power over all individuals, the strength of his power is itself a function of the *costs* of power he is prepared to bear. The greater efforts and sacrifices he is prepared to make, the stronger incentives for compliance he will be able to provide and the greater will be the strength of his power over them.

Therefore, a given individual's power can be described not only by stating the specific values of the five dimensions of his power (whether as single numbers, or as vectors, or as lists of specific items), but also by specifying the mathematical *functions* or *schedules* that connect the costs of his power with the other four dimensions. When power is defined in terms of the specific values of the five power variables we shall speak of power in a *point* sense, and when power is defined in terms of the functions or schedules connecting the other four power variables with the costs of power we shall speak of power in a *schedule* sense.[9]

Power in a schedule sense can be regarded as a "production function" describing how a given individual can "transform" different amounts of his resources (of his working time, his money, his political rights, his popularity, etc.) into social power of various dimensions (of various strengths, scopes, amounts, and extensions). The commonsense notion of social power makes it an *ability* to achieve certain things—an ability that the person concerned is free to use or to leave unused. It seems to me that this notion of power as an ability is better captured by our concept of power in a schedule sense than it is by the concept of power in a point sense. (The latter seems to better correspond to the commonsense notion of actually exerted *influence*, rather than to that of power as such.)

If a person's power is given in a mere schedule sense, then we can state the specific values of his five power dimensions only if we are also told how much of his different resources he is actually prepared to use in order to obtain social power of various dimensions—that is, if besides his power schedules we know also his *utility function*. Whereas his power defined in a schedule sense indicates the conditions under which his environment is ready to "supply" power to him, it is his utility function which determines his "demand" for power under various alternative conditions.

---

[9] In analogy to the distinction in economic theory between demand or supply in a point sense and in a schedule sense.

BILATERAL POWER AND THE "BLACKMAILER'S FALLACY"

So far we have tacitly assumed that, in situations where A has power over B, A is always in a position to determine, by his unilateral decision, the incentives he will provide for B's compliance, as well as the degree of compliance he will try to enforce. Situations in which this is actually the case may be called unilateral power situations. But it very often happens that not only can A exert pressure on B in order to get him to adopt certain specific policies, but B can do the same to A. In particular, B may be able to press A for increased rewards and/or decreased penalties, and for relaxing the standards of compliance required from him and used in administering rewards and penalties to him. Situations of this type we shall call bilateral or reciprocal power situations. In such situations, both the extent of B's compliant behavior (i.e., the scope and the amount of A's power over B) and the net incentives that A can provide for B (i.e., the net strength of A's power over B) will become matters of explicit or implicit *bargaining* between the two parties.

Of the four ways in which A can increase his strength of power discussed previously, we tend to obtain unilateral power situations in cases 1, 3, and 4, where A's power over B is based on providing *unconditional* advantages or disadvantages for B, on conveying information or misinformation to him, or on having legitimate authority over B and/or enjoying B's personal affection (though there are also exceptions where these cases give rise to bilateral power). For example, it is usually largely a matter for A's personal discretion whether he provides certain facilities for B, whether he discloses certain pieces of information to him, or whether he gives him an order as his legitimate superior. In case 2, on the other hand, when A's power over B is based on A's ability to set up rewards and/or punishments for B *conditional* upon B's behavior, normally we find bilateral power situations (though again there are important exceptions).[10] Here B can exert pressure on A by withholding his compliance, even though compliance would be much more profitable than noncompliance. He may also be able to exert pressure on A by making the costs of a conflict (including the costs of punishing B for noncompliance) very high to A.

For bilateral power situations Theorem I and Theorem I' do not hold true. For these conclusions have been completely dependent on the assumption that if a certain strategy s_1, involving some given degree of

---

[10] Viz. in cases when A is able to persuade B that he, A, has irrevocably committed himself in advance to not making any concessions to B.

compliance by B, is more profitable to B than any alternative strategy s_2 involving a lesser degree of compliance (or none at all), then B will always choose strategy s_1 and will never choose strategy s_2—not even as a result of dissatisfaction with the terms A offers in return for B's co-operation. While in unilateral power situations this assumption is perfectly legitimate (as it amounts to no more than assuming that B tries to maximize his utility or expected utility), in bilateral power situations this assumption would involve what I propose to call the "blackmailer's fallacy" (Harsanyi, 1956, p. 156).

A would-be blackmailer A once argued that as he was in a position to cause damage worth $1,000 to a certain rich man B, he should be able to extract from B any ransom r short of $1,000, because after payment of $r < \$1,000$, B would still be better off than if he had to suffer the full $1,000 damage.

But this argument is clearly fallacious. By similar reasoning, B could also have argued that A would accept any ransom r larger than nil, because after accepting a ransom $r > \$0$, A would still be better off than if no agreement were reached and he did not receive anything at all. What both of these arguments really show is that in any bargaining between two rational bargainers, the outcome must fall between what may be called the two parties' concession limits, which are defined by each party's refusal to accept any agreement that would make him actually worse off than he would be in the conflict situation. But the two arguments in themselves say nothing about where the two parties' agreement point will actually lie between these two limits. They certainly do not allow the inference that this agreement point will actually coincide or nearly coincide with one party's concession limit.[13] (Only if we know the two parties' attitudes towards risk-taking, and in particular towards risking a conflict rather than accepting unfavorable terms, can we make any predictions about where their agreement point will lie between the two concession limits.)

Either party's actual behavior will be a resultant of two opposing psychological forces. On the one hand, for example, B will admittedly have some incentive for agreeing to any ransom payment less than $1,000. But B will also know that A will likewise have some incentive for accepting any ransom payment greater than zero, and this fact will make B expect to get away with a ransom payment of much less than $1,000. This expectation in turn will provide B with some incentive to resist any ransom payment too close to $1,000. Any realistic theory of B's behavior must take full account of both of these psychological forces—both of B's motives for compliance, and of the reasons which make him expect some concessions on A's part which will render full compliance on his own part unnecessary. . . .

VI

TOWARD A THEORY OF COMMUNITY POWER— FUTURE RESEARCH DIRECTIONS

Where have the preceding sections taken us? In view of the complexity of the research and the results, is it possible to state some definitive theory of community power? We turn in this section to some thoughts which may point the way to answers.

The progress of ideas in intellectual discourse is not an orderly affair. The development of a complex concept and its empirical support proceeds disjointedly because many insights and much evidence stem from the different perspectives of the scholars involved. Scattered case studies or limited experiments which flow from different conceptual bases flood the field in the early stages of the search for a generalizing theory. This disorder tends to coalesce slowly into a limited number of approaches or to form "schools of thought." From the conflict arising among these schools, a dialectic process leads to modification of the original, simpler ideas of "truth" which had increasingly failed to meet more rigorous canons of logic and evidence. The resulting new perspectives contain some of the old views, of course. In time, continued research and rethinking operate to create even further revision of what was once thought by many (or even most) to be the ultimate answer. Thus the intellectual process never yields final truths—such absolutes are for the world of dogma—but only more and more proximate understandings.

The student newly come to the intellectual discourse of a field may initially experience disillusionment and frustration, especially in the social sciences. Everywhere he sees interpretive schools in conflict, and men whose names are held in respect by some are the objects of trenchant criticism by others. Yet in such seeming confusion there is often an underlying, if ill-defined, order which contains an opportunity. For when men differ and "truths" are in the process of becoming, there is opportunity to contribute new insights of concept and method.

In this book we have arranged the selections to emphasize both the evolution of ideas in the search for community power and to suggest that there is much that is not known. The preceding section focused upon some special problems still to be solved; in this section, we offer some of the work on the frontier of this field which suggests promising new directions for research in community power. If it is not yet clear that much remains to be done, it soon will be!

The first important step in the evolution of ideas from the simple to the sophisticated is the collection of available data and conclusions within the context of a comparative framework. Students of community power seem now to be making that step. But, as John Walton has noted, "To come to grips with the diverse social and political facets of community life in a comparative design remains the chief problem in this field" (225). Peter H. Rossi, in an article which follows, succinctly states the problem which exists as long as research remains with particular cases. Each is

> best characterized by the statement, "It is different here than elsewhere." . . . Each author owns his own town, defending it from the erroneous and somewhat heretical conceptualizations of others much the way a feudal lord defends the integrity of the local patron saint against the false counterclaims of nearby realms.

The common theme which pervades the articles in this section is the need for an effective approach to the comparative study of community power.

Robert Alford offers us a conceptual scheme which, in its wide reach of systems theory, seems to help sort out many of the variables we have encountered to this point; like other systems theories, it also should function to generate new research. Peter Rossi suggests at least two variables which in their interrelationship can yield the varieties of community power structures we have treated earlier. The selection from Charles Bonjean and David Olson proposes typologies for classifying leaders; they also stress the importance of evaluating both the precedents and consequences of specific leadership systems—a point we shall return to shortly.

Similarly, Robert Agger and his colleagues develop an elaborate and sophisticated multi-dimensional typology of power structures; in addition they suggest other dimensions, which, in their permutations, proliferate these structures to a degree far removed from earlier notions of elitism or pluralism. Their comments on the frustrations of the segregated minorities require reflection in light of contemporary racial conflict.

To these model-building efforts we have added two selections, based upon aggregate data analysis, which classify large numbers of communities by variables that might affect the structure of community power. Amos Hawley's article is an almost unique example of the application of this method. Hawley skips entirely the laborious study of the interpersonal milieu of power and examines the structural community characteristics and associated community policies. If this methodology could be validated generally, it would open the way to analysis of a large number of cities and to broadly applicable conclusions now impossible because of the slow and difficult process of constructing case studies. In the concluding article in this section John Walton utilizes existing case studies to extract conclusions about factors associated with different types of power structures. Unlike most other studies, he stresses the effect of factors external to communities which may account for their differing distribution of power.

The selections presented in this section do not exhaust future research directions. We are still in the early stages of the search for community power. Abstractly, we can hypothesize a continuum of structures, leading from a completely authoritarian-elite community to one in which almost all citizens participate in making all decisions. Obviously different mixes of these types should logically exist, but how are such mixes actually distributed among the thousands of American cities? We do not know.

Further, what are the consequences for American political and social values of a specific distribution of power? If all American cities were grouped on the authoritarian-elite end of our continuum, for example, we would regard this as antithetical to many of our basic values—especially liberty, equality, and diversity. But might there not be a "benevolent elite" which operates to maximize community preferences and requirements—even though retaining all power to initiate, decide, and administer policies? Agger, *et al*, suggest such a possibility. Or, contrariwise, if our cities were heavily concentrated on the extreme of full popular participation in all aspects of decision-making, would that necessarily promote our traditional values? Initiative and referendum—about as close to the popular democratic ideal as we get—in recent years have been used to veto greatly needed tax and expenditure programs for educational and other purposes, and to deny open housing to minority groups.

We raise these points to illustrate the need to examine the consequences of public policy as a result of various community power structures. There are dangers in overstating the importance of the form and in neglecting the actual policies of the community's political system. Participation in decision-making is desirable, but it is not the only goal of democratic politics.

It is unclear how far the study of community power can take us toward a fuller understanding of, and prescription for, a truly democratic polity. Nevertheless, we think that the continuing search these pages have traced will yield more information than has been known in the past. In any event it is time, it seems to us, to broaden the scope of our efforts to comprehend the nature and uses of political influence. It is time, too, to abandon those community studies which aim to strengthen an ideological conception of the current health or infirmity of American society. The search for community power has the potential to provide new insights which can help us with the many problems of our increasingly urban society: it is this potential above all other attractions which justifies further inquiry.

The Comparative Study of Urban Politics

Robert R. Alford

If community power study is to move from anecdotal case studies to comparative analysis, such research will necessitate the development of a comprehensive analytical scheme or field theory of grand scope. The next selection by Robert R. Alford is suggestive of what is needed. Alford considers community decisions to be affected by both long-run (structural, cultural, environmental) and short-run (situational) factors. Such systematic theory has the advantage of all field theories: it enables one to analyze common elements of unrelated case studies in the context of a more general conceptual framework. In most of the succeeding selections Alford's ideas find certain continuities. Further, the reader may wish to apply this schema to the case studies we have examined in earlier sections.

AN ANALYTICAL SCHEME

There have been three principal objects of study in the area of comparative urban politics: decisions, policies and roles of government. A *decision* is a particular act by a local government agency or other authoritative group. A *policy* is a series of decisions of a certain type, any one of which has a certain probability determined by the consistency of the policy, its legality, and support by political and economic forces. A *role of government* is a commitment to certain types of policies, established formally by law or informally by means of the dominance of groups in a community holding certain political values and goals.

Several classes of factors have been used to explain or to show the consequences and correlates of decisions, policies and governmental roles: situational, structural, cultural, and environmental. A *situational* factor is one pertaining to the particular sequence of events and balance of political and social forces bearing upon and determining a particular

From Robert R. Alford, "The Comparative Study of Urban Elites," in *Urban Research and Policy Planning*, Leo F. Schnore and Henry Fagin, eds., pp. 264–271, 301–302. Reprinted with permission of Sage Publications, Inc.

decision. Incumbent leadership, the strategies used, the motivations of participants, the coincidence of one decision with another, are all situational factors which determine the outcome of a particular decision-making process.

Structural factors include both long-term "situations" and relatively unchanging elements of the society and polity. What this means is that there are important subcategories of structural factors, which we do not have space to analyze here. The economic base of the community, its social and economic composition, the number and type of organizations which exist that play potential political roles, the legal power of governmental officials, the distribution of population in a community by class, age, and other characteristics, the amount of land reserve, are only a few examples of the many possible structural factors which for any given period of time are relatively constant. Clearly they differ considerably in their degree of permanence. Whether a chamber of commerce exists at the time that a decision is made may be regarded as a marginal case; the proportion of college educated persons in the community is far more stable than the existence of a particular organization, although the general density of organizations may be quite stable. Structural factors thus establish the framework within which situations for action arise, although the outcomes of those actions may in turn alter the structure.

Cultural factors are the value commitments of groups within the community as a whole, expressed through laws and policies. Preferred ranges of governmental action, the legitimacy of the demands of various groups, the types of pressures upon government regarded as appropriate, the norms attached to political participation, are examples of cultural factors.

Environmental factors are those which, for convenience, are considered to operate outside the boundaries of the community political system although affecting it. We shall not be able systematically to consider environmental factors in this chapter.

Structural factors may be regarded as those which are at least potentially quantifiable (e.g., size, density, mobility, unemployment, number of organizations) but which have an influence independent of their cultural content. Cultural factors are those which are qualitative in their intrinsic character (e.g., the strength and pervasiveness of norms, the degree of group solidarity) despite the fact that some quantitative indicators might be constructed to measure parts of their meaning.

Structural and cultural factors have consequences for community life which, at any given point in time, produce events that have no connection with the political system. If these events occur regularly, they become processes of various kinds—e.g., crime rates and divorce rates. Depending on situational factors, one or another such process may become important in the strategies and alliances of leadership. The crime rate may become visible after a particularly heinous murder. But the reason for the distinction between events and decisions is to make explicit the fact that there are many processes going on at any time which have no relation to the political system, and yet are potentially "available" to political actors, depending upon strategic considerations. Since the processes are not random, but depend upon structural and cultural features of the community, they must be taken into account in any systematic attempt at comparative political studies.

Also to be emphasized is that a number of processes taking place even within "government," however defined, may not be either a decision or a policy, in the sense that any person or group intends them to happen. Unanticipated consequences of structural and cultural factors, whether internal or external to government or politics, may occur and have great consequences for subsequent decision and policy processes, and yet have no purposeful relation to present decision and policy processes. The effects of increasing the size of a police department, for example, may be to decrease the span of control by central policy makers, and to increase the individual patrolman's area of discretion, without anyone intending it to happen. Such consequences of change impinge on policy in ways which have to be understood in order to explain what actually happens, but would be excluded from a mode of analysis which treats only consciously intended policies and decisions.

Figure 1 presents a graphic picture of this analytical scheme.

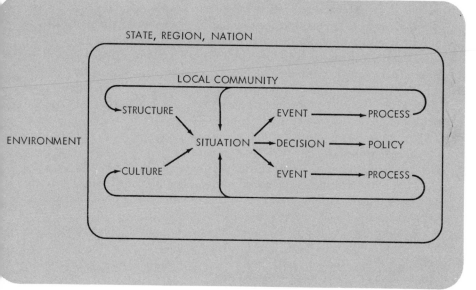

Figure 1

Each of the variables shown in the scheme can be regarded as a class of either independent or dependent variables. We cannot here deal with all of the complexities of these relationships, but must deal only with the general categories: the dependent variables of decisions and policies and the independent variables of situational, structural and cultural factors.

The regional, state, and national environment within which decisions are made and with which decision-makers must reckon also has situational, structural, and cultural components, but we cannot include these systematically, partly because no existing study has dealt with them. The economic base of the community is a constant at a given point in time—industrial composition, market position, employment stability and composition. Historically, the economic base of a given local political unit depends upon the environment—a given community will become economically differentiated by the various market and locational forces dealt with in studies of regional economics. How and why given concentrations of economic activities become marked off into political units depends on the relative advantages seen by local leaders at crucial decision-making points, and upon the successes of the strategies used in conflicts between various groups benefiting from or injured by a given political structure and boundaries.

Given a particular economic base, consequences follow for the demographic changes and composition of a city. Clearly the occupational and educational composition of a city, and its income distribution, are influenced by its economic base—the industrial and service "mix" of the city's economy. Given the technological level of development in the nation at a given time, the level of economic growth of the city's industries is also influenced, and therefore its population growth or decline. These factors in turn, by influencing the income structure of the population, will affect the proportion of home owners, population density and distribution (which in particular areas will be influenced by the particular climatic and geographic features of the land).

The previous factors will [shape] at any given time the political and social structure of the city. Given a certain income and occupational composition, racial and ethnic mixture, and political and economic values, a class structure will develop, as well as organizations expressing the needs and demands of various groups in the community, neighborhood groupings, and other forms of social organization.

The "problems" facing city government at any given point in time will be determined by the history of the city—its past social composition and wealth and how these have been translated into public and private action to serve what are defined as the proper services performed by government and public-spirited private groups. Political structures will have emerged which reflect the balance of forces between groups with conflicting interests and values. The strength of political parties, various forms of governmental organization, electoral systems, and the state of the government bureaucracy will at any given time reflect the past victories of particular groups competing for the allocations of community resources.

Existing concurrently with these social and political structures, providing them with meaning and legitimating them, are the local political cultures of the city. The historical cumulation of community experiences, combined with the values infused from the national political culture, will provide several sets of guiding norms which constrain particular leaders or free them to act. The expectations and demands of various groups in the electorate create a climate of public opinion which at any given time opens or closes paths for political action.

At any particular time, "issues" will arise in a city. Their content and form will depend upon the particular combination of all the other factors affecting the course of political and social development of the city. Which "issues" are seen as the legitimate subject of public action will vary in different historical periods. The line between "private" and "public" action is frequently an obscure one, with private groups contributing to public goals and public agencies contributing to goals of private groups.

The outcomes of particular decision-making struggles over issues will be influenced by the pattern of situational factors which exists at the time the decision is made: the incumbents in public office and their political values and skills, the strategic electoral situation, the "pileup" of issues of various kinds and the bargaining that goes on between interested parties for support, the particular national and state political situation at the given time, the resources which are able to be brought into play by activists, the visibility of the issues to the electorate, the resonance of the issues, against opinions of concerned publics, and many other factors which exist in a particular situation. All of these situational factors are conditioned by the underlying factors already summarized above: the local and national political culture, the social and political structure of the community, themselves shaped by the demographic and economic base of the community, and by the social and political environment.

Given a certain pattern of outcomes, "policies" emerge—sets of commitments to certain decisions which are set in motion by a particular outcome. One outcome may increase the chances of another and parallel outcome, other things being equal. Under certain conditions, of course, a particular outcome, if it is the result of a peculiar and unrepeated set of contingencies, may not have any impact upon future outcomes.

Once policies are settled (and clearly the conditions under which policies are reopened are an important problem), political "decisions" in the sense usually meant no longer are necessary, and routine actions may be institutionalized to carry out the policy. Administrative agencies may be created, or executive action may become routine, not requiring any legislative or judicial assent to carry out the policy. Depending upon the content of the policy, there are feedbacks to previous stages of the policy-making process. By removing certain areas of decision-making from the political process, the institutionalization of policies removes many "decisions" from the contingencies and "accidents" of the political situation in existence at any given time. Here the historical fact of the establishment of commitments must be taken into account in evaluating the nature of the political situation at a given time. Many factors which might affect the outcome of a given political struggle over an issue are not operating because the relevant actors, groups, and interests have removed themselves from the political arena by a previous victory or compromise. Thus, the establishing of a particular policy serves to affect future decision-making situations.

Decisions also change the political and economic structure of the city. By definition, a number of aspects of political and economic structure are subject to change, and the essential meaning of an open, democratic system is that a given system of allocation of resources to various groups is never final. It is always at least theoretically possible to reopen established policies embedded in the economic and political structure, even if the political and economic power of particular groups at any particular time makes basic changes difficult.

Established policies can also play an important part in controlling the demographic composition of a city, by zoning industry out or in, by restrictions on residential construction, by racial segregation, or by housing covenants and other controls designed to reinforce or change an existing economic and social composition. Once a given set of policies reflecting the interests of dominant groups is in force, it may be relatively difficult to shift, unless forces beyond the control of the locally dominant groups intervene in the form of state or national legislation, or market and other economic forces against which local leadership is relatively impotent.

The policy preferences of groups in a community are differentially transformed into effective city policies. Some groups with policy preferences are not internally cohesive enough to enable their preferences to become politically potent. If a group does achieve dominance in a community, whether by virtue of its strength, stability, and homogeneity of its preferences, or by default because of the weakness, vacillations, and heterogeneity of other groups, their preferences (and the ideologies attached to them) may become institutionalized to the point where they become part of the political culture of the community. By this is meant that governmental commitments are not easily changed by the accession of other groups to power. If this were not the case, then there would be no point in distinguishing political culture from policy preferences. City politics would merely be the arena of combat of competing interest groups, able to institute their programs at will as the aftermath of victory. There is reason to believe that this is not the case; a given set of goals and procedures established in institutionalized forms persists in spite of changes in incumbents. This is the implication, at any rate, of the conception of "roles of government" that Williams and Adrian present.

The above brief statement of the relations between the wide range of factors affecting urban policy-making is not intended to be an empirical prediction of their relative importance in any given situation. Nor is it intended to be an exhaustive summary of all the possible types of variables which might be included under one or another general class of factors. The assumption which the scheme reflects is that each class of factors has at least analytical, if not in each instance empirical, independence which requires that it be distinguished at a theoretical level. The studies summarized here have necessarily dealt with selected variables. We turn now to the five studies. . . .

CONCLUSIONS

I have argued that a critical distinction often ignored in studies of power and influence in urban political processes is the one between long-term and short-term factors, or what we have called here structural and cultural factors versus situational factors.

If opportunities are continually available to particular individuals or groups by virtue of their positions in particular institutions, then we might refer to the conduciveness of a structure or culture to the creation of certain situations. Social and political structures may provide situations continually favoring one group with greater political access, visibility of their interests, and various resources, and consequently with greater motivations, interest, and experience. Such individuals and groups may thereby have disproportionate chances to win when their interests are at stake in a decision. Such a statement is an attempt to link the long- with the short-range aspects of factors affecting decisions, not a hypothesis about the nature of structural conduciveness. Even such a link, if established, does not tell us what is likely to happen (who will win) in a unique sequence of events. Only relatively low probabilities can be established by knowledge of the structural and cultural factors creating opportunities for action. Prediction of which individuals will get involved and which strategies will be chosen and ultimately successful in such unique situations is probably a goal with little scientific pay-off.

As we have seen, a focus upon one or another object of study has been accompanied in these studies by a parallel focus upon a certain class of explanatory or correlated variables. Those who have studied particular decisions have usually sought their explanations in situational factors. Policies have usually been explained by structural factors and roles of government by cultural ones. Because of limitations of resources, few studies have systematically taken environmental factors into account. Most studies, either tacitly or explicitly, simply regard other objects of study and associated factors as either being "constant" and therefore capable of being ignored or as beyond their resources to study.

Our intention here has not been to evaluate existing studies, but rather the field of comparative studies of urban politics as a whole. Any particular study must make certain assumptions, must exclude problems which are vital for another, and must exploit resources available at the cost of neglecting certain aspects of the problem which may well be important. To have noted that a certain book fails to deal with a certain class of factors is thus not a criticism, unless its omission was vital for the task that the author set for himself. It is hoped that this sketchy review has brought out some of the possibilities for future comparative studies.

Although a major controversy in the area has concerned the nature of "community power structure," this concept has not been treated here as a major analytic category, because of the inconsistency of meanings and operations attached to the term. It is hoped, however, that the different sets of problems dealt with under the rubric of power structure have become clearer by treating the several studies with respect to their focus upon the influence of cultural, structural and situational factors in decisions and policy-making.

Whether a power structure, for example, is defined as a set of *persons* or as a set of *institutions* which provide such political resources as property, wealth, high status, communication networks, and legality to persons is an important distinction corresponding to the distinction between situational, structural and cultural factors. If a power structure is a set of persons, then finding different people involved in different issues might lead to the conclusion that a pluralistic power structure exists. If a power structure is a set of institutions, then it may be irrelevant whether or not the same individuals are involved in different situations. The point is not that individuals who have similar resources and institutional positions will always act in the same way. Rather, the two aspects must be considered separately, and resources must not be simply viewed as attributes of individuals who choose whether or not to act on behalf of political ends in particular situations, but also as systematically allocated consequences of the institutional structure of the society and political system.

Power and Community Structure

Peter H. Rossi

In this selection Peter H. Rossi offers a conceptual scheme for guiding further research in terms of class-status differentiation and of political institutions; he notes especially the impact of parties on policy-making within a community. He suggests that combinations of these variables will yield the distinctive patterns of the distribution of power. Rossi's ideas may be thought of as specific applications of Alford's general theory of the relationship between long-run and short-run factors. They also are linked to the typologies constructed by Agger et al in the article reproduced in this section, although Rossi's article preceded both works. The reader may ask whether this formulation of community power types might help account for the sociologists' emphasis upon business domination, and the political scientists' emphasis upon political domination, which we explored earlier.

A CONCEPTUAL SCHEME FOR THE POLITICAL STRUCTURE OF LOCAL COMMUNITIES

The purpose of the scheme to be described here is to account for the variations in power structures to be found among American local communities. It may also prove of some utility in other areas, for example, community conflicts. The general thesis underlying the scheme is a simple one: the pattern taken by the power structure of a community is a function of the kind of political life to be found therein. My reasons for postulating this relationship are also simple and somewhat obvious: the political institutions of a community are the ultimate locus of the decisions that are binding on the total community. Hence much of the power exercised is focused on the governmental institutions of the local community.

For our present purposes, it is useful to regard the political life of a community as occurring at two different levels, interrelated but to some

Reprinted from "Power and Community Structure," *Midwest Journal of Political Science*, IV (November, 1960), 394–401, by Peter H. Rossi by permission of the Wayne State University Press. Copyright 1960, by Wayne State University Press.

degree independent. On the one hand, there is a set of governmental institutions manned by officials and employees with defined functions and spheres of authority and competence. On the other hand, there is the electorate, the body of citizens with voting rights, organized to some degree into political parties. We expect that phenomena appearing on each of these levels dependently influence the forms taken by community power structures.

On the institutional level, there are several characteristics of local government that are of some consequence. First, communities vary according to the degree to which the roles of officials are *professionalized*. In many communities, mayors and city councilmen and often other officials are employed in their official capacities only part time and lack the opportunity to become fully engrossed in these roles. At the other extreme, some communities employ professionally trained officials—city managers, school superintendents, etc.—who are full time employees expecting to remain in their occupation—although not in any particular post—for long periods of time. In communities where local officials exercise their functions on a part time basis and where the qualifications for incumbency are not exacting, the incumbents are less likely to segregate their official roles from their other roles and hence extra-official considerations are more likely to play roles of some importance in their decisions. Thus the informal cabal which ran Springdale, as described by Vidich and Bensman, hardly distinguish between their roles as city fathers and their roles as businessmen and professionals. At the other extreme are the professional politicians who run Chicago, whose independence is curbed very little.

A second important structural characteristic of local government refers to the rules by which officials are selected. Two aspects of electoral rules are significant. Electoral rules can either retard or facilitate the development of enduring political alignments in the community, and the latter are important determinants of the forms of decision making. In this respect, the crucial differences lie between communities which have non-partisan and communities which have partisan elections. Non-partisan electoral rules discourage the development of enduring political alignments by reducing the advantages to candidates of appearing on slates, whereas partisan elections facilitate cooperation among candidates and the drawing of clear lines between opposing slates of candidates. It should be noted in this connection that primaries are in effect non-partisan elections in communities which are predominantly Democratic or Republican.[1]

---

[1] Non-partisan elections operate to the benefit of the highly organized political minority. Hence, usually, non-partisan elections operate to the benefit of the white collar groups in industrial communities and to the benefit of the Democratic Party in middle class suburbs.

Another structural characteristic which tends to reduce the importance of political organizations is the rule concerning the number of officials elected by popular vote. Short ballots on which only a few candidates compete for the major offices tend to reduce organizational importance by lowering the benefits to candidates of cooperation with each other.

These structural characteristics of the governmental institutions of the local community underlie the ability of these institutions to develop an independence of their own and also indicate the extent to which conflicts within the community are manifested in the political realm or in some other fashion.

Moving now to the level of the electorate and its organization, there are two important dimensions to be considered. First, we must consider the political homogeneity of the electorate, roughly defined as the extent to which the community is divided equally or unequally among the contending political factions of the community. The more unequally the community is divided, the less likely are open political struggles to be the major expressions of clashes of interest and the more likely is decision making to be a prerogative of a "cozy few."

Borrowing from Gerhard Lenski, a second characteristic of the electorate might be called "political crystallization": the extent to which the lines of political cleavage within the community coincide with major social structural differentiations. In this connection the crucial modes of social structural differentiation are along class and status lines. The more political lines coincide with class and status lines, the more likely are community clashes to take a political form. These are important lines of differentiation within communities because they are likely to endure over time.[2] Political differences which coincide with class and status differences are for these reasons likely to be reinforced by the double factors of differential association and connection with important interests.

If we now consider the entire set of community characteristics distinguished here, we see that they may be conceived of as indicators of two more abstract attributes of communities: first, the institutional indicators express the degree of segregation of political institutions from other community institutions; second, the indicators relating to the electorate reflect the extent to which partisan politics is a crucial arena for the important decision making within the community.

It is important to note that these characteristics of communities can be easily translated into operational forms. The city charter can tell us how officials are elected and whether their jobs are full or part time. Elec-

[2] On a large space scale—i.e., for regions and nations—regional differences would also play important roles, but since the micro-regional differences in the American city tend to be wiped out quickly by residential mobility, they play only a minor role within communities.

tion statistics and survey research can tell us the degree of political homogeneity and political crystallization.

Two broad hypotheses can be formulated at this point. (1) The more segregated are political roles from other roles played by incumbent officials, the more independent the governmental structure of a community from other institutional structures. (2) The more heterogeneous the electorate and the greater the degree of political crystallization, the more important the governmental institutions as loci for important decision making.

IMPLICATIONS FOR COMMUNITY POWER STRUCTURES

The studies of community power structures have universally found the upper levels of the occupational hierarchy to occupy prominent power positions. In no city—even heavily working class Stackton—have proprietors, managers, and professional men played insignificant parts. Often enough some members of these groups do not play as prominent a part as others, even though they are as wealthy and as important in the economic life of the city, but in all cities members of these groups were to be found in some kind of inner circle.

The disagreement among researchers concerns two important matters. First, there is disagreement over the pattern of power, with some researchers preferring the monolith as their model and others preferring polyliths or more complicated forms. Second, there is disagreement over the roles played by public officials and voluntary associations. Hardly anything could be written about Chicago, Stackton, or Philadelphia without reference to the mayor's office and other top level public officials. In contrast, in Regional City and some of the towns studied by C. P. Loomis and his research workers, public officials and often labor leaders appear as minor and insignificant personages. It should be noted that these two kinds of disagreements among researchers are related. A monolithic model for a power structure generally goes along with a very subordinate role for voluntary associations and public officials. Thus, in Hunter's Regional City public officials are explicitly viewed as the handmaidens of the elite group, and labor leaders are scarcely worth mentioning.

A polylithic power structure tends to mean a number of small monoliths each centering around a particular sort of activity. Thus in industrial Stackton, the civic associations and community service organizations were the preserves of the business community, whereas local government was safe in the hands of professional politicians resting on the mass base of the Democratic Party and its heavy support from among ethnic groups of relatively recent arrival from abroad. Indeed, respondents rarely reported that any one individual was powerful in all spheres of community life.

To some degree the disagreements among researchers on the forms taken by the power structures in communities and the place to be accorded public officials and associational leaders are functions of the different research techniques employed. Some approaches preclude the finding of polylithic power structures. However, in much larger part, the differences among researchers are functions of "reality," representing major ways in which communities *in fact* differ. My general thesis is that these differences are functions of the differences among communities in their political structures.

If we look carefully at the studies of community power structure we may discern the following types:

(1) *Pyramidal.* Lines of power tend to have their ultimate source in one man or a very small number of men. Decision making tends to be highly centralized, with lower echelons mainly carrying out major policy decisions made by the small group at the apex.

Examples: Middletown, Regional City

(2) *Caucus rule.* Lines of power tend to end in a relatively large group of men who make decisions through consensus. Decision making tends to be a matter of manufacturing consent among the "cozy few" who make up the caucus. Typical power structure in the small town or dormitory suburb.

Examples: Springdale, Mediana

(3) *Polylith.* Separate power structures definable for major spheres of community activity. Typically, local government in the hands of professional politicians backed by the solidary strength of voluntary associations, with the community service organizations in the hands of the business and professional subcommunity.

(4) *Amorphous.* No discernible enduring pattern of power. Logical residual category. No examples.

Note that the first two types of power structures are very similar, differing only in the number of decision makers who share power among themselves. The major differentiation is between the first two types wherein lines of power tend to converge and the last two types wherein lines of power tend to diverge.

The divergence of power lines has its source in the existence of the possibility for occupational groups other than business and professional to occupy positions of importance within major community institutions. This occurs typically when there is political crystallization in a community which is heterogeneous class wise or status wise. When the lower status or class levels have a political party representing them which has a chance to get into office, there is the possibility that public office can become one of the important sources of power.

The conditions under which the political parties have a vigorous life are defined by the structural features described earlier. Under partisan electoral laws, when officials are professionalized, when either the majority of the electorate favor the underdog party or when the parties are balanced in strength, then the political institutions and public officials assume a position of importance within the power structure of the community.

Another way of putting this thesis is to say that the leaders of the dominant economic institutions ordinarily wield power, but they are forced to take others into account when popular democratic rules allow the lower levels of the community an opportunity to place their representatives in public office. The elements of the community political structure we have distinguished here are those which facilitate the development of governmental independence from the business and professional community.

The general hypothesis may now be stated more precisely, as follows: *in communities with partisan electoral procedures, whose officials are full time functionaries, where party lines tend to coincide with class and status lines and where the party favored by the lower class and status groups has some good chance of getting elected to office, community power structures tend to be polylithic rather than monolithic.* Since these characteristics of community political structures are to some unknown degree independent of one another, different combinations of such characteristics can appear empirically. The patterns in such communities cannot be deduced from this hypothesis since we do not specify the weights to be assigned to each characteristic.

There are further expectations implied in the general hypothesis. Some examples follow:

(1) Homogeneous middle class communities, for example, dormitory suburbs and the like, will tend to have monolithic power structures, since the class basis for countervailing political power does not exist.

(2) In communities where the lower class party has a clear majority there will be moves on the part of the business and professional community to introduce structural changes in city government to undermine this majority, as for example, nonpartisan elections, short ballot, and the like.

(3) In polylithic communities, city government and private community organizations try to limit the sphere of each other's operations by moving more and more functions into their own spheres of authority.

(4) In communities with monolithic power structures, conflicts tend to take on the character of mass revolts in which small incidents are magnified out of proportion because there are no regularized means for the expression of conflict.

(5) Historically, the development of voluntary civic associations may be interpreted as a reaction to the loss of local political power by high status groups. Since these community organizations were not governed by the mass vote of the lower class groups, high status groups could keep control over them.

Additional similar propositions may be generated from the basic hypothesis set forth in this paper. Although I believe that such propositions will be upheld in general by empirical data, I am also sure that considerable modifications will be made in them. . . .

Community Leadership:
Directions of Research

Charles M. Bonjean

David M. Olson

The authors of this selection suggest the necessity of research in terms of typologies based upon the variables of leadership qualities such as legitimacy, visibility, scope of influence, and cohesiveness. Further, they emphasize that attention should be given not merely to the dynamics of the power structure at the time it is under investigation, but that one should also know the antecedents and consequences of that structure. That is, it is of equal importance to understand how some power structure characteristics "may be dependent on the nature of the society or community of which they are a part," and to know how such characteristics are related to "the effectiveness, efficiency, or quality of community projects, organizations, or institutions." This insistence is reminiscent of Alford's stress on the importance of long-run factors and of the ideas of Agger et al below, which stress the need to take different time periods into account when performing such studies. In the original, this article provides an extensive bibliographic review.

. . . The types of power structures that could function in American communities (and, in fact, have been described by the investigators cited in this paper) are many, and, indeed, little would be gained here from a brief description of each of them. Rather, what is needed is a means by which their main characteristics can be summarized and compared. One approach that has been successful in describing and comparing other types of social structures is the use of sets of ideal-type constructs. Entire societies, for example, have been described and compared by the degree to which they approximate folk societies or urban societies. Complex organizations are said to approximate the Weberian model of bureaucracy or the human relations model. There is no reason why this same ap-

From Charles M. Bonjean and David M. Olson, "Community Leadership: Directions of Research," *Administrative Science Quarterly*, VIII (December, 1964), 291–300.

proach could not be used in the study of community leadership. For example, using Hunter's findings and exaggerating the main characteristics of the leadership structure he found, an ideal type may be constructed that would logically fall at one extreme on our hypothetical yardstick and therefore could be used as a rough measure that would enable comparison and thus give some meaning to data that have been and will, no doubt, be found by others. One possible leadership model, then, is the Covert Power Elite, identified by the following characteristics: (1) leaders do not hold political offices or offices in associations, (2) they are not recognized by the community at large as key decision makers, (3) they are active in a wide range of decision areas, and (4) they work together as a group, rather than independently or in opposition.

Most ideal-type constructs have logical opposites, which, in this case, would be a leadership model where: (1) leaders hold political or associational office, (2) leaders are recognized by the community at large as key decision makers, (3) leaders are concerned only with those decisions related to official areas, and (4) group structure may not be present (certainly, at least, primary relations would be absent). These characteristics, of course, probably best describe that type of leadership structure most consistent with the political formula of our society—legitimate pluralism.[1] Between these two extremes one would find independent sovereignties (covert subgroupings concerned with one or a few decision areas), rival sovereignties (visible, though not legitimate, subgroupings competing on any number of decisions), and interest groups (leaders may hold associational, but not political, office; concern is with one or a few decisions; and leaders are recognized by the community).[2]

In short, the following four characteristics appear to be the most important in identifying the two ideal-type leadership structures and thus perhaps any structure falling between these two:

1. *Legitimacy.* Where leaders hold public or associational office, the leadership structure is, in fact, an authority structure. Legitimacy is easily measured by collecting information on each leader (identified by either the reputational or decisional approach) in regard to political or associational offices. One measure of the leadership structure's legitimacy, then, is simply the proportion of leaders who hold or have recently held such offices. The use of a percentage score enables the comparison of different communities that may have different numbers of leaders.

2. *Visibility.* This is a dimension separate from legitimacy. If all com-

---

[1] "Political formula" includes the system of beliefs and values which legitimize the democratic (or any other) system and specify the institutions (such as political parties, a free press, etc.) which allow for the distribution of power. See Seymour Martin Lipset, *Political Man* (New York: 1960), chs. ii and iii.

[2] The types are suggested by Dahl, *Who Governs?*

munity leaders held political or associational offices, perhaps the leadership structure would be clearly visible. But the reverse is not equally as true. Leaders who do not hold positions of authority may or may not be covert. Thus legitimacy tells us nothing about visibility unless all leaders *are* public or associational officers. To measure visibility necessitates the use of the reputational approach, at least to some degree. Visibility may be roughly measured if the nominations and rankings of a panel of judges (or better, the leaders themselves) are compared with the nominations and rankings of a sample of the general public or some other segment of the community. Comparing the rankings by sets of informants yields three possible types of leaders: *visible* (those recognized by both the judges and the general public), *concealed* (those recognized by the judges but not by the general public), and *symbolic* (those recognized by the general public, but not by the judges). The differential visibility of community leadership structures could be assessed by comparing the proportions of visible leaders.

3. *Scope of Influence.* One leader or set of leaders may participate in decision making in a wide range of issues in a community, or different leaders or sets of leaders may be active in different areas. Both types of leaders, in fact, could be found within the same community. Scope of influence could be measured in at least two different ways:

a. A list of actual or possible decisions in the community could be presented to each leader (or each informant), and he, in turn, could be asked to specify those decisions in which he (or his nominee) had participated in policy formation. Each leader could then be assigned a percentage score based on the number of decision areas in which he participated compared to the total number of decision areas. Scores within and between communities are important here, in that a summary score for any given community may be misleading if leaders of both types have been identified. A problem arises from the fact that the number of salient decisions may vary from community to community. If *possible* rather than *actual* decisions are used as the denominator, the total score will be affected by the number of actual decisions. The problem is minimized, of course, if the investigator limits his concern to actual decisions.

b. The second method of measuring scope of influence is possible only if the decisional approach is used to identify leaders. If several different types of decisions are analyzed, each leader's role in each type of decision may be carefully assessed. Indeed, participation in decision making in four different types of issues, for example, would be evidence of *general* leadership. Perhaps one criterion for selection using the decisional approach (or for inclusion on an interview schedule using the reputational approach) to assess scope of influence should be variability along the dimensions suggested by Barth and Johnson or by Banfield and Wilson.

4. *Cohesiveness.* Given legitimate or nonlegitimate, visible or concealed, and general or issue leaders, they may or may not interact as members of a group (or perhaps several groups). It is possible that cohesiveness, certainly one characteristic of a group, could be measured, at least roughly, by the degree to which leaders nominate one another. Indeed, one sociometric statistic, the ratio of interest, purports to measure this group characteristic in precisely such a manner. Interaction patterns, themselves, may be investigated by asking respondents to indicate those with whom they have worked (and in regard to which decisions). Cohesiveness has been treated in a particularly precise manner by Scoble. After finding three major factions by sociometric techniques, he determined that each was internally divided on policy preferences by using Rice's index of cohesion to measure their answers to a set of public opinion questions. Nevertheless, the factions possessed sufficient agreement for at least some members of each to participate as indentifiable cliques on most decisions. Other similar techniques, for example an acquaintanceship scale, have also been used to attempt to assess the group structure of leadership elites. Such techniques appear to identify unitary, bifactional, multifactional, and amorphous patterns. These patterns may be found within either a general- or issue-oriented elite. The analysis of clique or factional patterns is very similar to that used in discussion of political parties (one-, two-, or multiparty systems), intra-party factions (one-faction, two-faction, or multifactional parties), and industrial competition (monopoly, oligopoly, or competition).

In summary, legitimacy, visibility, scope of influence, and cohesiveness appear to be the most significant dimensions of community leadership structures in that (1) they have been the major sources of disagreement and criticism, (2) a review of leadership studies indicates that variation may, in fact, be found along all four dimensions, and (3) they are useful in the identification of different types or models of leadership structures.

Antecedents and Consequences of Leadership Structure Characteristics

Given the tentative conclusion that community leaders may be identified and that leadership structures vary along certain dimensions from community to community, what has been found to be related to leadership structure characteristics? The search for such relationships is a fairly recent trend. Most of the earlier investigations were simply case studies attempting to describe the leadership structure or processes in one community. Explanation, of course, usually requires the examination of two or more cases and an attempt to account for their differences or similarities. Only through a comparative approach—studies of large numbers of decisions on comparable issues within one community over time or in many different communities—is it possible to make generalizations in regard to those phenomena which might be related to leadership structure characteristics. The few comparative analyses of community leadership structures that have been undertaken usually deal with possible antecedents of community leadership structures or possible consequences of the same, but seldom, if ever, both. Many of these investigations have not been concerned with visibility, legitimacy, cohesiveness, or scope of influence as leadership structure characteristics per se; some, however, do offer insights into relationships between these characteristics and antecedents and consequences.

Antecedents

That the characteristics of influence structures may be dependent on the nature of the society or community of which they are a part has been the basic relationship investigated by those concerned with antecedents of community leadership structures.

A number of comparative analyses have been cross-cultural comparisons seeking to test the hypothesis that leaders represent those institutions that are the most powerful and influential in the society at large. Thus, as might be expected, Miller found that businessmen exerted a predominant influence in community decision making in two United States cities, but in a British city other institutions were better represented. According to Miller, this is in part a consequence of the higher social status of industry and its captains in the United States, and in part a function of city government in the British city—specifically an active community council requiring much time and work of its 112 members.

D'Antonio and his colleagues compared institutional and occupational representations in eight United States cities, the British city studied by Miller, and two Mexican cities. They found that business provided the largest number of top influentials in all the United States cities as well as in the two Mexican cities. The two Mexican cities, however, gave the strongest evidence of a challenge to business by another sector of the community—government. They explain this as a consequence of the dominance of the PRI (*Partido Revolucionario Institucional*) in Mexico. The role of economic dominants over time in one community was studied by Schulze. He noted, for example, that as the economic structure of the community changed, so did its leadership structure. As the community economic system became absorbed into the larger industrial complex of a nearby large city, local economic dominants participated less in community decision making, leaving it almost wholly in the hands of a group of middle-class business and professional men. The same relationship was observed by Clelland and Form in a more recent investigation of another community. One implication of those studies concerned with the relationship between the community's institutional structure and leadership structure is the greater probability of legitimate, visible structures with limited scopes of influence in communities with complex institutional structures, or at least in those where a single institution or organization is not dominant.

Not only may the relative importance of different institutions influence the nature of the leadership structure, but characteristics of a single institution may also be important. Perhaps the most obvious, as suggested by Miller above, is the political institution itself. The perceptions and values of public officials may, of course, vary between communities. While they may play merely formal ministerial roles, and therefore be rated low in reputation for power, they may also actively exercise independent and real power. On at least those issues which require government decision, government officers occupy potentially strategic positions. Studies of state legislators show that they vary considerably in their role orientations toward their jobs and toward other participants in the legislative process, and that these variations are linked systematically with their behavior as public officials. City officials, both elected and appointed, might also be expected to vary in these respects. One would expect, then, a positive relationship between activist role perceptions of public officials and the legitimacy, visibility, and definite scope of decision making.

Another institutional factor affecting community power is the party system. The boss of a cohesive political party who is also mayor has considerable independent power, though he, of course, does not lack external constraints on his behavior. Rossi has suggested that professionalization of political roles and electoral competition in a diverse electorate lead to an independence of government actors from economic influence.

The locale and procedures of decision making may have an important impact on leadership patterns. Some issues are public and are resolved only through a referendum. The referendum is potentially the least capable of control by a small covert elite. To have power, the leaders must be able to control both voter turnout and their voting.[3] Power is not subjected to this test if the issue is resolvable through private means, such as fund raising for an auditorium or hospital. Decisions resolvable through formal positions occupy an intermediate category. The holders of formal

---

[3] James S. Coleman, *Community Conflict* (Glencoe, Ill.: 1957), found that voter turnout and referendum defeats were positively correlated (p. 19).

positions may actually exercise power, or they may be open to degrees of influence from either covert elites or segments of the public.

The institutional structure of the community includes but one set of variables that may influence the nature of a community's leadership structure. Eighty-eight different community variables, ranging from population density to socioeconomic status, have been factor analyzed by Jonassen and Peres. Seven factors were identified that accounted for most of the variation: urbanism (population size, density, and hetero-geneity), welfare (health, wealth, employment, and education), influx (population growth), poverty (low income, dependent population), magnicomplexity (social, economic, and governmental complexity), educational effort, and proletarianism (propertyless, relatively poor, low-skilled and poorly paid workers). Bonjean examined four communities to see if any of these community factors were associated with any of the leadership structure characteristics discussed above. It was found that those characteristics most closely associated with the Covert Power Elite type of structure were population influx (for example, the greater the influx, the less visible the leadership structure), poverty (for example, the greater the community poverty, the less visible the leadership struc-ture), and magnicomplexity (for example, the less complex the com-munity, the less visible the leadership structure). Although the same factors per se were not used, Presthus studied similar relationships in two communities. His conclusions show a relationship between magnicom-plexity and the presence of a Covert Power Elite (in the same direction as was found in the investigation cited above), a relationship between poverty and Covert Power Elite characteristics (also consistent with the findings set forth above), and a negative relationship between urbanism and Covert Power Elite characteristics.

Consequences

Even fewer studies have been concerned with consequences of leader-ship structure characteristics than with antecedents. Sociologists' interest here seems to be relating leadership structure characteristics to the effec-tiveness, efficiency, or quality of community projects, organizations, or institutions. Belknap and Steinle, for example, studied relationships be-tween hospital systems and community leadership in two communities and found that the quality of hospital facilities, services, and so forth was higher in the community where the hospital board-members were also community leaders. Hunter, of course, was concerned with the same types of relationships, noting for example, that community agencies were extremely careful not to incur the displeasure of top leaders and thereby be excluded from their interest and beneficence. The same general type of relationship was studied by Dakin who was concerned with the relationship between variations in leadership structure and differences in the effectiveness with which four areas were organized for action on some area problem. He also found that group structure and legitimacy were positively related to effective organization.

The major consequence studied by political scientists is the "public interest." Interest group studies, and now community power-structure studies, cause political scientists to ask if a given distribution of power is in the public interest. While most investigators in this field distrust a monolithic power structure, especially if it is composed of economic rather than political actors, political scientists are generally content to raise the issue of the public interest without pronouncing a definitive answer.

CONCLUSIONS

Basic changes have taken place in the study of community leadership over the past decade. The changes seem to indicate that there have been perhaps more continuity and direction in this area of investigation than would appear to be the case at first glance. Briefly, the basic trends have been: (1) a shift in preference and use from the positional to the reputational to the decisional method, and finally to a combination of methods for the identification of leaders; (2) growing consensus in regard to the variability of leadership structure over time and place, and thus more concern with the salient dimensions along which the variation takes place—legitimacy, visibility, scope of influence, and cohesiveness; and finally, (3) less concern with descriptive case studies and greater interest in comparative analyses of explanatory utility—that is, more concern with those factors that may be related to variations in leadership structure.

Classifying Power Structures and Political Regimes

Robert E. Agger

Daniel Goldrich

Bert E. Swanson

The volume from which this selection is drawn continues, in our judgment, to be one of the most sophisticated analyses of community power by political scientists to date. Based on their ten year study of two towns in a western state, and a four to five year study of two southern cities, the authors derive a multi-dimensional model for categorizing community systems. They focus on limited variables to develop typologies of "power structure" and "regimes" which later are combined into "political systems." Further, they place great emphasis not only on the distribution of power but on the rules by which the "game" of politics is played, and on the interrelationship between these two elements.

Agger and his co-workers also suggest additional dimensions which can modify and proliferate the simple typologies into multi-faceted models which extend their many concepts to fit a range of real-world situations. The authors' use of the time factor, the importance of which was suggested earlier in the selections from Bonjean and Olson and from Alford, allows us to move from a "snapshot" to a "motion picture" of community politics.

FOUR TYPES OF POWER STRUCTURES

The conception of a community power structure as a functioning organization has led [us] to a typology of power structures based on two variables: the extent to which political power is distributed broadly or narrowly over the citizenry, and the extent to which the ideology of the political leadership is convergent and compatible or divergent and con-

From Robert E. Agger, Daniel Goldrich, and Bert E. Swanson, *The Rulers and the Ruled* (New York: John Wiley & Sons, Inc., 1964), pp. 73–112 (excerpts).

flicting.[1] By dichotomizing each variable, four types of power structure are delineated.

The typology indicates that if only one political leadership group shared a single ideology, the power structure would be consensual, whether mass or elite.[2] There may be two or more political leadership groups, whose ideologies could be either compatible or conflicting. An example of a condition of compatible ideologies would be two sets of political leaders representing different socio-economic interests but agreeing on a compromise-bargaining-trading perspective; an example of a conflicting-ideology condition would be two sets of political leaders who had such firm emotional commitments to an overall program for the scope of government relating to all areas of life that the loss of a single decisional battle or the prospect of compromise would be almost intolerable.[3] These conditions are based on the findings in the four communities, findings we would expect in communities throughout the United States. But if communities in nations marked by more violent ideological conflict were compared with these American communities, the American communities might all have to be classified as consensual in character rather than competitive.

This simple typology of power structures raises several points. As one example, the competitive-consensual dimension is based upon the state of ideology in the groups that have attained positions of political leadership in a power structure. However, two Consensual Elite structures may differ in the extent to which there are groups of people aspiring to enter the leadership. One may face no outside challenge; another may have to face a group that has been actively aspiring to take over leadership without success. Such differences are noted if they occur.

As another example of a point suggested by this typology, the broad-

[1] The analyst must decide which of the many aspects or dimensions of political-power relations merits investigation first. Additional subcategories of these two variables, as well as additional dimensions, may be introduced to produce a more complex set of power-structure types. We constructed the present typology by adapting and reducing much more complex, multidimensional schemes to the limited number of communities and measured variables available in this study.

[2] The terms "mass" and "elite" are used in a somewhat special sense to refer to the extent to which proportions of the citizens share in political power, that is, purposefully contribute in various ways to decisional outcomes. They do not refer to comparisons of the size of political leaderships, although it may be that elite distributions of power are associated with relatively small political leaderships—"elite" in a more traditional sense. Nor do these terms as used here have any connotation of permanence or long duration.

[3] We might point out here that the measurement of the relative degree of convergence or divergence of the political leadership's ideology rests on operations designed to establish the degree to which the opposition, if there is more than one political leadership group, is viewed as a power-monopolizing, mortal enemy which threatens the community's way of life or as a power-sharing opponent whose political success, while undesirable, will not injure the community irreparably.

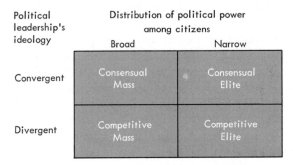

Figure 1.   Type of power structures.

narrow power dimension raises the question of the extent of overlap between the leadership and the rank and file. As has already been indicated, political leaders may comprise a small proportion of or be the entire working force in a community power structure. Power structures that are classified as mass in character might still have a minority of citizens sharing in power, although the minority would be larger than that of elite power structures. This also is an empirical question. Nor does this typology as it stands provide for classifying power structures according to the extent to which there are decisional conflicts with "winners" and "losers." A politics of personal or group interests theoretically may produce as intense a conflict as that of competing ideologies. Interest groups may be competing politically at the same time that ideological consensus exists at the leadership level of the power structure. Political participation may be high and political power broadly distributed whether there is a single ideology or convergent ideologies represented at the leadership level of the power structure. This is one reason for positing the possibility of a Consensual Mass power structure.[4]

The criteria used to classify a community power structure should be made explicit. For example, the problem of estimating and comparing distribution of political power among citizens in such a way that a community power structure can be classified as mass or elite depends directly upon the decisional processes selected for making the estimates. If one decision that has brought shares in political power to many citizens is

---

[4] A Consensual Mass power structure might exist even if there were no political-interest-group conflict within the framework of a single ideology, if some citizens feel strongly that their civic duty is to participate. It is important to understand, however, that in the absence of ideological conflict among the political leaders, the power structure is classified as consensual no matter how conflicting the interest-group politics may be.

overlooked, the distribution of power may be underestimated. We made our assessments from those decisions that a widely representative panel of officials of the communities' formally organized voluntary associations regarded as very important. These decisions will obviously differ from community to community in number and character. The specific political decisions that have emerged in each community and the sense of importance they evoke from the citizens are both relevant to the classification of power structure types. With the exceptions of school desegregation and school consolidation, decisions that were concerned with the functioning of the public schools were excluded from consideration, because we purposely phrased questions to elicit responses about decisions involving municipal government.[5] Otherwise the decisions in each community come from a variety of scope areas and are classified under one or more of the general categories of local government decisions: economic, social, governmental reorganization, or civic improvement. To classify power structures by type we must compare the distribution of power among citizens in each set of selected decisional processes that took place in a specific time period. The assessment of broad or narrow distribution of power is not specific to subdomains or subsets of decisions.[6]

The distribution of political power may vary from decisional process to decisional process within a community during a given time period. We classified a community power structure as mass to the extent that the distribution of power was broader in one or more decisional processes of the selected set than it was for any of the processes in another community.[7] In those communities classified as having mass power structures, there were ordinarily narrow or elite distributions of political power in most decisional processes. But the central interest here is in the gross differences in patterns of such distribution from community to community.

As with the other classificatory variables to be discussed, the categories used to define the power structure emerged from an interplay of theoretical interests and the actual comparisons of the four communities. The degree of ideological convergence or divergence of leadership and the degree to which power is distributed broadly or narrowly among the citizens are relative matters that depend on the comparison of real situa-

[5] For every question about participation in local government and community affairs, a corresponding question was asked about participation in school affairs. However, the data derived from the latter questions have not been included.

[6] As a result, we do not distinguish between and among common power structures even though they may differ in regard to the kinds of decisional categories under which citizens may have acquired their power.

[7] Future studies may classify types of power structures further by distributions of power by category or scope areas; they may use multiple classifications according to the distributions of power by particular decisions, or averages or other summary statistics.

tions, rather than upon an arbitrary yardstick.[8] If communities vary slightly on either count the use of different classificatory terms could lead a reader to focus on insignificant differences. Generally, however, the differences observed are sufficiently large to obviate this danger. For example, if we compared one of the four research communities to a power structure in still another community, our Competitive Mass power structures might be classified as Consensual Elite structures, thereby eliminating this basis of comparison among the original four. Rather than use categories with values fixed in an *a priori* fashion that would have masked important differences between and among the four research communities, we decided to use relative standards in classifying power structures. . . .

FOUR TYPES OF REGIMES

By "regime" we do not mean the structure of political power but rather the "rules of the game" in political decision-making as political leaders and other citizens in a polity conform to and interpret them.[9] Polities have both power structures and regimes; the term *democracy* is applied to regimes. By themselves, the four types of power structure reveal nothing about the state of democracy in the community. Theorists or philosophers of democracy do not insist that a single or convergent set of ideologies among political leaders is incompatible with democracy, nor that a broad distribution of political power is a necessary component of democracy.[10] In fact, a high level of satisfaction with life in a com-

---

[8] It should be stressed that the classification "mass" does not necessarily mean a majority—50 per cent or more—of the adults or of the eligible participant citizens. Cf. Robert A. Dahl, "The Analysis of Influence in Local Communities," in *Social Science and Community Action*, ed. by Charles R. Adrian (East Lansing, Michigan: by the Board of Trustees, 1960), p. 28; and Herbert McClosky, "Ideology and Consensus in American Politics" (unpublished paper delivered at the 1962 Annual Meeting of the American Political Science Association). McClosky defined "consensus" as a state of agreement equaling or exceeding 75 per cent, recognizing the arbitrariness of setting a specific figure for a continuous variable. Such specifications are in order when a sufficient number of readings have been taken on such variables as the distribution of power to ensure having cases on both sides of the specified figure, or when it is unimportant for a particular analysis that comparisons be made on the particular variable.

[9] This conception is more specific and narrower than, but congruent with, David Easton's definition of a regime in "An Approach to the Analysis of Political Systems," *World Politics*, IX, Number 3 (April, 1957), 392. See also Lasswell and Kaplan's use of the term "regime" in *Power and Society* (New Haven: Yale University Press, 1950), pp. 130–31, wherein they seem to refer primarily to the sense-of-electoral-potency variable. Our usage of regime is not the customary one, which refers only to the governors rather than to both the governors and the governed.

[10] This statement holds for both political power and political influence, as defined, subject to the qualifications introduced below.

munity and a low level of unsatisfied needs might be expected to produce or reinforce a Consensual Elite type of power structure in a democracy.[11]

The writings of political philosophers offer two variables for defining the extent to which a polity's regime, regardless of its type of power structure, is democratic. The first is a sense of electoral potency. This exists where citizens believe that they can attempt to obtain authorities responsive to their decisional preferences through elections without suffering illegitimate sanctions. . . . The second variable is the probability that citizens' efforts to shift or maintain the scope of government will be blocked by the use of illegitimate sanctions. The four types of regimes that result from dichotomizing each variable are presented in Figure 2.

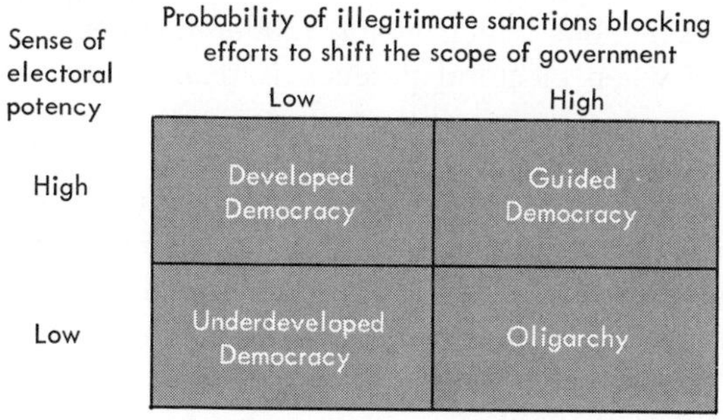

Sense of electoral potency	Probability of illegitimate sanctions blocking efforts to shift the scope of government	
	Low	High
High	Developed Democracy	Guided Democracy
Low	Underdeveloped Democracy	Oligarchy

Figure 2. Types of regimes.

One of the two variables defining regimes refers to elections rather than other forms of political participation. The constitutional guarantees of freedom of speech, right of assembly, and right of petition may be considered analogous to stages of decision-making: policy deliberation, organization of political support, and authoritative consideration. If citizens are deprived of any one of these rights—the right to become involved in any one of these stages—democracy becomes an empty symbol in reference to the political decision-making process.[12] Although these rights and stages are necessary for a fullblown democratic political process, they are not sufficient to guarantee it. The right to petition or to organize

[11] This proposition, of course, is testable. In the process of operationally defining such terms as "level of satisfaction with life in a community," some definitions may yield different empirical findings. It is so frequently taken for granted that Consensual Elite power structures are "undemocratic" that the reader needs to be specially sensitized to differences between power structures and regimes.

[12] Mass turnout at the polls is a well-known phenomenon in totalitarian countries but at variance with traditional conceptions of the democratic process, assuming that citizens have pre-electoral rights.

political support behind decisional preferences may be useless if the electoral process is controlled by and restricted to a small set of inaccessible people. The formal structure of democracy may exist without the core electoral process; in some nation-states, the electoral process only masks tightly controlled policy-deliberation, organization-of-political-support, and authoritative-consideration stages. It is assumed that the sense of *electoral* potency will be low if citizens do not feel that they can freely and effectively speak, assemble, or petition.[13]

An optimistic feeling about the right to use elections in order to express preferences is a necessary but insufficient element in a fully developed democracy: the optimism may be unjustified. It is possible that if such optimism were to lead citizens into attempting to use elections or other methods to affect the scope of government, they would be countered by illegitimate sanctions which would render their expectations invalid. Thus, it is only when electoral potency is realistically considered high, when there is a low probability of illegitimate sanctions' being used effectively to block efforts to shift the scope of government, that the regime is classified as a Developed Democracy. "Sense of electoral potency," then, refers to the expectations that citizens can use elections to obtain authorities responsive to their decisional preferences regarding the appropriate scope of government. It does not mean that they must feel sanguine about their prospects of electoral victory; only that this political channel is available.

If the sense of electoral potency is high but mistaken, the regime is labeled a Guided Democracy.[14] Oligarchy is the absence of either of these attributes of a democracy.[15] An Underdeveloped Democracy is a regime in which the electorate's sense of electoral potency is lower than it realistically should be: the probability that illegitimate sanctions will be used effectively is low. The term "democracy" is thus reserved for regimes in which at least one of the two attributes of democracy is present.

[13] This is a working assumption, which should be investigated in a cross-cultural study of politics where political cultures differ in the values placed on such stages.

[14] Argentina might be considered an example of a Guided Democracy when Peronistas were allowed officially to run for office in 1962, following which the Frondizi administration was overthrown by the military. Both before and after that period Argentina had a more oligarchic character. The sense of electoral potency apparently was high when the ban against Peronistas was lifted; at the same time, the military was prepared to use illegitimate sanctions to prevent the shifts in the scope of government expected if those elected took office.

[15] This restricted usage of the term "Oligarchy" to denote a type of regime is not common. "Oligarchy" usually refers to what we would call a type of power structure, in which political power is restricted to a small set of citizens. See Lasswell and Kaplan, *Power and Society*, p. 218; see also Robert A. Dahl, "The Analysis of Influence in Local Communities," p. 28.

It would be unrealistic and utopian to suggest that in real world politics men can interact and not sanction one another. An aspect of political maturity, as of human maturity, is the realization that it is not always possible to please everyone; loss of status or prestige is to be expected at some times in a political career. Social ostracism or economic boycotts, when applied for the first time in a polity, may effectively deactivate those who are making certain demands. Paradoxically, the more such sanctions are used, the more they may become both expected and accepted. Thus, they can lose their illegitimate character and their effectiveness. Changes may occur in the effectiveness and illegitimate character of sanctions as alternative social group satisfactions develop and alternative economic opportunities emerge from shifts in the local economy.[16] An analyst must keep these possibilities in mind when classifying regimes by type and assessing changes in regimes. Regardless of the difficulties introduced by the notion of "illegitimate" sanctions, our position in this study is that it is possible, useful, and, indeed, necessary to the scientific analysis of "democracy" to specify the importance of such sanctions in classifying regimes.

For our purposes we regard such sanctions as loss of employment opportunities in the private sectors of the economy and extreme social ostracism as among the major illegitimate political sanctions. However, we might also include the right to a job in the government itself, particularly in the established civil service. Ordinarily, civil servants are not as free to become involved in political activities as are private citizens. Because there may be some questions about this matter, we shall assume in this study that loss of government jobs, failure to be promoted or receive salary increases that are normally expected in the bureaucracy, or failure to obtain expected positions as a consequence of political activity are legitimate sanctions. This assumption might be thought incompatible with the classificatory prerequisites we have set up for a Developed Democracy. We do not think that any regime in the present study would need to be reclassified even if the operational definition of illegitimate sanctions were broadened in this particular regard. It should be stressed again that the effectiveness of illegitimate sanctions needs to be assessed for the purposes of classifying regimes.

The conception of illegitimate sanctions in the present context has a broad two-fold referent. On the one hand, they refer to a set of procedures wherein otherwise legitimate sanctions, including incarceration, capital punishment, fines, or restrictions on economic activities are re-

---

[16] The strength, flexibility, and continued growth, as well as some of the less ideal aspects, of the American constitutional system stem from the fact that the Bill of Rights does not to any great extent specify illegitimate deprivations, but broadly states that citizens may not be deprived of certain rights.

garded as illegitimate because of their use in an arbitrary, capricious, personalized, unpredictable, unequal, or unfairly discriminatory manner. In other words, the way they are used violates accepted norms of legal and judicial procedures. They apply legitimately to an act already declared unlawful by the constitutional authorities, but their application may not meet norms of due process. . . . In its second sense, the conception of illegitimate sanctions refers to relatively severe deprivations, excluding relatively minor withdrawals or withholding, of affection, respect, or money that are considered to be wrong when used for the purpose of preventing or punishing peaceful, politically motivated behavior. Although, normally, government officials are the potential violators of legal and judicial procedures, private citizens with either the knowing assistance or the unwitting cooperation of police, judges, or other government officials may be responsible for illegitimate sanctions in either sense.

Because of what historical analyses indicate to be the development of substantially juridical regimes—in the first, procedural sense of illegitimate sanctions—in all four of our research communities following the Second World War, the major concern herein is with assessing expectations of illegitimate sanctions in the second sense. Negro citizens, particularly in one of the Southern cities, feared that police and judicial procedures would be used in a discriminatory manner, violative of the equal-protection-of-law aspect of due process. However, the most likely sources of illegitimate sanctions were groups of private citizens, particularly those with relatively large amounts of economic, social, and political power. We look to the political leaderships, whether consisting of government officials, private citizens, or both, in estimating, at various points in time, the likelihood of the use of illegitimate sanctions, primarily in the second sense. . . .

The *permeability* of the power structure is another way of viewing the "probability" dimension of a regime: permeability varies with the probability that certain political demands can be pushed to the electoral process, it need be, without having illegitimate sanctions applied to those who make the demands. . . .

Our definition of permeability does not mean that a permeable set of power strata will necessarily be permeated, and thereby altered, in a subsequent period of time. Neither does it mean that certain political demands will be pushed to the electoral stage; nor that if so pushed, the demands would constitute the decisional outcomes, for they might be defeated by political opponents. Proponents may refrain from pushing their demands because they do not feel that the demands are sufficiently appealing to others, or because they believe the power structure to be impermeable, even if such is not the case.

An Underdeveloped Democracy exists when citizens who have political demands to make feel impotent because they erroneously expect that illegitimate sanctions will be used against them. A sense of electoral impotence may lead to a self-fulfilling expectation: a citizen who fears sanctions may not make his demands because of that fear; one who does not fear sanctions may make the sanctions ineffective by disregarding them. The mistaken belief that illegitimate sanctions will be used may result from the use of such sanctions in the past, and the failure of the potentially sanctionable to recognize a subsequent decrease in the disposition to use them. Or this mistaken belief may be rooted in a myth from the past maintained as an operative belief in the present.

In a Guided Democracy, as in an Oligarchy, illegitimate sanctions may or may not be actually invoked. Occasions for their application may not occur in either regime. Such sanctions accomplish their purpose through deactivating citizens who are making demands that are opposed by political leaders. Deactivation occurs not only when the consequences of continued participation are understood but also when a participant's energies are effectively redirected toward other ends. If a person begins to lose customers as a result of a politically inspired boycott, he may direct all of his efforts to his business and leave politics alone—at least for the while. He may even be unaware that the loss of customers is due to a politically inspired boycott. He may maintain his faith in democracy by treating this illegitimate sanction as an idiosyncratic event that will not be repeated. Guided Democracies may or may not be more stable than Oligarchies, in which the actual rules of the game are understood by the potentially sanctionable. In Oligarchies illegitimate sanctions may accomplish their purpose to greater degree by discouraging "undesirable" citizen political activity than by deactivating the desperate or the martyr.

Deviation from a Developed Democracy on either dimension of regimes constitutes a departure from the hitherto unmentioned principle "majority rules." Polities are Developed Democracies to the extent that an electoral outcome is determined by counting each citizen's ballot as equal to every other citizen's ballot, with the victory going to the man with the greatest number of votes—a majority or a plurality—and to the extent that citizens understand, correctly, that they may cast ballots without suffering illegitimate sanctions. The typology of regimes discussed here emphasizes the rights of minorities or powerless majorities to become the ruling majority; it stresses the fact that the spirit or intent of the democratic rule for weighing and counting votes can be violated in fact as well as through law. But since the compound democratic rules of one citizen, one vote, and victory to the man who gets more votes tend to be universal in modern cultures, this does not pose special classificatory problems, and certainly not in American communities. Infringement of these rules because of the use of an open rather than a secret ballot would be taken into account when one assessed the condition of the two defining variables of regimes. There is a special difficulty, however, if in some political systems such rules are not part of the political culture. . . .

RELATIONSHIPS OF REGIMES TO POWER STRUCTURES

A Developed Democracy theoretically may have any type of power structure; similarly, an oligarchic regime theoretically may have at least three, if not all four, types of power structure. Ordinarily, Oligarchies are thought of as regimes in which citizens justifiably feel that they are impotent as an electorate, and as power structures with a single, united political leadership sharing but one ideology, in which relatively few citizens share in political power. This is a Consensual Elite structure in the terms of our typology. However, a similar regime-power-structure combination where the leadership has become divided ideologically into two competing groups—a Competitive Elite structure—also is possible. It is even possible to conceive of an oligarchic regime to which citizens have become so accustomed that relatively large numbers of citizens contribute to decisional outcomes in one way or another—a Consensual Mass structure. An oligarchic regime with a Competitive Mass power structure is most difficult to imagine. Yet it is conceivable that two or more otherwise ideologically antagonistic leadership groups can agree upon who should not share in power.

Underdeveloped Democracies are theoretically and logically possible but, empirically, they may not exist as types of regimes. Similarly, although we can conceive of an Oligarchy with a Competitive Mass power structure, a regime and power-structure combination of that type may not exist in the real world. Theoretically, every one of the four types of regimes may exist with any one of the four types of power structures. The combinations and recombinations found in the four research communities over time are of central interest in the following chapters.

Actually, it is inaccurate to suggest that the writings of democratic theorists nowhere require that political power in a Democracy be distributed broadly. Because of their current prominence and appropriateness to this study, we shall re-examine the views of those modern democratic theorists referred to earlier as pluralists.[17] Although each pluralist has his own views, and ambiguity exists at a variety of crucial points, the following presentation of the pluralist position in regard to the inter-

---

[17] A recent criticism of pluralists and of power elitists that implies a commitment to a widespread sharing of political power as a fundamental component of democracy is to be found in Peter Bachrach, "Elite Consensus and Democracy," *The Journal of Politics*, 24, No. 3 (August, 1962), 439–52.

locking character of a democratic regime and type of power structure seems to be an accurate summary of major tenets that they share.
As one pluralist puts it:

A pair of competing party hierarchies, a polyarchal political structure in which many minorities participate, a pattern of interest groups and pressure politics appear as the most effective ways in which modern democracies can operate.

It would appear that in the pluralist view, regimes, or constitutional-legal orders, have primarily one dimension: a rule of law or the absence of illegitimate sanctions at one pole and rule by arbitrary fiat or the prevalence of illegitimate sanctions at the other. Types of power structures in American communities also are differentiated on the basis of one dimension: the degree to which citizens acquire political power when they oppose a political leadership, either through direct participation in decision-making or by using the ballot to replace an unresponsive set of officials. The term "democracy" is usually applied to those power structures that are inclined toward the appropriate pole on this dimension, the implicit assumption being that such democratic power structures have the appropriately "democratic" rules of law. Oligarchies are power structures in which the ruling minority is entrenched; this minority does not lose in decision-making conflicts. Oligarchies also are assumed to be regimes that rule by the threat or use of illegitimate sanctions, rather than by law.

Pluralists assume that few American communities are Oligarchies. The only community that has been described as an Oligarchy was New Haven, Connecticut, before the middle of the nineteenth century.[18] Yet pluralists seem to distinguish Democracies according to the degree to which they have institutionalized democratic processes or the extent to which they have become what might be called (in a different sense than we define this term) "Developed" Democracies.

They assume that in Democracies, whether developed or underdeveloped, some citizens whose political interests differ to some extent will periodically make conflicting political demands. In more developed Democracies, competitive and complementary political interests are organ-

---

[18] Robert A. Dahl, *Who Governs?*, pp. 11–24. Dahl's classification of New Haven as an Oligarchy prior to about 1840 apparently was not based on regime type. The classification seems to rest on the evidence that the political leadership was a single, unified group committed to a single ideology, with common upper-class backgrounds and interests, in whose hands rested top political, economic, and social power. This group had almost invariable success at the polls, the implication being that not only did other citizens fail to oppose them successfully but they also failed to make opposing political demands during that period. Thus the term Oligarchy seems to have been based on power structure assessments.

ized. Men who want to be elected to governmental positions because of personal or group interests tend to organize in parties. Usually, parties stand for somewhat different political programs. Since parties periodically must gain electoral support from the citizens at large, these programs must appeal to a relatively wide variety of political interests, thereby diluting what otherwise might tend to be an ideological politics. To gain and maintain elective office, officials must compromise conflicting demands; but they are likely to suffer decisional defeats periodically during their tenure in office or even be turned out of office on occasion, as minorities whose demands they could not meet rally to their electoral opponents.

A Developed Democracy in the pluralistic sense is more likely to exist, they suggest, in a large metropolis than in a small city or suburb. It is in the large, complex city that a heterogeneous citizenry is to be found; this citizenry is differentiated along social, economic, ethnic, and racial lines which become group interests and lead to, or facilitate, the formation of political interest groups. It is in the large metropolis that electoral competition is likely to develop. The pluralists expect to find in large cities the power structure that we call a Consensual Mass power structure. This, as we have mentioned, would have relatively broad distributions of power in elections and periodically in nonelectoral decision-making; and competitive parties and political interest groups would share pluralistically in the political power that accrues to those who, on occasion, successfully oppose the group in power or force the latter to compromise.

In the small city, according to the pluralists, the rule of law can be more easily undermined, so that an oligarchic regime and a Consensual Elite power structure might exist, representing a dominant interest.[19] Illegitimate social and economic sanctions are more likely to be used

---

[19] The dangers to the rule of law in small towns as a consequence of the operations of a spirit of fraternity are discussed by Robert C. Wood, *Suburbia: Its People and Their Politics* (Boston: Houghton Mifflin Co., 1959), pp. 276–80. Since the pluralists have not explored comparatively the distribution of political power among the citizens, we do not mean to imply that they have specifically indicated that a mass type of power structure is the norm in large American cities. Minority political participation has increasingly been recognized by all schools of thought as the norm in American community politics. Yet the dominant connotation seems to be that there is a wider distribution of political power over the citizens in larger than in smaller cities, in cities with a competitive party politics than in cities with one party dominance, etc. Although the extent of ideological divergence in the political leadership has rarely been studied in a conscious, systematic, comparative manner, the implication is clear that most pluralists do not think that ideology is a major variable at all. It is safer to conclude that they posit Consensual-power-structure situations as the norm, but we think that it is a fair statement that they also perceive relatively mass distributions of power as the other power-structure-dimension norm.

effectively in the "extended family" type of community, where political difference is seen by the father-leaders of the community as political deviance that threatens the whole group. Even if democracy exists in a small community, the power structure may be of the type that inhibits the expression of divergent political interests and that does not encourage the organization of opposition groups. Thus, there may be little overt opposition to the decisional preferences of the political leadership, which may itself not bother to run for elective office; electoral competition, which allows alternative programs to be offered to the voters, also may be absent. In our terminology, such polities would have democratic regimes, but such power structures would be Consensual Elite.[20]

Comparable situations presumably existed in the patrician communities of yesterday; perhaps they still exist in an occasional larger, but still homogeneous, simple city of today. The modern, metropolitan suburb is today's counterpart of yesterday's small city which had comparably "underdeveloped" democratic politics.

The present study is specifically interested in exploring the nexus assumed by the pluralists to be increasingly the norm in American communities: a democratic regime and Consensual Mass power structure. Because the present typology of regimes is based on two major dimensions, the connections presumed by pluralists between Developed Democracies and Consensual Mass power structures are of special interest. At the same time, we also shall explore the pluralist image of deviation from the norm: the existence of Oligarchy and a Consensual Elite power structure in small towns. One of our communities is very small; a second is much smaller than the third and fourth. Although a study of four communities can do very little in the way of assessing norms or typical patterns in the country as a whole, it is hoped that the findings will illuminate what are sometimes the hopes and values—rather than the empirical findings—of those democratic theorists who are committed to pluralism as the most desirable kind of political system for communities and nation-states. . . .

SOME CLASSIFACTORY CONSIDERATIONS: REGIMES

The assessment of the "probability" dimensions poses such special problems as how to classify sanctions as legitimate or illegitimate. Within the United States there is some degree of consensus on what constitute legitimate or illegitimate sanctions. In this cultural context, the major

---

[20] Springdale, as described by Arthur J. Vidich and Joseph Bensman, is in many ways of this character. See *Small Town in Mass Society* (Princeton, N.J.: Princeton University Press, 1958).

types of illegitimate sanctions are loss of job or economic advancement and extreme social ostracism, involving expulsion from formal or informal social organizations, because of "undersirable" political participation. . . .

The effectiveness of illegitimate sanctions must be assessed in the context of existing conditions. By "the context of existing conditions" we mean that a particular action, such as a boycott, loss of a job, or social ostracism, may not be an effective sanction if the sanctioned person has alternative sources of economic or social gratification. These acts may occur under various types of conditions and may vary in the extent to which they effectively block political participation. This also means that changing conditions may make an effective illegitimate sanction ineffective, and vice versa.

It is necessary to study prior time periods in order to assess the "probability" dimension, that is, what is likely to happen in a future time period. The state of the "probability" dimension can be assumed not to have changed if there is evidence that an effort to shift the scope of government has been blocked recently by the use of illegitimate sanctions, if the sanctioners are still able and disposed to act in the same way, and if the situation of the potentially sanctionable citizens has not changed. Given such conditions, the situation at Time M, the time of measurement, is projected and presumed to hold for the next period of time, Time M to $M + 1$. On the other hand, illegitimate sanctions may never have been used; they may never have occurred, or only in the distant past. The crucial consideration in such cases is the disposition of potential sanctioners in the event of certain political demands. . . .

Can regimes be compared and classified if, in a set of decisional questions selected for classifying purposes, one or more of the questions is of concern to people in one polity but of no concern to those in another polity? By "no concern" we mean that people never have had occasion to think or to formulate policy preferences about a question, or that they are indifferent to the matter. How can the potentially sanctionable be identified if a demand has never been deliberated?

One approach to the problem is to examine the perspectives of the people interested in the decisional question in the polity or polities in which it exists. From these perspectives it may be possible to identify the people in another polity who would be the potentially sanctionable, and then to classify regimes on the basis of the same kinds of potential political demands. However, we have rejected this approach in favor of one that classifies regimes on the basis of political demands that are extant in each polity, although these may vary by number and kind from polity to polity. A similar approach was taken in classifying power structures by type. . . .

The set of decisional processes selected as the basis for classifying regimes by type includes those that have become subjects of policy deliberation, at least of informal political discussion, in any of the four cities. It is ordinarily larger than that selected for classifying power structures, since it may include processes that have been repressed or tabled during a policy-deliberation stage, before reaching the point where political power can properly be assigned by the analyst. Although such processes are not included among those selected to classify power structures, they may differentiate one type of regime from another. Election and nomination decisions are considered but not actually used in classifying power structures. Since they are significant in the conception of regime, however, they are included in the sets of decisional processes used to classify regimes.

In selecting decisional questions in order to determine types of regimes, policy formulations not being deliberated were excluded from consideration. This was done on the assumption that the four communities were sufficiently "democratic" to allow for at least covert deliberation of intensely held political preferences. This, in turn, assumed that two or more persons with an intense preference wanted to deliberate it, and that people with such a preference had been able to find others who shared that preference so that they could at least discuss it.

Such conditions might not have existed. There is, therefore, the possibility that there may be serious repression of decisional preferences in at least one of the four research communities, so that classifying any of them as a Developed Democracy, for example, may distort reality. If decisional preferences for the establishment of a socialist city government were being repressed by some citizens because of the fear of illegitimate sanctions, but the proponents of the preference were unable to locate one another, so that a demand as we define it was not in being, a regime might still have been classified as a Developed Democracy. To the extent that people develop decisional preferences but do not let them be known for fear of being sanctioned illegitimately, the likelihood of even covert, informal deliberation may be reduced. A regime thus could be classified as a Developed Democracy when there were instances of severe repression of demands due to fears of illegitimate sanctions, either because classifications are relative to situations in other selected communities where there may be fewer such instances, or because the operational definitions used herein were insufficiently rigorous.

The estimate of permeability of the power structure is affected by assumptions about the form of political action in which the potential participants may engage. Theoretically, the effectiveness of sanctions is partly a function of the number of people participating, because this affects the alternative resources available to any one participant. The effectiveness of sanctions is also partly a function of the characteristics and relationships among these potentially sanctionable people. The effect of a given sanction may vary with the character of the political roles played by the potential participants, and with the connections and interrelationships such roles would have with each other.

The probable tactics of the potentially sanctionable thus need to be examined, as do the images held by the potential sanctioners of the tactics likely to be adopted by their opponents. These images may affect the disposition of the potential sanctioners to use illegitimate sanctions. Estimating the "probability" dimension is quite complicated because, at this stage, it involves speculation for which only further research and theoretical development can provide a firmer foundation. . . .

More Complex Regime Typologies for Future Studies

This examination of classificatory problems will conclude with suggestions for modifications that should be considered in future studies of regimes, particularly those of the Developed Democracy and Oligarchy types.

There are several ways of classifying types of Oligarchies which we shall mention. It has already been suggested that if it is probable that political participation within a polity will be met by the use of such illegitimate sanctions as death or imprisonment, the particular lines drawn for this study between an Oligarchy and other types of regimes may need to be redrawn. We shall elaborate on another way of distinguishing Oligarchies.

The traditional civil liberties are analogous to the stages of our decision-making model: free speech, free assembly, and the freedom to petition correspond in some ways to policy deliberation, organization of political support, and authoritative consideration. Free elections are the "last chance" to change the authorities who determine decisional outcomes and the scope of government. Freedom of thought is the basis of all civil liberties; policy formulation is basic to all decision-making processes. The more totalitarian the regime, the harder the rulers try to eliminate institutional mechanisms that produce uncontrolled political actions that take these forms or correspond to these stages. While control of any stage renders all prior stages futile, it is dangerous for rulers to permit any one of the stages to exist.

There seems to be a natural order of difficulty in suppressing these basic political liberties or in eliminating institutional mechanisms that facilitate uncontrolled expression of political behavior. Formal elections open to all adult citizens are the simplest to eliminate. Petitions, appeals, and demands made directly to the political leaders are fairly easily restricted to politically "eligible" segments of the citizenry. If necessary, ancestries can be checked, ghettos established, and yellow stars sewn on the garments of the ineligible. But the right to assemble is more difficult to control. Assembly does not need to take place in a public forum nor does it need to be formally organized. Political parties may be eliminated, but clandestine organizations dedicated to opposition or overthrow of the regime require more alert internal-security forces.

The formally organized opposition groups may be prevented more easily than may small informal groups which covertly deliberate policies and the possibilities of action. The most totalitarian rulers will not even stop here but will try to prevent the thinking that results in subversive policy formulations, to propagandize the younger generation and control dissident elements in the older. The family may find itself in a setting where no one may speak without fear that his mate or his child will serve as an informer. The difficulty in controlling the policy-formulation stage is attested by the tenacity of the family as an important unit of social organization in all regimes, and by the magnitude of efforts by totalitarian regimes to control it. . . .

The typology of regimes also may be elaborated and extended for Developed Democracies, as for Oligarchies. In some communities, regimes may be classified as Developed Democracies which have a highly effective propaganda system, controlled by a consensual political leadership and devoted to developing or maintaining citizen support for that leadership. In others, a Developed Democracy may be due more to political education and to a nonmanipulative political-socialization and information process. . . .

In Developed Democracies, as well as in other regimes, political values are inculcated in the young through what have been called political-socialization processes. Regimes of the same type, such as Developed Democracies, may be differentiated according to the degree to which communication from adults to children and from politicized adults to apolitical adults is propaganda or education. Estimates of the effects of intended deceit and the extent to which political manipulation is deliberate are also relevant to a classification of Developed Democracies or other types of regimes by such a dimension as political manipulation. . . .

Another dimension that might be introduced into the typology of regimes is citizen apathy. Two regimes, equally deserving to be classified as Developed Democracies, may differ considerably in the degree to which their citizens are indifferent to politics. Moreover, it is possible that Developed Democracies with mass power structures may differ sharply in the degree to which the citizens not sharing in political power are politically interested or apathetic. Even if the sense of electoral potency is high, and there is little fear of illegitimate sanctions, there may be variations among communities with Developed Democracies in citizen fear of legitimate sanctions, pessimism about the prospects of winning in an admittedly fair political fight, or cynicism about the responsiveness of officials in office or of those who might replace them. Apathy itself can be conceived as a multi-dimensional variable which necessitates further classifications, not only of Developed Democratic regimes, but also of all four types of regimes identified by the elementary fourfold classification used in this study. . . .

It is quite possible that a system of segregation by race or socio-economic class, whether maintained by law directly or indirectly, produces political conditions that constitute deviations from what we have termed Developed Democracy. On the other hand, it is conceivable that under some conditions, if not under most modern American conditions, communities with such segregation systems can have at the same time a relatively high sense of electoral potency among both segregators and segregated and a low probability that illegitimate sanctions would be used effectively by the former against the latter. Even with civil rights, a minority may be unable to convince the majority that government should do away with segregation. This is imaginable, however unlikely, if there were a very strong commitment to democratic rules of the game and a faith by the segregated that over the long run they would convince a sufficient number of segregators of the errors of their ways and that segregation would then be abolished by a majority. Since other kinds of reactions than these can easily be visualized, one might find few if any cases in the real world, but it would be useful to examine communities empirically in that connection. Given such special circumstances of the American Negro as his violent enslavement, the obliteration of any political heritage other than his new one in the New World, and his attainment of a nonslave status through the deeds of men who then preached inevitable progress by hard and good work and through faith in a just God and a fundamentally benevolent, manipulatable political order, it is not entirely surprising that in one of our two Southern cities such dynamics seemed to have produced prior to the time of field work just those kinds of reactions—to the point of that regime's deserving the classification Developed Democracy when compared to the other three regimes.

A system of segregation may take its political toll in other ways than by generating or reinforcing fears of illegitimate sanctions, producing a condition of low resistance to such sanctions and a disposition by segregators to exercise them to maintain political, racial, and/or socio-economic dominance. Assuming that such are not the consequences in a particular community of a system of sharp segregation, and theoretically they may well be the consequences, there are still other important political implications of systems of segregation that bear on the concept of Developed

Democracy. One might conceive of democracy as a political system that ensures not only permeability of the political leadership of the power structure in the sense of minimizing the role of illegitimate sanctions but also *maximum accessibility to top power positions*. This does not mean that democracy in that sense would require actual penetration by masses of people of the political leadership; a power structure in a democracy might still be a consensual or competitive, mass or elite type.

Some citizens' channels of access may be closed by the political actions of other citizens that, by definition, intentionally—as at least one end in view—are directed to that end. Besides such illegitimate sanctions that impair freedom of speech, assembly, petition, and electoral participation, there are a variety of extrapolitical conditions that can have the same effects. Such conditions are different in kind from illegitimate sanctions, in the sense that they can apply constantly to some categories of citizens in such a way as to make them relatively disadvantaged in exercising their political rights or in using the channels of political access to the political leadership, which rights and channels they may enjoy on an apparently equal basis with all citizens. Illegitimate sanctions, on the other hand, involve an actual or threatened or feared differential allocation of resources consequent upon someone's engaging in political activity permitted others in the polity.

In what ways does a system of segregation constitute ordinarily a set of constant political liabilties for the segregated? Assume for the moment that the segregated are not disqualified politically by formal or informal laws, such as the White primary, "grandfather" clauses, poll taxes, etc. Residential segregation makes it more difficult for the segregated, for example, to engage in personal political dialogues with the segregators. This constitutes a political impediment for minority points of view to become majority opinions over time. This is analogous to the political implications of socio-economic structures. The more sharply structured and differentiated are classes, the more likely it is that those at the bottom suffer the political disadvantages encountered by the poor —a fact of political life that has resulted in the unequal distribution of the political liabilities as well as the relative economic costs of the poll tax. Not all prisoners, whether physically in jail or in such socio-psychological prisons as ghettos, lose their civil rights, but their opportunities to participate politically in the larger community are less than perfect.

As segregation in school and society impairs personality development among its victims, their political personality may also be impaired. That is, segregation may result in the failure to develop political interest, competence, and a sense of political responsibility. The resulting political apathy means that the segregated may formulate no demands for a shift in the scope of government, and hence the regime can be, "by default," a Developed Democracy. This would be the case because, as we define it, regime type depends upon citizens' formulating demands.

If widespread political discourse and equal opportunity to obtain political influence and power are dimensions to be built into a typology of regimes, the more segregated comunities are less likely to be Developed Democracies, even if the sense of electoral potency and the permeability of the power structure were both high relative to illlegitimate sanctions.

The conceptual alternative adopted here was to reserve the term Developed Democracy to the more restricted sense. This means that such types of regimes are probably far from ideal not only relative to the two defining dimensions, and in the degree of citizen apathy, cynicism, or manipulation found therein, but also in terms of the distribution of such political disadvantages or liabilities as those associated with systems of segregation. By adopting that terminological convention self-consciously, and by pointing to such other options, we hope to reduce the ambiguities that ordinarily creep into discussions of democracy. By restricting the meaning of the term Developed Democracy to its narrow sense we also hope to underline the need for additional modifying objectives or alternative terms in thinking about such other dimensions of democracy as the patterns of political liabilities or disadvantages present in such regimes. Such classificatory labels as Equalitarian and Nonequalitarian Developed Democracies might be in order to enrich our vocabularies so that we could consider intelligently the riches to be mined from the various ways of conceiving political regimes. We would also hope that our use of the more restricted conception of political democracy would result in a greater realization that men may have other than political needs and values, e.g., for social or personal dignity, which may not automatically be realized by the improvement of Developed Democracy in the United States or by its establishment abroad, since in its narrow sense it could exist alongside racial, socio-economic, or cultural segregation. It is useful to be aware of the limitations of such regime constructs as they are used conventionally, but also of the possibility of elaborating and extending them to encompass specifically dimensions that are at issue in an ambiguous way and that need to be intentionally built into, or cast out of, political system concepts. . . .

Community Power and Urban Renewal Success

Amos H. Hawley

Starting from the premise that power is an attribute of a social system rather than of an individual, this study by Amos H. Hawley examines the relationship between the extent of power concentration and the success of urban renewal. The concentration of power (devised from the proportion of managers, proprietors, and officials in the total employed labor force) is found to be significantly related to policy success in urban renewal, even under a series of controlled conditions. Focusing upon structural characteristics of communities and policy outcome Hawley ignores the personal interactions of a power structure which were the central feature of earlier works by both sociologists and political scientists. This approach, if valid, allows one to consider large numbers of communities in an effort to identify the key structural elements in a pattern of influence. These elements may be thought of, in this case, as independent variables with actual policies considered as the independent variables. Hawley's approach is exploratory, and has not been free of criticism (213).

Power, in most sociological studies, is conceived as the ability to exercise influence in a decision-making process. It is viewed as a personal attribute that distinguishes leaders from followers. Working with that conception investigators normally proceed by inquiring into the reputations of members of a community, establishing juries to winnow the great from the small, constructing sociograms to determine who interacts with whom, and so on. No matter what the methodological apparatus, investigators are uniformly led to the discovery that managerial and proprietary personnel, with occasional exceptions, constitute the power figures. Some of the more sophisticated start with the assumption that managers and proprietors are the principal power figures and use their sociometric tools

Reprinted from "Community Power and Urban Renewal Success" by Amos H. Hawley, *American Journal of Sociology*, LXVIII (June, 1963), 422–431, by permission of The University of Chicago Press. Copyright 1963 by The University of Chicago.

to discover how members of an elite are grouped about various kinds of issues to form power centers. Both procedures, as Wolfinger has recently pointed out, often rest on certain unspoken and unwarranted assumptions. They appear to asume, for example, that lines of influence are clearly perceptible to respondents. They also assume a static distribution of power among certain personalities. But the chief difficulty with the usual approach is that it is only applicable in a case study; it offers no facility for quantitative and comparative studies of the phenomenon. And that, it seems to me, is a disability inherent in a social-psychological approach to the study of community structure.

Before turning to an alternative way of treating the matter, a prefatory comment on the nature of that which is in question seems to be appropriate. It should be obvious that power in the social sphere, as with energy in the physical world, is ubiquitous. It is like energy, too, in that it appears in many forms. Every social act is an exercise of power, every social relationship is a power equation, and every social group or system is an organization of power. Accordingly, it is possible to transpose any system of social relationships into terms of potential or active power. Perhaps such a transposition is nothing more than the substitution of one terminology for another. At the very least, however, it focuses attention on the instruments of control and causes a social system to be viewed as a control mechanism.

The community, for example, may be conceived as an energy system. That is, as a system of relationships among functionally differentiated units the community constitutes a mobilization of power—the capacity to produce results—for dealing with the environment, whether physical or social. Each unit or subsystem—family, church, store, industry—is also an organization of power for the conduct of a function. Both the system and its subsystems tend to approximate a single organization model. Moreover, since the performance of its function by any one part affects in greater or lesser degree the conditions under which other parts carry out their functions, the parent system and each subsystem is an arena in which a more or less continuous interplay of influence occurs. Power, then, is expressed in two ways: (1) as functional power—that required to execute a function; and (2) as derivative power—that which spills over into external relationships and regulates the interaction between parts. The two modes of manifestation are necessarily connected. The type of function performed determines the kind of derivative influence transmitted to other parts or subsystems. There might also be a quantitative association, though the magnitude of the derivative influence is a consequence not only of the scale to which a function has developed but also of its position in the system. Those subsystems that are most instrumental in relating the system to the environment doubtlessly exert a greater derivative effect than do subsystems one or more steps removed from the key position. Space does not permit a full exposition of a system conception of power. Perhaps enough has been said to indicate that power is a product of a system having developed, that it is lodged only in a system, and that it is most appropriately treated, therefore, as a system property. Whatever power an individual might appear to possess is in effect attached to the office he occupies in a system. He acquires power by attaining to an office and he loses it when he is separated from the office. But the acquiring and losing of power is illusory; the property belongs rather with the office or, better still to the system in which the office is a specialized function.[1]

In the conduct of its routine activties the system exercises its power through established and well-worn channels; the interplay of influence is institutionalized. But the structure of relationships through which power is communicated may leave various areas of interest or activity unattended, for example, private charity, religious digression and reform, the supervision of adolescents. When crises occur in such matters or when non-routine issues affecting the whole system arise, the existing structure is put to a test. It may or may not be effective in dealing with the exceptional circumstance. Whether it is effective would appear to be contingent on the way in which derivative power is distributed in the system. Where it is highly concentrated the community should be able to act as a unit in almost any emergency. On the other hand, where power is widely distributed a community may be able to act coherently only with great difficulty, if at all, when confronted with a novel problem.

This suggests a way of dealing with the variable quantitatively. A frustrating feature of studies of power has been the understandable failure to find a way to measure its amount. If, however, we can assume that an enduring system has sufficient force to regularly perform its normal functions, we can conclude that all systems of the same kind generate equivalent amounts of power. There remains a variable, namely, the way in which power is distributed. Any given amount may be in some instances concentrated in a small sector of the system or in other instances distributed more or less uniformly over all sectors or subsystems. The measurement of distribution appears to present fewer difficulties than does the measurement of the amount of power.

Now let me propose that the greater the concentration of power in a community the greater the probability of success in any collective action

---

[1] The conception of power developed here is interchangeable with the ecological concept of dominance. Ecologists, however, have been content to treat dominance as an attribute of location or type of place, though the concept has always carried overtones of organizational properties. They have neglected to exploit the concept as an entree into the general problem of organization.

affecting the welfare of the whole. This follows, if it be granted that (1) success in a collective action requires the ability to mobilize the personnel and resources of the community and (2) that ability is greatest where power is most highly concentrated. The proposition does not say that a concentration of power assures success in any community venture. Various factors might intervene to defeat a collective project. Moreover, a concentration of power might be used to block a course of action. Power concentration, however, is not needed to defeat an action on the part of a community. That might occur as a result of power being so diffusely held that mobilization of the community cannot be accomplished.

Proceeding from the notion that system power resides in the subsystems of functional units of a community, we can infer that it must be exercised through the managerial functions of the subsystems. For it is those functions that co-ordinate the several other functions in their respective subsystems and articulate the latter with the larger system. In the absence of data on the number of managerial functions, I shall use the number of managerial personnel, that is, the number of people who reported occupations as manager, proprietor, or official in the Population Census, to measure concentration of power. Personnel, it should be stressed, is used only as a substitute for, and as an index of, functions. Since the significance of the number of functions varies with the number of all other functions (i.e., the size of the employed labor force), it should be expressed as a ratio to the latter. Hence the lower the ratio of managers, proprietors, and officials [2] to the employed labor force the greater is the concentration of power. (This measure will hereafter be called the MPO ratio.)

As the dependent variable, that is, an example of collective action, I shall use success in urban renewal. Urban renewal, programed and administered by the Housing and Home Finance Agency, has the advantage of involving a standard procedure to which all participating communities must submit in like manner. Participation in the program by a municipality involves passage through a series of stages, differentiated by the extent to which the planning and other local arrangements required for federal financial support have been fulfilled. The stages are *planning, execution,* and *completion.* Arrival at the completion stage is unquestionably the best measure of success. Unfortunately only eighteen cities in the continental United States had by the end of 1959 advanced so far—hardly enough for statistical purposes. The next best indication of success in urban renewal

---

[2] For present purposes only managers, proprietors, and officials "not elsewhere classified" are used, this eliminating technical positions that have no management or policy-determining functions. The category, it should be noted, is not limited to management positions in pecuniary establishments. It includes managers of art galleries, libraries, community funds, welfare agencies, and others.

is arrival at the execution stage. At that stage a city has completed its planning and has satisfied all administrative requirements for the receipt of a capital grant from the Housing and Home Finance Agency. The city is then either at the point of, or has embarked upon, the acquisition of land, the relocation of current occupants, and clearing and improving the land. At the end of 1959, ninety-five cities with population of 50,000 or more (in 1950) had advanced to the execution stage.

For control purposes data on two other classes of cities of 50,000 or more population are employed. One class includes cities that entered the urban renewal program but for one reason or another abandoned their efforts sometime between 1950 and 1960. The thirty-eight cities that had that experience are called "dropouts." The second control class is made up of all cities, in states where urban renewal is legally permissible, that have not attempted urban renewal at any time. There are sixty-one such cities. All the members of this class, it is to be noted, are eligible for urban renewal assistance from the federal agency. There remains a sizable group of cities that are still in the planning stage. Eventually they will either pass into the execution stage or terminate their efforts; but at present their status is indeterminate. For that reason they are not included in the present study.

Whether urban renewal is a form of collective action that would call into operation the organization of the entire community may be debatable. . . . That urban renewal . . . represents a significant challenge to a community must be left as an unanswered question for the present. If it is regarded as a major undertaking in a community, it should certainly involve the local power structure. If it is considered to be a rather insignificant form of collective action, then as a dependent variable it provides a fairly severe test of the hypothesis.

It seems advisable to restate the hypothesis in the operational terms set forth. The hypothesis is: MPO ratios are lowest in urban renewal cities that have reached the execution stage and highest in cities that have never attempted urban renewal. Dropout cities are expected to occupy an intermediate position between the polar classes.

The hypothesis is to be examined with reference to cities of 50,000 population or more. The abundance of data available for cities in that size range offers considerable latitude for refining the measure of power concentration and for the development of controls. In the following, however, the analysis of power concentration as an independent variable is confined primarily to ratios for the entire class of MPO's. Differentials within that class will be investigated in a later report.

As a preliminary test of the representativeness of cities of 50,000 population or more, their MPO ratios, for each urban renewal status class, are compared with those for all cities of 15,000–50,000 population, in Table

1. Observe that the two series of ratios are very similar. Thus it seems possible that findings for large cities might apply to all cities regardless of size. Further, though somewhat tangential, support of that conclusion is found in the fact that the number of years spent in the planning stage before reaching the execution stage is unrelated to size of city. No further attempt to ascertain the representativeness of large cities has been made.

It is also to be noted in Table 1 that the ratios conform to the hypothesis. Power is most highly concentrated in the execution-stage cities and most diffusely distributed in the never-in-program cities. That the concentration of power, as represented by the ratio of all MPO's to the employed labor force, is significantly greater in cities that have reached the execution stage in urban renewal than in the other classes of cities is apparent in Table 2. The probability that the association shown there is due to chance is less than 1 in a 100.

The quintile distribution of cities shown in Table 2 displays a considerable spread over the ratio range in each urban renewal status class. That raises a question of how some cities manage to get to the execution stage without a concentration of power. The complementary question of

TABLE I

Number and MPO Ratios, Cities by Size Class and by
Urban Renewal Status

Urban Renewal Status	All Cities of 15,000 Population and Over		Cities of 50,000 Population and Over		Cities of 15,000– 50,000 Population	
Execution stage . . .	136	9.0	95	9.0	41	9.1
Dropout	79	10.0	38	10.1	41	9.8
Never in program .	402	11.0	61	10.8	341	11.1
Total	617	10.4	194	9.5	423	10.7

TABLE II

Quintile Distribution of Cities (MPO Ratios), by
Urban Renewal Status *

Urban Renewal Status	1st (Under 7.7)	2d (7.8– 8.9)	3d (9.0– 9.9)	4th (10.0– 11.7)	5th (11.8 and Over)
Execution stage	27	22	21	17	9
Dropout	3	9	8	8	7
Never in program . . .	9	9	8	13	22

* $X^2 = 23.516$, $C = .330$, $P < .01$.

how other cities with marked concentrations of power escape urban renewal may be given a tentative a priori answer: that is, they are susceptible and may yet enter the program. In any event, it is doubtlessly true that factors other than the distribution of power operate on urban renewal experience or the lack of it.

For example, the probability that urban renewal might recommend itself to a community as a course of action should be somewhat contingent on the state of its physical equipment. If the equipment, in this instance its buildings, is fairly new and in good condition, urban renewal would make little sense. But where buildings are old or dilapidated a proposal to renew or rehabilitate would appear to be appropriate. Two measures of the condition of buildings are used here: (1) the percentage of all residential units constructed before 1920, and (2) the percentage of all residential units reported as dilapidated. Cities are classified relative to the median for each characteristic, providing two dichotomies. "Young" cities have less than 65 per cent of their houses built before 1920, and "old" cities 65 per cent or more of their houses built prior to that date. Cities with less than 4.7 per cent of their houses dilapidated are described as "low" on that variable while those with 4.7 per cent and over are classified as "high."

It is conceivable, too, that some cities might have anticipated the problems that invite urban renewal by having established a well-financed and strongly supported planning agency. Cities that have done so might not have to seek federal assistance for improvements. A contrary argument can also be advanced. Perhaps cities with substantial commitments to planning are more prepared to enter into a renewal project than are cities in which planning has not been developed to any appreciable extent. Notwithstanding my inability to resolve this question, the size of the planning budget might prove to be a factor of some consequence. For the purpose of control, planning expenditures are expressed as a ratio to total government operating costs in 1955. Ratios of less than .4 are below the median and thus identify their respective cities as "low" with respect to planning budgets, while ratios of .4 and over indicate cities with "high" planning budgets.

There is a strong likelihood, too, that central cities of metropolitian areas might be more favorably disposed toward urban renewal than suburban cities. That should follow from the fact that central cities are generally older than are suburbs. But it should also derive from the deconcentration trend through which central cities have been losing population and industry to outlying areas. Many large suburban cities have also begun to experience declining growth rates, though in only a few cases has the trend reached a critical stage. Where substantial losses, real or threatened, have been encountered urban renewal might appear to offer a means by which to reverse the trend. There is a second factor that calls attention to the central city-suburb distinction. That is the peculiar residential distribution of managers, proprietors, and officials. Since members of those groups tend to live in suburbs while working in central cities their numbers as reported in the Census fail to reflect accurately the number of such positions in each place. The only practicable solution to this difficulty is to control for metropolitan status, that is, central city and suburb.

My operationalization of the concentration of power represents but one facet of a complex phenomenon. Other dimensions of that phenomenon should at least be admitted as control variables. For example, power may lie mainly in either the manufacturing or in the local service sector of a community's economy, whichever is most important. Relative importance is here measured by the ratio of manufacturing payroll to the combined payrolls in retailing, wholesaling, and service enterprises. Service cities have ratios of 1.5 or less and manufacturing cities have ratios of over 1.5.

The average size of manufacturing plant is another possible dimension of the distribution of power, especially if it may be construed as an indicator of the general scale of functional activities in the community. Size of plant is measured by the average number of employees per plant. Small-plant cities have averages of less than 70 employees; large-plant cities have over 70 employees per plant.

Still another expression of power distribution is found in the type of city government. In cities having a commission form of government, administrative responsibility is spread over a large number of non-elective officials. Such cities probably are unable to mobilize for action unless there is a fairly high concentration of power of the kind under study here. Administrative authority is more centralized where a mayor-council government exists. And in a city manager government administrative authority reaches its highest degree of centralization and articulation. Hence, contrary to the findings of another study that type of city government is not important in determining urban renewal success, I shall employ it as a control.

Two other controls having to do with the socioeconomic level of the resident population are used. Both assume that where the socioeconomic level is high the community may be prepared to act in a matter such as surban renewal independently of a concentration of power. The first, education, is represented by the proportion of the population with four or more years of college completed. The second, income, is measured by median income. Cities are dichotomized on the median for each variable. Cities with less than 6.0 per cent of their residents with four years or more of college education are "low," and those with over that proportion are "high." The median position for the median income array falls at $3,450; cities below and above that figure are "low" and "high," respectively.

Finally, region is included among the controls. To some extent regional differences combine differences in age of cities, dilapidation, income, education, and possibly other of the control variables discussed above. Thus it is reasonable to expect that the association of power distribution with urban renewal success might vary by region. Four regions are recognized for control purposes; northeast, north central, south, and west.[3]

MPO ratios for each urban renewal status class and with each of the ten controls applied successively [were shown]. In no instance does the introduction of a control vitiate the association of power concentration with urban renewal success, though in a number of instances the dropout cities fail to hold an intermediate position between execution stage and never-in-program cities. Although the averages for dropout cities are affected by small numbers of cities in many cases, it is also possible that power concentration has been employed to defeat urban renewal in those cities. It is worth noting that even where the concentration of power is relatively great, as in old cities, mayor-council cities, manufacturing cities, large-plant cities, low-education cities, and cities in the northeast, the concentration varies with urban renewal success. There is no indication, in short, that the importance attached to the concentration of power is peculiar to any one type of class of city. Despite the fact that suburban cities are the preferred places of residence for a large proportion of the holders of administrative positions, urban renewal success seems to require as great a concentration of power in suburbs as it does in central cities. Also of interest is the evidence that manager cities appear to be able to achieve urban renewal with less power concentration than do cities of other government classes.

To better assess the closeness of the association of power concentration with urban renewal success I have employed rank correlation analysis, using Kendall's tau-c. . . .

It is clear from the findings . . . that the concentration of power is positively and significantly associated with urban renewal success under virtually all conditions of control. Several exceptions occur, however. The relationship is not dependable for cities with mayor-council governments, with a predominance of service industry, with small proportions of college graduates among their residents, and with locations in the northeast and the west. Some of these exceptions appear to be contrary to

[3] Two other controls were used with similar results: population size and income as represented by the proportion of families with incomes of $10,000 or more per year.

the positive findings involving variables known to be closely associated with them (education and income, northeastern location, and manufacturing industry). Had it been possible to refine the controls, some of the inconsistencies doubtlessly would have disappeared.

The category of all managers, proprietors, and officials is quite heterogeneous; it embraces the full range of both size and type of unit in which such positions occur. Thus it is not unlikely that one or another subclass or industry group of managers, proprietors, and officials might be primarily responsible for the observed association. But the measures reported . . . indicate that that is not the case. The correlation is statistically significant for every industrial class of managers, proprietors, and official but one. The one, public administration, not only falls short of significance, it is negative. Why the prospects for urban renewal success should tend to increase with increases in the relative numbers of managers and officials in public administration poses an interesting problem. But that is not a question that can be pursued here. Nor is it possible to press the analysis of industry class of managers, proprietors, and officials further at present, though the fact that the relationship for each industry class taken separately responds differently to the application of controls clearly points to a need for a more intensive investigation.

While the findings reported in this paper should be regarded as exploratory, they clearly support the hypothesis that the lower the MPO ratio the greater the chance of succss in an action program such as urban renewal. They also demonstrate the facility and the economy in research of a conception of power as a system property. Much remains to be done, however, to develop knowledge about that property. A factor of some importance is the composition of managerial positions in a city. The relative numbers in the key industry should prove decisive, if my initial argument is correct. What constitutes a key industry, of course, is contingent upon the function the city performs for the regional and national society. The pursuit of that question will doubtlessly suggest further lines of investigation.

The Vertical Axis of Community
Organization and the Structure of Power

John Walton

In view of the many case studies of community power which have been carried out, it is surprising that so little systematic use has been made of the data they provide for comparative analysis of the factors associated with the distribution of influence. In the selection below John Walton examines the characteristics of a large number of communities and relates these characteristics to the structure of power which had been imputed to each community by the original researcher. David Rogers has noted the difficulties in accepting the validity of such conclusions (181).

On the bases of these secondary data, Walton finds that to the extent that the local community becomes increasingly interdependent with "extra-community institutions," the structure of power becomes more competitive, i.e., more pluralistic. This "vertical axis" of extra-community influence is a factor which many earlier studies allude to as being of possible significance, but here Walton not only focuses upon estimates of its significance but places it within a broader theoretical framework.

In the relatively brief period since its inception, the study of community power structure has attracted a wide range of enthusiasts. Researchers of diverse backgrounds have found their particular interests coalesce around the assumption that local leadership processes are of central importance to the explanation of community action. . . .

In addition to fertile substantive applications, much has been done to develop the research methods of power-structure studies. . . .

[H]owever, there has been almost no progress in one vital respect; the development of theoretical explanation of the reported findings. Elaborate documentation of the atheoretical character of the field hardly seems necessary. One has only to peruse a portion of the literature to discover

From *Community Structure, Power, and Decision-Making: Comparative Analysis,* ed., Terry N. Clark published by Chandler Publishing Company, San Francisco. Copyright 1968 by Chandler Publishing Company. Reprinted by permission.

that the principal issues are almost entirely concerned with method and conflicting interpretations of how broadly power is distributed. Only rarely do we find some of the initial steps in theorizing represented by conceptual considerations and the development of propositional inventories.

The purpose of this paper is to develop a theoretical explanation of how power is distributed in local communities, and to consider briefly how various power arrangements may account for different forms of community action. The analysis incorporates earlier theoretical discussions of the community and a systematic review of the power-structure literature. Anticipating the conclusions for a moment, it will be argued that as communities become increasingly interdependent with extracommunity institutions, changes in the local normative order ensue producing more competitive power arrangements. . . .

Findings of Previous Research

[A] screening of the [published] literature [on community power resulted in a] list of studies [which] was checked against several lengthy bibliographies to insure its inclusiveness. Thus the studies are regarded as a universe, defined by the above criteria, rather than a sample.

Each study was reviewed and, when sufficient information was available, coded in terms of a number of self-explanatory independent variables (*e.g.,* region, population size, industrialization, economic diversity, *etc.*). Similarly, the type of power structure identified in each report was coded in terms of four categories: 1) Pyramidal—a monolithic, monopolistic, or single cohesive leadership group; 2) Factional—at least two durable factions that compete for advantage; 3) Coalitional—leadership varies with issues and is made up of fluid coalitions of interested persons and groups; 4) Amorphous—the absence of any persistent pattern of leadership or power exercised on the local level. Table 1 indicates those few associations which were found to be significant or meaningful.[1]

In contrast to these positive findings, a large number of variables, including region, population size, population composition, industrialization, economic diversity and type of local government, were *not* found to be related to type of power structure.

Taking these results as a summary of the present status of research, it appears that no firm generalizations are suggested. The findings fail to conform to any neat pattern such as an association between competitive power structures and greater complexity of local social and economic

---

[1] The cell entries in the table represent communities, rather than studies, since a single study often dealt with two or more towns.

TABLE I

Community Characteristics and Community Power Structure [2]

	Pyramidal	Factional, Coalitional and Amorphous	Total
Absentee Ownership[3]			
Present	2	18	20
Absent	12	9	21
Total	14	27	41
	Q = — .85	.01 > p > .001	
Economic Resources Adequate	9	17	26
Inadequate	6	5	11
Total	15	22	37
	Q = —.39	.30 > p > .20	
Type of City			
Independent	14	22	36
Satellite	2	10	12
Total	16	32	48
	Q = — .52	.20 > p > .10	
Party Competition			
Competitive	0	10	10
Noncompetitive	10	12	22
Total	10	22	32
	Q = — 1.0	.02 > p > .01	
Change in Power Structure			
Dispersion	2	17	19
Concentration	0	0	0
No Change	3	4	7
Oscillation	2	1	3
Decline Locally	1	2	3
Total	8	24	32

[2] The variable power structure was originally coded in terms of four categories. The categories are collapsed here to avoid small N's and to provide a contrast between more and less concentrated power arrangements.

The N's in each of these subtables vary because the studies coded do not provide uniform data on each variable.

[3] Operational definitions of the following three variables are indicated by the type of information coded under such category. Adequate economic resources—includes towns with reportedly prosperous business communities and low rates of poverty and unemployment; inadequate economically—underdeveloped with high rates of poverty and unemployment. Independent city—includes central cities of metropolitan areas and independent manufacturing, commercial or agricultural centers; satellite city—suburb or town dominated by a nearby city. Party competition—the existence of two or more local parties (or affiliates in formally nonpartisan cities) which regularly contend for public office; noncompetitive—a one-party town.

organization. The inadequacies of such an explanation are underscored by the negative findings. The evidence may, however, be suggestive of some less obvious explanation. In order to explore that possibility we shall look at some implicitly theoretical positions in the area of community power and a major theoretical work on American communities, asking, in both cases, how they square with the above findings and how they might inform the present analysis.

THEORETICAL APPROACHES

In one of the first attempts to bring some order out of the confusion of results, David Rogers developed a series of propositions concerning community political systems. His dependent variable, type of political system, was made up of the categories monolithic and pluralistic. In stating the relationship between these and a number of characteristics of community social structure, Rogers hypothesized that the following would be associated with a pluralistic system: a high degree of industrialization, a large population, a socially heterogeneous population, a policy differentiated from the kinship and economic systems, a local government of extensive scope, two or more political parties and the unionization, or other political and economic organization, of working-class groups. The underlying theme in this series of propositions, what has been referred to as the implicit theory, centers on the effects of industrialization, and attendant processes of urbanization and bureaucratization, the outcome of these being structural differentiation which contributes to a pluralistic power situation. The approach is, of course, central to contemporary social science whether stated in terms of *gemeinschaft* and *gesellschaft* or any other of a variety of polar types.

Amos Hawley has presented a somewhat more specific approach. Here power is defined as a system property whose distribution can be measured by the ability to mobilize resources and personnel. In any total system, such as a community, this ability lies in the various component subsystems and is exercised through their managerial functions. Hence, operationally, the greater the number of managerial personnel, the greater the concentration of power. If we grant that success in a collective action requires the mobilization of resources and personnel, and that this ability is greatest where power is most highly concentrated, then it follows that the greater the concentration of power in a community the greater the *probability* of success in any collective action. In a recent paper, inspired in part by the Hawley piece, Edgar Butler and Hallowell Pope have suggested another measure of power concentration, the number of profile or key industries and the concentration of managerial functions within these.[4]

It should be noted that the Hawley and Butler and Pope papers are concerned chiefly with community action; for each the premise is that more concentrated power situations are conducive to concerted action. Unlike Rogers they are not trying to explain patterns of power distribution but, rather, employ these to explain community action. Nevertheless, they are pertinent here because they imply a theoretical position involving the saliency of managerial functions in the determination of community power structures.

How do these explanatory schemes square with the findings culled from the existing literature? Considering first the hypotheses formulated by Rogers, the evidence runs counter to his notions of the effects of industrialization, population size and population heterogeneity. On the positive side, his proposition about political parties, though not entirely equivalent to party competition, is supported. Unfortunately, no data are available on the remaining three propositions. What evidence we have, however, indicates that Roger's propositions do not fare very well within the present context, though they may have greater predictive power in a cross cultural or historical perspective. For our purposes the implication is that the theoretical approach implicit in these propositions is in need of revision. Perhaps it will be necessary to abandon the simplified notion of a unilinear relationship between the growing complexity of industrial society and more pluralistic local power arrangements, in favor of a more limited, yet more discriminating explanation.[5]

The evidence presented previously is not directly relevant to the Hawley and Butler and Pope approaches since these attempt to explain community action. If, however, we assume with these authors that concentrated power structures are associated with community action, and then examine the antecedent link in their chain of reasoning, we find that those community characteristics allegedly conducive to power concentration (*i.e.* ones engendering a large number of managerial functions)—industrialization, economic diversity, proportion of absentee ownership, and economic resources—are either unrelated or associated with the less concentrated power structures in our data. This fact can hardly be taken as a refutation of the positions presented. What it does indicate is that the number of managerial functions appears to be a poor indicator of type

[4] Edgar W. Butler and Hallowell Pope, "Community Power Structures, Industrialization and Public Welfare Programs," paper read at the 61st annual meeting of the American Sociological Association, Miami Beach, Florida, August, 1966.

[5] This conclusion applies to similar propositional inventories based on the "evolutionary" or "continuum" notion. See, for example, Delbert C. Miller and William H. Form, *Industry, Labor and Community* (New York: Harper Bros., 1960).

of power structure (though it may indicate the number of potentially powerful people in community action).

In short, the analysis thus far demonstrates the need for theoretical statements which are both more explicit and account better for the available data.

As we shall see, Roland Warren's analysis of *The Community in America* [6] provides a pertinent general framework for dealing theoretically with the specific questions of power structure. Warren's central thesis is that American communities are undergoing a drastic transformation of their entire structure and function; "[this] 'great change' in community living includes the increasing orientation of local community units toward extracommunity systems of which they are a part, with a decline in community cohesion and autonomy." Although Warren analyzes these changes along seven fundamental dimensions of community life, a summary statement indicates their relevance for present purposes:

> In the first place, they signalize the increasing and strengthening of the external ties which bind the local community to the large society. In the process, various parts of the community—its educational system, its recreation, its economic units, its governmental functions, its religious units, its health and welfare agencies, and its voluntary associations— have become increasingly oriented toward district, state, regional, or national offices and less and less oriented toward each other.
>
> In the second place, as local community units have become more closely tied in with state and national systems, much of the decision-making prerogative concerning the structure and function of these units has been transferred to the headquarters or district offices of the systems themselves, thus leaving a narrower and narrower scope of functions over which local units, responsible to the local community, exercise autonomous power.

On the basis of these observations concerning the "great change" and with the simultaneous recognition that communities (*i.e.* "combinations of social units and systems which perform the major functions having locality reference") do persist as meaningful units, Warren finds useful a distinction between the *horizontal* and *vertical axes* of community organization. The vertical axis refers to connections between community organizations and extracommunity centers, and the horizontal axis refers to connections between community organizations. The "great change" involves an increase in the former type of connections often at the cost of the latter.

In what follows several propositions will be developed which relate

---

[6] Roland L. Warren, *The Community in America* (Chicago: Rand McNally, 1963), and "Toward a Reformulation of Community Theory," *Human Organization*, 15 (Summer, 1962), pp. 8–11.

Warren's approach specifically to the question of how power is distributed on the local level. We will find that his concept of a vertical axis of community organization has particular importance for this analysis.

An Explanation of Differential Patterns of Community Power Structure

Power is defined here as *the capacity to mobilize resources for the accomplishment of intended effects with recourse to some type of sanction(s) to encourage compliance.* This definition includes the elements of both potential and actualized power in that capacity for mobilizing resources refers to potential while the application of sanctions refers to actualized power. *Capacity* also implies a distinction from *right* such that *authority* is not confused with the definition. Following Lasswell and Kaplan, the threat of sanctions, positive or negative, distinguishes *influence* from power—*i.e.* influence refers only to the capacity to mobilize resources.

Power structure is defined as *the characteristic pattern within a social organization whereby resources are mobilized and sanctions employed in ways that affect the organization as a whole.*

For the sake of simplicity we will deal here with competitive and monopolistic power structures. Monopolistic power structures characterize social organizations in which the capacity for mobilizing resources and recourse to sanctions are the exclusive property of a group with similar interests. In competitive situations the capacity for mobilizing resources and recourse to sanctions are possessed by two or more groups with different interests.

The basic assumption of the theoretical statement to be developed here is that a monopoly of power produces a situation in which consensus is the most important factor underlying the use of power. This consensus may, but need not imply agreement on values and objectives. What it does imply is agreement concerning the capabilities of those holding power to realize their own intentions over a wide range of community relevant issues. In such a monopolistic situation expectations concerning the norms prescribed by the existing power arrangement tend to be widely recognized. That is, the limits of allowable (nonsanctionable) deviance and opposition are narrow and clear. As a result of these congruent expectations, potential rather than manifest power is more commonly the mechanism by which compliance is encouraged; overt conflict and coercion are relatively infrequent occurrences because compliance can be realized without them. Merriam captured the sense of this assumption when he wrote "Power is not strongest when it uses violence, but weakest."

By contrast, in competitive situations the exercise of power moves from a reliance on consensus to more overt applications of sanctions. This becomes necessary to the extent that competing groups become capable of restricting the scope of each other's sanctions. Claims to power must be supported by effective action. Greater normative diversity, with attendant diversity in expectations, characterizes this situation. Such circumstances result in a greater incidence of conflict stemming from the fact that those who would exercise power are required to make evident their claim through the use of sanctions.

It should be added that each of these circumstances contains elements of the other. Monopolistic power arrangements do, at times, generate divergent norms and expectations just as they occasionally have recourse to overt applications of coercion. More importantly, the role of consensual expectations and potential power are critical to all forms of social organization and can be observed in many of the transactions carried on in competitive power settings. In this connection conflict is probably most characteristic of those transitional periods in which power is becoming more or less diffused since it is at this point that the normative order is most uncertain and expectations least clear. In the event that this transition is one from monopolistic to competitive it may culminate in a new set of rules defining community power arrangements which, while more conducive to conflict than the monopolistic situation, produces less conflict than the transitional phase.

Because at first glance this assumption may appear to be a truism, its nontrivial character will be demonstrated. Presthus' study of two New York communities which differed on a pluralist-elitist continuum is valuable here. Discussing the more elitist of the two, Presthus reasons:

> In Riverview sharper class and economic differences and resulting disparities in expectations, values and consensus seem to have placed a premium on more centralized, imperative leadership. As organizational theory and studies of group behavior suggest, social support, shared values, and common expectations make possible the minimization of overt power and authority. When community consensus is limited, leaders tend to function in a more unilateral manner.

Here the minimization of overt power and authority is equated with a more pluralistic (competitive) power situation. The present argument agrees with the prior notion that common expectations result in a minimization of overt power (and conflict), but this is taken to be characteristic of a monopolistic situation. Thus, when community consensus is limited the leadership process tends to be more competitive.[7]

---

[7] A more precise treatment of this relationship would specify types of conflict and how these are associated with various power arrangements. For example, monopolistic

Obviously the relationship identified in my assumption may operate in either direction—*i.e.* changes in the competitiveness of the power situation can produce changes in norms and expectations and, similarly, changes in norms and expectations can lead to changes in power arrangements. In this approach we are concerned with developing an explanation of the change in power structures, that is, in the latter direction of the causal complex.

In this section we have reasoned that normative expectations bear a particular relationship to power structure and that conflict can be taken as an indicator of that relationship. In what follows an attempt will be made to elaborate the connection between normative expectations and types of power structure in terms of the data drawn from existing community studies.

Returning to the data in Table 1, we can now raise the question of how the ideas presented would account for the findings. It will be recalled that the data indicate a relationship between competitive power structures and the presence of absentee-owned corporations, competitive party politics, adequate economic resources and satellite status. Further, in those communities where change was studied, the trend was in the direction of a greater dispersion of power. Do these findings suggest some underlying explanation?

Upon closer examination the evidence does point to an explanation. Each of the variables associated with competitive power structures reflects the interdependence of the community and extracommunity centers of power or increased emphasis on the vertical axis. For example, a high proportion of absentee-owned industry suggests that many community relevant decisions are controlled by the personnel and interests of national corporate bodies whose influence may stem from either a deliberate intervention in local affairs or from the more characteristic aloofness to local responsibility. Similarly competitive political parties may often reflect the involvement of county, state and national party organizations in a struggle for control of local constituencies. While it could be reasonably argued that inadequate economic resources result in substantial intervention and control by state and federal agencies which extend aid to local bodies, the position taken here is that communities with more adequate economic resources maintain a greater number of interdependent ties to extracommunity institutions such the suppliers, markets, investors and other economic units. Finally, in the case of type of city, the connection is apparent. Suburban municipalities and smaller towns which form satellites

---

power structures may suppress dissent and conflict, they may manage it within innocuous limits or they may engender revolutionary conflict. Competitive power structures, on the other hand, may encourage conflict which results in a stalemate or ineffective argument and nonrevolutionary change.

of large urban centers are interdependent in a variety of economic and political activities including municipal services, jobs, consumer behavior, etc. If, at points, the relationship between each of these variables and community interdependence is not unambiguous, the position taken here is enhanced by the pattern they suggest when taken together.

Drawing together all that has been said up to this point, the proposition which seems best to account for the findings can be stated as follows: to the extent that the local community becomes increasingly interdependent with respect to extra-community institutions (or develops along its vertical axis) the structure of local leadership becomes more competitive.

Theoretically this proposition derives from the more general statement concerning norms and power arrangements. That is, the mechanism by which interdependence, or increasing relevance of the vertical axis of community organization, affects the distribution of community power is the disruption of the local normative order associated with the existing power structure. Development along the vertical axis involves the introduction of new interests and new institutional relationships implying new definitions of the community, and these have the effect of disrupting consensual normative expectations.

In addition to a differentiation of allegiances, these changes include the introduction of new *resources* and *sanctions* into the community. Local organizations with vertical ties to extracommunity institutions frequently share in the capital and human resources of the larger entity making it possible for them to sustain a broader scope of activities than would otherwise be the case. For example, absentee-owned corporations may receive funds and skilled personnel for a desired expansion of local operations making them more important as local tax contributors, employers and suppliers. Such resources carry with them potention sanctions. In the above example some of these would include the threat to locate elsewhere, threat of cutbacks or other actions having an adverse effect on the local economy, support or nonsupport in local elections. What has been said here of absentee-owned corporations could also be said, though perhaps in less dramatic ways, of other vertical community organizations. The point to be emphasized is that these organizations introduce new sources of power into the local picture and, being interdependent, they also have stakes in the local decision-making process which occasionally must be defended. The greater the number of community organizations with vertical ties, the more frequent and the more inclusive are contests surrounding the decision-making process. . . .

Accordingly, variables which reflect the interdependence of the community and the "carrying society"—absentee ownership, party competition, adequate economic resources and satellite status—are associated with competitive power structures; whereas those variables which reflect only intracommunity changes—economic diversity, population increase, *etc.*— are not so associated.[8] . . .

The findings on change in Table 1 indicated that community power structures are tending to become more competitive. This trend is a predictable consequence of the spread of "metropolitan dominance" and its implications for greater community interdependence. That is, . . . the spread of metropolitan dominance would lead one to predict a corresponding trend toward competitive power arrangements. Such is, in fact, what the findings indicate. . . .

METROPOLITAN POLITICS AND COMMUNITY ACTION

Since the purpose of this paper was to develop an explanation of how power is distributed in local communities, *and* how power arrangements may account for community action, some comments on the latter question are called for. This may be particularly useful for two reasons; first, the foregoing analysis bears directly on the subject of community action and, second, the discussion serves to integrate another perspective on power and decision-making into this explanation.

In his well known essay describing the local community as an "ecology of games," Norton Long argues that the concept of "power structure" suffers from misplaced concreteness, that when we look more closely at cities we find no such structured decision-making institution.

What is characteristic of metropolitan areas is the lack of overall decision-making institutions. This does not mean that there are not institutions with power in metropolitan areas. It does mean that there are no institutions with sufficient power and overall responsibility to make decisions settling metropolitan issues and solving metropolitan problems . . .[9]

Rather, Long conceives of metropolitan issues as having careers in which interested and powerful parties—governments, groups and institutions—

---

[8] The point to be emphasized here is that greater complexity and specialization are not necessarily conducive to the changes under consideration, but only insofar as these developments produce greater interdependence. At some point, of course, complexity and specialization do necessitate greater interdependence, but it would seem that this is not always the case at every level of community development. We would expect that some of these variables are confounded in such a way that increasing size, for example, will be related to competitive power structures at that point in a community's development when size and interdependence vary together. According to this argument, such an association would be spurious. This may be the case though the available data are too crude and provide too few observations to allow an unequivocal solution.

[9] Norton E. Long, *The Polity* (Chicago: Rand McNally, 1962), p. 157.

interact and "develop a system of largely unintended cooperation through which things get done . . ."[10] In this process actors deal with metropolitan problems from a limited point of view: *i.e.* one confined to their particular interest and institutional base.

There are at least two reasons why Long's empirically persuasive approach has stymied students of community power. One would appear to be the fact that much of this research has been conducted in places other than metropolitan areas where decisions settling local issues are possible. Second, the well known controversy over pluralism and elitism in the literature—because it is a debate over who makes local decisions, a small, cohesive group or a large, diverse one—may have obscured the possibility that no one makes such decisions.

In the present explanation metropolitan areas are prototypes of interdependent, vertically organized communities. Here we would expect a highly fragmented and competitive power arrangement in which the scope of any group or institution would be limited to prime interest areas. That is, the competitive process would militate against generalized influence and require that actors work to maintain their position within the system. Long and Banfield concur with this prediction in the stress they put on metropolitan politics as going systems in which institutions and groups seek to maintain and enhance their power in particular areas, public policy representing the results of their cooperation.

Under these circumstances we would expect to find a fragmented and competitive pattern of community action. Community action in American cities seems increasingly to fit this pattern. The most apparent illustrations are found in the activities of civil rights, anti-poverty and peace groups which often possess resources conferred by extracommunity institutions and which are beginning to seriously involve themselves in the local political process. Here, of course, they encounter opposition from other local and vertically organized groups. As a result coordinated community action becomes more problematic and public policy represents less a reflection of consensus than a byproduct of the competitive process in which power is differentially exercised. . . . In another vein, several studies which have touched on the consequences of increasing involvement of the federal government in local affairs find, contrary to political folklore, an enhancement of competitive processes.[11]

Notable among deviant cases is the Vidich and Bensman study [Ed. See Section III.] where involvement of state and county governments resulted in an abdication of responsibility on the part of local leaders. While

---

[10] *Ibid.*

[11] Presthus, *Men at the Top;* William V. D'Antonio, "Community Leadership in an Economic Crisis: Testing Ground for Ideological Cleavage," *American Journal of Sociology,* 71 (May, 1966), pp. 688–700.

it is significant that these changes diluted the power of Springdale's elite, it is also recognized that the consequences of extracommunity involvement were not those we would predict. In this regard the theory presented here may be in need of modification. Recalling that Springdale is a town of 2,500 people and that its extracommunity ties center chiefly around state subsidies, it is reasonable to infer that both the nature of the community and of the vertical ties are contingent elements in the theory presented here. Perhaps it is the case, for example, that changes along the vertical axis lead to greater competitiveness only in those communities which possess a certain minimum of institutional viability and that without this the same changes spell the demise of local leadership.

Conclusions

The explanation offered here represents an attempt to push the study of community power beyond a disproportionate emphasis on technique and toward a concern for testing propositions derived from explicit theoretical statements. There seems little doubt that this alternative is best suited for resolving the controversies over how power is distributed in local communities, and for generalizing research in this area to the larger problems of social organization and change.

The theory developed in this paper states that the introduction into the local community of the institutions and influence of national-urban culture produces a "fragmentation of local normative order" or a disruption of consensual expectations concerning the norms prescribed by existing power arrangements. As expectations are altered and interests are differentiated, new resources are exploited for the creation of competing power groups.

The theory, as we have said, focuses on one direction of influence in what is undoubtedly a complex process. In so doing, however, it has the virtue of generating a number of testable propositions. Future comparative studies could evaluate, on the basis of first-hand data, the fundamental proposition regarding community interdependence and the advent of competitive power arrangements. A sampling of related propositions includes:

1. Changes, other than interdependence, which challenge the local normative order lead to more competitive power arrangements.
2. Intracommunity change which does not challenge the normative order does not lead to greater competitiveness.
3. Vertical ties which do not alter the normative order do not lead to the exploitation of new resources and more competitive power arrangements.

4. Normative diversity within a community leads to a greater frequency of application of overt sanctions (Presthus).

5. The greater the number of vertical ties in a community, the smaller the scope of local power groups.

6. The greater the number of vertical ties (and competitiveness) the more difficult (less frequent) is coordinated community action.

In addition to suggesting propositions the theory implies a new direction for research in that it locates the source of local change in the relationship between the community and extracommunity institutions. It is expected that researchers will find this theory informative as they become increasingly aware of what it implies for the choice of an appropriate unit of analysis in future community power studies. If the theory is correct the appropriate unit of analysis is not the community per se but, rather, the relationship between the community and the institutions of national-urban culture.

Bibliographic Appendix

ABBREVIATIONS

AJS —American Journal of Sociology

APSR—American Political Science Review

ASQ —Administrative Science Quarterly

ASR —American Sociological Review

1. Abu-Laban, Baha, "Leader Visibility in a Local Community," *Pacific Sociological Review*, IV (Fall, 1961), 73–78.
2. ————, "The Reputational Approach in the Study of Community Power: A Critical Evaluation," *Pacific Sociological Review*, VIII (Spring, 1965), 35–42.
3. Adrian, Charles R., "The Community Setting," *Social Science and Community Action*, ed. Charles R. Adrian. East Lansing: Michigan State University, 1960, pp 1–8.
4. ————, "Leadership and Decision-Making in Manager Cities: A Study of Three Communities," *Public Administration Review*, XVIII (Summer, 1958), 208–213.
5. ————, "Metropology: Folklore and Field Research," *Public Administration Review*, XXI (Summer, 1961), 148–157.
6. ————, "Power and City Officials," *Community Leadership and Decision-Making*. Iowa City, Iowa: Institute of Public Affairs, University of Iowa, 1966, pp. 35–47.
7. ————, ed., *Social Science and Community Action*. East Lansing: Michigan State University, 1960.
8. Agger, Robert E., "Power Attributions in the Local Community: Theoretical and Research Considerations," *Social Forces*, XXXIV (May, 1956), 322–331.
9. ————, and Daniel Goldrich, "Community Power Structures and Partisanship," *ASR*, XXIII (August, 1958), 383–392.
10. ————, Daniel Goldrich, and Bert E. Swanson, *The Rulers and the Ruled*. New York: John Wiley & Sons, Inc., 1964.

11. ————, and Vincent Ostrom, "The Political Structure of a Small Community," *Public Opinion Quarterly*, XX (Spring, 1956), 81–89.

12. ————, Bert E. Swanson, Daniel Goldrich, and Marshall Goldstein, "Political Influence Structures: Some Theoretical and Empirical Considerations," *Current Trends in Comparative Community Studies*, ed. Bert E. Swanson. Kansas City, Missouri: Community Studies, Inc., 1962, 81–88.

13. Alford, Robert, "The Comparative Study of Urban Politics," *Urban Research and Policy Planning*, eds. Leo F. Schnore and Henry Fagin. Beverly Hills: Sage Publications, 1967, 263–302.

14. Anton, Thomas J., "Power, Pluralism, and Local Politics," *ASQ*, VII (March, 1963), 425–457.

15. ————, "Rejoinder to Robert Dahl's critique of 'Power, Pluralism and Local Politics,'" *ASQ*, VIII (September, 1963), 257–268. (See Item 53).

16. Arensberg, Conrad M., "The Community Study Method," *AJS*, LX (September, 1954), 109–124.

17. Babchuck, Nicholas, Ruth Marsey, and C. Wayne Gordon, "Men and Women in Community Agencies: A Note on Power and Prestige," *ASR*, XXV (June, 1960), 399–403.

18. Bachrach, Peter, *The Theory of Democratic Elitism*. Boston: Little, Brown & Co., 1967.

19. ————, and Morton S. Baratz, "Decisions and Nondecisions: An Analytical Framework," *APSR*, LVII (September, 1963), 632–642.

20. ————, "Two Faces of Power," *APSR*, LVI (December, 1962), 947–952.

21. Baltzell, E. Digby, *Philadelphia Gentlemen: The Making of a National Upper Class*. New York: Free Press of Glencoe, Inc., 1958.

22. Banfield, Edward C., *Big City Politics*. New York: Random House, 1965.

23. ————, *Political Influence*. New York: Free Press of Glencoe, Inc., 1961).

24. ————, and James Q. Wilson, *City Politics*. Cambridge: Harvard and MIT Press, 1963).

25. Barth, Ernest A. T., "Community Influence Systems: Structure and Change," *Social Forces*, XL (October, 1961), 58–63.

26. ————, and Baha Abu-Laban, "Power Structure and the Negro Sub-Community," *ASR*, XXIV (February, 1959), 69–76.

27. ————, and Stuart D. Johnson, "Community Power and a Typology of Social Issues," *Social Forces*, XXXVIII (October, 1959), 29–32.

28. Belknap, George M., and Ralph H. Smuckler, "Political Power Relations in a Mid-West City," *Public Opinion Quarterly*, XX (Spring, 1956), 73–81.

29. Belknap, Ivan, and John Steinle, *The Community and Its Hospitals*. Syracuse: Syracuse University Press, 1963.

30. Bell, Wendell, Richard J. Hill, and Charles R. Wright, *Public Leadership*. San Francisco: Chandler Publishing Company, 1961.

31. Bensman, Joseph, and Arthur J. Vidich, "Social Theory in Field Research," *AJS*, LXV (May, 1960), 577–584.

32. Bierstedt, Robert, "An Analysis of Social Power," *ASR*, XV (December, 1950), 730–738.

33. Blackwell, Gordon W., "A Theoretical Framework for Sociological Research in Community Organization," *Social Forces*, XXXIII (October, 1954), 57–64.

34. ————, "Community Analysis," in Roland Young (ed.), *Approaches to the Study of Politics*. Evanston, Ill.: Northwestern University Press, 1958), 305–317.

35. Blankenship, L. Vaughn, "Community Power and Decision-Making: A Comparative Evaluation of Measurement Techniques," *Social Forces*, XLIII (December, 1964), 207–216.

36. Bloomberg, Warner, Morris H. Sunshine, and Thomas J. Fararo, *Suburban Power Structures and Public Education: A Study of Values, Influence and Tax Effort*. Syracuse: Syracuse University Press, 1963.

37. Bonjean, Charles M., "Class, Status, and Power Reputation," *Sociology and Social Research*, XLIX (October, 1964), 69–75.

38. ————, "Community Leadership: A Case Study and Conceptual Refinement," *AJS*, LXVIII (May, 1963), 672–681.

39. ————, and Lewis F. Carter, "Legitimacy and Visibility: Leadership Structures Related to Four Community Systems," *Pacific Sociological Review*, VIII (Spring, 1965), 16–20.

40. ————, and David Olson, "Community Leadership: Directions of Research," *ASQ*, IX (December, 1964), 278–300.

41. Booth, David A., and Charles R. Adrian, "Power Structure and Community Change: A Replication Study of Community A," *Midwest Journal of Political Science*, VI (August, 1962), 277–296.

42. Bradley, Donald S., and Mayer L. Zald, "From Commercial to Political Administrator: The Recruitment of the Mayors of Chicago," *AJS*, LXX (September, 1965), 153–167.

43. Burgess, Elaine M., *Negro Leadership in a Southern City*. Chapel Hill: University of North Carolina Press, 1962.

44. Clark, Terry N., ed. *Community Structure and Decision Making: Comparative Analyses*. San Francisco: Chandler Publishing Co., 1968.

45. Clelland, Donald A., and William H. Form, "Economic Dominants and Community Power: A Comparative Analysis," *AJS*, LXIX (March, 1964), 511–521.

46. Coleman, James S., *Community Conflict*. New York: Free Press of Glencoe, Inc., 1957.

47. Cowgill, Donald O., "Power as Process in an Urban Community," *Approaches to the Study of Urbanization*, ed. Richard Stauber. Lawrence, Kansas: University of Kansas Publications, Government Research Center Series, No. 27, 168–175.

48. Dahl, Robert A., "A Critique of the Ruling Elite Model," *APSR*, LII (June, 1958), 463–469.

49. ————, "Business and Politics: A Critical Appraisal of Political Science," *APSR*, LIII (March, 1959), 1–34.

50 ————, "The Concept of Power," *Behavioral Science*, II (July, 1957), 201–215.

51. ————, "Further Reflections on 'The Elitist Theory of Democracy,'" *APSR*, LX (June, 1966), 296–305. [See item 219.]

52. ————, "The Analysis of Influence in Local Communities," *Social Science and Community Action*, ed. Charles R. Adrian. East Lansing: Michigan State University, 1960, 25–42.

53. ————, "Reply to Thomas Anton's 'Power, Pluralism and Local Politics,'" *ASQ*, VII (March, 1963), 250–256. [See Item 14.]

54. ————, *Who Governs? Democracy and Power in an American City.* New Haven: Yale University Press, 1960.

55. Dakin, Ralph E., "Variations in Power Structures and Organizing Efficiency: A Comparative Study of Four Areas," *Sociological Quarterly*, III (July, 1962), 228–250.

56. Daland, Robert T., *Dixie City: A Portrait of Political Leadership.* University of Alabama, Bureau of Public Administration, 1956.

57. D'Antonio, William V., "Community Leadership in an Economic Crisis: Testing Ground for Ideological Cleavage," *AJS*, LXXI (May, 1966), 688–700.

58. ————, and H. J. Ehrlich, eds., *Power and Democracy in America.* South Bend: University of Notre Dame Press, 1961.

59. ————, Howard J. Ehrlich, and Eugene C. Erickson, "Further Notes on the Study of Community Power," *ASR*, XXVII (December, 1962), 848–853.

60. ————, and Eugene C. Erickson, "The Reputational Technique as a Measure of Community Power: An Evaluation Based on Comparative and Longitudinal Studies," *ASR*, XXVII (June, 1962), 362–376.

61. ————, and William H. Form, *Influentials in Two Border Cities: A Study in Community Decision-Making.* South Bend: University of Notre Dame Press, 1965.

62. ————, William H. Form, Charles P. Loomis, and Eugene C. Erickson, "Institutional and Occupational Representations in Eleven Community Influence Systems," *ASR*, XXVI (June, 1961), 440–446.

63. Danzger, M. Herbert, "Community Power Structure: Problems and Continuities," *ASR*, XXIX (October, 1964), 707–717.

64. Dick, Harry R., "A Method for Ranking Community Influentials," *ASR*, XXV (June, 1960), 395–399.

65. Domhoff, William G., *Who Rules America?* Englewood Cliffs, New Jersey: Prentice-Hall, Inc., 1967.

66. Dye, Thomas, "Popular Images of Decision-Making in Suburban Communities," *Sociology and Social Research*, XLVII (October, 1962) 75–85.

67. Ehrlich, Howard, and Mary Lou Bauer, "Newspaper Citation and Reputation for Community Leadership," *ASR*, XXX (June, 1965), 411–415.

68. ————, "The Reputational Approach to the Study of Community Power," *ASR*, XXVI (December, 1961), 926–927.

69. Fanelli, A. Alexander, "A Typology of Community Leadership Based on Influence and Interaction Within the Leader Subsystem," *Social Forces,* XXXIV (May, 1956), 332–338.

70. Faunce, William A., and Donald H. Clelland, "Professionalization and Stratification Patterns in an Industrial Community," *AJS,* LXXII (January, 1967) 341–350.

71. Fisher, Sethard, "Community Power Studies: A Critique," *Social Research,* XXIX (Winter, 1962), 449–466.

72. Form, William H., "Organized Labor's Place in the Community Power Structure," *Industrial and Labor Relations Review,* XII (July, 1959), 526–539.

73. ————, and William V. D'Antonio, "Integration and Cleavage Among Community Influentials in Two Border Cities," *ASR,* XXIV (December, 1959), 804–814.

74. ————, and Delbert C. Miller, *Industry, Labor and Community.* New York: Harper & Row, Publishers, 1960.

75.————, and Warren L. Sauer, *Community Influentials in a Middle-Sized City: A Case Study.* East Lansing: Michigan State University, 1960.

76. ————, "Organized Labor's Image of Community Power Structure," *Social Forces,* XXXVIII (May, 1960), 332–341.

77. Fowler, Irving A., "Local Industrial Structure, Economic Power and Community Welfare," *Social Problems,* VI (Summer, 1958), 41–51.

78. Freeman, Charles, and Selz C. Mayo, "Decision-Makers in Rural Community Action," *Social Forces,* XXXV (May, 1957), 319–322.

79. Freeman, Linton C., Warner J. Bloomberg, Jr., Stephen P. Koff, Morris H. Sunshine, and Thomas J. Fararo, *Local Community Leadership.* Syracuse, New York: University College, Paper #15, 1960.

80. ————, Thomas J. Fararo, Warner J. Bloomberg, Jr., and Morris H. Sunshine, "Locating Leaders in Local Communities: A Comparison of Some Alternative Approaches," *ASR,* XXVIII (October, 1963), 791–798.

81. ————, *et al., Metropolitan Decision-Making.* Syracuse, New York: University College, 1962.

82. Friedrich, Carl, ed., *Community.* New York: Liberal Arts Press, 1959.

83. Gamson, William A., "Reputation and Resources in Community Politics," *AJS,* LXXII (September, 1966), 121–131.

84. Goldhamer, Herbert, and Edward Shils, "Types of Power and Status," *AJS,* XLV (September, 1939), 171–182.

85. Goldstein, Marshall N., "Absentee Ownership and Monolithic Power Structures: Two Questions for Community Studies," *Current Trends in Comparative Community Studies,* ed. Bert E. Swanson. Kansas City: Community Studies, Inc., 1962, 49–59.

86. ————, "A Review of *Who Governs? Democracy and Power in an American City,* by Robert A. Dahl," *ASR,* XXVII (December, 1962), 860–862.

87. Gore, William J., and Fred S. Silander, "A Bibliographical Essay on Decision Making," *Administrative Science Quarterly*, IV (June, 1959), 97–121.

88. Grant, Daniel R., "Metropolitics and Professional Political Leadership: The Case of Nashville," *Annals of the American Academy of Political and Social Sciences*, CCCLIII (May, 1964), 73–81.

89. Greer, Scott, *Metropolitics: A Study of Political Culture*. New York: John Wiley & Sons., Inc., 1963.

90. Haer, John L., "Social Stratification in Relation to Attitude Toward Sources of Power in a Community," *Social Forces*, XXXV (December, 1956), 137–142.

91. Hanson, Robert C., "Predicting a Community Decision: A Test of the Miller-Form Theory," *ASR*, XXIV (October, 1959), 662–671.

92. Harsanyi, John, "Measurement of Social Power in N–Person Reciprocal Power Situations," *Behavioral Science*, VII (January, 1962), 81–91.

93. ————, "Measurement of Social Power, Opportunity Costs and the Theory of Two Person-Bargaining Games," *Behavioral Science*, VII (January, 1962), 67–80.

94. Hawley, Amos H., "Community Power and Urban Renewal Success," *AJS*, LXVIII (June, 1963), 422–431. [See Item 213.]

95. Herson, Lawrence J. R., "In the Footsteps of Community Power," *APSR*, LV (December, 1961), 817–830.

96. Hohle, Raymond, and John M. Foskett, "The Measurement of Influence in Community Affairs," *Research Studies of the State College of Washington*, XXV (June, 1957), 148–154.

97. Holden, Matthew, Jr., "The Governance of the Metropolis as a Problem of Diplomacy," *Journal of Politics*, XXVI (August, 1964), 627–647.

98. Hollingshead, August B., *Elmtown's Youth*. New York: John Wiley & Sons, Inc., 1949.

99. Hunter, Floyd, *The Big Rich and the Little Rich*. Garden City, New York: Doubleday & Company, Inc., 1965.

100. ————, *Community Power Structure*. Chapel Hill: University of North Carolina Press, 1953.

101. ————, *Top Leadership, U.S.A.* Chapel Hill: University of North Carolina Press, 1959.

102. ————, "A Review of *Who Governs? Democracy and Power in an American City*, by Robert A. Dahl," *ASQ*, VI (March, 1962), 517–519.

103. ————, Ruth C. Schaffer, and Cecil G. Sheps, *Community Organization: Action and Inaction*. Chapel Hill: University of North Carolina Press, 1956.

104. Janowitz, Morris, ed., *Community Political Systems*. New York: Free Press of Glencoe, Inc., 1961.

105. ————, "Community Power and 'Policy Science' Research," *Public Opinion Quarterly*, XXVI (Fall, 1962), 398–410.

106. Jennings, M. Kent, *Community Influentials: The Elites of Atlanta*. New York: Free Press of Glencoe, Inc., 1964.

107. ———, "Public Administrators and Community Decision Making," *ASQ*, VIII (June, 1963), 18–43.

108. ———, "Study of Community Decision-Making," *Current Trends in Comparative Community Studies*, ed. Bert E. Swanson. Kansas City: Community Studies, Inc., 1962, 18–30.

109. Jonassen, Christen T., "Community Typology," *Community Structure and Analysis*, ed. Marvin B. Sussman. New York: Thomas Y. Crowell Company 1959, 15–36.

110. Kammerer, Gladys M., "The Politics of Metropolis: Still a Frontier," *Public Administration Review*, XXIII (December, 1963), 240–246.

111. ———, Charles D. Farris, John M. DeGrove, Alfred B. Clubok, *The Urban Political Community: Profiles in Town Politics*. Boston: Houghton Mifflin Company, 1963.

112. Katz, Elihu, and Paul Lazarsfeld, *Personal Influence*. New York: Free Press of Glencoe, Inc, 1955.

113. Kaufman, Herbert, and Victor Jones, "The Mystery of Power," *Public Administration Review*, XIV (Summer, 1954), 205–212.

114. Keller, Suzanne, *Beyond the Ruling Class*. New York: Random House, 1963.

115. Kellstedt, Lyman, "Atlanta to 'Oretown'—Identifying Community Elites," *Public Administration Review*, XXV (June, 1965), 161–168.

116. Kimbrough, Ralph B., *Political Power and Educational Decision-Making*. Chicago: Rand McNally & Co., 1964.

117. Klapp, Orrin, and L. Vincent Padgett, "Power Structure and Decision-Making in A Mexican Border City," *AJS*, LXV (January, 1960), 400–406.

118. Knepper, David W., A Review of *Decisions in Syracuse: A Metropolitan Action Study*, by Roscoe C. Martin, Frank J. Munger, *et al.*, *The Journal of Politics*, XXIV (August, 1962), 622–623.

119. ———, "A Review of *Who Governs? Democracy and Power in An American City*, by Robert A. Dahl," *The Journal of Politics*, XXIV (August, 1962), 620–622.

120. Kornhauser, Arthur, ed., *Problems of Power in American Society*. Detroit: Wayne State University Press, 1957.

121. Kornhauser, William, " 'Power Elite' or 'Veto Groups,' " in *Culture and Social Character*, Seymour Martin Lipset and Leo Lowenthal. New York: Free Press, 1961, 252–267.

122. Lane, Robert E., "The Decline of Politics and Ideology in a Knowledge-able Society," *ASR*, XXXI (October, 1966), 649–662.

123. Lasswell, Harold, "The Decision Process: Seven Categories of Functional Analysis," in *Politics and Social Life*, eds. Nelson W. Polsby, Robert A. Dentler, and Paul Smith. Boston: Houghton Mifflin Company, 1963, 93–105.

124. ———, and Abraham Kaplan, *Power and Society*. New Haven: Yale University Press, 1950.

125. Laumann, Edward O., *Prestige and Association in an Urban Community*

—An Analysis of An Urban Stratification System. Indianapolis: Bobbs-Merrill Company, Inc., 1967.

126. Lenski, Gerhard, *Power and Privilege*. New York: McGraw-Hill Book Company, 1966.

127. London, Jack, A Review of *Community Power Structure*, by Floyd Hunter, *AJS*, LX (March, 1955), 522–523.

128. Long, Norton E., "Aristotle and the Study of Local Government," *Social Research*, XXIV (Autumn, 1957), 287–310.

129. ————, "Community Decision-Making," *Community Leadership and Decision-Making*. Iowa City, Iowa: Institute of Public Affairs, University of Iowa, 1966, 1–10.

130. ————, "The Local Community as an Ecology of Games," *AJS*, LXIV (November, 1958), 251–261.

131. ————, "Political Science and the City," in *Urban Research and Policy Planning*, eds. Leo F. Schnore and Henry Fagin. Beverly Hills: Sage Publications, 1967, 243–262.

132. ————, "Sayre and Kaufman's New York: Competition Without Chaos," *Public Administration Review*, XXI (Summer, 1961), 23–30.

133. ————, "Some Observations Toward a Natural History of Metropolitan Politics," *The Polity*. Chicago: Rand McNally & Co., 1962, 196–214.

134. ————, "Who Makes Decisions in Metropolitan Areas?" *The Polity*. Chicago: Rand McNally & Co., 1962, 156–164.

135. Lowry, Ritchie P., *Who's Running This Town? Community Leadership and Social Change*. New York: Harper & Row, Publishers, 1965.

136. Lynd, Robert S., and Helen M. Lynd, *Middletown*. New York: Harcourt, Brace & World, Inc., 1929.

137. ————, *Middletown in Transition*. New York: Harcourt, Brace & World, Inc., 1937.

138. Mack, Raymond, and Richard C. Snyder, "An Analysis of Social Conflict —Toward an Over View and Synthesis," *Conflict Resolution*, I (June, 1959), 212–248.

139. March, James G., "An Introduction to the Theory and Measurement of Influence," *APSR*, XLIX (June, 1955), 431–451.

140. ————, "Measurement Concepts in the Theory of Influence," *Journal of Politics*, XIX (May, 1957), 202–226.

141. ————, "The Power of Power," in *Varieties of Political Theory*, ed. David Easton. Englewood Cliffs, New Jersey: Prentice Hall, Inc., 1966, 39–70.

142. Martin, Roscoe C., *et al.*, *Decisions in Syracuse: A Metropolitan Action Study*. Bloomington, Indiana: Indiana University Press, 1961.

143. Masotti, Louis H., *Education and Politics in Suburbia: The New Trier Experience*. Cleveland: Western Reserve University Press, 1967.

144. McClain, Jackson M., and Robert B. Highsaw, *Dixie City: A Study in Decision-Making*. Birmingham: Bureau of Public Administration, University of Alabama, 1962.

145. McFarland, Andrew S., *Power and Leadership in Pluralist Systems*. Stanford: Stanford University Press, forthcoming.

146. McKee, James B., "Community Power and Strategies in Race Relations: Some Critical Observations," *Social Problems*, VI (Winter, 1958–59), 195–203.

147. ————, "Status and Power in The Industrial Community: A Comment on Drucker's Thesis," *AJS*, LVIII (January, 1953), 364–370.

148. Merton, Robert K., "Patterns of Influence: Local and Cosmopolitan Influentials," *Social Theory and Social Structure*. New York: Free Press of Glencoe, Inc., 1957, 387–420.

149. Miller, Delbert C., "Decision-Making Cliques in Community Power Structures: A Comparative Study of an American and an English City," *AJS*, LXIV (November, 1958), 299–310.

150. ————, "Industry and Community Power Structure: A Comparative Study of an American and English City," *ASR*, XXIII (February, 1958), 9–15.

151. ————, "The Prediction of Issue Outcome in Community Decision-Making," *Research Studies of the State College of Washington*, XXV (June, 1957), 137–147.

152. ————, "Town and Gown: The Power Structure of a University Town," *AJS*, LXVIII (January, 1963), 432–443.

153. ————, and James L. Dirksen, "The Identification of Visible, Concealed, and Symbolic Leaders in a Small Indiana City: A Replication of the Bonjean-Noland Study of Burlington, North Carolina," *Social Forces*, XLIII (May, 1965), 548–555.

154. Mills, C. Wright, "The Middle Classes in the Middle-Sized Cities," *ASR*, XI (October, 1946), 520–529.

155. ————, "A Review of *Community Power Structure*, by Floyd Hunter," *Social Forces*, XXXII (October, 1953), 92–93.

156. ————, and Melvin Ulmer, *Small Business and Civic Welfare: Report on Smaller War Plants Corporation to the Special Committee to Study Problems of American Small Business*, Senate Document No. 135, 79th Congress, 2d sess., 1946. Washington, D.C.: Government Printing Office, 1946.

157. Mowitz, Robert J., and Deil S. Wright, *Profile of a Metropolis: A Case Book*. Detroit: Wayne State University Press, 1962.

158. Muir, William K., Jr., *Defending "The Hill" Against Metal Houses*. (Inter-University Case Program, University, Alabama: University of Alabama Press, 1958).

159. Mulford, Charles L., "On Role Consensus About Community Leaders," *Sociological Inquiry*, XXXVI (Winter, 1966), 15–18.

160. Myerson, Martin, and Edward C. Banfield, *Politics, Planning and the Public Interest*. New York: Free Press of Glencoe, Inc., 1955.

161. Olmstead, Donald W., "Organizational Leadership and Social Structure in a Small City," *ASR*, XIX (June, 1954), 273–281.

162. Parenton, Vernon J. and Roland J. Pellegrin, "Social Structure and the

Leadership Factor in a Negro Community in South Louisiana," *Phylon,* XVII (First Quarter, 1956), 74–78.

163. Parsons, Talcott, "The Distribution of Power in American Society," *World Politics,* X (October, 1957), 123–143.

164. ———, "On the Concept of Political Power," *Proceedings of the American Philosophical Society,* CVII (June, 1963), 232–262.

165. Payne, Raymond, "Leadership and Perceptions of Change in a Village Confronted with Urbanism," *Social Forces,* XLI (March, 1963), 264–269.

166. Pellegrin, Roland J., and Charles H. Coates, "Absentee-Owned Corporations and Community Power Structure," *AJS,* LXI (March, 1956), 413–419.

167. Pfautz, Harold W., "The Power Structure of the Negro Sub-Community: A Case Study and a Comparative View," *Phylon,* XXIII (Summer, 1962), 156–166.

168. Polsby, Nelson W., *Community Power and Political Theory.* New Haven: Yale University Press, 1963.

169. ———, "Community Power: Some Reflections on the Recent Literature," *ASR,* XXVII (December, 1962), 838–841.

170. ———, "How to Study Community Power: The Pluralist Approach," *The Journal of Politics,* XXII (August, 1960), 474–484.

171. ———, "Power in Middletown: Fact and Value in Community Research," *The Canadian Journal of Economics and Political Science,* XXVI (November, 1960), 592–603.

172. ———, "The Sociology of Community Power: A Reassessment," *Social Forces,* XXXVII (March, 1959), 232–236.

173. ———, "Three Problems in the Analysis of Community Power," *ASR,* XXIV (December, 1959), 796–803.

174. ———, and Wallace S. Sayre, "American Political Science and the Study of Urbanization," in *The Study of Urbanization,* eds. Leo Schnore and Phillip Hauser. New York: John Wiley & Sons, Inc., 1965, 115–156.

175. Press, Charles, *Main Street Politics.* East Lansing, Michigan: Institute for Community Development, 1962.

176. Presthus, Robert, *Men at the Top: A Study in Community Power.* New York: Oxford University Press, 1964.

177. Price, Hugh Douglas, "A Review of *Who Governs? Democracy and Power in An American City,* by Robert A. Dahl," *Yale Law Journal,* LXXI (July, 1962), 1589–1596.

178. Rhyne, Edwin Hoffman, "Political Parties and Decision-Making in Three Southern Counties," *APSR,* LII (December, 1958), 1091–1107.

179. Riker, William H., "Some Ambiguities in the Notion of Power," *APSR,* LVIII (June, 1964), 341–349.

180. ———, *The Theory of Political Coalitions.* New Haven: Yale University Press, 1962.

181. Rogers, David, "Community Political Systems: A Framework and Hypothesis for Comparative Studies," in *Current Trends in Comparative Community Studies,* ed. Bert E. Swanson. Kansas City: Community Studies, Inc., 1962, 31–48.

182. ———, "A Review of *Who Governs? Democracy and Power in An American City*, by Robert A. Dahl," *AJS*, LXVIII (September, 1962), 271–272.

183. Rose, Arnold M., *The Power Structure: Political Processes in American Society*. New York: Oxford University Press, 1967.

184. Rossi, Peter H., "Community Decision-Making," *ASQ*, I (March, 1957), 415–443.

185. ———, "The Organizational Structure of an American Community" in *Complex Organizations: A Sociological Reader*, ed. Amitai Etzioni. New York: Holt, Rinehart & Winston, Inc., 1961, 301–312.

186. ———, "Power and Community Structure," *Midwest Journal of Political Science*, IV (November, 1960), 390–401.

187. ———, "A Review of *Community Influentials: The Elites of Atlanta*, by M. Kent Jennings," *AJS*, LXXI (May, 1966), 723–725.

188. ———, "Theory, Research and Practice in Community Organization" in *Social Science and Community Action*, ed. Charles R. Adrian. East Lansing: Michigan State University, 1960, 9–23.

189. Russell, Bertrand, *Power: A New Social Analysis*. New York: W. W. Norton & Company, Inc., 1938.

190. Salisbury, Robert H., "St. Louis Politics: Relationships Among Interests, Parties, and Governmental Structure," *Western Political Quarterly*, XIII (June, 1960), 498–507.

191. ———, "Urban Politics: The New Convergence of Power," *Journal of Politics*, XXVI (November, 1964), 775–797.

192. Sayre, Wallace S., and Herbert Kaufman, *Governing New York City: Politics in the Metropolis*. New York: Russell Sage Foundation, 1960.

193. Schattschneider, E. E., *The Semisovereign People*. New York: Holt, Rinehart & Winston, Inc., 1960.

194. Schmandt, Henry J., Paul G. Steinbicker, George P. Wendel, *Metropolitan Reform in St. Louis*. New York: Holt, Rinehart & Winston, Inc., 1961.

195. Schulze, Robert O., "The Bifurcation of Power in a Satellite City" in *Community Political Systems*, ed. Morris Janowitz. New York: Free Press of Glencoe, Inc., 1961, 19–80.

196. ———, "The Role of Economic Dominants in Community Power Structure," *ASR*, XXIII (February, 1958), 3–9.

197. ———, and Leonard U. Blumberg, "The Determination of Local Power Elites," *AJS*, LXIII (November, 1957), 290–296.

198. Scoble, Harry M., "A Review of *Community Power and Political Theory*, by Nelson W. Polsby," *ASQ*, IX (December, 1964), 313–315.

199. ———, "Leadership Hierarchies and Political Issues in a New England Town," in *Community Political Systems*, ed. Morris Janowitz. New York: Free Press of Glencoe, Inc., 1961, 117–145.

200. Seasholes, Bradbury, "Patterns of Influence in Metropolitan Boston: A Proposal for Field Research," in *Current Trends in Comparative Community Studies*, ed. Bert E. Swanson. Kansas City: Community Studies, Inc., 1962, 60–68.

201. Siegel, Roberta S., and H. Paul Friesema, "Urban Community Leaders'

Knowledge of Public Opinion," *Western Political Quarterly*, XVIII (December, 1965), 881–895.

202. Simon, Herbert A., "Notes on the Observation and Measurement of Power," *Journal of Politics*, XV (November, 1953), 500–516.

203. Smith, Joel, and Thomas Hood, "The Delineation of Community Power Structure by a Reputational Approach," *Sociological Inquiry*, XXVI (Winter, 1966), 3–14.

204. Smith, Louis, "Review of *Community Power Structure*, by Floyd Hunter," *Journal of Politics*, XVI (February, 1954), 146–150.

205. Smith, Paul A., "The Games of Community Politics," *Midwest Journal of Political Science*, IX (February, 1965), 37–60.

206. Smith, Ted C., "The Structuring of Power in a Suburban Community," *Pacific Sociological Review*, III (Fall, 1960), 83–88.

207. Sofen, Edward, *The Miami Metropolitan Experiment*. Bloomington: Indiana University Press, 1963.

208. ————, "Problems of Metropolitan Leadership: The Miami Experience," *Midwest Journal of Political Science*, V (February, 1961), 18–38.

209. Spinrad, William, "Power in Local Communities," *Social Problems*, XII (Winter, 1965), 335–356.

210. Stauber, Richard L., ed., *Approaches to the Study of Urbanization*. Lawrence, Kansas, University of Kansas Publications, Government Research Center Series No. 27, 1964.

211. Stewart, Frank, "A Sociometric Study of Influence in Southtown," *Sociometry* X (February and August, 1953) 11–31, 273–286.

212. Stone, Robert C., "Power and Values in Trans-Community Relations" in *Current Trends in Comparative Community Studies*, ed. Bert E. Swanson. Kansas City: Community Studies, Inc., 1962, 69–80.

213. Straits, Bruce C., "Community Adoption and Implementation of Urban Renewal," *AJS*, LXXI (July, 1965), 77–82. (See Item 94.)

214. Strong, Donald S., "Review of *Community Power Structure*, by Floyd Hunter," *APSR*, XLVIII (March, 1954), 235–237.

215. Swanson, Bert E., "Community Leadership and Policy Implementation," *Community Leadership and Decision-Making*. Iowa City, Iowa: Institute of Public Affairs, University of Iowa, 1966, 48–57.

216. ————, ed., *Current Trends in Comparative Community Studies*. A Report on the 1961 Kansas City Conference on Community Policy-Making. Kansas City: Community Studies, Inc., 1962.

217. Thometz, Carol E., *The Decision-Makers: The Power Structure of Dallas*. Dallas: Southern Methodist University Press, 1963.

218. Vidich, Arthur J., and Joseph Bensman, *Small Town in Mass Society*. Princeton: Princeton University Press, 1958.

219. Walker, Jack L., "A Critique of the Elitist Theory of Democracy," *APSR*, LX (June, 1966), 285–295, 391–392. [See item 51.]

220. Walter, Benjamin, "On the Logical Analysis of Power-Attribution Procedures," *Journal of Politics*, XXVI (November, 1964), 850–866.

221. ———, "Political Decision-Making in Arcadia," in *Urban Growth Dynamics*, eds. F. Stuart Chapin, Jr. and Shirley F. Weiss. New York: John Wiley & Sons., Inc., 1962, 141–187.

222. ———, "Political Decision-Making in North Carolina Cities," *PROD*, III (May, 1960), 18–21.

223. Walton, John, "Discipline, Method and Community Power: A Note on the Sociology of Knowledge," *ASR*, XXXI (October, 1966), 684–689.

224. ———, "A Review of *Influentials in Two Border Cities: A Study in Community Decision-Making*, by William V. D'Antonio and William H. Form," *AJS*, LXXI (May, 1966), 725–726.

225. ———, "Substance and Artifact: The Current Status of Research on Community Power Structure," *AJS*, LXXI (January, 1966), 430–438.

226. ———, "The Vertical Axis of Community Organization and the Structure of Power," *Southwestern Social Science Quarterly*, XLVIII (December, 1967), 353–368, and in Terry Clark (ed.) *Community Structure and Decision Making: Comparative Analyses*. San Francisco: Chandler, 1968.

227. Warner, William Lloyd, *et. al.*, *Democracy in Jonesville*. New York: Harper & Row, Publishers, 1949.

228. ———, *Yankee City*. New Haven: Yale University Press, 1963.

229. Warren, Roland L., "Toward a Typology of Extra-Community Controls Limiting Local Community Autonomy," *Social Forces*, XXXIV (May, 1956), 338–341.

230. Weber, Max, "Class Status and Party" in *From Max Weber*, eds. Hans Gerth and C. Wright Mills. New York: Oxford Galaxy, 1958.

231. Westby, David L., "The Civic Sphere in the American City," *Social Forces*, XLV (December, 1966), 161–170.

232. Wildavsky, Aaron, *Leadership in a Small Town*. Totowa, New Jersey: Bedminster Press, 1964.

233. Williams, Oliver P., "A Typology for Comparative Local Government," *Midwest Journal of Political Science*, V (May, 1961), 150–164.

234. ———, and Charles R. Adrian, *Four Cities: A Study in Comparative Policy Making*. Philadelphia: University of Pennsylvania Press, 1963.

235. Wolfinger, Raymond E., "A Plea for A Decent Burial," *ASR*, XXVII (December, 1962), 841–847.

236. ———, "Reputation and Reality in the Study of Community Power," *ASR*, XXV (October, 1960), 636–644.

237. Wood, Robert C., *Suburbia, Its People and Their Politics*. Boston: Houghton Mifflin Company, 1958.

238. Wood, Thomas J., "Dade County: Unbossed, Erratically Led," *Annals of the American Academy of Political and Social Science*, CCCLIII (May, 1964), 64–71.

239. Young, Roland A., *Approaches to the Study of Politics*. Evanston: Northwestern University Press, 1958.

240. Zelditch, Morris, Jr., "Some Methodological Problems of Field Studies," *AJS*, LXVII (March, 1962), 566–576.